Lecture Notes in Com

Founding Editors

Gerhard Goos
Juris Hartmanis

Editorial Board Members

Elisa Bertino, USA
Wen Gao, China
Bernhard Steffen, Germany
Moti Yung, USA

Formal Methods

Subline of Lecture Notes in Computer Science

Subline Series Editors

Ana Cavalcanti, *University of York, UK*
Annabelle McIver, *Macquarie University, Sydney, NSW, Australia*

Subline Advisory Board

Manfred Broy, *TU Munich, Germany*
Marieke Huisman, *University of Twente, The Netherlands*
André Platzer, *Karlsruhe Institute of Technology, Germany, and Carnegie Mellon University, PA, USA*
Erik de Vink, *Eindhoven University of Technology, The Netherlands*
Pamela Zave, *AT&T Laboratories Research, Bedminster, NJ, USA*

More information about this series at https://link.springer.com/bookseries/558

Nikolai Kosmatov · Laura Kovács
Editors

Integrated Formal Methods

19th International Conference, IFM 2024
Manchester, UK, November 13–15, 2024
Proceedings

Springer

Editors
Nikolai Kosmatov
Thales Research and Technology
Palaiseau, France

Laura Kovács
TU Wien
Vienna, Austria

ISSN 0302-9743 ISSN 1611-3349 (electronic)
Lecture Notes in Computer Science
ISBN 978-3-031-76553-7 ISBN 978-3-031-76554-4 (eBook)
https://doi.org/10.1007/978-3-031-76554-4

© The Editor(s) (if applicable) and The Author(s), under exclusive license to Springer Nature Switzerland AG 2025

This work is subject to copyright. All rights are solely and exclusively licensed by the Publisher, whether the whole or part of the material is concerned, specifically the rights of translation, reprinting, reuse of illustrations, recitation, broadcasting, reproduction on microfilms or in any other physical way, and transmission or information storage and retrieval, electronic adaptation, computer software, or by similar or dissimilar methodology now known or hereafter developed.
The use of general descriptive names, registered names, trademarks, service marks, etc. in this publication does not imply, even in the absence of a specific statement, that such names are exempt from the relevant protective laws and regulations and therefore free for general use.
The publisher, the authors and the editors are safe to assume that the advice and information in this book are believed to be true and accurate at the date of publication. Neither the publisher nor the authors or the editors give a warranty, expressed or implied, with respect to the material contained herein or for any errors or omissions that may have been made. The publisher remains neutral with regard to jurisdictional claims in published maps and institutional affiliations.

This Springer imprint is published by the registered company Springer Nature Switzerland AG
The registered company address is: Gewerbestrasse 11, 6330 Cham, Switzerland

If disposing of this product, please recycle the paper.

Preface

This volume contains the papers presented at the 19th International Conference on integrated Formal Methods (iFM 2024), held at the University of Manchester, UK, during November 13–15, 2024.

In the last decades, we have witnessed a proliferation of approaches that integrate several modelling, verification and simulation techniques, facilitating more versatile and efficient analysis of software-intensive systems. These approaches provide powerful support for the analysis of different functional and non-functional properties of the systems, complex interaction of components of different nature as well as validation of diverse aspects of system behaviour. The iFM conference series is a forum for discussing recent research advances in the development of integrated approaches to formal modelling and analysis. The conference covers all aspects of the design of integrated techniques, including language design, verification and validation, automated tool support and the use of such techniques in software engineering practice.

The iFM 2024 conference solicited high-quality papers reporting research results and/or experience reports related to the overall theme of formal methods integration. The conference interleaved various disciplines in formal methods, including formal verification, system refinement, quantitative and static analysis, cybersecurity, learning, monitoring and automated reasoning. There were two submission categories for iFM 2024:

1. **Regular research papers** presenting original scientific research results, foundation and evaluations of tools, or applications of formal methods, including rigorous evaluations and case studies,
2. **Short papers** describing works in the area of formal methods, including work-in-progress and preliminary results that are sufficiently interesting for the iFM community.

Regular research paper submissions were restricted to 16 pages, and short papers to 6 pages, excluding the bibliography and appendices. Two additional pages were granted for accepted papers, for revising and finalizing the camera-ready contributions included in these proceedings.

The Program Committee (PC) received a total of 58 paper submissions from authors in 21 different countries: 45 regular papers and 13 short papers. Each submission was rigorously reviewed by three PC members, who further relied on subreviewers. All submissions were reviewed using a single-blind reviewing process. Based on the review reports, the PC had a thorough discussion on each paper. As a result, the PC decided to accept 19 papers, out of which there were 12 regular research papers and 7 short papers. This corresponds to an overall acceptance rate of 33%. Each accepted paper at iFM 2024 had either all positive reviews or a "championing" PC member who argued in favor of accepting the paper.

To improve and reward reproducibility and to give more visibility and credit to the efforts of tool developers in our community, authors of accepted papers at iFM 2024 were invited to submit possible artifacts associated with their papers for evaluation. An artifact might consist of a tool, models, proofs or other data required for validation of the results of the paper. Artifact submission was voluntary at iFM 2024 and the result of the artifact evaluation did not alter the respective paper's acceptance decision. The Artifact Evaluation Committee (AEC) was tasked with reviewing the submitted artifacts, based on their availability, ease of use, and, most importantly, whether the results presented in the corresponding paper could be accurately reproduced. In total, artifacts of 10 acccepted papers at iFM 2024 were submitted to artifact evaluation and each submission successfully passed artifact evaluation. In addition to an availability badge, each of the 10 artifacts received either a functional or a (functional and) reusable badge. As a a result, at iFM 2024 we awarded 20 artifact badges, using the EAPLS artifact badging. Papers with artifacts that were successfully evaluated by the AEC include the awarded badges on their first page in these proceedings.

We are proud to award the **Distinguished Reviewer Award** to **Katherine Kossain** (Iowa State University, USA) for her very careful analysis of papers and proactive investment in the reviewing and selection process.

The PC also shortlisted three papers as **candidates for the Best Paper Award**. These papers are (in no specific order):

- "PLACIDUS: Engineering Product Lines of Rigorous Assurance Cases", co-authored by Logan Murphy, Torin Viger, Alessio Di Sandro and Marsha Chechik;
- "Stateful Functional Modeling with Refinement (a Lean4 framework)", by Frederic Peschanski;
- "Modeling Register Pairs in CompCert", co-authored by Alexander Loitzl and Florian Zuleger.

The decision on the iFM 2024 best paper award was taken during the iFM 2024 conference, by taking into account also the presentation of the paper at the conference.

The iFM 2024 conference featured **keynotes** by

- **Daniel Kröning** (Amazon Web Services and University of Oxford, UK), delivering a talk about *"Proof for Industrial Systems using Neural Certificates"*,
- **Philippa Gardner** (Imperial College London, UK), discussing *"Compositional Symbolic Execution for Over-approximating and Under-approximating Reasoning"*, and
- **Alessandro Cimatti** (Fondazione Bruno Kessler, Italy), presenting *"A Formal Approach to Railways Interlocking Design"*.

In addition, an invited tutorial by **Frédéric Loulergue** (Université d'Orléans, France) on *"The Frama-C Software Verification Platform"* was part of the iFM 2024 programme.

iFM 2024 also hosted the iFM Doctoral Programme 2024, providing PhD students a forum to present early results and to receive constructive feedback and mentoring. Further, the workshops on "Formal Methods for Autonomous Systems" and "Formal Ethical Agents and Robots" were organized as affiliated events of iFM 2024.

We would like to thank everyone who helped to make iFM 2024 successful. A huge thanks goes to our

- **authors** for submitting or presenting their works at iFM 2024,
- **invited speakers** who kindly accepted to give keynote talks or an invited tutorial during the conference,
- **PC members** and **additional reviewers** for providing detailed reports on papers they reviewed and actively engaging themselves in the PC discussions,
- artifact evaluation committee chairs **Daniela Kaufmann** (TU Wien, Austria) and **Mathias Fleury** (University of Freiburg, Germany),
- **AEC members** for their timely reviews during artifact evaluation,
- **steering committee** and, in particular, **former PC chairs** for valuable advice,
- PhD Symposium Chairs **Mădălina Eraşcu** (West University of Timişoara, Romania) and **Mattias Ulbrich** (Karlsruhe Institute of Technology, Germany), as well as all members of the **PhD Symposium Program Committee**,
- Web Chair **Conor Reynolds** (University of Manchester, UK),
- Local Organising Committee members **Hazel Taylor**, **Diana Benjumea Hernandez**, and **Noriko Griffiths** (each from the University of Manchester, UK), and
- *last but not least:* special thanks to our General Co-Chairs **Marie Farrell** (University of Manchester, UK) and **Mohammad Reza Mousavi** (King's College London, UK) for all their efforts to make iFM 2024 a wonderful event in Manchester.

We acknowledge the financial support provided by Springer and the general support of the Royal Academy of Engineering, InnovateUK and EPSRC. We are grateful for the institutional support iFM 2024 received from King's College London, Thales Research and Technology, University of Manchester and TU Wien. We are also grateful for the invaluable support provided by the EasyChair developers.

November 2024

Nikolai Kosmatov
Laura Kovács

Organization

Programme Committee Chairs

Nikolai Kosmatov   Thales Research & Technology, France
Laura Kovács   TU Wien, Austria

Programme Committee

Wolfgang Ahrendt   Chalmers University of Technology, Sweden
Ezio Bartocci   TU Wien, Austria
Maurice ter Beek   CNR, Italy
Dirk Beyer   Ludwig Maximilian University of Munich, Germany
Milan Ceska   Brno University of Technology, Czechia
Christian Colombo   University of Malta, Malta
Pedro R. D'Argenio   Universidad Nacional de Córdoba – CONICET, Argentina
Richard DeFrancisco   Augusta University, USA
Tom van Dijk   University of Twente, The Netherlands
Claire Dross   AdaCore, France
Catherine Dubois   ENSIIE-Samovar, France
Marco Eilers   ETH Zürich, Switzerland
Gidon Ernst   Ludwig Maximilian University of Munich, Germany
Marie Farrell   University of Manchester, UK
Mathias Fleury   University of Freiburg, Germany
Hadar Frenkel   CISPA – Helmholtz Center for Information Security, Germany
Carlo A. Furia   Università della Svizzera italiana, Switzerland
María del Mar Gallardo   University of Málaga, Spain
Angelo Gargantini   University of Bergamo, Italy
Paula Herber   University of Münster, Germany
Marieke Huisman   University of Twente, The Netherlands
Einar Broch Johnsen   University of Oslo, Norway
Amir Kafshdar Goharshady Hong Kong University of Science and Technology, China
Daniela Kaufmann   TU Wien, Austria
Katherine Kosaian   Iowa State University, USA
Frédéric Loulergue   Université d'Orléans, France
Vince Molnár   Budapest University of Technology and Economics, Hungary
Rosemary Monahan   Maynooth University, Ireland
Peter Ölveczky   University of Oslo, Norway
Virgile Prevosto   Université Paris-Saclay, France

Tim Quatmann	RWTH Aachen University, Germany
Giles Reger	Amazon Web Services and University of Manchester, UK
Cristina Seceleanu	Mälardalen University, Sweden
Emil Sekerinski	McMaster University, Canada
Abhishek Kr Singh	Tel Aviv University, Israel
Serdar Tasiran	Amazon Web Services, USA
Elena Troubitsyna	KTH, Sweden
Miroslav Velev	Aries Design Automation, USA
Willem Visser	Stellenbosch University, South Africa
Tomas Vojnar	Brno University of Technology, Czechia
Anton Wijs	Eindhoven University of Technology, The Netherlands
Kirsten Winter	University of Queensland, Australia
Emily Yu	Institute of Science and Technology Austria, Austria
Naijun Zhan	Chinese Academy of Sciences, China

Artifact Evaluation Committee Chairs

Mathias Fleury	University of Freiburg, Germany
Daniela Kaufmann	TU Wien, Austria

Artifact Evaluation Committee

Bruno Andreotti	Universidade Federal de Minas Gerais, Brazil
Chen Chen	Hong Kong University of Science and Technology (Guangzhou), China
César Cornejo	Universidad Nacional de Rio Cuarto, Argentina
Mario Frank	University of Potsdam, Germany
Bernhard Gstrein	University of Freiburg, Germany
Thomas Hader	TU Wien, Austria
Simone Heisinger	Johannes Kepler University Linz, Austria
Maurice Laveaux	Eindhoven University of Technology, The Netherlands
Yong Li	University of Liverpool, UK
Anik Momtaz	Michigan State University, USA
Andy Oertel	Lund University, Sweden and University of Copenhagen, Denmark
Alex Ozdemir	Stanford University, USA
Danilo Pianini	University of Bologna, Italy
Florian Pollitt	University of Freiburg, Germany
Mouhammad Sakr	University of Luxembourg, Luxembourg
Dimitrios Thanos	Leiden University, The Netherlands
Dieter Vandesande	Vrije Universiteit Brussel, Belgium

Additional Reviewers

Ádám, Zsófia
Adelt, Julius
An, Jie
Audrito, Giorgio
Ballenghien, Benoît
Becker-Kupczok, Jonas
Demasi, Ramiro
Di Stefano, Luca
Dust, Lukas
Ferrari, Alessio
Gu, Rong
Heemstra, Jan
Hu, Guangyu
Ischard, Jordan
Laarman, Alfons
Lluch Lafuente, Alberto
Muroya Lei, Stefanie
Nagy, Simon
Osama, Muhammad
Pferscher, Andrea
Schlatte, Rudolf
Síč, Juraj
Tan, Yong Kiam
Tappler, Martin
Wu, Hao
Xu, Xiong

Abstracts of Invited Speakers

A Formal Approach to Railways Interlocking Design

Alessandro Cimatti[ID]

Fondazione Bruno Kessler, Italy
cimatti@fbk.eu

Abstract. Many railways interlocking systems are still based on electromechanical solutions. They are hard to understand and costly to modify, and can be considered legacy systems. In this talk I will present the research underlying a novel process for the development of interlocking applications. The proposed methodology is able on one side to analyze and reverse-engineer legacy relay-based interlocking systems, and on the other to support the specification and verification of interlocking procedures by means of a model-based approach. Research challenges include modeling and verification of continuous-time, real-valued transition systems, automated abstraction for reverse engineering and specification mining, automated test generation, and parameterized verification.

Compositional Symbolic Execution for Over-approximating and Under-approximating Reasoning

Philippa Gardner

Imperial College London, UK
p.gardner@imperial.ac.uk

Abstract. A relatively recent challenge has been to develop symbolic-execution techniques and tools that are functionally compositional with simple function specifications that can be used in broader calling contexts. The technical breakthrough came with the introduction of separation logics for reasoning about partial mutable state, leading to compositional symbolic execution tools being developed in academia and industry. Many of these tools have been grounded on a formal foundation, but either the function specifications are validated with respect to the underlying symbolic semantics of the engine, with no meaning outside the tool, or there is a large gulf between the theory and the implementations of the tools. In this talk, I will introduce a formal compositional symbolic execution engine which creates and uses function specifications from an underlying separation logic and provides a sound theoretical foundation for, and indeed was partially inspired by, the Gillian platform. This is achieved by providing an axiomatic interface which describes the properties of the consume and produce functions for updating the symbolic state when calling function specifications, a technique used by VeriFast, Viper and Gillian but not previously characterised independently of the tool. A surprising property is that our semantics provides a common foundation for both correctness and incorrectness reasoning, with the difference in the underlying engine only amounting to the choice to use satisfiability or validity. We use this insight to extend the Gillian platform with incorrectness reasoning, developing automatic true bug-finding using incorrectness bi-abduction, which our engine incorporates by creating fixes from missing-resource errors. We have shown that the Gillian implementation of the consumer and producer functions satisfy the properties described by our axiomatic interface, and evaluate our new Gillian platform by using the Gillian instantiation to C. This instantiation is the first tool to support both correctness and incorrectness reasoning, as well as being grounded on a common formal compositional symbolic execution engine.

This talk is loosely based on the paper "Compositional Symbolic Execution for Over-approximating and Under-approximating Reasoning" by Andreas Lööw, Daniele Nantes Sobrinho, Sacha-Elie Ayoun, Caroline Cronjäger, Petar Maksimović and Philippa Gardner, ECOOP 2024, distinguished paper.

Proof for Industrial Systems Using Neural Certificates

Daniel Kröning [ID]

Amazon Web Services and Magdalen College, Oxford, UK
dkr@amazon.co.uk

Abstract. We introduce a novel approach to model checking software and hardware that combines machine learning and symbolic reasoning by using neural networks as formal proof certificates. We train our neural certificates from randomly generated executions of the system and we then symbolically check their validity which, upon the affirmative answer, establishes that the system provably satisfies the specification. We leverage the expressive power of neural networks to represent proof certificates and the fact that checking a certificate is much simpler than finding one. As a result, our machine learning procedure is entirely unsupervised, formally sound, and practically effective. We implemented a prototype and compared the performance of our method with the state-of-the-art academic and commercial model checkers on a set of Java programs and hardware designs written in SystemVerilog.

Contents

Software Verification

A Formal Tainting-Based Framework for Malware Analysis 3
Andrei Mogage and Dorel Lucanu

A Systematic Literature Review on a Decade of Industrial TLA$^+$ Practice 24
Roman Bögli, Leandro Lerena, Christos Tsigkanos, and Timo Kehrer

Implementing, Specifying, and Verifying the QOI Format in Dafny:
A Case Study 35
Ștefan Ciobâcă and Diana-Elena Gratie

VeriCode: Correct Translation of Abstract Specifications to C Code 53
Gerhard Schellhorn, Stefan Bodenmüller, and Wolfgang Reif

Proving Termination via Measure Transfer in Equivalence Checking 75
Dragana Milovančević, Carsten Fuhs, Mario Bucev, and Viktor Kunčak

Verification and Refinement

PLACIDUS: Engineering Product Lines of Rigorous Assurance Cases 87
Logan Murphy, Torin Viger, Alessio Di Sandro, and Marsha Chechik

Stateful Functional Modeling with Refinement (a Lean4 Framework) 109
Frédéric Peschanski

Modeling Register Pairs in CompCert 128
Alexander Loitzl and Florian Zuleger

Quantitative Analysis

Monitoring Extended Hypernode Logic 151
Marek Chalupa, Thomas A. Henzinger, and Ana Oliveira da Costa

Towards Quantitative Analysis of Simulink Models Using Stochastic
Hybrid Automata 172
Pauline Blohm, Paula Herber, and Anne Remke

Monitoring Real-Time Systems Under Parametric Delay 194
*Martin Fränzle, Thomas M. Grosen, Kim G. Larsen,
and Martin Zimmermann*

System Analysis and Security

VeyMont: Choreography-Based Generation of Correct Concurrent
Programs with Shared Memory................................... 217
    Robert Rubbens, Petra van den Bos, and Marieke Huisman

Correct and Complete Symbolic Execution for Free.................... 237
    *Erik Voogd, Einar Broch Johnsen, Åsmund Aqissiaq Arild Kløvstad,
Jurriaan Rot, and Alexandra Silva*

Solvent: Liquidity Verification of Smart Contracts..................... 256
    *Massimo Bartoletti, Angelo Ferrando, Enrico Lipparini,
and Vadim Malvone*

StEVe: A Rational Verification Tool for Stackelberg Security Games 267
    Surasak Phetmanee, Michele Sevegnani, and Oana Andrei

Learning and Reasoning

PyQBF: A Python Framework for Solving Quantified Boolean Formulas..... 279
    Mark Peyrer, Maximilian Heisinger, and Martina Seidl

Improving SAT Solver Performance Through MLP-Predicted Genetic
Algorithm Parameters 288
    Sabrine Saouli, Souheib Baarir, and Claude Dutheillet

Active Learning of Runtime Monitors Under Uncertainty................ 297
    Sebastian Junges, Sanjit A. Seshia, and Hazem Torfah

Specify What? Enhancing Neural Specification Synthesis by Symbolic
Methods.. 307
    George Granberry, Wolfgang Ahrendt, and Moa Johansson

Author Index 327

Software Verification

A Formal Tainting-Based Framework for Malware Analysis

Andrei Mogage[1,2](✉) and Dorel Lucanu[1]

[1] Alexandru Ioan Cuza University, Iași, Romania
andrei.mogage@gmail.com
[2] Bitdefender, Iași, Romania

Abstract. In this paper, we propose a new approach of combining formal methods and malware analysis for quickly determining if an application has specific malicious capabilities. The proposed solution is a Formal Tainting-Based Framework that uses a combination of binary instrumentation, taint analysis, and temporal logic in order to selectively extract behavioral properties of a malware. These are then formalized in order to check if the application expresses certain capabilities. The findings are accompanied by a concrete implementation, which proved effective and efficient against real-life malware, as highlighted by an evaluation. Furthermore, the framework has been used in actual cyber forensics investigations, reducing the time and efforts of security researchers.

Keywords: temporal logic · taint analysis · malware analysis · formal methods

1 Introduction

Highly complex and evasive malware has been on an increasing trend for the last few years [9,10,17]. Extracting the behavior of a malware is a critical task, especially during an urgent forensics investigation. However, an exhaustive report regarding the behavior of a malware is not always necessary. A rapid verification of a potential capability is more desired, in situations where a quick triage is necessary. For instance, a more useful and meaningful solution is to automatically get a verdict/hint of what the program is capable of, e.g.: *Does it steal data? Is it a ransomware?* Moreover, it is very helpful *to know the arguments that led to that verdict*. Knowing which semantic correlations have been made in order to reach a verdict might allow us to determine the correctness of the assessment. For instance, we want to know which chain of relating events has led to the verdict that the program has the capability of stealing data. This is in contrast with the AI-based approaches, e.g. machine learning, where such correlations are merely statistical.

Contribution. One of the best ways to ensure the correctness of the checking process, along with its results, is to formalize the behavior of the malware, using a formal logic. Our contribution consists in a Formal Tainting-Based Framework (FTBF) which uses ① binary instrumentation to control an application; ② taint analysis to extract relevant behavioral properties into a trace; ③ a new temporal logic to analyze the tainted trace, Tainting-Based Logic (TBL); ④ a formally described behavior that the user wishes to check. Despite usual usage of taint analysis to detect vulnerabilities or input reaching certain *sinks*, we use it to extract complex behavioral properties, that are later formally checked against malicious capabilities. To our best knowledge, this is the first time when dynamic instrumentation, tainting analysis, and temporal-logic-based checking are integrated into a formal framework for malware analysis. The result is a sound confirmation of whether the application has a specific capability, ensured through the formal checking process. The framework is presented along with concrete implementation details and experiments using actual malware, testing its efficiency in capturing various capabilities (e.g. code injection, encryption, deobfuscation, privilege escalation). Moreover, the system has been used in real-life scenarios, during cyber forensics, proving useful for speeding up the process of analysis and filtering data.

Paper Structure. The paper continues as follows: We present the prerequisites for our solution, along with related work, in Sect. 2, while FTBF will be described in Sect. 3. Concrete implementation details are introduced in Sect. 4, while the evaluation results of the implementation against malware families are presented in Sect. 5. We conclude and discuss the next steps in Sect. 6.

2 Preliminaries and Related Work

The proposed solution, at its core, lays at the intersection of three main "ingredients": *Binary Instrumentation* (for full control over the execution), *Taint Analysis* (required for providing the raw results), and *Linear Temporal Logics (LTL)*, on which the proposed *Tainting-Based Logic (TBL)* is based. This allows us to reach the ultimate goal, *Malware Analysis*.

2.1 Binary Instrumentation

Binary instrumentation [3] represents an analysis technique, at a binary level, which leverages a program's instructions and can alter, modify, suppress, or execute them. Moreover, additional code may be injected into the target program for gaining a better control of the execution. This allows for a thorough analysis of every step taken by the program. Similar to other analysis methods, binary instrumentation may be used statically or dynamically [7].

A few examples of the most popular Dynamic Binary Instrumentation (DBI) tools or frameworks are: *Intel PIN* [15], *DynamoRIO* [1], *Valgrind* [20].

While not included in the technique itself, the binary instrumentation process is usually configured to generate a trace, consisting of execution-related information. We use the operational semantics of the binary language to formally specify the instrumentation. We assume that a *program configuration* is a pair $\langle S, \sigma \rangle$, where S is the program to be executed and σ is the current state. The *one-step execution* relation is defined as follows: $\langle S, \sigma \rangle \rightarrow \langle S', \sigma' \rangle$ if executing the first statement of S in the state σ, the program remaining to execute is S' and the new obtained state is σ'. Let $\rightarrow^*$ denote the reflexive and transitive closure of $\rightarrow$, meaning that $\langle S', \sigma' \rangle$ is obtained after zero, one or more one-step executions.

An *instrumented execution step* is formally written as $\langle S, \sigma, \tau \rangle \rightsquigarrow \langle S', \sigma', \tau' \rangle$, where $\langle S, \sigma \rangle \rightarrow^* \langle S', \sigma' \rangle$ and the instrumentation of this execution fragment correspondingly appends facts to the *trace* τ, obtaining τ'. Naturally, the trace will be updated by adding new information to it. A complete instrumented execution is represented as $\langle S, \sigma, nil \rangle \rightsquigarrow^* \langle \cdot, \sigma', \tau \rangle$, where the trace τ is the result of instrumenting the whole execution.

2.2 Taint Analysis

Taint Analysis [24], in its standard approach, refers to tracing or following the information flow throughout an application. This can be achieved statically, usually on source code, dynamically, at execution time, or via a combination of those two. The rules which describe when, where, and which pieces of information should be tainted, are grouped under taint policies [24]. Therefore, we can decide when to insert, propagate, or remove certain taint elements. Any element which is altered by or derived from tainted information will also be tagged.

Taint Analysis provides an insight over a multitude of types of applications and scenarios, such as malware analysis, code coverage or testing [19,21]. Examples of applications using taint analysis include TaintDroid [8], Libdft [13], TaintGrind [26], or Neutaint [25].

Our use of taint analysis will be applied to malware analysis. In common approaches, information is followed from *source* to *sink*. However, here it is the first time, to our knowledge, when complex behavioral properties of tainted executions are used to extract (malicious) capabilities of an application. During binary instrumentation, *instances of behavioral patterns (i.e. predicates) are inserted into the generated trace, which describe various behavioral properties of the execution, that also carry tainted information.*

3 Formal Tainting-Based Framework (FTBF)

This section introduces our proposed Formal Tainting-Based Framework(FTBF), which uses taint analysis and temporal logic to extract and formalize a subset of actions performed by an application. This process verifies if it meets certain rules of the form: *behavioral properties imply capability*. These rules are specifications of possible capabilities exposed by applications, and checking them ultimately determines if the application has such behavior.

The taint analysis process requires a taint policy, dictating for which information new taint symbols should be introduced, alongside how they propagate to information-containing elements, such as memory or CPU registers.

FTBF uses a formal specification of tainting policies, leading to different outputs in the form of tainted traces. The next step is to use a temporal logic for reasoning with the tainted trace, in order to analyze if the application expresses specific capabilities.

3.1 Specification of Tainting Policies

The first component of the FTBF is given by the specification of tainting policies, which are essential in defining the syntax of the temporal logic TBL and its models.

The formal specification of tainting policies is an important factor because it dictates which information will be included in the tainted trace. If the captured behavioral properties are incomplete or insufficient, the verification process for capabilities will fail.

The specification of a tainting policy consists of:

- a set of predicates $P(x_1, \ldots, x_k)$ describing *behavioral facts* observed during an execution and that are stored in the tainting trace, and
- a set of *policy rules* that describe when a fragment of an execution observes a behavioral fact and adds it to the tainting trace.

Some examples of behavior facts, along with policies that dictate their insertion, are listed below:

- $Tainted(X)$ - A new taint symbol, X, has been introduced;
- $PropToReg(R, X)$, $PropToMem(M, SZ, X)$ - Taint propagation to register R or memory area $[M, M + SZ]$
- $TaintedAPI(A)$ - The execution has reached API A, which is a taint source;
- $PropToAPI(A, X)$ - A tainted value, with symbol X, has been propagated as parameter to API A.

A policy rule saying that a fragment of execution $\langle S, \sigma \rangle \rightarrow^* \langle S', \sigma' \rangle$ observes a behavioral fact $P(x_1, \ldots, x_k)$ is written as

$$\langle \widetilde{S}, \widetilde{\sigma} \rangle \rightarrow^* \langle \widetilde{S'}, \widetilde{\sigma'} \rangle \models P(x_1, \ldots, x_k) \tag{PR}$$

where $\langle \widetilde{S}, \widetilde{\sigma} \rangle$ and $\langle \widetilde{S'}, \widetilde{\sigma'} \rangle$ are *configuration specifications* using the variables $x_1, \ldots, x_k$. A DBI, instructed to taint by following a tainting policy, will update the *tainted trace* τ by applying the policy rules. A *tainted execution step* corresponds to the application of such a rule and can be written as

$$\langle S, \sigma, \tau \rangle \rightsquigarrow \langle S', \sigma', \tau \mathbin{\raisebox{0.2ex}{\scriptsize$\circ$}} P \langle v_1, \ldots, v_k \rangle \rangle$$

where $\langle S, \sigma \rangle$ and $\langle S', \sigma' \rangle$ are instances of the specifications $\langle \widetilde{S}, \widetilde{\sigma} \rangle$ and $\langle \widetilde{S}', \widetilde{\sigma}' \rangle$, respectively, $P\langle v_1, \ldots, v_k \rangle$ is an instance of a behavioral fact $P(x_1, \ldots, x_k)$, and $\S$ denotes the concatenation of traces. A sequence of such steps describes a *tainted DBI execution*.

3.2 Tainting-Based Logic (TBL)

A *behavioral property* is described as a sequence of relating behavioral facts. We use a particular class of temporal formulas for specifying behavioral properties. A *capability* is a consequence of a behavioral property, and we use capability rules to specify that: in order to check if a program has a certain capability, we produce a tainted trace using DBI and taint analysis, followed by the verification of the trace against a behavioral property, specified as a temporal formula. In this section we introduce Tainting-Based Logic, a formalism where all these ingredients are defined.

Alphabet. A TBL *alphabet* $\mathbb{A} = (\Pi, \Gamma, \mathcal{X}, \mathcal{C})$, over which the patterns and rules are defined, consists of the following elements:

- A set Π of predicate symbols, used for expressing *behavioral facts*. We use $P, P_0, P_1, \ldots$ to range over Π.
- A set Γ of predicate symbols, used for expressing *capabilities*. Π and Γ are disjoint sets. We use $C, C_0, C_1, \ldots$ to range over Γ.
- A set of *variables* $\mathcal{X}$. We use $X, Y, Z, X_0, Y_0, Z_0, X_1, Y_1, Z_1, \ldots$ to range over $\mathcal{X}$.
- A set of *constant names* $\mathcal{C}$. We use $c, c_0, c_1, \ldots$ to range over $\mathcal{C}$.

Remark 1. We assume that each behavioral/capability predicate Q has a fixed arity k and we often use a Prolog-like notation Q/k to specify the arity of a predicate.

Formulas. A *behavioral pattern* is

- either an *atomic pattern* (*behavioral fact*):

$$p ::= \top \mid P(z_1, \ldots, z_k)$$

where z_i is a variable or a constant, $P \in \Pi$;
- or a *linear temporal pattern*:

$$\phi ::= p \mid \neg \phi \mid \phi_1 \vee \phi_2 \mid \mathsf{X} \phi \mid \phi_1 \text{ andthen } \phi_2$$

The logical conjunction is extended as follows:

$$\phi_1 \wedge \phi_2 = \neg(\neg \phi_1 \vee \neg \phi_2)$$

We use $var(\phi)$ to denote the set of variables occurring in ϕ.

The only specific temporal operator is andthen that describes the fact that a property ϕ_2 occurs at a certain time in the future after another one ϕ_1. The other operators are directly borrowed from linear temporal logic, X describing the next state.

An example of a behavioral pattern is:

$$(TaintedAPI(\texttt{CreateFile}) \land \mathsf{X}(Tainted(T)))$$
$$\text{andthen } PropToAPI(\texttt{ReadFile}, T)$$

that, intuitively, says that in the current state a file is created or accessed the first time and at some later state it is read. The parameter T is the tainting tag used to track the file.

A *capability pattern* is an atomic formula:

$$p ::= C(z_1, \ldots, z_k)$$

where z_i is a variable or a constant, $C \in \Gamma$.

An example of a capability pattern is:

$$FileRead(T)$$

where the predicate describes the capability of a program to read the contents of a file, where the T variable will be instantiated by a behavioral pattern (see the definition for capability rules below).

A *capability rule* is used to specify a relationship between behavioral properties and a capability and its generic form is:

$$\phi \vdash C(z_1, \ldots, z_k)$$

where ϕ is a behavioral pattern and $C(z_1, \ldots, z_k)$ is a capability pattern s.t. $var(C(z_1, \ldots, z_k)) \subseteq var(\phi)$.

A simple example of rule is

$$(TaintedAPI(\texttt{CreateFile}) \land \mathsf{X}(Tainted(T)))$$
$$\text{andthen } PropToAPI(\texttt{ReadFile}, T)$$
$$\vdash$$
$$FileRead(T)$$

that helps us to deduce that our program has the capability of reading the contents of a file. Despite its name, CreateFile is also used to open existing files. The behavioral pattern is the same introduced earlier, where we expect a propagation of the taint symbol, T (and its associated tainted data), from the CreateFile API to ReadFile.

Models. Given a TBL alphabet $\mathbb{A} = (\Pi, \Gamma, \mathcal{X}, \mathcal{C})$, a $\mathbb{S}$-*structure* $\mathbb{S} = (D, \rho, \tau)$ consists of:

- a domain D, which is a non-empty set;
- an interpretation ρ that assigns a value $\rho(c) \in D$ for each constant name c, and a relation $\rho(Q) \subseteq D^k$ for each predicate symbol $Q/k, Q \in \Pi \cup \Gamma$;
- a finite trace $\tau = (\tau_0, \ldots, \tau_{n-1})$, where τ_i is a set of instances of atomic patterns, written as $P\langle d_1, \ldots, d_k \rangle$ with $\langle d_1, \ldots, d_k \rangle \in \rho(P), P \in \Pi$.

An example of a trace is given by the following sequence:

$$\tau = (\{TaintedAPI\langle \texttt{CreateFile} \rangle\},$$
$$\{Tainted\langle t_1 \rangle\},$$
$$\{TaintedAPI\langle \texttt{VirtualAlloc} \rangle\},$$
$$\{Tainted\langle t_2 \rangle\},$$
$$\{PropToAPI\langle \texttt{ReadFile}, t_1 \rangle\},$$
$$\{PropToAPI\langle \texttt{CryptEncrypt}, t_2 \rangle\}$$
$$)$$

where $D = \mathbb{CT} \cup \mathbb{T}$, $\mathbb{CT} = \{CreateFile, ReadFile, \ldots\}$ is the set of constant values, $\mathbb{T} = \{t_1, t_2, \ldots\}$ is the set of tainting tags, and the interpretation of predicate symbols satisfies $\rho(Tainted) \subseteq \mathbb{T}$, $\rho(TaintedAPI) \subseteq \mathbb{CT}$, $\rho(PropToAPI) \subseteq \mathbb{CT} \times \mathbb{T}$, $\rho(c) = c$ for any constant c.

Remark 2. While $\mathbb{CT}$ might seem to describe actions (due to the naming of these constants), they are considered constants because they express names of Windows API functions used by the analyzed application. Usually, the constant values are specific to particular operating systems.

Satisfaction Relation $\models_{TBL}$ We use the following notations:

- $|\tau|$ - the length of the trace τ;
- $\tau[i..]$ - the sub-trace $(\tau_i, \ldots, \tau_{|\tau|-1})$;
- $\tau[..j]$ - the sub-trace $(\tau_0, \ldots, \tau_j)$.

The satisfaction relation between traces τ and behavioral patterns ϕ is defined as follows:

$$\tau \models_{TBL} \phi \text{ iff there is a variable assignment } \alpha : var(\phi) \to D$$
$$\text{such that } \tau, \alpha \models_{TBL} \phi$$

where

- $\tau, \alpha \models_{TBL} \top$;
- $\tau, \alpha \models_{TBL} P(z_1, \ldots, z_n)$ iff $P\langle \gamma(z_1), \ldots, \gamma(z_n) \rangle \in \tau_0$, where $\gamma(z_i) = \alpha(z_i)$ if z_i is variable and $\gamma(z_i) = \rho(z_i)$ if z_i is constant symbol;
- $\tau, \alpha \models_{TBL} \neg \phi$ iff $\tau, \alpha \not\models_{TBL} \phi$;

- $\tau, \alpha \models_{\text{TBL}} \phi_1 \vee \phi_2$ iff $\tau, \alpha \models_{\text{TBL}} \phi_1$ or $\tau, \alpha \models_{\text{TBL}} \phi_2$;
- $\tau, \alpha \models_{\text{TBL}} \mathsf{X}\phi$ iff $\tau[1..], \alpha \models_{\text{TBL}} \phi$;
- $\tau, \alpha \models_{\text{TBL}} \phi_1$ andthen ϕ_2 iff $\exists j, k, j < k$ s.t. $\tau[..j] \models_{\text{TBL}} \phi_1 \wedge \tau[k..] \models_{\text{TBL}} \phi_2$.

For instance, the previous trace τ satisfies the following behavioral pattern:

$$(TaintedAPI(\texttt{CreateFile}) \wedge \mathsf{X}(Tainted(T)))$$
$$\text{andthen } PropToAPI(\texttt{ReadFile}, T)$$

using the assignment $\alpha(T) = t_1$.

Proposition 1 (Associativity). *The operator* andthen *is associative.*

The associativity is used later for defining a sugar-syntax for the TBL formulas.

A *capability* is an instance $\langle d_1, \ldots, d_k \rangle \in \rho(C), C \in \Gamma$. We often denote capabilities by $C\langle d_1, \ldots, d_k \rangle$.

Definition 1. *A trace τ has capability $C\langle d_1, \ldots, d_k \rangle$ if there exist α and i s.t. $\tau[i..], \alpha \models \phi$ for some rule $\phi \vdash C(z_1, \ldots, z_k) \in \mathbb{SP}$, where*

$$d_i = \begin{cases} \alpha(z_i) & , z_i \in \mathcal{X} \\ \rho(z_i) & , otherwise \end{cases} \qquad for\ i = \overline{1, k}$$

A capability rule can be seen as a particular kind of implication between two behavioral properties of the whole execution. For instance, the previous trace τ satisfies the following behavioral pattern:

$$(TaintedAPI(\texttt{CreateFile}) \wedge \mathsf{X}(Tainted(T)))$$
$$\text{andthen } PropToAPI(\texttt{ReadFile}, T)$$

using the assignment $\alpha(T) = t_1$. This means that the application (from which τ was generated) has the capability *FileRead(T)*.

3.3 An Algorithm for Behavioral Satisfaction

The Algorithm 1, which makes use of its recursive version Algorithm 2, is used for rules verification. It returns true and the variable assignment α if the trace satisfies the behavioral patterns. Considering that the pattern might be included in a sub-trace starting at an arbitrary position, $\tau[i..]$, the initial algorithm calls the recursive version in a loop, incrementing the start position after each call, until either the trace has been exhausted or the pattern has been satisfied.

Algorithm 1: ModelCheck

Input: τ - trace, ϕ - formula
Output: α and **true** if $\tau, \alpha \models \phi$, **false** otherwise

$index \leftarrow 0$
repeat
  $\alpha \leftarrow \varnothing$
  if $ModelCheckRec(index, \phi).first$ **then**
    return true
  end if
  $index \leftarrow index + 1$
until $index \geq |\tau|$
return false

Lemma 1 (Correctness of *ModelCheckRec*). *The function* ModelCheckRec *given by Algorithm 2 returns* (**true**, j) *for the input* (τ, i, ϕ) *and the global* α, *iff* $\tau[i..j], \alpha \models \phi$.

The proof is by structural induction on ϕ. The most tricky is the base case, where the pattern is an atomic one, because it makes use of the *IsValidAtom* function, which also updates α. The first step of the function is to compare the atom parameter with the one in the current position in trace. If they are different, the function terminates and returns a *false* value. Otherwise, the next step checks if the variables of the atom parameter are not already part of α, case in which the variables are assigned to the values from the trace and updated in α and a *true* value is returned. Lastly, the return value also depends on the equality of the variables' values. □

Theorem 1 (Correctness of *ModelCheck*). *The function* ModelCheck *given by Algorithm 1 (and Algorithm 2) returns* α *and* **true** *for the input* (τ, ϕ) *iff* $\tau, \alpha \models \phi$.

Time Complexity. Considering that FTBF is based on temporal logics on finite traces [6], we would expect a similar complexity, see e.g., [11,14]. However, in our case, the complexity of the algorithm depends on the size of the trace and the size of the pattern. The worst case scenario is given by a pattern which includes the **andthen** operator. Considering the size of ϕ_1 **andthen** ϕ_2 is $m_1 + m_2$, we have the recurrence $T(n, m_1 + m_2) = \sum_{0}^{n-1}(T(i, m_1) + \sum_{i+1}^{n-1} T(n-j, m_2))$. The sum provides a rough estimate of the worst case, where the ϕ_2 pattern represents a negation, because it demands a verification of all the events in the remaining sub-trace $\tau[i+1..]$. This highlights the importance of how capability rules are formulated and how optimization techniques are implemented, e.g., by reducing the size of the trace.

Algorithm 2: ModelCheckRec

Input: τ, index, ϕ - formula
Output: (true, j) if $\tau[index..j], \alpha \models \phi$,
(false, -1) otherwise
Modifies: α

```
if index ≥ |τ| then
    return (false, -1)
end if
switch (φ)
case ¬φ₁:
    (val, j) ← ModelCheckRec(index, φ₁)
    if val then
        return (false, -1)
    end if
    return (true, index)
case X φ₁:
    return
        ModelCheckRec(index + 1, φ₁)
case φ₁ ∨ φ₂:
    (val, j) ← ModelCheckRec(index, φ₁)
    if val then
        return (val, j)
    end if
    return ModelCheckRec(index, φ₂)
case φ₁ andthen φ₂:
    (val, j) ← ModelCheckRec(index, φ₁)
    index ← j + 1
    if index ≥ |τ| then
        return (false, -1)
    end if
    repeat
        (val, j) ←
            ModelCheckRec(index, φ₂)
        index ← index + 1
    until val ∨ index ≥ |τ|
    return (val, j)
default:
    if IsValidAtom(τ[index], φ) then
        return (true, index)
    end if
    return (false, -1)
end switch
```

3.4 Sound by Construction

The soundness of the whole approach is ensured by the rigorous construction of the actual formal specification of the taint policy, along with the behavioral pattern described by the capability rule:

If $\langle S, \sigma, nil \rangle \leadsto^* \langle \cdot, \sigma', \tau \rangle$ and $\tau, \alpha \models_{\text{TBL}} \phi$ for some α,
then $\langle S, \sigma \rangle \to^* \langle \cdot, \sigma' \rangle \models \phi$
meaning that the execution $\langle S, \sigma \rangle \to^* \langle \cdot, \sigma' \rangle$ has the behavioral property ϕ.

Note that the variable assignment α is computed by analyzing τ, and it is consistent with the states obtained during the instrumented execution due to the taint policy:

if $\langle S, \sigma, nil \rangle \leadsto^* \langle \cdot, \sigma', \tau \rangle$ then $\langle S, \sigma \rangle \leadsto^* \langle \cdot, \sigma' \rangle \models \tau$
meaning that the instrumented execution ensures that the native execution has the behavioral property described by the whole tainting trace τ.

Therefore, the soundness of checking that an execution $\langle S, \sigma \rangle \leadsto^* \langle \cdot, \sigma' \rangle$ reveals a capability, defined by $\phi \vdash C$, is ensured by $\langle S, \sigma \rangle \leadsto^* \langle \cdot, \sigma' \rangle \models \tau$ and $\tau, \alpha \models_{\text{TBL}} \phi$, for α found by the checking algorithm.

Concluding, when checking if a program has a specific capability using FTBF, the correctness of the results is rendered by:

- *Taint policy*: The tainted trace must include all facts relevant to the behavioral pattern of the rule. Therefore, the taint policy must be properly configured to capture all relevant behavioral properties.

- *Behavioral pattern*: The capability is described by the behavioral pattern. Therefore, the pattern must capture the specific properties, but also to be generic enough, in order to encompass various ways a capability might be expressed through behavioral patterns.
 - *Correct Implementations* of the taint policy and of the algorithm checking the behavioral property.

4 Implementation

We have implemented the FTBF in the form of an analysis solution integrating all necessary elements: binary instrumentation, taint analysis, and TBL. The last two components are combined, for efficiency reasons that will be discussed later. Moreover, only the binary instrumentation component is based on an external tool, while the most important parts (taint analysis, formalization, and rule checking) were fully implemented by us.

Binary Instrumentation Component

We have integrated our system into Intel PIN [15]. It is a versatile and generic DBI framework, allowing us to have full control over the execution of the analyzed program. This feature is important in the process of taint analysis, making sure that all tainted information is correctly monitored and propagated throughout the execution of the program.

The tainting and formalization processes are practically implemented as a tool/plugin for PIN. The instrumented application follows its natural execution, without any disruption, but we install specific functions to be called when specific events occur, such as API calls, or data transfer instructions. We have chosen PIN for our convenience, but the framework can be easily integrated in other DBIs, as well.

Taint Analysis and TBL Component

The callbacks installed and executed during instrumentation are dependent on the granularity of the analysis, which is ultimately controlled by the taint policy. The user can specify both APIs and CPU instructions as part of the taint sources, instructing the taint analysis component to insert, propagate, or eliminate taint symbols, depending on how they are used throughout the execution. Taint policies and rules are provided as inputs to this component as files in the JSON format.

Examples of JSON descriptions of a taint policy and a TBL rule are included in Listings 1.1 and 1.2. They are accompanied by a trace in Listing 1.3, generated using this taint policy.

Listing 1.1. Taint sources, dictated by the taint policy

```
"taint_sources": {
    "OpenSCManager": [
        {
            "type": "reg",
            "reg": "gax"
        }
    ],
    "OpenService": [
        {
            "type": "reg",
            "reg": "gax"
        }
    ],
    "QueryServiceStatusEx": [
        {
            "type": "ptr",
            "index": 2,
            "ptr_length": {
                "len_param_index": 3,
                "len_param_type": "int"
            }
        }
    ],
    ....
}
```

Listing 1.2. Behavioral Pattern of the rule

```
"pattern": {
    "andThen": [
        {
            "and": [
                {
                    "TaintedAPI": [
                        "A"
                    ]
                },
                {
                    "Next": {
                        "Tainted": [
                            "X_0"
                        ]
                    }
                }
            ]
        }
```

```
18                },
19                {
20                  "and": [
21                    {
22                      "PropToAPICond": [
23                        "B",
24                        "X_0",
25                        [
26                          {
27                            "index": 1,
28                            "type": "str",
29                            "value": "
                                      EventLog"
30                    }]]
31    ...
```

Listing 1.3. Fragment of a Tainted Trace

{TaintedAPI(OpenSCManager)}
{Tainted(T0)}
{PropToReg(rax, T0)}
{PropToReg(rcx, T0)}
{PropToAPI(OpenService, T0)}
{TaintedAPI(OpenService)}
{Tainted(T1)}
...
{PropToReg(rcx, T1)}
{PropToAPI(QueryServiceStatusEx, T1)}
{TaintedAPI(QueryServiceStatusEx)}
{Tainted(T2)}
{PropToMem(0xBB702FF7C0, 0x24, T2)}

As an efficiency feature, the taint analysis and the formalization processes are combined, leading to the insertion of formal behavioral facts in the tainted trace, instead of raw information. This makes the analysis faster, and also reduces the amount of memory required.

Another step taken for the reduction of the analysis overhead is the possibility of specifying which events (e.g., specific behavioral facts) can trigger the rule checking process. This is important because the user does not have to wait until the end of the execution - especially helpful for large applications or in scenarios where the target enters an infinite loop.

An important aspect is the level of knowledge required to create new capability rules. While it is true that a basic understanding is necessary, it is not required to know beforehand an application's behavior or implementation in order to capture its capabilities (this would be redundant). The rules can and should be created by having an overall idea as to what functions or instructions can be chained in order to achieve a specific behavior (i.e. by induction, where API X is required by API Y and so on). Moreover, the most common way of defining a rule is to chain several APIs, instead of relying on predicates involving instructions, as this represents the main interaction with the operating system. The taint analysis component will ensure that taint symbols are properly propagated through relevant APIs by monitoring them through other instructions, registers, memory and even other APIs.

In the following section, we provide a brief evaluation of our implementation along with the obtained results.

5 Evaluation

In this section, we present the potential of the analysis tool described in Sect. 4 by testing it against a suite of malicious applications.

Method. We have selected eight malware families and created one rule for each family, such that each will capture a different capability that a malicious application may express. The selection process has been random, but with a focus on selecting malware families that are still relevant (i.e. seen in recent attacks or that represented a strong inspiration for subsequent cyber threats).

The number of samples for each family varies between 6 and 37, depending on their public availability. All applications have been collected from two publicly available sources: VirusTotal[1] and Malpedia[2]. Each malware family is briefly described below:

Al-Khaser[3]: An application which deploys a myriad of malicious techniques, borrowed from complex malware, in order for analysts to test analysis solutions. While not an actual malware (the only one in this situation in our test suite), it is relevant for capturing anti-analysis capabilities;

Avaddon [27]: A ransomware family initially seen in 2020, with a strong Ransomware-as-a-Service (RaaS) model, which affected a high number of victims spanning multiple industries and countries. Even if the RaaS has been shutdown 2021, the malware is still being distributed worldwide and several new ransomware families emerged later on and share common practices and even source code [2];

RokRat [22]: A Remote Administration Tool (RAT), first reported in 2017, RokRat is a malware distributed in multiple malicious campaigns and makes use of numerous attack vectors and techniques in order to infiltrate a victim and then start an entire chain of receiving and executing commands. While it has not suffered significant changes at its core lately, it has been combined with new techniques to ensure its success in affecting victims [23];

---

[1] https://www.virustotal.com
[2] https://malpedia.caad.fkie.fraunhofer.de/
[3] https://github.com/LordNoteworthy/al-khaser

Darkside [5]: A ransomware family renowned for high-impact attacks targeting large corporations and governments, culminating with the attack on the Colonial Pipeline in the United States;

CobaltStrike Beacon [4]: A beacon is a payload from Cobalt Strike[4] which mimics attacker activities seen in the wild. However, beacons have been used directly in actual attacks as an initial step for deploying other malware tools on the systems of affected victims;

Phant0m[5]: A tool capable of tampering with the Event Logging Service integrated into the Windows OS, resulting in the operating system not logging critical events that occur. This leads to attacks that are more stealthy and harder to investigate;

HermeticWiper [12]: A malware involved in cyber-attacks targeting Ukraine, emerged during the recent war, which disrupts the functionality of systems;

Makop [16]: An infamous ransomware family and group, which has been active for at least the last 4 years.

Capability Rules. As previously mentioned, we have created one capability rule for each malware family. The rules are constructed based on each malware's purpose and modus operandi, as described by public reports. The taint sources are also included in the description of the rules - *for source APIs with no special mentions, we considered that the output of that API is tainted with the freshly introduced taint symbol*. Recall that the `"eax"` (for 32-bit architecture) or `"rax"` (for 64-bit) registers hold the output value upon function return. Due to space constraints, we will only include two representative rules.

Remark 3. For ease of use, we allow a flexible syntax for the binary operators (∨, ∧, andthen), and allow them to be used with an arbitrary number of operands, using associativity.

Code Injection: Verify if the malware uses code injection, i.e. injecting and executing a payload in a separate process.

Brief Description. Code Injection represents a malicious technique in which an application injects a payload into a different process - usually legitimate. This allows the attacker to spread the infection throughout the system, while also keeping a low profile, since the legitimate processes have a higher degree of trust. The code injection is usually performed by either starting a new, normally legitimate, process (`CreateProcess`) or obtaining a handle to an existing one (`OpenProcess`), allocating a new memory region inside it (`VirtualAllocEx`) in order to place the malicious payload(`WriteProcessMemory`) and finally executing it - this is achieved by either creating a new thread to execute the code (`CreateRemoteThread`) or by hijacking a suspended thread to point to the payload and resuming it (`ResumeThread`).

Capability Rule (TBL notation)

---

[4] https://www.cobaltstrike.com/product/features/beacon
[5] https://github.com/hlldz/Phant0m

andthen$((($ $TaintedAPI(A) \vee TaintedAPI(E)) \wedge ($ X $Tainted(X_0))),$
$(PropToAPI(B, X_0) \wedge ($ X $TaintedAPI(B)) \wedge ($ X X $Tainted(X_1))),$
$(PropToAPI(C, X_0) \wedge ($ X $PropToAPI(C, X_1)))$
$((PropToAPI(D, X_0) \wedge ($ X $PropToAPI(D, X_1))) \vee PropToAPI(F, X_0))$
$)$
⊢ Code Injection

where:
A = `CreateProcess`   B = `VirtualAllocEx`
C = `WriteProcessMemory` D = `CreateRemoteThread`
E = `OpenProcess`   F = `ResumeThread`

The taint sources include the following: `CreateProcess` - monitoring the 9th parameter, a pointer to a memory area, which includes the handle to the process; `OpenProcess` - the output value; `VirtualAllocEx` - the output value.

Deobfuscation: Highlight an obfuscated code that is deobfuscated and executed.

Brief Description. Data and code obfuscation is another strategy used by threat actors in order to strengthen their applications against analysis. It involves concealing parts of a malware using encryption, packing, or some other computations (e.g. using XOR operations), which will only be revealed during execution. In this scenario, we rely on one deobfuscation algorithm discovered in some CobaltStrike Beacons, which involves XOR-ing the bytes of an obfuscated area, representing a malicious payload, which will be executed after.

Capability Rule (TBL notation)

andthen$($
    $(Tainted(X) \wedge ($ X $PropToMem(M, SZ, X))),$
    $TaintedCodeExecute(M, X)$
$)$
⊢ Payload deobfuscation

The taint sources includes the following regex code:
- `"xor (.+), .+"`;
- `"mov byte ptr \[(.+)\]+.+\],\1"`.

The first instruction captures the result byte, because it will be referred in the second instruction (using the first capture group, `"\1"`). In turn, the result buffer will be captured in the second instruction. This is relevant because the taint policy, in addition to the sources, instructs the taint analysis module to insert a new symbol for it. In other words, if the code is satisfied by the execution (i.e. the sequence of instructions is executed), a new symbol is introduced, and the memory area described by the second captured group (the buffer referenced by `mov byte ptr`) is also tainted. Hence, two new predicates will be introduced: *Tainted* and *PropToMem*. Moreover, a new predicate will be introduced when executing a tainted area: *TaintedCodeExecute*. This will allow us to define a rule chaining these events: a symbol is introduced and propagated to a memory area, which is later executed.

Results. All experiments have been conducted inside a virtual machine (using VMWare Workstation 16), with a Windows 10 as guest with 8 GB of RAM, 4 cores and virtualization enabled, while the host uses Windows 11 on an Intel i7-11800H CPU @2.30 GHz and 32 GB of RAM.

Due to space restrictions, we have summarized the results for each test in Table 1. We have computed each average by ignoring the timeout entries, but marked the column entry as *TIMEOUT* where all instances have exceeded the timeout of 10 min. All experiments were successful (i.e. the capability has been correctly identified). Moreover, each analysis instance was achieved under 30 s, except for a sample for Makop ransomware, where some anti-analysis tricks were deployed, which slowed the analysis process.

Table 1. Summary of results

Malware Family	Avg. Analysis (s.)	Avg. Native execution (s.)
Al-Khaser	7.73	TIMEOUT
Avaddon	14.375	TIMEOUT
RokRat	22.69	19.72
DarkSide	15.87	14.68
CobaltStrike	4.13	TIMEOUT
Phant0m	6.22	1.22
HermeticWiper	9	TIMEOUT
Makop	20.42	TIMEOUT

These experiments bring forward the potential of such an analysis solution to quickly identify if a program expresses a specific capability or not. Naturally, the analysis process will bring an additional overhead compared with the program executing outside an execution environment. Because of this, we have also tested the duration under native execution. However, while the analysis time represents only duration until the capability is expressed, we could not verify at which exact moment the same capability is expressed natively without tampering with the applications. Therefore, we have chosen to estimate the total time necessary to complete the execution, with a provided timeout of **10 min**. This lead to three scenarios of comparison:

- **TIMEOUT** on native execution - this was caused by applications that either take longer than 10 min to complete their execution, or continue executing endlessly, e.g. waiting for network commands or scanning possibly new files. This category only applies to native execution, while all analysis instances ended successfully.
- Native duration is **longer** than analysis duration - this is directly related to the fact that the analysis process has ended once the capability has been expressed, as part of the optimizations described in Sect. 4.

– Native duration is **shorter** than analysis duration - this represents the overhead of the analysis solution.

We have summarized how many of samples per malware family fall under these three scenarios in Table 2.

Table 2. Evaluation scenarios per malware family

Malware Family	TIMEOUT	LONGER NATIVE	LONGER ANALYSIS
Al-Khaser	15	0	0
Avaddon	8	0	0
RokRat	1	1	24
DarkSide	0	4	12
CobaltStrike	37	0	0
PhantOm	0	22	0
HermeticWiper	6	0	0
Makop	19	0	0

Nonetheless, an actual real-life comparison is not against a native execution, but rather takes into account the effort, especially regarding the time consumed, of an analyst. Another important remark relates to the generality of these rules, i.e. how well they can capture a capability. This is directly influenced by how well a rule is constructed and if it considers multiple scenarios, because there might be multiple ways of implementing a capability, e.g. by combining different APIs or instructions.

In this regard, a prerequisite for a user of this analysis solution is to have some general information on such combinations that might lead to an expected output. Nonetheless, the effort required to construct a rule, along with the analysis duration, are significantly lower than manually analyzing an application or by filtering and correlating a myriad of results provided by other automated solutions, such as a sandbox. Furthermore, the process of crafting rules for capturing capabilities can be simplified by using Large Language Models (LLMs), as presented in [18]. The user can query a LLM for an overall idea of how capabilities can be implemented, and then proceed with the formalization process.

Real-Life Use. Apart from the evaluation, the FTBF implementation has been used in actual forensics investigations in the Bitdefender Research Labs[6], helping in filtering multiple files uncovered in the initial steps of these investigations. Some rules presented during the evaluation were inspired by these cases, e.g. *Ransomware encryption, Code Injection, Data Exfiltration*. While the base set of rules will be expanded to capture a broader range of capabilities, the analysis

---

[6] https://www.bitdefender.com/.

solution has presented enthusiastic results so far, even for security researchers with no knowledge of formal methods or temporal logics. For example, it proved to be useful for junior colleagues that, while having basic understanding on how some Windows APIs can be combined to achieve a capability, currently lack experience in complex malware analysis. This gap was reduced with the help of our analysis tool, allowing novice analysts to quickly verify malware capabilities without the classical approach of manual analysis.

6 Conclusion and Future Work

In this paper, we introduced FTBF, a framework that can be used to formally and selectively express behavioral properties of an application, in order to check if they lead to a specific capability. The main motivation stems from the necessity of having a sound, and hence trustworthy, mechanism of capability verification, while also doing it fast.

FTBF achieves its goals of capabilities extraction through three main components: binary instrumentation for control over the execution, a taint tracking process in which sensitive data and behavior is tainted and monitored throughout the execution, and a comprehensive and formal behavioral analysis component in which the formally generated trace is evaluated along with the rules describing program capabilities.

An implementation of FTBF was already experimented in practice and the results are promising. It uses Intel PIN [15] as the DBI engine, while the remaining components (taint analysis, TBL, formal checking) were entirely implemented by us. The framework was also useful in real world cyber investigations, for quickly filtering out malware that would not express certain capabilities.

Future Work. The adaptable format of our solution, along with the thorough verifications of a formal system, allow us a future development and extension of the current work. First, we are currently working on the creation of more rules, directly inspired by malware behavior, that will capture a broader range of capabilities spanning different categories of malicious applications. Another important aspect, also currently in work, is the ability of defining new rules based on pre-existing ones, i.e. using capabilities as behavioral predicates for other rules. If needed, we may also increase the expressivity of TBL with new temporal operators. At the implementation level, we also intend to integrate FTBF with other DBIs, especially those focused on transparency and anti-anti-analysis tricks.

References

1. Dynamorio public repository. https://github.com/DynamoRIO/dynamorio. Accessed 19 Mar 2024
2. One source to rule them all: Chasing avaddon ransomware. https://www.mandiant.com/resources/blog/chasing-avaddon-ransomware. Accessed 13 Mar 2024
3. Bala, V., Duesterwald, E., Banerjia, S.: Dynamic binary translation and optimization. ACM Comput. Surv. (CSUR) **37**(2), 1–52 (2005)

4. Mar 10339794-1.v1 - cobalt strike beacon. https://www.cisa.gov/news-events/analysis-reports/ar21-148a. Accessed 13 Mar 2024
5. Darkside ransomware explained: How it works and who is behind it. https://www.csoonline.com/article/570723/darkside-ransomware-explained-how-it-works-and-who-is-behind-it.html
6. De Giacomo, G., Vardi, M.Y.: Linear temporal logic and linear dynamic logic on finite traces. In: Proceedings of the Twenty-Third International Joint Conference on Artificial Intelligence. IJCAI '13, pp. 854–860. AAAI Press (2013)
7. D'Elia, D.C., Coppa, E., Nicchi, S., Palmaro, F., Cavallaro, L.: SOK: using dynamic binary instrumentation for security (and how you may get caught red handed). In: Proceedings of the 2019 ACM Asia Conference on Computer and Communications Security, pp. 15–27 (2019)
8. Enck, W., et al.: Taintdroid: an information-flow tracking system for realtime privacy monitoring on smartphones. ACM Trans. Comput. Syst. **32**(2) (2014). https://doi.org/10.1145/2619091
9. Evasive malware threats on the rise despite decline in overall attacks. https://www.infosecurity-magazine.com/news/evasive-malware-rise-decline/
10. New research: Fileless malware attacks surge by 900% and cryptominers make a comeback, while ransomware attacks decline. https://www.globenewswire.com/en/news-release/2021/03/30/2201173/0/en/New-Research-Fileless-Malware-Attacks-Surge-by-900-and-Cryptominers-Make-a-Comeback-While-Ransomware-Attacks-Decline.html
11. Fionda, V., Greco, G.: The complexity of LTL on finite traces: Hard and easy fragments. In: Proceedings of the Thirtieth AAAI Conference on Artificial Intelligence. AAAI'16, pp. 971–977. AAAI Press (2016)
12. Hermeticwiper: A detailed analysis of the destructive malware that targeted Ukraine. https://www.malwarebytes.com/blog/threat-intelligence/2022/03/hermeticwiper-a-detailed-analysis-of-the-destructive-malware-that-targeted-ukraine. Accessed 13 Mar 2024
13. Kemerlis, V.P., Portokalidis, G., Jee, K., Keromytis, A.D.: Libdft: Practical dynamic data flow tracking for commodity systems. In: Proceedings of the 8th ACM SIGPLAN/SIGOPS Conference on Virtual Execution Environments. pp. 121–132. VEE '12, Association for Computing Machinery, New York, NY, USA (2012). https://doi.org/10.1145/2151024.2151042
14. La Torre, S., Parlato, G.: On the complexity of LTL model-checking of recursive state machines. In: Arge, L., Cachin, C., Jurdziński, T., Tarlecki, A. (eds.) ICALP 2007. LNCS, vol. 4596, pp. 937–948. Springer, Heidelberg (2007). https://doi.org/10.1007/978-3-540-73420-8_80
15. Luk, C.K., et al.: Pin: building customized program analysis tools with dynamic instrumentation. In: Proceedings of the 2005 ACM SIGPLAN Conference on Programming Language Design and Implementation. PLDI '05, New York, NY, USA, pp. 190–200. Association for Computing Machinery (2005). https://doi.org/10.1145/1065010.1065034
16. Dissecting the malicious arsenal of the makop ransomware gang. https://securityaffairs.com/143452/malware/dissecting-makop-ransomware.html. Accessed 13 Mar 2024
17. The hidden picture of malware attack trends. https://www.helpnetsecurity.com/2023/04/06/malware-attack-trends-q4-2022/
18. Mogage, A.: A.I. Assisted Malware Capabilities Capturing. Procedia Computer Science (2024). In the proceedings of the 28th International Conference on Knowledge-Based and Intelligent Information & Engineering Systems (KES 2024)

19. Moser, A., Kruegel, C., Kirda, E.: Exploring multiple execution paths for malware analysis. In: Proceedings of the 2007 IEEE Symposium on Security and Privacy. SP '07, USA, pp. 231–245. IEEE Computer Society (2007). https://doi.org/10.1109/SP.2007.17
20. Nethercote, N., Seward, J.: ValGrind: a framework for heavyweight dynamic binary instrumentation. SIGPLAN Not. **42**(6), 89–100 (2007). https://doi.org/10.1145/1273442.1250746
21. Qiu, J., Yadegari, B., Johannesmeyer, B., Debray, S., Su, X.: A framework for understanding dynamic anti-analysis defenses. In: Proceedings of the 4th Program Protection and Reverse Engineering Workshop. PPREW-4, New York, NY, USA. Association for Computing Machinery (2014). https://doi.org/10.1145/2689702.2689704
22. Introducing rokrat. https://blog.talosintelligence.com/introducing-rokrat/. Accessed 13 Mar 2024
23. Chain reaction: Rokrat's missing link. https://research.checkpoint.com/2023/chain-reaction-rokrats-missing-link/. Accessed 13 Mar 2024
24. Schwartz, E.J., Avgerinos, T., Brumley, D.: All you ever wanted to know about dynamic taint analysis and forward symbolic execution (but might have been afraid to ask). In: 2010 IEEE Symposium on Security and Privacy, pp. 317–331 (2010). https://doi.org/10.1109/SP.2010.26
25. She, D., Chen, Y., Shah, A., Ray, B., Jana, S.: Neutaint: efficient dynamic taint analysis with neural networks. In: 2020 IEEE Symposium on Security and Privacy (SP), pp. 1527–1543 (2020). https://doi.org/10.1109/SP40000.2020.00022
26. Taintgrind. https://github.com/wmkhoo/taintgrind
27. Yuste, J., Pastrana, S.: Avaddon ransomware: an in-depth analysis and decryption of infected systems. Comput. Secur. **109**, 102388 (2021). https://www.sciencedirect.com/science/article/pii/S0167404821002121

A Systematic Literature Review on a Decade of Industrial TLA[+] Practice

Roman Bögli[1(✉)], Leandro Lerena[1], Christos Tsigkanos[1,2], and Timo Kehrer[1]

[1] Institute of Computer Science, University of Bern, Bern, Switzerland
{roman.boegli,christos.tsigkanos,timo.kehrer}@unibe.ch
[2] Department of Aerospace, University of Athens, Athens, Greece

Abstract. TLA[+] is a formal specification language used for designing, modeling, documenting, and verifying systems through model checking. Despite significant interest from the research community, knowledge about usage of the TLA[+] ecosystem in practice remains scarce. Industry reports suggest that software engineers could benefit from insights, innovations, and solutions to the practical challenges of TLA[+]. This paper explores this development by conducting a systematic literature review of TLA[+]'s industrial usage over the past decade. We analyze the trend in industrial application, characterize its use, examine whether its promised benefits resonate with practitioners, and identify challenges that may hinder further adoption.

Keywords: Formal Methods · TLA[+] · PlusCal · Literature Review · Industry

1 Introduction

Despite the potential of increasing dependability of software-intensive systems, formal methods are still scarcely adopted in industry [26]. A prominent example is the formal specification language TLA[+] (*Temporal Logic of Actions*) [22], which was designed for modeling, specifying, and verifying a variety of systems. It provides a high-level mathematical notation to describe system behavior over time using temporal logic [25] and set theory, making it particularly well-suited for distributed or concurrent systems. TLA[+] specifications can be verified using the *TLC model checker*, which systematically explores all possible states and highlights property violations using counterexamples. As the syntax of TLA[+] closely relates to the underlying mathematical notation, it can be challenging for software engineers that are accustomed to imperative programming languages. Thus, Lamport [23] introduced *PlusCal*, a C-like programming language that translates into TLA[+] specifications and therewith aims to bridge the gap between conventional programming practices and formal methods. Unless stated otherwise, we use TLA[+] to refer to both TLA[+] and PlusCal in this paper.

TLA$^+$ promises several benefits in software development. First, it allows for precise specification and verification of system behaviors and properties, substantially reducing the likelihood of fundamental design flaws or subtle bugs that traditional testing methods might miss. Examples of these notoriously hard-to-detect errors include, for instance, race conditions and deadlocks. Second, TLA$^+$ promotes clear and unambiguous system documentation, preventing misinterpretations that can arise from informal specifications written in natural human language. This eases the integration of new system features and streamlines staff onboarding. Lastly, the similarity of PlusCal's syntax to conventional programming languages lowers the entry barrier and encourages the adoption of formal methods in mainstream software development.

From an academic perspective, TLA$^+$ is appreciated due to its promising benefits, which is why it is suggested to practitioners in industry. However, little is known about the actual adoption of TLA$^+$ in real-world settings and whether its promises resonate with practitioners. To address this gap, we conduct a *Systematic Literature Review* (SLR), guided by the following research questions:

RQ1: What is the trend in TLA$^+$ usage in industry over the past decade?
RQ2: How are industrial applications of TLA$^+$ characterized?
RQ3: Do the promised benefits of TLA$^+$ resonate in industry reports?
RQ4: What challenges hinder the adoption of TLA$^+$ in industry?

2 Review Methodology

In terms of our SLR, we followed the guidelines in [21,24] for collecting, filtering, and analyzing existing literature. Moreover, following the guidelines by Carrera-Rivera et al. [18], we employed *Parsifal* to streamline the SLR. This online tool aids in creating the review protocol, including formulating inclusion and exclusion criteria, a quality assessment checklist, and a data extraction form. Note that we use the term *paper* as a synonym for publication, resource, report, or document.

Figure 1 visualizes the paper gathering and reduction process over the sampled time period. Each bar's total length corresponds to the number of optimistically found papers in a given year. The subfigure on the right subsumes the totals per phase, which are further explained in the rest of this section. The entire SLR was conducted by two researchers independently and disagreements were discussed and eliminated among all four authors.

2.1 Optimistic Search

Since this SLR focuses on the use of TLA$^+$ in industry, we chose to rely exclusively on *Google Scholar* search results. This platform includes grey literature, such as industrial reports, which may not be published in peer-reviewed academic publication outlets [28].

```
      ( "verification" OR "correctness" OR "model checking" )
  AND ( "TLA+" OR "PlusCal" )
  AND ( "experience" OR "application" OR "insight" OR
        "lesson" OR "practical" OR "practice" OR "usage" )
  AND ( "industry" OR "cloud" OR "blockchain" OR "transportation" OR
        "railway" OR "healthcare" OR "aerospace" OR "control systems" OR
        "hardware design" OR "internet of things" )
```

Listing 1. Google Scholar search string used for the optimistic search of our SLR.

The first phase involves creating a search string that is specific yet broad enough for comprehensive results. We targeted the topic and combined it with overlapping synonyms and industry names (see Listing 1). Besides the hypernym *industry*, we additionally included more specific industry names such as *blockchain* or *aerospace* as these domains are known to entail software use cases predestined for formal methods. This approach aims to optimistically balance the reach and relevance of the search results. We further limited the search using two inclusion criteria: (1) English language and (2) published within the last 11 years (2013–2023). After configuring the search settings according to these criteria, we collected a total of 290 papers[1].

2.2 Reduction

After the initial paper gathering phase, we reduced the scope in the three consecutive phases, namely deduplication, exclusion, and affinity filter.

Deduplication: First, a total of 29 duplicate papers were removed. This concerned, for example, papers with prior preprints or search results listing a paper once isolated and once in the context of an entire volume such as conference proceedings.

Rejection: In a second phase, we rejected papers that did match any of our four exclusion criteria. Namely, these are (1) no access to paper over university network, (2) not covering a case in industry, (3) neither TLA$^+$ nor PlusCal are the selected formal methods, or (4) neither TLA$^+$ nor PlusCal appear in abstract, introduction, conclusion or discussion. A total of 224 papers were rejected in this phase.

Affinity Filter: The final reduction phase involved the quality assessment. However, we denote this phase as *affinity filter* as it concerns the paper's suitability for answering our research questions rather than the paper's overall objective quality. We quantified a given paper's affinity using four questions, which can either be fully (1 point), partially (0.5 points) or not answered (0 points). Specifically, we questioned whether the paper addressed: (1) the reason for using formal methods, (2) assumptions for creating the model, (3) the link between model and implementation, and (4) drawbacks from practical experiences. Papers with ≥ 3.5 points passed this affinity filter, reducing the set of 37 accepted papers

---
[1] Measurement from last execution on May 28, 2024.

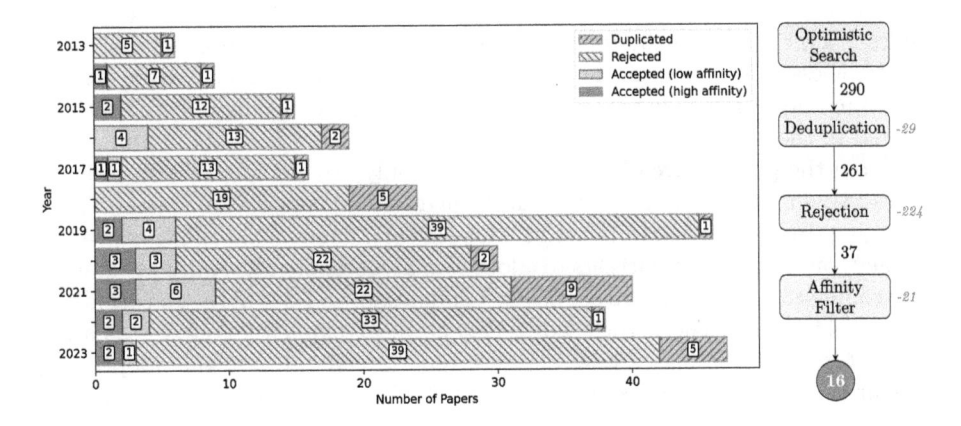

Fig. 1. Paper qualifying process, resulting in 16 relevant ones for this SLR.

further by 21. The resulting 16 accepted high-affinity papers are included in this SLR[2]. To differentiate these from other references in this paper, we have numbered them accordingly (1–16) and subdivided the bibliography into two sections.

3 Results

The 16 included papers could be linked to some well-known companies or products. This includes Abaco Autoscaler [11], Alibaba Group (Alibaba PolarDB) [4], Amazon Web Services (including S3 and DynamoDB) [10], Audi [7], eBay [13], Huawei Cloud (Taurus Distributed Database, now called GaussDB) [3], Informal Systems [1], Microsoft (Cosmos DB) [5,6], MongoDB [2,16], PharOS [8] and Thales [12]. The remainder of this section highlights interesting findings and answers the four research questions stated at the end of Sect. 1.

3.1 RQ1: Trend

The number of publications on TLA[+] in industrial settings has been growing over the last decade, as shown in Fig. 1. Although only 16 papers qualified for this SLR, the initially considered 290 papers support this claim. A linear regression analysis of the total unique papers points to statistical significance of the upward trend. Specifically, the total deduplicated papers (261) exhibit a $S = 3.67$ upward slope with $p < 0.001$.

This insight of a growing overall trend, however, should be interpreted with caution for two reasons. First, the adoption of innovative technologies typically follows non-linear evolution curves or hype cycles [20,27]. Given the relatively short time frame considered in this SLR, accurately pinpointing the current stage of this cycle is challenging. Second, the overall growth trend does not directly

---
[2] See data set on doi.org/10.5281/zenodo.13629185.

address TLA+ usage in industrial settings, as posed in this research question. Nevertheless, the increasing number of unique papers listed in Google Scholar matching the search string is noteworthy, as it suggests ongoing research activity related to the topic.

From the perspective of industry practice only, we record that this growing overall trend resonates in some of the 16 high-affinity papers. For instance, the emerging trend is carried from within MongoDB [2], Huawei [3], and Amazon [10] as they convinced other partners to adopt formal methods. The Amazon paper by Newcombe et al. [10] appears particularly impactful, as 7 out of the 16 considered papers (44%[3]) referenced their work. Gao et al. [3] explicitly stated it as a key motivator. This showcases how industry reports can catalyze the adoption of similar practices by other companies.

> *Summarized answer to RQ1:* There is a significant upward trend in TLA+ papers in general, which is likely to continue due to success stories recommending its adoption in industry. The report by Amazon [10] can be seen as a guiding factor in this development.

3.2 RQ2: Application Settings

We identified that 8 of the papers (50%) applied pure TLA+ while sole PlusCal applications were only recorded in 3 papers (19%). The remaining 5 papers (31%) mention to use both languages in combination. Papers that utilize PlusCal justify this solely by its intuitive and programmer-friendly syntax. They appreciate its readability for engineers [7,12] without extensive training in formal methods. Consequently, it is also said to be easier to start with [9]. Reasons for using plain TLA+ include its records of successful examples in industry [3] or because it has previously been used within the company [16].

To analyze the domain of application, we classified each of the 16 high-affinity papers based on their most fitting industry affiliation based on an open card sorting approach [29]. While these industry categories resemble those in our initial search string, they were chosen independently and are unrelated to its design. The search string was crafted for broad scoping, whereas the industry affiliations of high-affinity papers aim to cluster the TLA+ application domains.

We found the majority focuses on cloud applications (63%), followed by 2 papers for railway and control systems (13% each), and only 1 paper for blockchain and transportation (6% each). This distribution aligns with TLA+'s suitability for distributed systems [2,4] and the fact that today's heavy reliance on cloud infrastructure on software-intensive systems makes minimizing downtime crucial [17].

In addition to industry affiliation, we examined the stage in the system lifecycle where TLA+ was predominantly applied. We depicted these stages with three labels and assigned one or more of them to each of the 16 papers. Namely, these

---

[3] All percentages in this paper are rounded to the nearest integer for readability.

labels are *early design*, *implementation*, and *debugging*. By counting the total number of label occurrences, we conclude that TLA[+] was mostly used during early design (81%), followed by debugging (44%), and implementation (38%). From these 16 papers, 9 were labelled only with one purpose (7 for early design and 2 for debugging) while the remaining 7 exhibited a combination of purposes.

Keeping a model in sync with an actual implementation is costly. Therefore, we specifically checked if a paper highlights the link between model and implementation during the affinity filtering phase. Notably, 3 papers (19%) discussed automated synchronization between TLA[+] specifications and productive system implementation. Salierno et al. [15] proposed a translation algorithm to generate relay logic[4] from the model to verify interlocking components. Methni et al. [8] introduced C2TLA+, a tool that automatically derives TLA[+] specification from given C code. Similarly, Resch and Paulitsch [12] translated C code to PlusCal using scripts.

> *Summarized answer to RQ2:* TLA[+] is mostly applied directly or in combination with PlusCal. Its predominant application area resides in the cloud industry. It is mainly used during the early system design stage, followed by debugging purposes. Despite its importance, efforts to synchronize models with implementations have been only marginally addressed.

3.3 RQ3: Fulfillment of Promised Benefits

All papers highlight several benefits of using TLA[+]. Primarily, it effectively helped to identify subtle system errors or bugs that are difficult to reproduce with conventional testing methods. Examples include fixing stack overflow errors [2], race-conditions [11], or deadlocks [13]. Jakobs et al. [7] emphasize that, unlike testing, which can only be performed after development, formal verification can be applied from the beginning.

The benefits of improved system design and a better overall understanding of system behavior were equally prominent. Examples include non-trivial system executions [1], considering all possible system states in aggregate [5], and detecting anomalous but correct behaviors not mentioned in the system's documentation [6]. Furthermore, Salierno et al. [15] benefited from TLA[+]'s hardware modelling capabilities and Newcombe et al. [10] could confidently perform aggressive system optimizations.

> *Summarized answer to RQ3:* TLA[+] is reported to successfully identify bugs, contribute to better system design, and overall system understanding – therewith validating its potential.

---

[4] Referring to control systems using electrical relays to perform logical operations.

3.4 RQ4: Identified Challenges

On the drawback side, two major aspects were mentioned. One is the steep learning curve of formal methods, as software engineers are usually unfamiliar with them [3,12]. Although PlusCal was praised in the papers considered for mitigating this, modeling existing systems remains an effortful task that threatens scalability [7].

Another challenge is choosing the right level of abstraction [3] and necessary assumptions [13] for the formal model. Overly detailed models are costly and prone to state space explosion [19], while overly simple models reduce the added value of applying formal methods. Note that compositional model checking was reported as a technique to help to mitigate state space explosion [4]. Sabraoui et al. [14] also followed such a component-based architecture but later combined them to test the model as a whole.

> *Summarized answer to RQ4:* TLA$^+$'s steep learning curve, compared to common imperative languages, demands notable effort, especially when applied retrospectively. Besides this, selecting the right level of model abstraction remains challenging.

4 Threats to Validity

As a threat to validity, we acknowledge that other industrial uses of TLA$^+$ may exist but are not publicly reported due to intellectual property (IP) issues. As such, we only considered papers indexed by Google Scholar. We noticed that using this search engine for the SLR presented challenges, such as slightly varying search results and query rate limits.

In addressing RQ1, we concluded that there is a significant upward trend in the use of TLA$^+$. However, this conclusion is based on the deduplicated number of papers (261) rather than the 16 high-affinity papers, due to the latter's poor sample size. The larger set, however, may include irrelevant or nonsensical papers, which potentially skews our trend analysis and leading to misleading conclusions.

For RQ2, RQ3, and RQ4, our conclusions are derived from manually scanned arguments concerning benefits, challenges, or the affiliations regarding industry and deployment stages. As with any manual process, there is a risk of incompleteness or subjective interpretation. As mentioned earlier, we mitigated this risk by having two researchers independently conduct the SLR to ensure consistency and reduce bias. However, this risk cannot be completely eliminated.

Finally, it is important to acknowledge that there are likely very few papers that exclusively document the limitations that make TLA$^+$ impractical for industry use. As a result, the identified high-affinity papers may be positively biased towards the usefulness of TLA$^+$ as they primarily showcase success stories.

5 Conclusion and Future Work

With this SLR we analyzed the surface of TLA$^+$'s industry adoption using our RQs. We conclude that TLA$^+$ usage has surged since 2015, especially in the cloud industry and is mainly applied during early system design and debugging. It effectively uncovers deep bugs, enhances system design, and improves overall understanding. However, its adoption is hindered by a steep learning curve and the challenge of selecting appropriate model abstractions, despite PlusCal's help in easing this difficulty.

With this contribution we shed light on the actual use of formal methods in industry and its consequences, focusing on TLA$^+$ and the last decade. We believe the resulting curated list of relevant papers and our findings serve as a foundation for two stakeholders. First, interested practitioners that have more specific questions in favor of a potential adoption can use it to bootstrap their consultation. Second, the identified reported challenges from adopting TLA$^+$ serve academics for directing future optimization efforts effectively.

Based on the curated list of papers, future work could more broadly address practical challenges and produce valuable lessons learned regarding introducing formal methods in industrial settings. Case studies, structured interviews of experts and other empirical studies with industry software engineers and formal method researchers could explore their experiences with system design issues and hard-to-reproduce bugs when using formal methods. Such investigations would improve understanding of their needs and promote TLA$^+$ adoption in industrial software.

Regarding the systematic literature review performed in this paper, future work can mitigate limitations and address threats to validity. Naturally, extending the time range beyond 10 years, to other search engines and beyond scientific works may provide further insights. Findings themselves as presented in this paper can be further confirmed through other empirical methods, such as expert surveys, interviews or through informal company documents. Generality of findings can be also increased by employing a less restrictive affinity filter. Finally, we addressed TLA$^+$ and its use in practice. Analyzing such trends in the industrial application of formal methods in general can help assess (and ensure) that their benefits resonate with practitioners and can be valuable for the broader scientific community.

Acknowledgments. This work has been supported by the Swiss National Science Foundation (SNSF) within project "RUNVERSPACE: Runtime Verification for Space Software Architectures", grant no. 220875.

References

The 16 High-Affinity Papers

1. Braithwaite, S., et al.: A Tendermint Light Client (2020). https://doi.org/10.48550/arXiv.2010.07031
2. Davis, A.J.J., Hirschhorn, M., Schvimer, J.: eXtreme modelling in practice. Proc. VLDB Endowment **13**(9), 1346–1358 (2020). https://doi.org/10.14778/3397230.3397233
3. Gao, S., et al.: Formal verification of consensus in the Taurus distributed database. In: Huisman, M., Păsăreanu, C., Zhan, N. (eds.) FM 2021. LNCS, vol. 13047, pp. 741–751. Springer, Cham (2021). https://doi.org/10.1007/978-3-030-90870-6_42
4. Gu, X., Cao, W., Zhu, Y., Song, X., Huang, Y., Ma, X.: Compositional model checking of consensus protocols via interaction-preserving abstraction. In: 2022 41st International Symposium on Reliable Distributed Systems (SRDS), pp. 82–93 (2022).https://doi.org/10.1109/SRDS55811.2022.00018
5. Hackett, F., Rowe, J., Kuppe, M.A.: Going Beyond an Incident Report with TLA[+] (2023). https://www.usenix.org/sites/default/files/login_-_going_beyond_an_incident_report_with_tla_.pdf
6. Hackett, F., Rowe, J., Kuppe, M.A.: Understanding inconsistency in azure cosmos DB with TLA+. In: 2023 IEEE/ACM 45th International Conference on Software Engineering: Software Engineering in Practice (ICSE-SEIP), pp. 1–12. IEEE (2023). https://doi.org/10.1109/ICSE-SEIP58684.2023.00006
7. Jakobs, C., Werner, M., Schmidt, K., Hansch, G.: Following the white rabbit: integrity verification based on risk analysis results. In: Proceedings of the 5th ACM Computer Science in Cars Symposium. CSCS '21, pp. 1–9, New York, NY, USA. Association for Computing Machinery (2021). https://doi.org/10.1145/3488904.3493377
8. Methni, A., Lemerre, M., Ben Hedia, B., Haddad, S., Barkaoui, K.: Specifying and verifying concurrent C programs with TLA+. In: Artho, C., Ölveczky, P.C. (eds.) FTSCS 2014. CCIS, vol. 476, pp. 206–222. Springer, Cham (2015). https://doi.org/10.1007/978-3-319-17581-2_14
9. Newcombe, C.: Why Amazon Chose TLA[+]. In: Ait Ameur, Y., Schewe, K.D. (eds.) Abstract State Machines, Alloy, B, TLA, VDM, and Z. pp. 25–39. Springer, Berlin, Heidelberg (2014). https://doi.org/10.1007/978-3-662-43652-3_3
10. Newcombe, C., Rath, T., Zhang, F., Munteanu, B., Brooker, M., Deardeuff, M.: How Amazon web services uses formal methods. Commun. ACM **58**(4), 66–73 (2015). https://doi.org/10.1145/2699417
11. Padhy, S., Stubbs, J.: Designing and proving properties of the abaco autoscaler using TLA+. In: Bloem, R., Dimitrova, R., Fan, C., Sharygina, N. (eds.) Software Verification, pp. 86–103. Springer, Cham (2022). https://doi.org/10.1007/978-3-030-95561-8_6
12. Resch, S., Paulitsch, M.: Using TLA+ in the development of a safety-critical fault-tolerant middleware. In: 2017 IEEE International Symposium on Software Reliability Engineering Workshops (ISSREW), pp. 146–152 (2017). https://doi.org/10.1109/ISSREW.2017.43
13. Roohitavaf, M., Ren, K., Zhang, G., Ben-romdhane, S.: LogPlayer: fault-tolerant exactly-once delivery using gRPC asynchronous streaming (2019). https://doi.org/10.48550/arXiv.1911.11286

14. Sabraoui, M., Hieb, J., Lauf, A., Graham, J.: Modeling and machine-checking bump-in-the-wire security for industrial control systems. In: ICCIP 2019. IAICT, vol. 570, pp. 271–288. Springer, Cham (2019). https://doi.org/10.1007/978-3-030-34647-8_14
15. Salierno, G., Morvillo, S., Leonardi, L., Cabri, G.: Specification and verification of railway safety-critical systems using TLA$^+$: a case study. In: 2020 IEEE 29th International Conference on Enabling Technologies: Infrastructure for Collaborative Enterprises (WETICE), pp. 207–212 (2020). https://doi.org/10.1109/WETICE49692.2020.00048
16. Schultz, W., Zhou, S., Dardik, I., Tripakis, S.: Design and analysis of a logless dynamic reconfiguration protocol (2021). https://doi.org/10.48550/arXiv.2102.11960

Other

17. Buyya, R., et al.: A manifesto for future generation cloud computing: research directions for the next decade. ACM Comput. Surv. **51**(5), 105:1–105:38 (2018). https://doi.org/10.1145/3241737
18. Carrera-Rivera, A., Ochoa, W., Larrinaga, F., Lasa, G.: How-to conduct a systematic literature review: a quick guide for computer science research. MethodsX **9**, 101895 (2022). https://doi.org/10.1016/j.mex.2022.101895
19. Clarke, E.M., Klieber, W., Nováček, M., Zuliani, P.: Model checking and the state explosion problem. In: Meyer, B., Nordio, M. (eds.) LASER 2011. LNCS, vol. 7682, pp. 1–30. Springer, Heidelberg (2012). https://doi.org/10.1007/978-3-642-35746-6_1
20. Dedehayir, O., Steinert, M.: The hype cycle model: A review and future directions. Technological Forecasting and Social Change **108**, 28–41 (2016). https://doi.org/10.1016/j.techfore.2016.04.005
21. Kitchenham, B.A., Charters, S.: Guidelines for performing systematic literature reviews in software engineering. Technical rep.ort EBSE 2007-001, Keele University and Durham University Joint Report (2007). https://www.elsevier.com/__data/promis_misc/525444systematicreviewsguide.pdf
22. Lamport, L.: Specifying Systems: The TLA+ Language and Tools for Hardware and Software Engineers. Addison-Wesley (2002). https://www.microsoft.com/en-us/research/uploads/prod/2018/05/book-02-08-08.pdf
23. Lamport, L.: The PlusCal algorithm language. In: Leucker, M., Morgan, C. (eds.) ICTAC 2009. LNCS, vol. 5684, pp. 36–60. Springer, Heidelberg (2009). https://doi.org/10.1007/978-3-642-03466-4_2
24. Petersen, K., Vakkalanka, S., Kuzniarz, L.: Guidelines for conducting systematic mapping studies in software engineering: An update. Inf. Software Technol. **64**, 1–18 (2015). https://doi.org/10.1016/j.infsof.2015.03.007
25. Pnueli, A.: The temporal logic of programs. In: 18th Annual Symposium on Foundations of Computer Science (sfcs 1977), pp. 46–57 (1977). https://doi.org/10.1109/SFCS.1977.32
26. Reid, A., Church, L., Flur, S., de Haas, S., Johnson, M., Laurie, B.: Towards making formal methods normal: meeting developers where they are (2020). https://doi.org/10.48550/arXiv.2010.16345
27. Rogers, E.M.: Diffusion of Innovations. Social science, Free Press, New York London Toronto Sydney, 5 edn. (2003). ISBN: 978-0-7432-2209-9

28. Yasin, A., Fatima, R., Wen, L., Afzal, W., Azhar, M., Torkar, R.: On using grey literature and google scholar in systematic literature reviews in software engineering. IEEE Access **8**, 36226–36243 (2020). https://doi.org/10.1109/ACCESS.2020.2971712
29. Zimmermann, T.: Card-sorting: from text to themes. In: Menzies, T., Williams, L., Zimmermann, T. (eds.) Perspectives on Data Science for Software Engineering, pp. 137–141. Morgan Kaufmann, Boston (2016). https://doi.org/10.1016/B978-0-12-804206-9.00027-1

Implementing, Specifying, and Verifying the QOI Format in Dafny: A Case Study

Ştefan Ciobâcă[✉] and Diana-Elena Gratie

Alexandru Ioan Cuza University, Iasi, Romania
{stefan.ciobaca,diana.gratie}@uaic.ro

Abstract. We present as a case study a verified implementation in Dafny for the Quite OK Image Format, a recently introduced lossless image compression/decompression algorithm that aims to be simple, have a good compression ratio and be fast to execute. We present the choices we make in the implementation and the specification, which enable the verification effort.

Keywords: QOI Format · Dafny · Formal Verification · Image Compression · Satisfiability Modulo Theories · Program Proof · Deductive Verification · Case Study

1 Introduction

The Quite OK Image (QOI) format [16] was introduced by Dominic Szablewski in 2022 as a high-performance lossless format for image compression that is very simple. The English-language specification of the format consists of a single A4 page document [16] and the reference implementation of the encoder and decoder has around 300 lines of C code [15]. Not only is QOI simpler than other lossless image compression algorithms, but QOI allows for typically 20% better compression than the more mainstream PNG format. Additionally, the QOI compression algorithm is typically 20 to 50 times as fast as PNG, while the decompression algorithm is typically 3 to 4 times as fast according to benchmarks performed by the author of the QOI format (https://qoiformat.org/benchmark/).

QOI is inherently sequential and it combines, in a clever manner, several well-known techniques for compression, such as run-length encoding, dictionary-based compression, and delta encoding. We briefly describe the format in Sect. 2 and refer to its specification [16] for reference. QOI is not difficult to implement, but the potential for edge cases makes it an interesting and non-trivial target for formal verification. Edge cases could include off-by-one errors, infinite loops when decoding or encoding, out-of-bounds array accesses or other types of crashes, incorrect encoding or decoding. While typical implementations are validated by testing, our verified implementation gives a higher degree of confidence in the lack of such errors.

We implement, specify, and formally verify the functional correctness of QOI in the Dafny [10] language. Our proof ensures there are no runtime errors such as

© The Author(s), under exclusive license to Springer Nature Switzerland AG 2025
N. Kosmatov and L. Kovács (Eds.): IFM 2024, LNCS 15234, pp. 35–52, 2025.
https://doi.org/10.1007/978-3-031-76554-4_3

out-of-bounds array accesses, but also that encoding and decoding match their specification, ensuring that decoding is the inverse of encoding. We chose Dafny because it supports autoactive verification of imperative programs. A similar choice could be Why3 [7], but Isabelle/HOL [13] and the Coq proof assistant [17] could also be used, although these approaches would require a different style of verification involving either a program logic such as Iris [8] or VST [2] or a refinement logic such as proposed by Lammich [9]. In this paper, we present our approach to the entire verification process as a case study in formal verification.

Dafny is an imperative language with some functional and object-oriented features, and it features an auto-active verifier based on translation into Boogie [3], which discharges verification conditions using the Z3 solver [12]. We feature a very brief overview of Dafny in Sect. 3 and we refer to the Dafny reference manual [18] for more details.

In Sect. 4 we describe the main formalisation effort. We focus on the architecture of our formalisation, with the encoding and decoding process being split into two phases, which is, to our knowledge, novel. These phases enable an efficient verification process by separating concerns. We discuss related work in Sect. 5 and we conclude with a brief discussion in Sect. 6.

2 Preliminaries: The QOI Format

The QOI file format starts with a header: 14 bytes consisting of the "qoif" identifier, the width and height of the image, each 4 bytes in length, one byte for the number of channels used (3 for RGB, 4 for RGBA), and the last byte for the colorspace (0 for sRGB with linear alpha; 1 for all channels linear). The header is followed by a number of data chunks that encode the pixel data. The file ends with an 8-byte end marker (seven 0 bytes and one byte with a value of 1). There are six possible data chunks of various sizes (all with a bit length multiple of 8), each starting with either a 2-bit or an 8-bit tag. The 8-bit tags have precedence over the 2-bit ones. Further details can be found in the QOI specification [15].

2.1 Image Encoding

The images are processed in a single pass, from left to right, top to bottom (row-major order). Each pixel is internally represented using a structure that gives the (r,g,b,a) values of the pixel. A pixel can be encoded in one of four ways:

1. As a run of the previous pixel (QOI_OP_RUN)
   A variable run is used to count the number of consecutive pixels that coincide. If the value of the current pixel px is the same as the previous pixel, pxPrev (initialized to r=g=b=0, a=255), increase the run length by one, up to a value of 62. If px $\neq$ pxPrev, the current pixel is encoded using one of the other methods.

2. As an index into an array of previously seen pixels (QOI_OP_INDEX)
An array `index` is used to remember 64 of the previously seen pixels. For each pixel `px`, a hash value (0..63) is computed that represents the index of `px` into the `index` array. Let `pos(px)` denote this hash value. If `index[pos(px)]` and `px` have the same value (the exact same color values are encoded in the `index` array), an index chunk is written to the stream. Otherwise (a different color with the same hash code is encoded in the `index` array), `index[pos(px)]` is updated and the pixel is encoded using one of the remaining methods.
3. As a difference to the `r,g,b` values of the previous pixel
    3.1 As a small difference (QOI_OP_DIFF)
    If the difference between the current and the previous pixel for each of the `r,g,b` channels is small enough (between -2 and 1 for each color channel), encode this difference on two bits for each color channel, and write a diff chunk to the stream.
    3.2 As a significant difference (QOI_OP_LUMA)
    If the difference between the current (`px`) and previous pixel (`pxPrev`) for at least one of the `r,g,b` channels is outside of the [-2,1] interval, more bits are needed for the encoding. The green channel difference from `pxPrev` is encoded on 6 bits, and indicates the general direction of the change (values between -32 and 31). The red and blue channels' differences are computed relative to the green difference, and stored on 4 bits each (values between -8..7). The luma 2-byte chunk is written to the stream.
4. As full `r,g,b` or `r,g,b,a` values
    4.1 For the same alpha channel value (QOI_OP_RGB)
    If the alpha values of `px` and `pxPrev` are the same, encode the `r,g,b` channel values in an RGB chunk and write it to the stream (a leading 8-bit b11111110 tag is used).
    4.2 For different alpha channel values (QOI_OP_RGBA)
    If the alpha values of `px` and `pxPrev` differ, encode the `r,g,b,a` channel values in an RGBA chunk and write it to the stream (a leading 8-bit b11111111 tag is used).

2.2 Image Decoding

The decompression of QOI images is also single-pass. The decoder first identifies the image width, height, the number of channels and colorspace from the header bytes, then iterates through the data chunks doing the reverse operations to get the pixel information. We present an example of the decoding process for the QOI format using the compressed image in Fig. 1. The thicker boxes denote chunks, while the squares are bytes in hexadecimal.

The first four bytes are dedicated to the magic number ("qoif"), the next two groups of 4 bytes give the width and height of the picture (3 pixels for each, in our example). The two trailing bytes of the header give the number of

	magic number	width=3	height=3	
Header	71 6F 69 66	00 00 00 03	00 00 00 03	03 01

Data chunks | 55 | C2 | 9B EE | 26 | 17 | FE 46 46 46 | 17 |

55	01010101	QOI_OP_DIFF
C2	11000010	QOI_OP_RUN
9BEE	1001101111101110	QOI_OP_LUMA
26	00100110	QOI_OP_INDEX
17	00010111	QOI_OP_INDEX
FE46	1111111001000110	QOI_OP_RGB
4646	0100011001000110	

End marker | 00 | 00 | 00 | 00 | 00 | 00 | 00 | 01 |

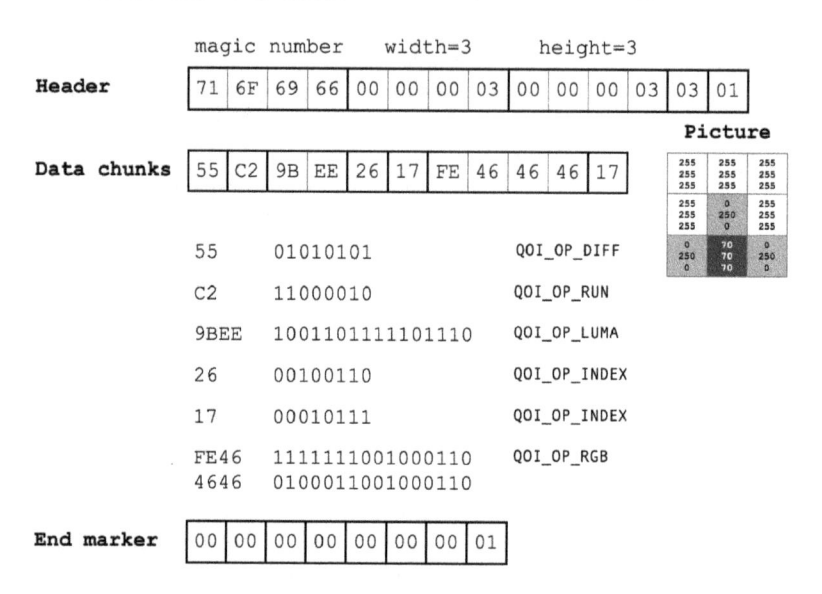

Fig. 1. Example of a compressed image in QOI format. Each color has its r,g,b code displayed.

channels (3, for r,g,b in our case) and the colorspace (1, for all channels linear, in the example).

There are seven data chunks encoded. 0x55 is decoded as a QOI_OP_DIFF, because an 8-bit valid tag is absent, and the 2-bit tag indicates a small difference (namely of -1 on each channel) between the first pixel of the picture and the default previous pixel, which is considered to be black and opaque. Due to the wraparound operation there is a difference of -1 between black $(0,0,0)$ and white $(255,255,255)$, so a small difference. The white pixel is stored in the index array.

The next byte, 0xC2, is identified as a QOI_OP_RUN of length 3, so 3 more white pixels. The third chunk, consisting of two bytes, 0x9BEE, is decoded as a QOI_OP_LUMA, with a difference of -5 on the g channel (250), and differences of 6 between the red/blue channels' differences and the green channel difference, so a green hue pixel $(0,250,0)$. It is stored in the index array. The next two chunks are QOI_OP_INDEX chunks, with the indices of the white and green (respectively) pixels decoded previously.

The 0xFE tag indicates a QOI_OP_RGB chunk, so together with the next 3 bytes it is decoded as a new color pixel, distant to the previously read ones, namely a dark grey $(70,70,70)$. It is also added to the index array. The last data chunk is an index, decoded as the position of the green color pixel. The compressed image file ends with the 8-byte end marker.

3 Preliminaries: Dafny

Dafny is an imperative language and verifier supporting classes and dynamic allocation. Its methods contain specification constructs (preconditions - introduced by **requires** -, postconditions - introduced by **ensures** -, framing constructs, invariants, and termination metrics). The features of the language allow for modular verification, where the correctness of a program is implied by the verification of each of its parts. The verification is auto-active, which implies an automatic verification part, and an interactive one. The preconditions and postconditions are automatically checked. For more complex code involving loops, the user can define loop invariants, variants, and other helper annotations, this being the interactive part.

A Dafny program is verified by translating it into Boogie [3] (such that the correctness of the translation implies that of the original program), which is then used to generate verification conditions that are passed on to the Z3 solver [12].

Figure 2 contains an example of a Dafny method implementing binary search. The precondition (Line 2) of the method requires that the input array a be sorted increasingly. It ensures that the output index p is either the index on which value key is found in the array (if that is the case), or negative (−1), if key is not among the values in a. The first while loop invariant (Line 9) specifies that l and r are indices between 0..a.Length. The second loop invariant (Line 10) specifies that key is surely not found in a before position l or after position r. The variant **decreases** r - 1 on Line 11 gives a termination metric. More information on Dafny can be found in the user manual [18].

```
1   method BinarySearch(a: array<int>, key: int) returns (p: int)
2     requires forall j, k :: 0 <= j < k < a.Length ==> a[j] <= a[k]
3     ensures 0 <= p ==> p < a.Length && a[p] == key
4     ensures p < 0 ==> forall k :: 0 <= k < a.Length ==> a[k] != key
5   {
6     var l :int := 0;
7     var r :int := a.Length;
8     while (l < r)
9       invariant 0 <= l <= r <= a.Length
10      invariant forall i :: 0 <= i < a.Length && !(l <= i < r) ==> a[i] != key
11      decreases r - l
12    {
13      var mid := (l + r) / 2;
14      if a[mid] < key {
15        l := mid + 1;
16      } else if key < a[mid] {
17        r := mid;
18      } else {
19        return mid;
20      }
21    }
22    return -1;
23  }
```

Fig. 2. An example of verified Dafny code.

4 Formalisation

We now describe the formalisation of the compression and decompression algorithms. The full source code can be found at https://github.com/ciobaca/qoi-dafny/. The high-level architecture of the Dafny development is summarized in Fig. 3.

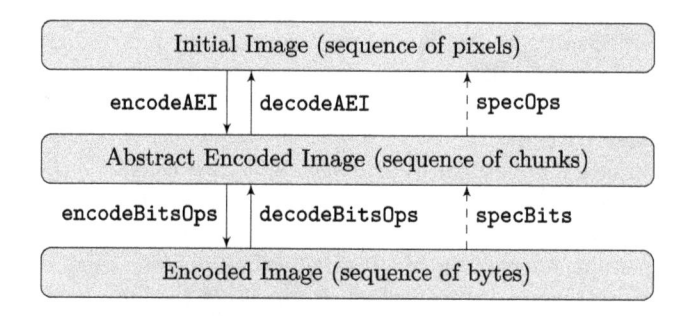

Fig. 3. The architecture of the development.

In order to simplify the compression (encoding) and decompression (decoding) processes, we use an intermediate layer for representing images that sits between the initial image (seen as a sequence of pixels) and the compressed image (seen as a sequence of bytes). This intermediate layer stores the encoded image as a list of chunks, but the chunks are represented at the logical level, not as bytes.

This makes the verification and development effort more clear by separating two orthogonal concerns: • the generation (respectively interpretation) of the logical chunks and • the encoding (respectively decoding) of the chunks into bytes.

Using the three-layer approach described above, we implement compression as the composition of two phases:

1. The method `encodeAEI` (AEI stands for Abstract Encoded Image) takes as input an image and computes the chunks.
2. The method `encodeBitsOps` takes as input the chunks and encodes them as a sequence of bytes.

Similarly, we use two phases for decompression:

1. The method `decodeBitsOps` takes as input a sequence of bytes and decodes it into a sequence of chunks.
2. The method `decodeAEI` takes as input the chunks, represented at the logical level, and computes the image.

The end-to-end decompression phase is the composition of the two methods.

We formally verify that the implementation terminates, does not have memory errors such as out-of-bounds accesses, and is functionally correct, in the sense that encoding and decoding meet their specification. The specification is given by the `specOps` function (respectively by the `specBits` function), shown in the diagram in Fig. 3 on the right. These specification-level functions specify the decoding process.

As part of the verification process, we show that the decoding methods (`decodeAEI`, `decodeBitsOps`) match these two functions exactly. For the encoding process, we show that applying these two functions on the result yields back the initial input. From this it follows immediately that decoding is the inverse of encoding. We choose to specify the decoding phase (instead of encoding, or both) since it is deterministic, while the encoding can be nondeterministic: there can be several encodings for the same image (for example, for a pixel that is close to the previous pixel, and that is also stored in the index, an encoder could emit either an `OpIndex` or an `OpDiff`).

We now present the core data structures that we use and we explain the implementation choices.

4.1 Representing the Initial Image

We represent one pixel by an algebraic data type: either `RGB` if the image has three color channels, or `RGBA` if there is an additional *alpha* channel.

```
1   datatype RGB = RGB(r : byte, g : byte, b : byte)
2   datatype RGBA = RGBA(r : byte, g : byte, b : byte, a : byte)
```

The identifier `RGB` (respectively `RGBA`) doubles as both the name of the data type and the name of the only constructor for the data type. The names r, g, b (and respectively a) act as destructors.

The number of channels is represented as a refinement type which will be extracted to a byte.

```
1   newtype {:nativeType "byte"} Channels = x : int | 3 <= x <= 4 witness 3
```

The color space is represented as an enumeration and it is used only for storing in the file header – it does not impact the compression or decompression process in any way.

```
1   datatype ColorSpace = SRGB | Linear
```

Images are represented by metadata (the data type `Desc`) and the sequence of bytes representing the pixel data.

```
1   datatype Desc = Desc(width : uint32,
2                        height : uint32,
3                        channels : Channels,
4                        colorSpace : ColorSpace)
5   datatype Image = Image(desc : Desc, data : seq<byte>)
```

We define `bytes` (respectively `uint32s`) to represent 8-bit unsigned integers (respectively 32-bit unsigned integers).

```
1  newtype {:nativeType "byte"} byte = x:int | 0 <= x < 256
2  newtype {:nativeType "uint"} uint32 = x:int | 0 <= x < 4294967296
```

As is usual in Dafny, we define a validity predicate that is responsible for identifying valid **Image**s. In our case the validity predicate simply checks that the image data contains enough bytes to represent the entire image.

```
1  predicate validImage(image : Image)
2  {
3    |image.data| == image.desc.width as int *
4      image.desc.height as int *
5      image.desc.channels as int
6  }
```

4.2 Representing the Chunks at the Logical Level

We represent chunks by using an algebraic data type. Each type of chunk has one constructor.

```
1  datatype Op = OpRun(size : Size)        // chunk represents a segment of the same color
2              | OpIndex(index : Index64)  // index into previously seen colors
3              | OpDiff(diff : RGBDiff)    // delta encoding (first type)
4              | OpLuma(luma : RGBLuma)    // delta encoding (second type)
5              | OpRGB(rgb : RGB)          // pixel value (3 channels)
6              | OpRGBA(rgba : RGBA)       // pixel value (4 channels)
```

The arguments of each constructor are defined using refinement types so that only valid values can be represented.

```
1  newtype {:nativeType "byte"} Size = x : int | 1 <= x <= 62 witness 1
2  newtype {:nativeType "byte"} Index64 = x : int | 0 <= x <= 63
3  newtype {:nativeType "short"} Diff64 = x : int | -32 <= x <= 31
4  newtype {:nativeType "short"} Diff16 = x : int | -8 <= x <= 7
5  newtype {:nativeType "short"} Diff = x : int | -2 <= x <= 1
6  datatype RGBDiff = RGBDiff(dr : Diff, dg : Diff, db : Diff)
7  datatype RGBLuma = RGBLuma(dr : Diff16, dg : Diff64, db : Diff16)
```

The type **Size** denotes integers between 1 and 62, which represent valid lengths for the run-length encoding operator **OpRun**. The type **Index64** represents integers between 0 and 63, which are valid indices into the dictionary for the compression operator **OpIndex**. The difference-based operators **OpDiff** and **OpLuma** use the **Diff64**, **Diff16**, and **Diff** types to store the color differences from the previous pixel.

Finally, to represent an encoded image at the abstract level of chunks, we use the type

```
1  datatype AEI = AEI(width : uint32, height : uint32, ops : seq<Op>)
```

The **AEI** datatype does not recall the header information other than **width** and **height**. The additional information will be stored elsewhere to save it into the final byte stream.

4.3 Specification

To prove that the encoding and decoding processes are correct, we need a specification. We specify the meaning of one chunk using the function `specDecodeOp`:

```
1  function specDecodeOp(state : State, op : Op) : seq<RGBA>
2    requires validState(state)
3  {
4    match op {
5    case OpRGB(RGB(r, g, b)) => [ RGBA(r, g, b, state.prev.a) ]
6    case OpRun(size) => seq(size, i => state.prev)
7    case OpIndex(index) => [ state.index[index] ]
8    case OpDiff(RGBDiff(dr, dg, db)) =>
9      [ RGBA(add_byte(state.prev.r, byte_from(dr as int)),
10             add_byte(state.prev.g, byte_from(dg as int)),
11             add_byte(state.prev.b, byte_from(db as int)),
12             state.prev.a ) ]
13   case OpLuma(RGBLuma(dr, dg, db)) =>
14     [ RGBA(add_byte(add_byte(state.prev.r, byte_from(dg as int)), byte_from(dr as int)),
15            add_byte(state.prev.g, byte_from(dg as int)),
16            add_byte(add_byte(state.prev.b, byte_from(dg as int)), byte_from(db as int)),
17            state.prev.a ) ]
18   case OpRGBA(rgba) => [ rgba ]
19   }
20 }
```

This function returns a sequence of pixels represented by one chunk. Sequences, represented by `seq`, are immutable data structures. Because this function is only used at the specification level, the runtime overhead induced by immutability is not relevant. We do not show the functions `add_byte`, `byte_from` to save space. In order to remove duplication, we define the function to return RGBAs, independently of the number of channels of the image. For 3-channel images, the *alpha* components will be 255. The decoding function depends crucially on the current *state* of the encoder (the first argument), as defined in the QOI format specification. We represent the state at the specification level as a pair consisting of the previous pixel and a sequence of 64 previously-seen pixels (as defined in the QOI format specification):

```
1  datatype State = State(prev : RGBA, index : seq<RGBA>)
2  ghost predicate validState(state : State)
3  {
4    |state.index| == 64
5  }
```

We specify how the state changes after visiting one pixel and what the initial state is by following the official specification:

```
1  function updateState(previous : State, pixel : RGBA) : State
2    requires validState(previous)
3    ensures validState(updateState(previous, pixel))
4  {
5    State(prev := pixel, index := previous.index[hashRGBA(pixel) := pixel])
6  }
7  function initState() : State
8  {
9    State(prev := RGBA(0, 0, 0, 255), index :=
10        seq(64, i => RGBA(r := 0, g := 0, b := 0, a := 255)))
11 }
```

We specify the meaning of an **AEI** as a sequence of pixels by concatenating the information given by subsequent calls to `specDecodeOp`:

```
1   function spec(aei : AEI) : seq<RGBA>
2     requires validAEI(aei)
3   {
4     specOps(aei.ops)
5   }
6   function specOps(ops : seq<Op>) : seq<RGBA>
7   {
8     specOpsAux(ops, initState())
9   }
10  function specOpsAux(ops : seq<Op>, state : State) : seq<RGBA>
11    requires validState(state)
12  {
13    if |ops| == 0 then []
14    else var pixels : seq<RGBA> := specDecodeOp(state, ops[0]);
15      pixels + specOpsAux(ops[1..], updateStateStar(state, pixels))
16  }
```

For brevity, we skip the function `updateStateStar`, which uses `updateState` repeatedly to specify how the state should be updated after visiting *several* pixels. We also specify the meaning of a sequence of bytes as a chunk at the logical level:

```
1   function decodeBits(bits : seq<byte>) : Op
2     requires validBits(bits)
3   {
4     match opTypeOfBits(bits[0]) {
5     case TypeRun => OpRun((bits[0] - 128 - 64 + 1) as Size)
6     case TypeLuma => OpLuma( RGBLuma( ((bits[1] / 16) as int - 8) as Diff16,
7       ((bits[0] - 128) as int - 32) as Diff64, ((bits[1] % 16) as int - 8) as Diff16))
8     case TypeDiff => OpDiff( RGBDiff( (((bits[0] - 64) / 16) as int - 2) as Diff,
9       (((bits[0] / 4) % 4) as int - 2) as Diff, ((bits[0] % 4) as int - 2) as Diff))
10    case TypeIndex => OpIndex(bits[0] as Index64)
11    case TypeRGBA => OpRGBA(RGBA(bits[1], bits[2], bits[3], bits[4]))
12    case TypeRGB => OpRGB(RGB(bits[1], bits[2], bits[3]))
13    }
14  }
```

For brevity, we do not show the `validBits` predicate, nor the `opTypeOfBits` function. We concatenate the results of the `decodeBits` function to obtain the sequence of chunks represented by a sequence of bytes.

```
1   function specBits(bits : seq<byte>) : seq<Op>
2     requires validBitSeq(bits)
3   {
4     if |bits| == 0 then []
5     else ( var len := sizeBitEncoding(opTypeOfBits(bits[0]));
6       [ decodeBits(bits[0..len]) ] + specBits(bits[len..]) )
7   }
```

We would like to emphasize the recursion pattern in `specBits` above, which has a significant influence on proofs later in the paper. Note that `bits` is a concatenation of potentially variably-sized chunks. There, we cannot know beforehand at which point one chunk ends and another starts. In order to find this information, we need to inspect the first byte (`bits[0]`), which contains enough information to determine the size of the first chunk (saved in the variable `len`). The function `opTypeOfBits` computes the type of the chunk depending on the first byte and `sizeBitEncoding` computes the length, in bytes, of such a chunk. These functions are not shown to save space. Once we know where the first chunk ends, we can perform the recursive call. For brevity, we do not show the `validBitSeq` function, which uses a similar recursion pattern to check whether the input data is a valid concatenation of chunks.

```
1   method encodeAEI(image : seq<RGBA>) returns (r : array<Op>, len : int)
2     ensures 0 <= len <= r.Length
3     ensures specOps(r[..len]) == image
4   {
5     r := new Op [|image|];
6     var prev : RGBA := RGBA(r := 0, g := 0, b := 0, a := 255);
7     var index : array<RGBA> := new RGBA[64](i => RGBA(r := 0, g := 0, b := 0, a := 255));
8     var i : int := 0;
9     var wh : int := |image|;
10    len := 0;
11    ghost var state := initState();
12    while (i < wh)
13      invariant 0 <= len <= i <= wh
14      decreases wh - i
15      invariant state == updateStateStar(initState(), image[..i])
16      invariant state.prev == prev
17      invariant state.index == index[..]
18      invariant specOps(r[..len]) == image[..i]
19    {
20      var curr := image[i];
21      len := encodePixelAEI(curr, prev, index, state, r, len);
22      state := updateState(state, curr);
23      prev := curr;
24      i := i + 1;
25    }
26  }
```

```
1   method encodePixelAEI(curr : RGBA, prev : RGBA, index : array<RGBA>,
2     ghost state : State, encoding : array<Op>, len : int) returns (newlen : int)
3     ensures specOps(old(encoding[..len])) + [ curr ] == specOps(encoding[..newlen])
4   {
5     newlen := len + 1;
6     if (curr == prev) {
7       if (len > 0 && encoding[len - 1].OpRun? && encoding[len - 1].size < 62) {
8         encoding[len - 1] := OpRun(encoding[len - 1].size + 1);
9         newlen := len;
10      } else {
11        encoding[len] := OpRun(1);
12      }
13    } else if (index[hashRGBA(curr)] == curr) {
14      encoding[len] := OpIndex(hashRGBA(curr) as Index64);
15    } else if (canDiff(curr, prev) != None) {
16      var result := canDiff(curr, prev).some;
17      encoding[len] := OpDiff(result);
18    } else if (canLuma(curr, prev) != None) {
19      var result := canLuma(curr, prev).some;
20      encoding[len] := OpLuma(result);
21    } else if (curr.a == prev.a) {
22      encoding[len] := OpRGB(RGB(curr.r, curr.g, curr.b));
23    } else {
24      encoding[len] := OpRGBA(RGBA(curr.r, curr.g, curr.b, curr.a));
25    }
26    var h := hashRGBA(curr);
27    index[h] := curr;
28  }
```

Fig. 4. The functions that compute the chunks representing an image.

4.4 Encoding

The encoding function that takes images into abstract encoded images, shown in Fig. 4 follows typical encoder logic.

At each step, we show that the state of the algorithm (stored in the variables prev and index) matches the specification (Line 16) and that what was encoded so far matches a corresponding prefix of the image data (Line 18). The main postcondition (Line 3) establishes that decoding the result yields back the original image data. The method `encodePixelAEI(curr, prev, index, state, r, len)` does the work for a single pixel (several verification conditions removed for brevity).

Encoding an abstract encoded image as a sequence of bytes (Fig. 5) is straightforward (some verification conditions removed to save space).

```
1    method encodeBitsOps(ops : array<Op>, opsLen : int, result : array<byte>,
2      pos : int) returns (newpos : int)
3      requires 0 <= opsLen <= ops.Length
4      ensures result[pos..newpos] == encodeOpsSpec(ops[..opsLen])
5    {
6      var i := 0;
7      newpos := pos;
8      while (i < opsLen)
9        invariant 0 <= i <= opsLen
10       invariant pos <= newpos
11       invariant newpos + 5 * (opsLen - i) + 8 <= result.Length
12       invariant result[..pos] == old(result[..pos])
13       invariant result[pos..newpos] == encodeOpsSpec(ops[..i])
14     {
15       ghost var oldpos := newpos;
16       newpos := writeBitsOp(ops[i], result, newpos);
17       i := i + 1;
18     }
19   }
```

Fig. 5. The method for encoding an abstract encoded image as a sequence of bytes. The helper method `writeBitsOp` (not shown to save space) encodes a single chunk.

4.5 Decoding

Decoding an abstract encoded image (Fig. 6, top) into an image is relatively straightforward (some helper assertions are removed from the code for brevity).

Decoding one chunk is done by `decodeOp` (not shown to save space).

Decoding a byte stream into a sequence of chunks (Figure 6, bottom) is significantly more difficult to prove, because each chunk is represented using a potentially variable number of bytes. This means that not all prefixes of the byte stream are valid representations of chunks. We walk the byte stream and check at each step the type of the first potential chunk and its length, `len` (Line 16). If the byte stream contains at least `len` bytes, and they represent a valid chunk (Line 23), we store the decoding of the `len` bytes into the `result` and we advance the index `i` by `len` positions (Line 28). Crucially, we use as an invariant (Line 14) that what was stored so far is the decoding of everything up to the current position `i`. But we never know until the very end if the remaining stream (after position `i`) is valid or not. In order to keep track of this, we use an invariant (Line 12) stating that the full byte stream is valid iff what is left is also valid. This invariant crucially allows us to prove the postcondition when the byte stream given as input is not valid.

```
1   method decodeAEI(ops : array<Op>, size : int) returns (r : array<RGBA>, ok : bool)
2     ensures ok ==> r[..size] == specOps(ops[..])
3   {
4     var i := 0;
5     var state := initState();
6     var len := 0;
7     r := new RGBA [size];
8     ok := true;
9     while (i < ops.Length)
10      invariant specOps(ops[..i]) == r[..len]
11    {
12      var op := ops[i];
13      var ok' : bool;
14      len, state, ok' := decodeOp(state, op, len, r);
15      if (!ok')
16      {
17        ok := false;
18        return;
19      }
20      i := i + 1;
21    }
22    if (ok) {
23      if (len != size)
24      {
25        ok := false;
26        return;
27      }
28    }
29  }
```

```
1   method decodeBitsOps(bits : array<byte>, start : int, end : int)
2     returns (r : Option<array<Op>>, lenr : int)
3     ensures !validBitSeq(bits[start..end]) ==> r.None?
4     ensures validBitSeq(bits[start..end]) ==>
5       r.Some? && r.some[..lenr] == specBits(bits[start..end])
6   {
7     var i := 0;
8     var j := 0;
9     var result : array<Op> := new Op [end - start];
10    while (i < end - start)
11      invariant 0 <= j <= i <= end - start
12      invariant validBitSeq(bits[start + i..end]) == validBitSeq(bits[start..end])
13      invariant validBitSeq(bits[start..start + i])
14      invariant result[..j] == specBits(bits[start..start + i])
15    {
16      var len := sizeBitEncoding(opTypeOfBits(bits[start + i]));
17      if (i + len > end - start)
18      {
19        return None, j;
20      }
21      else
22      {
23        var b := areValidBits(bits, start + i, len);
24        if (b)
25        {
26          result[j] := decodeBits(bits[start + i..start + i + len]);
27          j := j + 1;
28          i := i + len;
29        }
30        else
31        {
32          return None, j;
33        }
34      }
35    }
36    return Some(result), j;
37  }
```

Fig. 6. The methods that decodes chunk into a image and a stream of bytes into a stream of chunks. Some verification conditions are not shown to save space.

4.6 Statistics

The core development is structured into 4 files:

Name	Line Count	Purpose
helper.dfy	69	Bytes, Helper Functions
spec.dfy	329	AEI, Specification
specbit.dfy	540	Chunks as bytes, Specification
qoi.dfy	792	Encoding and Decoding

The Dafny lines of code quoted above include specification, lemmas, helper assertions, comments, white lines. The development has 131 methods, lemmas, and functions to verify. Together, they take around 42 seconds to verify on a modern computer (2,4 GHz 8-Core Intel Core i9, 16 GB 2667 MHz DDR4) in single threaded mode. We estimate that the entire Dafny development took approximately a month of part-time work, stretched over a longer period.

The largest verification time (a bit more than 10 seconds) is required by the `canLuma` function:

```
1   function canLuma(curr : RGBA, prev : RGBA) : Option<RGBLuma>
2     ensures forall luma ::  canLuma(curr, prev) == Some(luma) ==>
3       curr.r == add_byte(add_byte(prev.r, byte_from(luma.dg as int)),
4         byte_from(luma.dr as int)) &&
5       curr.g == add_byte(prev.g, byte_from(luma.dg as int)) &&
6       curr.b == add_byte(add_byte(prev.b, byte_from(luma.dg as int)),
7         byte_from(luma.db as int)) &&
8       curr.a == prev.a
9   {
10    var dr : int := curr.r as int - prev.r as int;
11    var dg : int := curr.g as int - prev.g as int;
12    var db : int := curr.b as int - prev.b as int;
13    var da : int := curr.a as int - prev.a as int;
14    if (-32 <= dg <= 31 && -8 <= (dr - dg) <= 7 &&
15        -8 <= (db - dg) <= 7 && da == 0) then
16      // ... (some assertions removed for brevity)
17      Some(RGBLuma((dr-dg) as Diff16, dg as Diff64, (db-dg) as Diff16))
18    else
19      None
20  }
```

This checks whether a pixel is close enough to the previous one to be represented by a `QOI_OP_LUMA` chunk and the large verification time is likely due to the SMT solver performing bit-blasting. Most of the other functions and methods are much quicker to verify, with most verifying instantly and just 7 taking more than a second.

Here is a summary of the entire development:

Item	Count
Number of lemmas	25
Number of methods	16
Number of preconditions	81
Number of postconditions	99
Number of invariants	35
Number of helper assertions	161
Number of calculational [11] proofs	5
Number of comments	94
Number of white lines	129

To check interoperability, we extract the above code, which was formally verified in Dafny, into C#. We choose C# because this is the backend that Dafny supports best. We link it with some unverified C#/Dafny code (files `file_input.cs`, `file_input.dfy`, `entry.dfy`) that performs file IO and we validate that the resulting executable interoperates with other implementations of the QOI format. In preliminary testing, we time our implementation at 1.9 mega pixels per second for encoding and 0.17 mega pixels per second for decoding, while the fast reference C implementation delivers a bit more than 100 megapixels per second. In future work, we plan to optimize the implementation further for runtime efficiency and benchmark it more thoroughly against the reference C implementation.

5 Related Work

To our knowledge, no other attempts at implementing, specifying and verifying the QOI format encoding and decoding algorithms using Dafny have been published so far. A presentation of a preliminary version of our implementation using Dafny was given by the first author of this paper at the Tenth Congress of Romanian Mathematicians in 2023. There was no formal publication and the Dafny development has since changed significantly.

A similar line of work on the QOI format encoding and decoding algorithms is by Bucev and Kunčak [4] using the Stainless verifier. It is worth noting that the code extracted from this development is very fast, but the development itself takes much more to verify. To our understanding, the authors manage to prove that decoding is the inverse of encoding without relying on a separate specification. However, the code is written in a functional style, which makes the proof simpler. In future work, it is worth investigating in more depth this asymmetric difference in performance. On the one hand, we suspect that the architecture of our development, using an intermediate encoding at the abstract level, makes the verification process much more feasible. On the other hand, this could impact performance in a non-negligible way.

A formally verified Ada/SPARK implementation was announced in a blog post in [6], proving the absence of runtime errors, but without a full functional correctness proof.

Loosely related to our work, we mention other instances where specific algorithms were formally verified. For example the Deflate [5] compressed data format algorithm was formalized, implemented and verified using Coq, see [14]. A couple of standard lemmas in data compression were formally proven in Coq, with application to the Shannon-Fano codes in [1].

Other approaches aim to verify other tasks that do not imply compression, for example serialization tasks. A compiler for the Protocol Buffer serialization format implemented in Coq was formally verified in [19], proving the correctness of every generated serializer/deserializer.

6 Discussion

We have implemented, specified, and verified the algorithms for encoding and decoding images into the QOI format. The main novelty of our work is the modular architecture, where we use an intermediate level for representing a compressed image at the abstract level. This allows the verification time to stay reasonable and separates concerns nicely between the bitwise representation of the encoded image and its logical counterpart. Subjectively, this separation of concerns enables the entire verification effort. It might be possible to preserve this modularity at the specification-level only and merge the two phases into one at the implementation level. In future work, we will test whether this approach works and if it improves runtime efficiency.

There are several directions for future work. First of all, there are still many known places in the decoding and encoding implementation where performance can be optimised for runtime efficiency. For example, we rely on `int` in several places in the code, which is extracted as a `BigInteger`, slowing down the encoding/decoding process. We should move towards machine integers. Moreover, especially in the decoding phase, we rely on some immutable data structures, which are slower because they involve copying memory. Furthermore, currently Dafny does not fully support extraction to `C++`. Instead, we use extraction to `C#`, which can be slower as a language than `C++`. Improving support for extracting to `C++` in Dafny would improve the running time. Another approach to obtain a verified efficient implementation would be to use a refinement calculus in the style of Lammich [9].

An open problem which would be interesting to attack is to prove that the encoding and decoding methods (`encodeAEI` and `decodeAEI`, respectively `encodeBitsOps` and `decodeBitsOps`) are reverses one of the other, but without relying on the intermediate specification-level functions (`specOps`, respectively `specBits`). This could prove challenging given that these are methods (imperative code), but it would remove some of the duplication. Additionally, it seems that many of our helper lemmas could be generalized and potentially reused in other types of encoding/decoding processes. For example, the technique we use to verify the decoding of the byte stream into abstract chunks could be useful in other contexts where a variable-length encoding is used. Finally, there is a requirement in the QOI format specification which we do not formalise and leave for future work instead: a valid encoder is required not to issue 2 or more consecutive QOI_OP_INDEX chunks to the same index (instead, QOI_OP_RUN should be used). While our encoder does satisfy this requirement, we do not currently formalise, nor prove, this. In contrast, the specification has nothing more to say about optimality: an encoder could simply issue a QOI_OP_RGB(A) for each pixel. Some form of minimality for the encoder would be an interesting additional requirement to formalize and verify in future work.

Acknowledgements. We would like to thank the reviewers for their thoughtful comments and suggestions and for the interesting questions, which helped improve the paper.

References

1. Affeldt, R., Garrigue, J., Saikawa, T.: Examples of formal proofs about data compression. In: International Symposium on Information Theory and Its Applications, ISITA 2018, Singapore, October 28–31, 2018, pp. 633–637. IEEE (2018). https://doi.org/10.23919/ISITA.2018.8664276
2. Appel, A.W.: Verified software toolchain. In: Barthe, G. (ed.) ESOP 2011. LNCS, vol. 6602, pp. 1–17. Springer, Heidelberg (2011). https://doi.org/10.1007/978-3-642-19718-5_1
3. Barnett, M., Chang, B.-Y.E., DeLine, R., Jacobs, B., Leino, K.R.M.: Boogie: a modular reusable verifier for object-oriented programs. In: de Boer, F.S., Bonsangue, M.M., Graf, S., de Roever, W.-P. (eds.) FMCO 2005. LNCS, vol. 4111, pp. 364–387. Springer, Heidelberg (2006). https://doi.org/10.1007/11804192_17
4. Bucev, M., Kunčak, V.: Formally verified Quite OK Image Format. In: Griggio, A., Rungta, N. (eds.) 22nd Formal Methods in Computer-Aided Design, FMCAD 2022, Trento, Italy, October 17–21, 2022. pp. 343–348. IEEE (2022). https://doi.org/10.34727/2022/ISBN.978-3-85448-053-2_41
5. Deutsch, L.P.: DEFLATE Compressed Data Format Specification version 1.3. RFC 1951 (1996). https://doi.org/10.17487/RFC1951, https://www.rfc-editor.org/info/rfc1951
6. Fabien Chouteau, J.H.: Quite proved image format. https://blog.adacore.com/quite-proved-image-format
7. Filliâtre, J.-C., Paskevich, A.: Why3 — where programs meet provers. In: Felleisen, M., Gardner, P. (eds.) ESOP 2013. LNCS, vol. 7792, pp. 125–128. Springer, Heidelberg (2013). https://doi.org/10.1007/978-3-642-37036-6_8
8. Jung, R., Krebbers, R., Jourdan, J., Bizjak, A., Birkedal, L., Dreyer, D.: Iris from the ground up: a modular foundation for higher-order concurrent separation logic. J. Funct. Program. **28**, e20 (2018). https://doi.org/10.1017/S0956796818000151
9. Lammich, P.: Refinement to Imperative HOL. J. Autom. Reason. **62**(4), 481–503 (2019). https://doi.org/10.1007/S10817-017-9437-1
10. Leino, K.R.M.: Dafny: an automatic program verifier for functional correctness. In: Clarke, E.M., Voronkov, A. (eds.) LPAR 2010. LNCS (LNAI), vol. 6355, pp. 348–370. Springer, Heidelberg (2010). https://doi.org/10.1007/978-3-642-17511-4_20
11. Leino, K.R.M., Polikarpova, N.: Verified calculations. In: Cohen, E., Rybalchenko, A. (eds.) VSTTE 2013. LNCS, vol. 8164, pp. 170–190. Springer, Heidelberg (2014). https://doi.org/10.1007/978-3-642-54108-7_9

12. de Moura, L., Bjørner, N.: Z3: an efficient SMT solver. In: Ramakrishnan, C.R., Rehof, J. (eds.) TACAS 2008. LNCS, vol. 4963, pp. 337–340. Springer, Heidelberg (2008). https://doi.org/10.1007/978-3-540-78800-3_24
13. Nipkow, T., Paulson, L.C., Wenzel, M.: Isabelle/HOL - A Proof Assistant for Higher-Order Logic, LNCS, vol. 2283. Springer, Heidelberg (2002). https://doi.org/10.1007/3-540-45949-9
14. Senjak, C., Hofmann, M.: An implementation of Deflate in Coq. CoRR abs/1609.01220 (2016). http://arxiv.org/abs/1609.01220
15. Szablewski, D.: QOI - the "Quite OK Image Format" for fast, lossless image compression. https://github.com/phoboslab/qoi
16. Szablewski, D.: The Quite OK Image Format specification. https://qoiformat.org/qoi-specification.pdf
17. The Coq Development Team: The Coq reference manual – release 8.19.0 (2024). https://coq.inria.fr/doc/V8.19.0/refman
18. The dafny-lang community: Dafny reference manual (2024). https://dafny.org/dafny/DafnyRef/DafnyRef
19. Ye, Q., Delaware, B.: A verified protocol buffer compiler. In: Mahboubi, A., Myreen, M.O. (eds.) Proceedings of the 8th ACM SIGPLAN International Conference on Certified Programs and Proofs, CPP 2019, Cascais, Portugal, January 14–15, 2019. pp. 222–233. ACM (2019). https://doi.org/10.1145/3293880.3294105

VeriCode: Correct Translation of Abstract Specifications to C Code

Gerhard Schellhorn[✉], Stefan Bodenmüller, and Wolfgang Reif

Institute for Software and Systems Engineering, University of Augsburg, Augsburg, Germany
{schellhorn,stefan.bodenmueller,reif}@informatik.uni-augsburg.de

Abstract. The semantics of logics is based on valuations that map variables to values, while programming languages cannot store complex values atomically. They have a pointer semantics where complex data is stored on the heap, linked with pointers. The standard approach to bridge the semantic gap between algebraic specifications and executable programs is to translate algebraic data types, recursive definitions and programs to functional code with immutable data types. Since functional programs are often less efficient than C programs due to the lack (or limited use) of mutation and the requirement of using garbage collection, we develop a different approach in this paper that is based on always mutating data structures but keeping different ones disjoint. The approach generates efficient C programs from the specifications, which have a pointer semantics and explicitly allocate and free memory on the heap. Formal specifications are given for the semantics of a core source and target language that allow to demonstrate the main transformations necessary and prove their correctness. The approach has been implemented for the full language and produces working C code.

Keywords: Code Generation · Algebraic Specifications · Efficient C Code · Pointer Semantics · Small-Step Semantics · Separation Logic

1 Introduction

Abstract specifications of software systems usually work with abstract data types like sets, lists, or free algebraic data types, like the ones supported by SMT provers (e.g., [3,12]). These have the standard *value semantics* of predicate logic, i.e., the semantics is based on a *valuation* that stores a value for each variable.

Verification of abstract (functional or imperative) programs over such data types is the typical approach to formal verification in theorem provers, since it is sufficient to capture the essential correctness arguments of programs and software systems. However, programs in real programming languages cannot store non-primitive data structures as values. They have a *pointer semantics* which has to deal with aliasing.

Supported by the Deutsche Forschungsgemeinschaft (DFG), "Correct translation of abstract specifications to C-Code (VeriCode)" (grant RE828/26-1).

This paper defines an approach that compiles abstract programs and algebraic definitions to C programs, which bridges the gap between value semantics and pointer semantics, where explicit allocation and deallocation of heap memory is necessary. We define syntax and semantics of a core source and target language and show the central concepts used in the translation. The approach is based on keeping data structures disjoint and should be contrasted with the standard approach of many theorem provers to compile to a functional language (often their own implementation language), which allows sharing but not mutation and requires garbage collection. It is well-known that such functional code can usually not compete with efficient implementations in C, which is still the standard language used where efficiency is critical.

The topic of translating formal specifications to working code of a programming language is not new. Therefore, we will first motivate the approach, define its scope, and give an overview of how it fits into related work in Sect. 2. Since a formal model of the full language including all data types and features would be much too big to fit into this paper, Sect. 3 will give a prototypical model of the specification language. The core language defines the data types of lists and pairs only and specifies a simple imperative programming language with a small-step semantics. Section 4 then lays the foundations for translating abstract programs to concrete programs by defining heap structures and formulas of separation logic. Again, we will formally define these for our core language and indicate informally how other data structures are represented. Section 5 details the translation process to a language with pointer semantics. The translation ensures that the behavior of the resulting code matches its specification, i.e., that the small-step semantics of the target language allows transitions only that match those of the value semantics. Section 6 gives a formal small-step semantics of the target language, which allows to prove correctness of the translation. The specifications of syntax and semantics defined in Sects. 4-6 have been formalized using KIV and are available at [30]. A full mechanized verification of the translation correctness is still work in progress. Section 7 outlines some optimizations already implemented in the code generator, which result in more efficient code. One of them is a fine grained liveness analysis that allows for the reduction of necessary copying. Finally, Sect. 8 concludes and gives an outlook on future work.

2 Motivation, Scope and Related Work

Our work on correct and efficient code generation is motivated by the Flashix project [6], a large-scale verification project that developed a fully verified file system for flash memory. Its focus was on verifying functional correctness with regards to an abstract specification of the POSIX interface as well as on guaranteeing various non-functional correctness properties like crash-safety. For this, the file system was modeled completely in the abstract programming language of the KIV theorem prover [29]. A prototypical code generator was developed to evaluate modifications or extensions to the file system quickly. This initial version provided a first translation of the KIV models resulting in 15k lines of executable C code[1], allowing the file system to be integrated and tested within the Linux operating system. However, comparisons to state-of-the-art flash file systems like UBIFS [15] showed that the in-memory performance of the resulting code, which heavily relies on copying in order to avoid side effects by destructive updates, lags noticeably behind that of hand-written implementations, cf. [6].

The VeriCode project aims to develop a systematic approach for translating abstract specifications to efficient C code that uses destructive updates and minimizes copying while maintaining correctness. This paper lays the foundation for the project by providing formal semantics of both the specification and the target language and presenting the fundamental translation mechanism.

Scope. The specification language is based on simply typed lambda calculus. Data types include the standard primitive types, i.e., booleans, natural numbers, integers, and strings, all free data types (see example below), but also important non-free data types like arrays, sets, bags, and maps. Axioms for well-founded recursive definitions of (total) first-order functions are supported. Operators like *map*, *filter*, and *fold* are available, but not arbitrary higher-order definitions.

Based on these, standard imperative abstract programs can be formulated and encapsulated as procedures supporting value and reference parameters (cf. methods in object-oriented programming languages or functions in C). These are a superset of first-order recursive functional programs as well as of imperative ones, since they allow mutable reference parameters.

Abstract programs have *value semantics* (detailed in the next section for a subset of the language): programs modify a state, which is simply a mapping of variables to values. Having programs that explicitly use the heap is possible (the heap can be specified as a map from references to objects). However, the heap is then an explicit argument that is manipulated by the program. This is in contrast to real programming languages where the heap is implicit and plays a central role in the semantics of the language, from now on called *pointer semantics*. This paper focuses on a translation of value semantics to pointer semantics, which uses a heap to store non-primitive data types and has to deal with aliasing and the avoidance of memory leaks.

Programs, more precisely procedures, can be structured using *components*: each component consists of an interface and an implementation, see [6]. The approach also supports concurrent libraries where the abstract specification consists of atomic operations, but the implementation is allowed to be concurrent using mutexes, reader-writer locks and conditions[2]. We plan to make the source language available as a DSL for Scala, so other verification tools can easily translate to it.

Related Work. As mentioned in the introduction, theorem provers have long supported translating abstract specifications to functional languages. Typically, the implementation language of the prover is supported: PVS supports compi-

---

[1] Additionally, a backend for producing Scala code was implemented too.
[2] Not using other primitives than locks allows to avoid considering weak memory models.

lation to LISP [26], Isabelle to ML [24], Coq translates to OCamL [5], etc. Of course, a translation to C with a garbage collector added is possible too, e.g., the Lean prover supports compilation to C using a reference counting garbage collector [11]. However, code that requires garbage collection is often not feasible or useful (and in particular, reference counting is difficult to interface with existing libraries that must be used in our context).

Since it is well known that the resulting functional code is often inefficient, many optimizations have been proposed, e.g., [18,33]. Most common is to support an analysis that checks for the linear propagation of values which then can be mutated, e.g., [7]. An extreme approach in this direction is the one of Cogent [25] that already restricts the specification language to a linear type system. Another attempt to optimize is the use of immutable (sometimes also called persistent) data structures. These have sophisticated implementations, which allow non-mutating updates that do not need to copy the data structure as a whole. However, it seems common knowledge that there is still a big gap, and we can confirm this for the Flashix project: if we generate code (except for additional deallocation instructions) with the same optimizations for our case study, we find that the Scala code is a factor of at least 10 slower than the C code. If we generate code in Scala that uses the immutable `Vector` type of Scala instead of the mutable `Array` type, the code becomes so slow that it is practically unusable. This is not surprising as any file system must deal with pages, i.e., parts of file content. All of these are arrays of (32- or 64-bit) words, that must be read from/written to hardware, cached in buffers, concatenated with management data, etc.

There are several approaches for achieving actual verified C code. One is direct verification of C programs using verification tools such as VCC [8], VeriFast [16], or Frama-C [4]. In addition to the task of verifying algorithmic correctness, this approach immediately has to deal with pointer semantics, the problems associated with aliasing, and memory leaks. Despite the advances using Separation Logic [27] or Dynamic Frames [17], this is still significantly more challenging than abstract verification, where algorithmic problems can be tackled without having to consider pointers all the time.

Another possibility is to prove correctness of an abstract algorithm and then to prove a refinement to a corresponding algorithm with pointer semantics. This is the approach followed for example in Isabelle-LLVM [19–21]. We have tried this approach but found it difficult to realize. Proving that an abstract while-loop modifying an array is refined by the same program in C requires proving that the C program does no out-of-bounds accesses within the loop. If this is the case due to a complex loop invariant that already has been established on the abstract level, this invariant has to be re-established for the C program, causing a significant amount of re-verification.

Refining to a heap-based program is sometimes necessary, though (and supported by our approach as basic programs may use explicit heap structures). Examples are efficient implementations of basic data types, where we found a way to separate out small refinements dealing with pointers in some cases (see

$$S = Atom \mid L(S) \mid P(S,S) \qquad E = X \mid C^+ \mid F^+(E) \mid G(E,E)$$
$$C^+ = C \uplus \{\mathtt{nil, true, false}\} \qquad F^+ = F \uplus \{\mathtt{head, tail, first, second}\}$$
$$G = \{\mathtt{cons, mkpair, .==., ..setHead(.), ..setFirst(.), ..setSecond(.)}\}$$

$$\mathcal{A} = (\{U, \{c^{\mathcal{A}} : c \in C^+\}, \{f^{\mathcal{A}} : f \in F^+\}, \{g^{\mathcal{A}} : g \in G\}, \{proc^{\mathcal{A}} : proc \in Proc\}) \qquad (1)$$

$$U = \bigcup_{s \in S} U_s \qquad \{\mathtt{tt, ff, \circ}\} \subseteq U_{Atom} \qquad U_{L(s)} = \{[u_1, \ldots, u_n] : u_i \in U_s\} \qquad (2)$$
$$U_{P(s_1, s_2)} = \{(u_1, u_2) : u_1 \in U_{s_2}, u_2 \in U_{s_2}\}$$

$$[\![c]\!](v) = c^{\mathcal{A}} \quad [\![x]\!](v) = v[x] \quad [\![f(e)]\!](v) = f^{\mathcal{A}}([\![e]\!](v)) \quad [\![g(e_1, e_2)]\!](v) = g^{\mathcal{A}}([\![e_1]\!](v), [\![e_2]\!](v)) \quad (3)$$

Fig. 1. Syntax and Semantics of Expressions

[28,31]). For most of the code used in the Flashix project, we found that explicit refinements to heap structures for each component would have duplicated all verification without leading to any new insights. The approach given here instead uniformly proves that a (verified) program with value semantics can be translated to an equivalent C program with pointer semantics.

Translation to C without using dynamic (heap-allocated) data is, e.g., done in EB2C [23] for Event-B models or in SCADE [9]. These focus for example on MISRA C [2], which is relevant for embedded systems with hard real-time constraints, where the use of heap-allocated memory is explicitly ruled out. Our approach instead wants to support such data types as they are relevant in compilers, operating systems, file systems, and other correctness-critical software.

Finally, PVS2C [10,13] is related. The approach translates programs using non-nested data types (arrays of integers are formalized) to C. It is based on reference counting, which however does not guarantee that mutation of nested structures like lists of lists is side-effect free.

3 Abstract Language and Value Semantics

The syntax of the source language supported is based on polymorphic types that include primitive types like *Int* for integers or *Bool* for booleans as well as non-primitive types such as $List(\alpha)$, $Set(\alpha)$, $Array(\alpha)$, $Map(\alpha, \beta)$ using type variables α, β. Free data types are available, as an example consider the following definition of binary trees with the polymorphic element type α.

$Bintree(\alpha) = \mathtt{node}(.\mathtt{left} : Bintree(\alpha); .\mathtt{elem} : \alpha; .\mathtt{right} : Bintree(\alpha)) \mid \mathtt{leaf}$

Field access for a node is written $bt.\mathtt{left}$, and respective field setters $bt.\mathtt{setLeft}(bt_0)$ (with result $\mathtt{node}(bt_0, bt.\mathtt{elem}, bt.\mathtt{right})$ for a node) are available as well. Axioms for free data types can be generated automatically.

Since the full language is too big to formalize here, we focus on a core language and assume polymorphism has been removed already.[3] Figure 1 gives the syntax

---
[3] Since the C language does not support polymorphism, we first traverse all the algebraic definitions and programs to find all concrete instances of types. Code is then generated separately for each instance, e.g., for lists of *Int* and lists of *Bool*.

$RHS = E \mid Proc(E; X)$
$P = RHS \mid X := RHS \mid P; P \mid \textbf{let}(X = RHS, P) \mid \textbf{if}(E, P, P) \mid \textbf{while}(E, P) \mid \textbf{pop}(X) \mid \varepsilon$

$$\frac{[\![rhs]\!](v, v', u')}{\langle \textbf{let}(x = rhs, p), v, \circ \rangle \Longrightarrow \langle p; \textbf{pop}(x), v'[x := u'], \circ \rangle} \qquad \frac{\langle p, v, u \rangle \Longrightarrow \langle p', v', u' \rangle}{\langle \varepsilon; p, v, u \rangle \Longrightarrow \langle p', v', u' \rangle}$$

$$\frac{[\![rhs]\!](v, v', u')}{\langle x := rhs, v, \circ \rangle \Longrightarrow \langle \varepsilon, v'[x := u'], \circ \rangle} \qquad \frac{\langle p, v, \circ \rangle \Longrightarrow \langle p', v', u' \rangle \quad p \neq \varepsilon}{\langle p; p_0, v, \circ \rangle \Longrightarrow \langle p'; p_0, v', u' \rangle}$$

$$\frac{[\![e]\!](v) = \textbf{tt}}{\langle \textbf{if}(e, p_1, p_2), v, \circ \rangle \Longrightarrow \langle p_1, v, \circ \rangle} \qquad \frac{[\![rhs]\!](v, v', u')}{\langle rhs, v, \circ \rangle \Longrightarrow \langle \varepsilon, v', u' \rangle}$$

$$\frac{[\![e]\!](v) \neq \textbf{tt}}{\langle \textbf{if}(e, p_1, p_2), v, \circ \rangle \Longrightarrow \langle p_2, v, \circ \rangle} \qquad \frac{}{\langle \textbf{pop}(x), v, u \rangle \Longrightarrow \langle \varepsilon, v \text{ -- } x, u \rangle}$$

$$\frac{[\![e]\!](v) = \textbf{tt}}{\langle \textbf{while}(e, p), v, \circ \rangle \Longrightarrow \langle p; \textbf{while}(e, p), v, \circ \rangle} \qquad \frac{[\![e]\!](v) \neq \textbf{tt}}{\langle \textbf{while}(e, p), v, \circ \rangle \Longrightarrow \langle \varepsilon, v, \circ \rangle}$$

Fig. 2. Syntax and Semantics of Programs

and semantics of expressions E of the core language. Expressions are based on sorts S, where primitive types are collected in one type $Atom$ to keep the type system simple. The non-primitive types used are lists $L(S)$ and pairs $P(S, S)$, representing typical container types. These can be nested, so more complex types like lists of pairs of lists can be built.

Expressions (with standard typing constraints) are constructed from a set of variables X, constants C^+ and applications of unary (F^+) and binary (G) functions to arguments. Constants in C and unary functions in F can be axiomatized by the user, C^+ additionally includes the predefined boolean literals and the constant nil for the empty list. Unary functions F^+ contain the predefined standard selectors for lists and pairs. G consists of the predefined equality predicate, the constructors cons and mkpair of lists and pairs, and their respective field setters. For simplicity, boolean operations and user defined functions of arity greater than one are left out (they can be imitated by if-then-else programs and pairs).

The semantics is a standard value semantics[4], where an algebra $\mathcal{A}$ is assumed with carrier sets U_s for every sort s and interpretations for all constants and functions (as well as for procedures $proc$, which are used in programs), see (1) in Fig. 1. U_{Atom} includes at least the boolean literals and an element $\circ$ representing the empty result of programs. The carrier sets of lists and pairs are constructed from the carrier sets of their element sorts ((2) in Fig. 1). Predefined functions in $(C^+ \setminus C) \cup (F^+ \setminus F) \cup G$ have standard semantics, e.g.,

$$[u_1, u_2, \ldots, u_n].\texttt{setHead}^{\mathcal{A}}(u) = [u, u_2, \ldots, u_n]$$

---
[4] The C++ language also uses the term *value semantics*. However, this is not synonymous with value semantics used in logics since explicit memory management is still necessary, and recursive data structures (of arbitrary size) must be implemented using pointers.

As usual in predicate logic, field accesses (including updates) return an unspecified result when called on an empty list. For code generation, it is assumed that the programs of the source language are *defined*, i.e., their runs do not have such calls, which can be ensured by verification.

The semantics $[\![e]\!](v)$ of expressions ((3) in Fig. 1) is standard, for the general polymorphic case see, e.g., [14]. The result is a value u of the sort of e, based on a valuation $v : Map(X, U)$ that maps finitely many variables x (at least those in e) of each type s to elements of U_s. We write $v[x]$ for the value stored for x, $v[x := u]$ for the valuation that has updated (or added) $v[x]$ to be u, and $v -- x$ for the valuation that has removed the entry of x. The empty map is $\emptyset$, and $x \in v$ determines whether there is an entry for x in v. The same notation is used for other maps used in the semantics[5].

The programs considered are Scala-like, where each program has a result, and if there is no result, the atom ∘ is returned (in C/Scala this is of type void/Unit). The syntax and semantics of programs $p \in P$ is given in Fig. 2. Right hand sides $rhs \in RHS$ of assignments may either be algebraic ('pure') expressions or calls of procedures $proc \in Proc$. Procedure calls have value parameters that can not be modified by the body of the procedure and reference parameters which are variables that can be assigned. Procedures return a value, which again may be ∘. For simplicity, the formal definition has a single value parameter and a single reference parameter, which is sufficient to explain their different roles[6]. The semantics of right hand sides is defined as a relation $[\![rhs]\!] \subseteq V \times V \times U$ between initial valuation v, final state v' (the reference parameter of a procedure may change), and result value u':

$[\![e]\!](v, v', u')$ iff $[\![e]\!](v) = u'$ and $v' = v$

$[\![proc(e; x)]\!](v, v', u')$ iff there is u_0 with $proc^A([\![e]\!](v), [\![x]\!](v), u_0, u')$
and $v' = v[x := u_0]$

The relation $proc^A(u_1, u_2, u_3, u_4)$ holds if the procedure – when started with values u_1 and u_2 for the two parameters – terminates, modifies the reference parameter to be u_3, and returns u_4. Defining the semantics of procedures in the algebra has the advantage that it can be constrained using, e.g., contracts. Of course, mutually recursive procedure declarations $proc(x; y)\{p\}$ (program p then can read x, y and update y only) with a least fixed point semantics are possible.

A program can be a right hand side rhs that returns its computed value. An assignment with rhs binds this value to variable x and returns nothing. The compound (';') executes the first program (which must return nothing) and then the second one (which determines the value returned). **let** binds a local variable to the computed value of rhs and executes its body p. **if** and **while** work as usual. **let** and **if** return whatever the last program they execute returns, **while**

---

[5] The specification of (syntactic) maps supported by the full language uses the same notation.

[6] For several reference parameters the code generator must ensure that they do not alias, just as it guarantees that the two components of a pair do not alias.

returns nothing. Finally, the **pop**(x) program and the empty program ε are not used in the input language. They are needed for the definition of the small step semantics below.

The operational semantics of programs (see Fig. 2) is defined as a small step semantics $\langle p, v, u \rangle \Longrightarrow \langle p', v', u' \rangle$ that transforms a configuration into another by executing one step of p, resulting in p'. An empty program ε can not execute any further step and signals termination. A configuration consists of a program p that is executed, a valuation v that is modified, and a result value u. The initial result value is ∘ and ignored. Most rules must just propagate ∘, since the constraints guarantee that only the last statement of a program can compute a value[7]. The rule for **pop** and the rule for $\varepsilon; p$ must propagate any value u to u': the program could have form $\mathbf{let}(x = 1, \mathbf{let}(y = 2, x + y))$ which results in configurations $\langle \mathbf{pop}(y); \mathbf{pop}(x), v', 3 \rangle$ and then $\langle \varepsilon; \mathbf{pop}(x), v'', 3 \rangle$ where propagation of the result 3 is required.

It is always assumed that variables bound by **let** are pairwise different and different from the other variables used in the program[8], so the update $v[x := u]$ adds an entry for the local x to v. Conversely, the **pop** instruction added to the end of the **let**-body p deallocates the variable again, resulting in $v -- x$.

The approach can easily be extended to nondeterministic or concurrent programs with standard interleaving semantics. It follows the standard literature (e.g., [1]) except for adding a result value. This is useful for functional programs and for modeling return values or exceptions as extra result values (which result in program parts being skipped) in the full language.

4 Heaps and Separation Logic

Algebraically defined heap structures and Separation Logic [27] formulas play a key role in the formalization of the concepts used in the translation from value to pointer semantics. This section defines the basic formulas and the relevant predicates on heaps that are used to specify the semantics of the target language.

In general, a heap $h : Heap(O)$ is a finite map $Map(Ref(O), O)$ from references $r : Ref(O)$ to objects of type O, where the special reference `null` is never allocated in any heap. To characterize heap content, we use Separation Logic formulas hP of type $Heap(O) \to Bool$ (abbreviated $HeapPrd$), which describe arbitrary heap parts. Predicate **emp** describes an *empty* heap, and *maplet* $r \mapsto o$ describes a singleton heap with only one reference r mapping to object o. More complex heaps are constructed using *separating conjunction* $hP_1 * hP_2$. This asserts that the heap consists of two disjoint parts, one satisfying hP_1 and one satisfying hP_2, respectively[9]:

$$\mathbf{emp}(h) \leftrightarrow h = \emptyset \qquad (r \mapsto o)(h) \leftrightarrow h = \emptyset[r := o]$$
$$(hP_1 * hP_2)(h) \leftrightarrow \exists\, h_1, h_2.\ h = h_1 \uplus h_2 \wedge hP_1(h_1) \wedge hP_2(h_2)$$

---

[7] Scala is more liberal: a program like 3; 5 is legal. It discards the 3 and computes 5.
[8] A simple initial pass during code generation can make sure of that.
[9] $h_1 \uplus h_2$ denotes the disjoint union of two heap parts h_1 and h_2, which is defined if they have disjoint allocated references (**dom** h_1 ∩ **dom** $h_2 = \emptyset$).

VeriCode: Correct Translation of Abstract Specifications to C Code   61

The heap stores container objects $o : O$, in our formal model these are lists or pairs. We abstract from the actual representation of container objects (e.g., doubly linked lists) by leaving the exact structure of type O open.

All we care about is that any representation will give access to the elements of the container. When an element is primitive, it is stored directly as part of the structure, if it is non-primitive, e.g., a list again, the container will store a reference that points to the element. We therefore define a type Val of values

$$Val = \text{R}(Ref(O)) \mid \text{V}(U_{Atom})$$

and provide a function $\text{mk}(s, vl)$ for constructing objects on the heap, which has a list of values $vl : List(Val)$ as input, representing the elements of the structure. Additionally, the sort $s : S$ of the structure is given as an argument, which allows to have different representations for different types. A list with values $val_1, \ldots, val_n$ of sort s (which again can be complex) is constructed with $\text{mk}(L(s), [val_1, \ldots, val_n])$, a pair object with values val_1 and val_2 representing elements of types s_1 and s_2 is constructed with $\text{mk}(P(s_1, s_2), [val_1, val_2])$[10]. The recursively defined heap predicate $\text{abs} : Val \times U \to HeapPrd$ characterizes a heap portion that stores a particular (complex) element in this representation:

$$\text{abs}(\text{V}(at), u)(h) \leftrightarrow u = at \land \text{emp}(h)$$
$$\text{abs}(\text{R}(r), [u_1, \ldots, u_n])(h) \leftrightarrow$$
$$\exists val_1, \ldots, val_n. \ (r \mapsto \text{mk}(L(s), [val_1, \ldots, val_n]) * \overset{n}{\underset{i=1}{*}} \text{abs}(val_i, u_i))(h)$$
$$\text{abs}(\text{R}(r), (u_1, u_2))(h) \leftrightarrow$$
$$\exists val_1, val_2. \ (\ r \mapsto \text{mk}(P(s_1, s_2), [val_1, val_2])$$
$$* \ \text{abs}(val_1, u_1) * \text{abs}(val_2, u_2))(h)$$

Note that primitive elements do not occupy additional heap space, i.e., are stored directly in the parent structure, and each element of a complex structure is again stored in a disjoint (*separated*) part of the heap. Thus, when lifted to the full state of a program, the heap basically consists of a set of disjoint heap structures.

In concrete programs, updates to substructures (identified via *selector chains*) are allowed in assignments, see Sect. 6. As a consequence, intermediate states can occur in which the abstraction of a substructure no longer holds, e.g., an old substructure must be freed just before the new value is set. In this situation, the heap predicate variant $\text{absNull} : SC \times Val \times U \to HeapPrd$ is used for describing the heap, based on a selector chain $sc \in SC$ given as a list of field selections:

$$SC = List(\text{head} \mid \text{first} \mid \text{second})$$

---

[10] Similarly, in the full language, arrays and sets are constructed from their elements; maps from a list of keys and values.

absNull(sc, val, u)(h) gives the same abstraction as abs(val, u)(h) but drops the substructure identified by applying the field selections of sc in order. Instead, the corresponding value must be set to the null reference. For brevity, we only give the definition of a head selection on a list object here; the cases for first and second selection of pairs are analogous.

$$\text{absNull}(sc, \text{V}(at), u)(h) \leftrightarrow sc = [\,] \wedge u = at \wedge \text{emp}(h)$$
$$\text{absNull}([\,], \text{R}(r), u)(h) \leftrightarrow r = \text{null} \wedge \text{emp}(h)$$
$$\text{absNull}([\text{head}, sel_2, \ldots, sel_m], \text{R}(r), [u_1, \ldots, u_n])(h) \leftrightarrow$$
$$\exists\, val_1, \ldots, val_n.\ \Big(\ r \mapsto \text{mk}(L(s), [val_1, \ldots, val_n]) \ * \ \overset{n}{\underset{i=2}{*}}\ \text{abs}(val_i, u_i)$$
$$*\ \text{absNull}([sel_2, \ldots, sel_m], val_1, u_1)\Big)(h)$$

Furthermore, $.\rightsquigarrow.\ :\ Ref(O) \times Ref(O) \to HeapPrd$ is used to mark references that point to a substructure of the object stored under some starting reference: $(r \rightsquigarrow r')(h)$ denotes that r' can be reached by applying a valid sequence of field selections (i.e., a selector chain), starting from the object stored in h under r.

5 Translation

In this section, we define the concrete programs that we translate to, give an informal semantics, and define the concepts used in the translation.

The concrete programs have a pointer semantics. They use a store st : $Map(X, Val)$ that maps variables to either primitive values or to references (type Val) in the heap h. The heap is specified with formulas of Separation Logic as defined in the previous section, so the language is still somewhat more abstract than C. It however has instructions that allocate/free heap space and can express aliasing. Therefore, it is sufficient to cover all important aspects of the translation. Generating C code from the concrete programs is a straightforward 1:1 translation. The translation consists of three steps. The first two are already done on the source language.

First Step: Moving Update Operations to Access Forms. In concrete programs, field updates like .setHead, .setFirst and .setSecond are no longer allowed. Instead, the left hand sides of assignments now use access forms Acc (see Fig. 3). These consist of a variable with a sequence of selectors applied. An

$$Id = X \mid C \mid \text{true} \mid \text{false} \qquad Acc = X \mid \text{head}(Acc) \mid \text{first}(Acc) \mid \text{second}(Acc)$$
$$IdAcc = Id \mid Acc \qquad CE = IdAcc \mid IdAcc == IdAcc$$
$$CRHS = \text{Proc}(Id; X) \mid F(X) \mid \text{copy}(Acc) \mid CE \mid \text{nil} \mid \text{mkpair}(Id, Id)$$
$$CP = CRHS \mid Acc := CRHS \mid CP; CP \mid \text{let}(X = CRHS, CP) \mid \text{pop}(X) \mid \text{free}(Acc)$$
$$\mid \text{if}(CE, CP, CP) \mid \text{while}(CE, CP) \mid \text{addHead}(Id, X) \mid \text{rmHead}(X) \mid \varepsilon$$

Fig. 3. Subtypes of expressions and concrete programs

$$x := x.\mathtt{setSecond}(a) \qquad\qquad x \rightarrow \mathtt{second} := a \qquad\qquad (4)$$
$$x := x.\mathtt{setHead}(\mathtt{head}(x).\mathtt{setFirst}(a)) \qquad x \rightarrow \mathtt{head} \rightarrow \mathtt{first} := a \qquad (5)$$
$$acc := acc.\mathtt{setHead}(a) \qquad\qquad acc \rightarrow \mathtt{head} := a \qquad\qquad (6)$$
$$y := x.\mathtt{setFirst}(a) \qquad\qquad y := x; y \rightarrow \mathtt{first} := a \qquad (7)$$
$$\mathbf{let}(y = x.\mathtt{setFirst}(a),\ p) \qquad\qquad \mathbf{let}(y = x,\ y \rightarrow \mathtt{first} := a;\ p) \qquad (8)$$
$$f(x.\mathtt{setFirst}(a)) \qquad\qquad \mathbf{let}(y_0 = x.\mathtt{setFirst}(a),\ f(y_0)) \qquad (9)$$

Fig. 4. Trading update functions for access forms

example in the core language is $\mathtt{first}(\mathtt{head}(x))$. In C, such a left hand side will be written as $x \rightarrow \mathtt{head} \rightarrow \mathtt{first}$, so we will write an access form as $x \rightarrow sc$ where $sc \in SC$. The full language also has access forms for arrays, maps and fields of free data types. An example is $ar\mathtt{[}n\mathtt{]}.\mathtt{field[}key\mathtt{]}$ when ar is an array that stores elements of a free data type with a $\mathtt{field}$ that is a map.

The first step eliminates such updates of fields by *shifting* them to access forms. Examples for shifting are given in Fig. 4. Transformation (4) shows the basic case, which can be iterated as in the second example (5); the general case of iteration is (6). If the assigned variable is different from the one a field is updated, an additional variable assignment is introduced to enable shifting, as shown in (7). Example (8) shows that a **let** with an update on the right hand side can be transformed, too. Finally, if the update is not on the top-level of a right hand side as in (9), the update expression itself must be bound to a new local variable, which then allows the previous transformation (8).

Recall that this transformation is performed on the source language: as an example, $y := x$ in (7) assigns the *value* of x to y, the assignment $y \rightarrow \mathtt{first} := a$ just modifies y. The switch to pointer semantics only happens in the third step below.

Second Step: Flattening of Expressions. Another required transformation is the flattening of expressions using new local variables. As an example, $f_1(f_2(x))$ must be transformed to $\mathbf{let}(y = f_2(x), f_1(y))$ in order to properly deallocate the intermediate result (bound to y) once it has been used in the call of f_2. The programs that result from flattening already obey the restrictions on expressions that are necessary for the concrete programs defined in Fig. 3. They use function calls (including $\mathtt{cons}$, $\mathtt{tail}$, $\mathtt{mkpair}$) and procedure calls only in **let**-bindings and on the right hand side of assignments. The arguments of calls must be variables or constants, those of equations must be access forms or constants.

Third Step: Translation to Concrete Programs. The main translation results in the programs given in Fig. 3. It is built on the principle to keep data structures disjoint. Without optimizations an abstract valuation $v : Map(X, U)$ corresponds to a concrete state $st : Map(X, Val), h : Heap(O)$ via

$$\mathsf{Abs}(v, st)(h) = \left(\underset{x \in v}{*}\ \mathsf{abs}(st[x], v[x]) \right)(h)$$

$x := \mathtt{tail}(x)$	$\mathbf{rmHead}(x)$	(10)
$x := \mathtt{cons}(a, x)$	$\mathbf{let}^c(a_0 = a, \mathbf{addHead}(a_0, x))$	(11)
$y \to sc := \mathtt{tail}(x)$	$\mathbf{let}^c(x_0 = x, \mathbf{rmHead}(x_0); \mathbf{free}(y \to sc); y \to sc := x_0)$	(12)
$y := \mathtt{cons}(z \to sc, x)$	$\mathbf{let}^c(x_0 = x, \mathbf{let}^c(a_0 = z \to sc, \mathbf{addHead}(a_0, x_0); \mathbf{free}(y); y := x_0))$	(13)
$\mathbf{let}(y = \mathtt{tail}(x), p)$	$\mathbf{let}^{cf}(y = x, \mathbf{rmHead}(y); p)$	(14)
$\mathbf{let}(y = \mathtt{cons}(a, x), p)$	$\mathbf{let}^{cf}(y = x, \mathbf{let}^c(a_0 = a, \mathbf{addHead}(a, y)); p)$	(15)
$z := \mathtt{mkpair}(x, y)$	$\mathbf{let}^c(x_0 = x, \mathbf{let}^c(y_0 = y, z := \mathtt{mkpair}(x_0, y_0)))$	(16)

Fig. 5. Translation of elementary instructions. Programs $\mathbf{let}^{cf}(y = x, p)$ and $\mathbf{let}^c(y = x, p)$ abbreviate $\mathbf{let}(y = \mathtt{copy}(x), p; \mathbf{free}(y))$ and $\mathbf{let}(y = \mathtt{copy}(x), p)$, respectively.

The formula implies that there is never any unreachable heap part (which would be a memory leak) and that all updates to data can be done by mutation. The next section will give a formal small step semantics for the concrete language that is suitable to prove that $\mathtt{Abs}(v, st)(h)$ is indeed preserved, and Sect. 7 will discuss optimizations that will introduce sharing where possible.

In concrete programs, memory has to be freed explicitly to avoid leaks. $\mathbf{free}(x \to sc)$ frees the data structure reachable from x via sc (including all substructures). The two typical cases are freeing the old data structure that is about to be overwritten by an assignment and freeing a local variable at the end of its **let** block. To keep data structures disjoint, operation $\mathtt{copy}(x \to sc)$ creates a disjoint copy of the structure at $x \to sc$. It is used exclusively for a value bound to a local variable in **let** to help with optimization. Therefore, we define the abbreviation $\mathbf{let}^{cf}(y = x \to sc, cp)$ for $\mathbf{let}(y = \mathtt{copy}(x \to sc), cp; \mathbf{free}(y))$, where the structure bound to the local variable y is copied and this copy is freed at the end of the **let** block. Similarly, we write $\mathbf{let}^c$ or $\mathbf{let}^f$ if the **free** or the call to $\mathtt{copy}$ are missing. In any case, $\mathbf{let}^{cf}$ does add neither of them if x has the primitive type *Atom*.

Conditionals and while loops are translated one-to-one, **let** is usually translated to $\mathbf{let}^f$, which frees the local variable at then end. Taking a copy by translating to $\mathbf{let}^{cf}$ is necessary when the value bound to the local variable is an access form (all other results are freshly allocated memory).

The instructions $\mathbf{rmHead}(x)$ and $\mathbf{addHead}(a, x)$ are typical examples for the translation of modification operations on data structures. $\mathbf{rmHead}(x)$ *mutates* the list x removing its first element, which is deallocated (including all substructures). Like for $\mathtt{tail}$, it is assumed that $\mathbf{rmHead}$ is never called on an empty list. Other examples in the full language include removing one or all occurrences of an element from a collection, e.g., a list or a set. Like all *mutating operations*, it returns no result. Translation of the source instruction $x := \mathtt{tail}(x)$ gives this result as shown as the first line (10) in Fig. 5.

This figure lists several more compilation results. $\mathbf{addHead}(a, x)$ also mutates the list x. It adds the element stored in a as the first element of the list *without copying it*: we say that the operation *steals* its first argument. Since variables a and x then share, this would cause side-effects when a or the first element of x are mutated subsequently. Therefore, the result of compiling $x := \mathtt{cons}(a, x)$

first takes a copy of a (when non-primitive) that is then added to x, as shown in (11). Note that the copy does not need to be freed since it is integrated into x. Other examples that steal are adding an element to a set, adding an element to the end of a list, or appending two lists with $x := \mathtt{append}(x, y)$: the result is a call **append**(x, y) that mutates x and steals y.

If the assigned variable y is different from the modified variable x or an access form compilation is more complex as shown in (12) for `tail`, the old value stored in $y \to sc$ must be deallocated, and the content of x has to be copied to x_0. (13) shows a similar case for `cons` where the element added to x is now computed via an access form. The use of an access form for the first argument of `cons` or on the left hand side of the assignment is possible in the other cases, too. Compiling **let** programs that call `tail` or `cons` is similar, see (14) and (15): x is copied to a local variable y, which then can be mutated by **rmHead/addHead** (and further in the body cp) and is finally deallocated at the end.

In general, the translation uses stealing wherever possible: all arguments of constructors of free data types, like `mkpair`, are stolen. Translating $z := \mathtt{mkpair}(x, y)$ therefore needs to copy x and y as shown in (16). Having an explicit copy that can be optimized away in many cases (see Sect. 7) is always preferred over having the operation itself (here `mkpair`) copying its arguments. Similarly, operations that mutate a data structure need copying only when the modified data structure is bound to another variable.

6 Correctness of the Translation

The small step semantics for our concrete language is based on heaps $h : Heap(O)$ and variable stores $st : Map(X, Val)$, storing the values (primitive elements or reference in the heap) of variables in the current program scope.

In contrast to the abstract semantics (cf. Sect. 3), the semantics $[\![e]\!](st, h)$ of an expression $e \in CE$, see Fig. 6, returns a *Val* rather than an element of the respective carrier set. This value contains the evaluated atom if e is of primitive type, e.g., when it is a constant or an equality check, or the reference to the substructure selected by an access form.

Transitions that execute one step of a concrete program cp leading to a remaining program cp' now have the form $\langle cp, st, h, val \rangle \Longrightarrow \langle cp', st', h', val' \rangle$. A transition may modify both the store st and the heap h. Like for the abstract programs, the result value (now either a primitive value or a pointer in the heap) is computed at the end of a program, so most rules have $val = val' = \circ$. Since right hand sides $crhs \in CRHS$ can also modify st and h, e.g., when a procedure is called, their semantics is given similarly as step transitions $\langle crhs, st, h \rangle \Rightarrow \langle st', h', val \rangle$, calculating a result value $val \in Val$.

For the correctness of the translation, it is essential that runs of translated programs never produce memory leaks or – even worse – access dangling pointers. The key to verifying this property is that our semantic rules already ensure that small steps are possible only when this does not happen. Therefore, the rules that evaluate right hand sides resp. execute basic instructions have the general forms

$[\![x]\!](st, h) = st[x]$ $\qquad$ $[\![c]\!](st, h) = \mathtt{V}(c^{\mathcal{A}})$
$[\![\mathtt{first}(e)]\!](st, h) = val_1$ iff $[\![e]\!](st, h) = \mathtt{R}(r)$ and $h[r] = \mathtt{mk}(P(S_1, S_2), [val_1, val_2])$
$[\![\mathtt{second}(e)]\!](st, h) = val_2$ iff $[\![e]\!](st, h) = \mathtt{R}(r)$ and $h[r] = \mathtt{mk}(P(S_1, S_2), [val_1, val_2])$
$[\![\mathtt{head}(e)]\!](st, h) = val_1$ iff $[\![e]\!](st, h) = \mathtt{R}(r)$ and $h[r] = \mathtt{mk}(L(S), [val_1, \ldots val_n])$
$[\![e_1 == e_2]\!](st, h) = \mathtt{V}(\mathtt{tt})$ iff there is a common u with[11]

$$(\mathtt{abs}([\![e_1]\!](st, h), u) * \mathtt{true})(h) \text{ and } (\mathtt{abs}([\![e_2]\!](st, h), u) * \mathtt{true})(h)$$

$$\frac{[\![e]\!](st, h) = val, e \in CE \vdash}{\langle e, st, h \rangle \Rightarrow \langle st, h, val \rangle} \quad (1) \qquad \frac{hP(h) \vdash (\mathtt{abs}(\mathtt{R}(r), [\,]) * hP)(h')}{\langle \mathtt{nil}, st, h \rangle \Rightarrow \langle st, h', \mathtt{R}(r) \rangle} \quad (2)$$

$$\frac{(\mathtt{abs}(st[x], u) * hP)(h) \vdash (\mathtt{abs}(val, f^{\mathcal{A}}(u)) * \mathtt{abs}(st[x], u) * hP)(h')}{\langle f(x), st, h \rangle \Rightarrow \langle st, h', val \rangle} \quad (3)$$

$$\frac{(\mathtt{abs}(st[x], u) * hP)(h), (x \to sc).sort \neq Atom}{\vdash (\mathtt{abs}(\mathtt{R}(r), u[sc]) * \mathtt{abs}(st[x], u) * hP)(h')}{\langle \mathtt{copy}(x \to sc), st, h \rangle \Rightarrow \langle st, h', \mathtt{R}(r) \rangle} \quad (4)$$

$$\frac{(\mathtt{abs}([\![id_1]\!](st, h), u_1) * \mathtt{abs}([\![id_2]\!](st, h), u_2) * hP)(h)}{\vdash (\mathtt{abs}(\mathtt{R}(r), \mathtt{mkpair}^{\mathcal{A}}(u_1, u_2)) * hP)(h')}{\langle \mathtt{mkpair}(id_1, id_2), st, h \rangle \Rightarrow \langle st, h', \mathtt{R}(r) \rangle} \quad (5)$$

$$\frac{proc^{\mathcal{A}}(u_1, u_2, u_2', u), (\mathtt{abs}(st[x_1], u_1) * \mathtt{abs}(st[x_2], u_2) * hP)(h)}{\vdash (\mathtt{abs}(val, u) * \mathtt{abs}(st[x_1], u_1) * \mathtt{abs}(st[x_2], u_2') * hP)(h') \wedge st' \stackrel{x_2}{=} st}{\langle proc(x_1; x_2), st, h \rangle \Rightarrow \langle st', h', val \rangle} \quad (6)$$

Fig. 6. Semantics of expressions CE (top) and right hand sides $CRHS$ (bottom)[11] (The abs-formulas express that the heap stores u under $[\![e_i]\!](st, h)$, together with arbitrary other data (that just satisfy $\mathtt{true}$), so equality is structural equality as on the abstract level.)

$$\frac{(hpred * hP)(h) \vdash (hpred' * hP)(h')}{\langle crhs, st, h \rangle \Rightarrow \langle st', h', val \rangle} \qquad \frac{(hpred * hP)(h) \vdash (hpred' * hP)(h')}{\langle cp, st, h, val \rangle \Longrightarrow \langle cp', st', h', val' \rangle}$$

The precondition $(hpred * hP)(h)$ expresses that the heap must have a specific shape for the step to be applicable. The shape contains a heap part hP that is unaffected by the rule and a part $hpred$ specifically characterized for the rule. This part typically uses the formulas $\mathtt{abs}(val, u)$ and $\mathtt{absNull}(sc, val, u)$, characterizing heap parts that store a structure representing u or u with a $\mathtt{null}$ reference at the selector chain sc, respectively (see Sect. 4). Similar to the precondition, the postcondition $(hpred' * hP)(h')$ characterizes the shape of the heap after the step: the stable heap portion hP is unchanged while a modified part characterized by $hpred'$ is now in place of $hpred$. So in summary, such small step rules can be viewed as a kind of *contract* that the steps satisfy.

A listing of the semantic rules for concrete programs resulting from the translation process described in the previous section is given in Fig. 6 and Fig. 7. We will explain some interesting semantic rules in detail to demonstrate the concepts.

Figure 6 gives the rules for right hand sides $CRHS$ as they are used within concrete programs. Note that most $CRHS$ steps (except for the call rule (6)) do not update the store st, but their result is directly used within a corresponding program step, e.g., it may be assigned to some variable.

Rule (1) covers the simplest case where an expression e is evaluated without producing or modifying any memory, e.g., when e is a variable or access form. The step does not modify store st or heap h but only computes the semantic value val of e.

The rule for `nil` ((2) in Fig. 6) extends the heap (satisfying an arbitrary heap predicate hP) by a *separate* junk representing the empty list ($\text{abs}(\text{R}(r), [\,])$), yielding a fresh reference r pointing to this new heap part.

Rule (4) gives the heap transformation for a **copy** step. The step requires that x stores a heap structure that represents data structure u, which is separate (note the separating conjunction *) from the remaining heap hP. The substructure of u accessed via sc, that should be copied, is written $u[sc]$. The postcondition ensures that the substructure is actually copied by storing $u[sc]$ in a new part *disjoint* to the parts of x and hP.

Conversely, rule (5) gives the semantics for the **mkpair** constructor that *steals* its arguments. The rule requires both arguments to be initially stored in separate heap parts, but then combines them into a single part representing the resulting pair (u_1, u_2). Note that this rule is already restricted to arguments $id_1, id_2 \in Id$, typically variables, since the semantics expect all transformations of Sect. 5 to be performed. Here in particular that (complex) arguments of stealing operations are bound to (copying) **let** instructions, as shown for example in (13) of Fig. 5.

Finally, rule (6) covers procedure calls. Noticeably, a call step updates the store st as it can alter the value of its reference argument x_2. Since we do not want to make any assumptions about the actual implementation of the procedure, which could for example store the resulting x_2 under another reference, the rule does not specify the resulting store st' precisely. It just restricts updates of st to the affected variable x_2 (written $st' \stackrel{x_2}{=} st$).

Based on the semantics of right hand sides, Fig. 7 shows the rules for programs statements. For brevity, we omit the rules for compound, **if**, and **while** since they are analogous to those of the abstract semantics given in Fig. 2.

For a result statement $crhs$, rule (1) simply reduces to the corresponding $CRHS$ rule of Fig. 6, returning the calculated result value val. The semantics for assignments, which now may update a substructure of the left hand side destructively, is given with rule (2). In order to prevent memory leaks, the rule requires that the location to be overwritten has been *nulled* beforehand (it must satisfy `absNull`), which enforces a prior **free** step for $x \to sc$, see rule (6). Similar to the step of a stealing operation, the assignment step combines the two heap parts of the result val of $crhs$ and the nulled parent data structure x of the left hand side, yielding a complete abstraction (without a hole at sc) of the updated element $u[sc := u']$ (where the element at sc in u is replaced with u'). The store st''

$$\frac{\langle crhs, st, h\rangle \Rightarrow \langle st', h', val\rangle}{\langle crhs, st, h, \circ\rangle \Longrightarrow \langle \varepsilon, st', h', val\rangle} \quad (1)$$

$$\frac{\langle crhs, st, h\rangle \Rightarrow \langle st'', h'', val\rangle, (\textsf{abs}(val, u') * \textsf{absNull}(sc, st''[x], u) * hP)(h'')}{\vdash (\textsf{abs}(st'[x], u[sc := u']) * hP)(h') \wedge st' = \textbf{if } sc = [\,] \textbf{ then } st''[x := val] \textbf{ else } st''} \quad (2)$$
$$\langle x \to sc := crhs, st, h, \circ\rangle \Longrightarrow \langle \varepsilon, st', h', \circ\rangle$$

$$\frac{(\textsf{abs}(\llbracket id \rrbracket(st, h), u_1) * \textsf{abs}(st[x], u_2) * hP)(h)}{\vdash (\textsf{abs}(st'[x], \textsf{cons}^A(u_1, u_2)) * hP)(h') \wedge st' \stackrel{x}{=} st} \quad (3)$$
$$\langle \textbf{addHead}(id, x), st, h, \circ\rangle \Longrightarrow \langle \varepsilon, st', h', \circ\rangle$$

$$\frac{(\textsf{abs}(st[x], u) * hP)(h) \vdash (\textsf{abs}(st'[x], \textsf{tail}^A(u)) * hP)(h') \wedge st' \stackrel{x}{=} st}{\langle \textbf{rmHead}(x), st, h, \circ\rangle \Longrightarrow \langle \varepsilon, st', h', \circ\rangle} \quad (4)$$

$$\frac{\langle crhs, st, h\rangle \Rightarrow \langle st', h', val\rangle}{\langle \textbf{let}(x = crhs, cp), st, h, \circ\rangle \Longrightarrow \langle cp; \textbf{pop}(x), st'[x := val], h', \circ\rangle} \quad (5)$$

$$\frac{(\textsf{abs}(st[x], u) * hP)(h)}{\vdash (\textsf{absNull}(sc, st'[x], u) * hP)(h') \wedge st' = \textbf{if } sc = [\,] \textbf{ then } st[x := \texttt{R}(\texttt{null})] \textbf{ else } st} \quad (6)$$
$$\langle \textbf{free}(x \to sc), st, h, \circ\rangle \Longrightarrow \langle \varepsilon, st', h', \circ\rangle$$

$$\frac{st[x] = \texttt{R}(\texttt{null}) \vee x.sort = Atom \vdash}{\langle \textbf{pop}(x), st, h, \circ\rangle \Longrightarrow \langle \varepsilon, st \mathbin{\text{-}\!\text{-}} x, h, \circ\rangle} \quad (7)$$

$$\frac{st[x] = \texttt{R}(r), r \neq \texttt{null}, st[x'] = \texttt{R}(r'), (r' \rightsquigarrow r)(h) \vdash}{\langle \textbf{pop}(x), st, h, \circ\rangle \Longrightarrow \langle \varepsilon, st \mathbin{\text{-}\!\text{-}} x, h, \circ\rangle} \quad (8)$$

Fig. 7. Semantics of concrete programs CP

after the $crhs$ step is updated only if the top-level variable is assigned directly, i.e., the selector chain sc is empty: then x is updated to store val, otherwise the values of variables are unchanged since only an *unshared* substructure was manipulated.

Rules (3) and (4) give the steps for mutating operations **addHead** and **rmHead**. As they *mutate* the argument list x, the step modifies the respective heap part $\textsf{abs}(st[x], \ldots)$ to store the updated list. Additionally, **addHead** *steals* the element id, thus its heap part is integrated into the one of x. Again, the precise updates to $st[x]$ are left open to allow various implementations of the list operations.

Finally, rules (7) and (8) for **pop** are formulated so that no memory leaks can occur from local variables: removing a variable x from st at the end of a **let** block is allowed only if (7) it has been freed before or (8) there is some other variable x' still pointing to the heap location of x, which is the case when it has been stolen. That way, the global abstraction **Abs**, see Sect. 5, is directly maintained by these rules.

As an example, consider the abstract program $x_2 := \textsf{cons}(x_1 \to sc, x_2)$, where the element $x_1 \to sc$ should be prepended to the list x_2. Applying the transformations described in Sect. 5 yields the concrete program **let**($x_3 = \textsf{copy}(x_1 \to sc)$, **addHead**($x_3, x_2$)). The upper sequence in Fig. 8 depicts the heap transformations caused by this result: the initial heap has a valid form satisfying

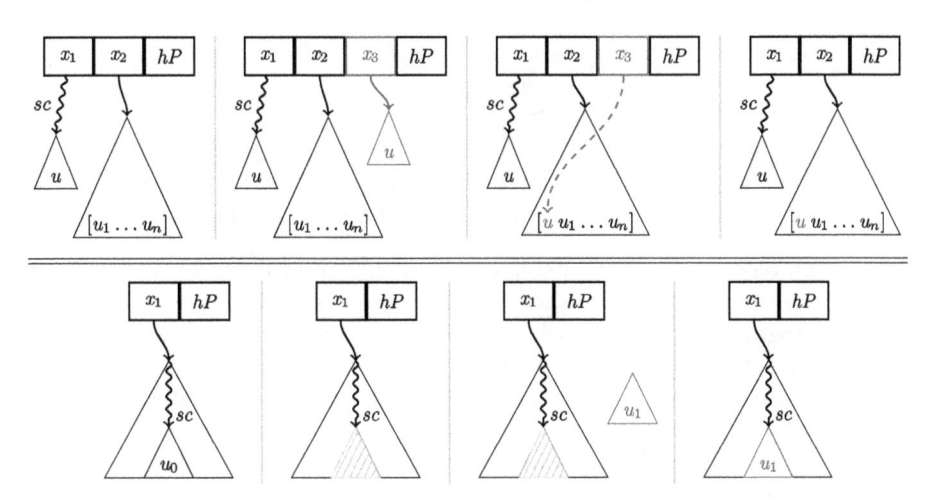

Fig. 8. Exemplary heap transformations: an **addHead** call stealing the element at $x_1 \to sc$ (top), and an assignment to access form $x_1 \to sc$ (bottom).

$(\mathtt{abs}(st[x_1], \ldots) * \mathtt{abs}(st[x_2], [u_1 \ldots u_n]) * hP)$, where $x_1 \to sc$ points to some element u. Since **addHead** *steals* its head argument, a copy of u is bound to a new variable x_3 using a **let** construct in a first step (recall that due to stealing, no freeing is required). Applying **copy** on $x_1 \to sc$ produces a new disjoint heap part $\mathtt{abs}(val, u)$ (rule (4) in Fig. 6), which can be bound to x_3 (rule (5) in Fig. 7), resulting in the additional heap part $\mathtt{abs}(st[x_3], u)$. In the next step, this heap part of x_3 is consumed by the actual **addHead** instruction, transforming the heap part of x_2 to $\mathtt{abs}(st[x_2], [u\; u_1 \ldots u_n])$ (rule (3) in Fig. 7). At this point however, x_3 still points to the stolen element (it is *shared*), so in the final step, this entry is removed from st (rule (8) in Fig. 7).

The lower sequence in Fig. 8 shows a second example: an assignment to an access form $x_1 \to sc$ (resulting from an abstract program $x_1 := x_1.\mathtt{setField}\ldots$). Initially, the heap has the form $(\mathtt{abs}(st[x_1], u) * hP)$ storing some complex element u under x_1, and the selector chain sc points to a part representing an element u_0, which is about to be overwritten. At first, this substructure is freed to avoid memory leaks (rule (6) in Fig. 7), resulting in the transformed heap part $\mathtt{absNull}(sc, st[x_1], \ldots)$ with "a hole" at sc (hatched part in the figure). Then, the right hand side of the assignment is evaluated, producing some new heap part $\mathtt{abs}(val, u_1)$ (see Fig. 6). Finally, these two heap parts are linked (rule (2) in Fig. 7), yielding the combined part $\mathtt{abs}(st[x_1], u[sc := u_1])$.

Based on these semantic rules, our main correctness property can be formulated (where $\mathtt{comp}(p)$ applies the transformations outlined in Sect. 5 to the program p).

Lemma 1. *For each abstract configuration* $\langle p, v, u \rangle$ *and a corresponding concrete configuration* $\langle \mathtt{comp}(p), st, h, val \rangle$ *satisfying* $(\mathtt{Abs}(v, st) * \mathtt{abs}(val, u))(h)$, *the following two properties hold:*

1) *For every abstract step* $\langle p, v, u \rangle \Longrightarrow \langle p', v', u' \rangle$, *there is a positive number of concrete steps* $\langle \texttt{comp}(p), st, h, val \rangle \Longrightarrow^+ \langle \texttt{comp}(p'), st', h', val' \rangle$ *such that* $(\texttt{Abs}(v', st') * \texttt{abs}(val', u'))(h')$.
2) *Each concrete run* $\langle \texttt{comp}(p), st, h, val \rangle \Longrightarrow^+ \ldots$ *reaches a configuration* $\langle cp', st', h', val' \rangle$ *in a finite number of steps such that a step* $\langle p, v, u \rangle \Longrightarrow \langle p', v', u' \rangle$ *exists with* $cp' = \texttt{comp}(p')$ *and* $(\texttt{Abs}(v', st') * \texttt{abs}(val', u'))(h')$.

Part 1) ensures that an abstract step can be simulated by concrete steps without violating any preconditions of the concrete semantics. Part 2) ensures that the concrete program has no extra behavior the abstract one does not have. Lemma 1 gives the inductive argument for constructing $1 : n$ commuting diagrams for runs of abstract programs and their translated concrete programs. Recall that we only consider defined programs that do not call selectors outside of their domain, e.g., **head** on the empty list. Lifting this argument to complete program runs, we get our main theorem.

Theorem 1. *If the original program p terminates, i.e., $\langle p, v, u \rangle \Longrightarrow^* \langle \varepsilon, v', u' \rangle$ holds, and if $(\texttt{Abs}(v, st) * \texttt{abs}(val, u))(h)$ holds at the start, then the compiled program $cp = \texttt{comp}(p)$ terminates as well, i.e., $\langle cp, st, h, val \rangle \Longrightarrow^* \langle \varepsilon, st', h', val' \rangle$ holds, and the return values and states are still an abstraction of each other, i.e., the heap h' satisfies $(\texttt{Abs}(v', st') * \texttt{abs}(val', u'))(h')$.*

Proof. Simple induction over the number of steps done by p. Each step is mapped to a finite number of steps by Lemma 1.

7 Optimization

In general, optimizations improve over the basic translation given in two ways: they avoid copying wherever possible, and they weaken the strict disjointness $\texttt{Abs}(u, st)(h)$ for all variables to disjointness for a subset only.

Avoiding copying can be exemplified with a program that *moves* data from one data structure to another as given in (17).

$$y := \texttt{cons}(\texttt{first}(\texttt{head}(x)), y); x := \texttt{tail}(x) \tag{17}$$

$$\texttt{let}(a = \texttt{copy}(x \rightarrow \texttt{head} \rightarrow \texttt{first}), \textbf{addHead}(a, y); \textbf{rmHead}(x)) \tag{18}$$

$$\texttt{let}(a = x \rightarrow \texttt{head} \rightarrow \texttt{first}, x \rightarrow \texttt{head} \rightarrow \texttt{first} := \texttt{null}; \textbf{addHead}(a, y); \textbf{rmHead}(x)) \tag{19}$$

The example assumes that $x : L(P(s, s'))$ and $y : L(s)$. The standard translation (18) copies the substructure to a local variable a and then adds a to x. Finally, **rmHead**(x) deallocates $x \rightarrow \texttt{head}$. However, a fine grained liveness analysis, that determines which access forms are *live/dead*, shows that $x \rightarrow \texttt{head}$ (and therefore $x \rightarrow \texttt{head} \rightarrow \texttt{first}$, too) is dead already when a is bound. Thus, a does not need to be copied if deallocating $x \rightarrow \texttt{head}$ in **rmHead** can be prevented from freeing a. This is simply done by setting the reference to it to $\texttt{null}$ as shown in (19).

There is another case where copying and freeing can be avoided: the program $\mathbf{let}^{cf}(x = y \to sc, cp)$ can be replaced with $\mathbf{let}(x = y \to sc, cp)$ letting x share with y when neither x nor $y \to sc$ are mutated in cp. This requires a careful analysis of whether a program mutates an access form.

There are a number of further optimizations for algebraic functions specified with axioms that define them recursively. The standard translation will give a recursive program that uses value parameters as arguments. However, turning the parameters into reference parameters is often strictly more efficient when operations like `tail`(x) are called on the parameter x which would require copying. With a reference parameter the caller has to make a single copy of x while the recursion can mutate x freely. Sometimes it is even possible to use an iterator, a concept that is completely absent in the source language. As an example, the code generator turns a list parameter x into an iterator when the body only calls `head`(x), `tail`(x) or checks for $x = $ `nil`. For example, if `sum`(x) for a list of values is defined as $x.\mathtt{fold}(0)(\_+\_)$, the code generator first expands the `fold` to a while loop that iterates over the list (as if the function were defined tail-recursively). It then optimizes the code to use an iterator (implemented as usual as a pointer that just traverses the linked list). Thus mutating the list is avoided completely.

We are currently investigating under which conditions lifting stealing from primitive operations (like `mkpair` or **addHead**) to full procedures (where then a value parameter is stolen) yields benefits.

8 Conclusion and Outlook

The paper presents a translation of an imperative language that uses abstract data types and is based on the standard value semantics of predicate (first- and higher-order) logic to a language with pointer semantics. Formal definitions of the translation to a language with pointer semantics have been given for a core language, which is sufficient to express the most important translation concepts and to express and verify the translation's correctness. The concrete level is sufficient to express optimization concepts.

This is only the first step of the project that aims at a formal verification of these concepts. We have started to set up a formal specification of the syntax and semantics given in this paper using our theorem prover KIV. Some cases of Lemma 1 already have mechanized proofs. These are available at [30].

Of course there is lots of work ahead. The specification has to be enhanced to include all supported data types. The concrete language is still not C, and another translation step is necessary. We plan to use a formal semantics specification of C (candidates are the semantics of C in Coq [22] or Isabelle [32]) and to verify this translation, too.

Remarkably, the concepts we use in the formal models of syntax and semantics of the languages are all concepts that are allowed as inputs of the existing code generator, so C code can be generated from the specification of the translation.

Finally, there are some interesting parallels between our target language and the concepts used by the Rust language. A detailed comparison is not in the scope of this paper, a rough idea would be that value parameters correspond to immutable ("borrowed") parameters, while reference parameters correspond to mutable parameters. Rust does not seem to directly support the concept of "stealing". However, it seems that in Rust libraries, a stolen parameter is implemented as a mutable parameter where the called routine, instead of deallocating the memory itself, modifies the parameter to be empty, e.g., the `append` function on `LinkedList`. Freeing memory by the caller is then essentially an empty operation. We are currently looking into whether generating Rust programs from our intermediate language is possible and what we can learn from it.

Acknowledgments. We would like to thank Alexander Knapp and the anonymous reviewers for many helpful comments.

References

1. Apt, K.R., de Boer, F.S., Olderog, E.-R.: Verification of Sequential and Concurrent Programs, 3rd edn. Springer, London (2009). https://doi.org/10.1007/978-1-84882-745-5
2. Bagnara, R., Bagnara, A., Hill, P.M.: The MISRA C coding standard and its role in the development and analysis of safety- and security-critical embedded software. In: Podelski, A. (ed.) SAS 2018. LNCS, vol. 11002, pp. 5–23. Springer, Cham (2018). https://doi.org/10.1007/978-3-319-99725-4_2
3. Barbosa, H., et al.: cvc5: a versatile and industrial-strength SMT solver. In: TACAS 2022. LNCS, vol. 13243, pp. 415–442. Springer, Cham (2022). https://doi.org/10.1007/978-3-030-99524-9_24
4. Baudin, P., et al.: The dogged pursuit of bug-free C programs: the Frama-C software analysis platform. Commun. ACM **64**(8), 56–68 (2021)
5. Bertot, Y., Castéran, P.: Interactive Theorem Proving and Program Development. Texts in Theoretical Computer Science, Springer, Heidelberg (2004). https://doi.org/10.1007/978-3-662-07964-5
6. Bodenmüller, S., Schellhorn, G., Bitterlich, M., Reif, W.: Flashix: modular Verification of a Concurrent and Crash-Safe Flash File System. In: Raschke, A., Riccobene, E., Schewe, K.-D. (eds.) Logic, Computation and Rigorous Methods. LNCS, vol. 12750, pp. 239–265. Springer, Cham (2021). https://doi.org/10.1007/978-3-030-76020-5_14
7. Boyer, R.S., Strother Moore, J.: Single-threaded objects in ACL2. In: Krishnamurthi, S., Ramakrishnan, C.R. (eds.) PADL 2002. LNCS, vol. 2257, pp. 9–27. Springer, Heidelberg (2002). https://doi.org/10.1007/3-540-45587-6_3
8. Cohen, E., et al.: VCC: a practical system for verifying concurrent C. In: Berghofer, S., Nipkow, T., Urban, C., Wenzel, M. (eds.) TPHOLs 2009. LNCS, vol. 5674, pp. 23–42. Springer, Heidelberg (2009). https://doi.org/10.1007/978-3-642-03359-9_2
9. Colaço, J.-L., Pagano, B., Pouzet, M.: SCADE 6: a formal language for embedded critical software development. In: Proceedings of International Symposium on Theoretical Aspects of Software Engineering (TASE), pp. 1–11. IEEE (2017)
10. Courant, N., Séré, A., Shankar, N.: The correctness of a code generator for a functional language. In: Beyer, D., Zufferey, D. (eds.) VMCAI 2020. LNCS, vol. 11990, pp. 68–89. Springer, Cham (2020). https://doi.org/10.1007/978-3-030-39322-9_4

11. Moura, L., Ullrich, S.: The lean 4 theorem prover and programming language. In: Platzer, A., Sutcliffe, G. (eds.) CADE 2021. LNCS (LNAI), vol. 12699, pp. 625–635. Springer, Cham (2021). https://doi.org/10.1007/978-3-030-79876-5_37
12. de Moura, L., Bjørner, N.: Z3: an efficient SMT solver. In: Ramakrishnan, C.R., Rehof, J. (eds.) TACAS 2008. LNCS, vol. 4963, pp. 337–340. Springer, Heidelberg (2008). https://doi.org/10.1007/978-3-540-78800-3_24
13. Férey, G., Shankar, N.: Code generation using a formal model of reference counting. In: Rayadurgam, S., Tkachuk, O. (eds.) NFM 2016. LNCS, vol. 9690, pp. 150–165. Springer, Cham (2016). https://doi.org/10.1007/978-3-319-40648-0_12
14. Gordon, M.J.C., Melham, T.F.: Introduction to HOL: A Theorem Proving Environment for Higher Order Logic. Cambridge University Press, Cambridge (1993)
15. Hunter, A.: A brief introduction to the design of UBIFS (2008). http://www.linux-mtd.infradead.org/doc/ubifs_whitepaper.pdf
16. Jacobs, B., Smans, J., Philippaerts, P., Vogels, F., Penninckx, W., Piessens, F.: VeriFast: a powerful, sound, predictable, fast verifier for C and Java. Proc. of NASA Formal Methods (NFM) **6617**, 41–55 (2011)
17. Kassios, I.T.: Dynamic frames: support for framing, dependencies and sharing without restrictions. In: Misra, J., Nipkow, T., Sekerinski, E. (eds.) FM 2006. LNCS, vol. 4085, pp. 268–283. Springer, Heidelberg (2006). https://doi.org/10.1007/11813040_19
18. Lameed, N., Hendren, L.: Staged static techniques to efficiently implement array copy semantics in a MATLAB JIT compiler. In: Knoop, J. (ed.) CC 2011. LNCS, vol. 6601, pp. 22–41. Springer, Heidelberg (2011). https://doi.org/10.1007/978-3-642-19861-8_3
19. Lammich, P.: Generating verified LLVM from Isabelle/HOL. In: Proceedings of International Conference on Interactive Theorem Proving (ITP). LIPIcs, vol. 141, pp. 22:1–22:19. Schloss Dagstuhl – Leibniz-Zentrum für Informatik (2019)
20. Lammich, P.: Efficient verified implementation of Introsort and Pdqsort. In: Peltier, N., Sofronie-Stokkermans, V. (eds.) IJCAR 2020. LNCS (LNAI), vol. 12167, pp. 307–323. Springer, Cham (2020). https://doi.org/10.1007/978-3-030-51054-1_18
21. Lammich, P.: Refinement of parallel algorithms down to LLVM. In: Proceedings of International Conference on Interactive Theorem Proving (ITP), LIPIcs, vol. 237, pp. 24:1–24:18. Schloss Dagstuhl – Leibniz-Zentrum für Informatik (2022)
22. X. Leroy. The Clight language: a simplified version of Compcert C. http://compcert.inria.fr/doc/html/compcert.cfrontend.Clight.html
23. Méry, D., Singh, N.K.: Automatic code generation from Event-B models. In: Proceedings of Symposium on Information and Communication Technology (SoICT), pp. 179-188. ACM (2011)
24. Nipkow, T., Paulson, L.C., Wenzel, M.: Isabelle/HOL – A Proof Assistant for Higher-Order Logic. LNCS, vol. 2283. Springer, Heidelberg (2002). https://doi.org/10.1007/3-540-45949-9
25. O'Connor, L., et al.: Refinement through restraint: bringing down the cost of verification. In: Proceedings of International Conference on Functional Programming (ICFP), pp. 89-102. ACM (2016)
26. Owre, S., Rajan, S., Rushby, J.M., Shankar, N., Srivas, M.: PVS: combining specification, proof checking, and model checking. In: Alur, R., Henzinger, T.A. (eds.) CAV 1996. LNCS, vol. 1102, pp. 411–414. Springer, Heidelberg (1996). https://doi.org/10.1007/3-540-61474-5_91
27. Reynolds, J.C.: Separation logic: a logic for shared mutable data structures. In: Proceedings of IEEE Symposium on Logic in Computer Science (LICS), pp. 55–74. IEEE (2002)

28. Schellhorn, G., Bodenmüller, S., Bitterlich, M., Reif, W.: Separating separation logic – modular verification of red-black trees. In: Lal, A., Tonetta, S. (eds.) VSTTE 2022. LNCS, vol. 13800, pp. 129–147. Springer, Cham (2022). https://doi.org/10.1007/978-3-031-25803-9_8
29. Schellhorn, G., Bodenmüller, S., Bitterlich, M., Reif, W.: Software & System Verification with KIV. In: Ahrendt, W., Beckert, B., Bubel, R., Johnsen, E.B. (eds.) The Logic of Software. A Tasting Menu of Formal Methods. LNCS, vol. 13360, pp. 408–436. Springer, Cham (2022). https://doi.org/10.1007/978-3-031-08166-8_20
30. Schellhorn, G., Bodenmüller, S., Reif, W.: KIV Specifications for the Code Generator (2024). https://kiv.isse.de/projects/VeriCodeLP.html
31. Schellhorn, G., Bodenmüller, S., Reif, W.: Refinement and separation: modular verification of wandering trees. In: Herber, P., Wijs, A. (eds.) iFM 2023. LNCS, vol. 14300, pp. 214–234. Springer, Cham (2024). https://doi.org/10.1007/978-3-031-47705-8_12
32. N. Schirmer. *Verification of Sequential Imperative Programs in Isabelle/HOL*. Ph.D. thesis, TUM (2006)
33. Shankar, N.: Static analysis for safe destructive updates in a functional language. In: Pettorossi, A. (ed.) LOPSTR 2001. LNCS, vol. 2372, pp. 1–24. Springer, Heidelberg (2002). https://doi.org/10.1007/3-540-45607-4_1

Proving Termination via Measure Transfer in Equivalence Checking

Dragana Milovančević[1](✉)[iD], Carsten Fuhs[2](✉)[iD], Mario Bucev[1](✉), and Viktor Kunčak[1](✉)[iD]

[1] EPFL, Station 14, 1015 Lausanne, Switzerland
{dragana.milovancevic,mario.bucev,
viktor.kuncak}@epfl.ch
[2] Birkbeck, University of London, London, UK
c.fuhs@bbk.ac.uk

Abstract. Program verification can benefit from proofs with varied induction schemas. A natural class of induction schemas, functional induction, consists of those derived from definitions of functions. For such inductive proofs to be sound, it is necessary to establish that the functions terminate, which is a challenging problem on its own. In this paper, we consider termination in the context of equivalence checking of a candidate program against a provably terminating reference program annotated with termination measures. Using equivalence checking, our approach automatically matches function calls in the reference and candidate programs and proves termination by transferring measures from a measure-annotated program to one without annotations. We evaluate this approach on existing and newly written termination benchmarks, as well as on exercises in programming courses. Our evaluation corpus comprises around 10K lines of code. We show empirically that the termination measures of reference programs often successfully prove the termination of equivalent candidate programs, ensuring the soundness of inductive reasoning in a fully automated manner.

Keywords: Equivalence checking · Termination analysis · Termination measures

1 Introduction

Termination is a prototypical liveness property of programs; verifying program termination is a long-standing problem in computing. Termination is also an interesting property for practical program verification because it is *implicit*, in the sense that it does not require developers to write specifications. It is important because non-interactive non-terminating computations fail to deliver any useful functionality. Furthermore, programs can be used to encode proofs and proof hints through ghost state or proof irrelevance. Termination of such programs is crucial for the soundness of all reasoning, even when reasoning applies to safety.

© The Author(s), under exclusive license to Springer Nature Switzerland AG 2025
N. Kosmatov and L. Kovács (Eds.): IFM 2024, LNCS 15234, pp. 75–84, 2025.
https://doi.org/10.1007/978-3-031-76554-4_5

In this paper, we focus on termination analysis in the context of program equivalence. Equivalence checking has applications in proving program optimizations [27], regression verification [9,28], refactoring [19], and automated grading [21]. However, while termination is often a prerequisite for the soundness of an equivalence proof, many existing approaches put termination analysis aside and leave it as the responsibility of end users [7,9]. Approaches that omit termination checks can result in unsound equivalence proofs, leading to incorrect conclusions. To illustrate this problem, we tried feeding the following (non-equivalent) functions to the REVE equivalence checker [9], and got the following verdict: "The programs have been proved equivalent"! As the authors of REVE state in [9], their approach indeed proves equivalence under the

```
int foo(int x) {
  int r;
  if (x == 1) r = 1;
  else r = foo(x);
  return r;
}
```

```
int foo(int x) {
  int r;
  if (x == 1) r = 1;
  else r = 2;
  return r;
}
```

assumption of termination, which does not hold here. On the other hand, in tools that do integrate equivalence checking with termination analysis, termination checks may fail systematically [21]. As a result, such tools often need many manual annotations, reducing the opportunities for fully automated deployment.

Researchers have built dedicated tools for automated termination checking [2,6,10,15,16,30]. Termination analysis is also integrated in proof assistants [13,24] and program verifiers such as Dafny [18] or Stainless [17], by means of synthesizing and verifying *termination measures*, also known as *ranking functions*. Termination checking in Stainless was in part carried over from Leon [29], along with support for generic types and quantifiers [31]. Subsequent work introduced a foundational type system that enforces termination [12].

Tools like Stainless are good at *verifying* that a given termination measure for a program is a valid termination proof. However, they are less good at *synthesizing* termination measures. Those limitations of termination analysis in Stainless are evidenced in recent case studies, including the LongMap proof [5], which modifies the implementation to add loop counters to prove termination, and the QOI proof [3], with 23 measure annotations for 313 lines of implementation.

In this paper, we consider the automatic transfer of termination measures between potentially-equivalent programs to facilitate equivalence checking. We extend the equivalence checking functionality of the Stainless verifier [21] to perform measure transfer along with its automated equivalence proof generation. We build on Stainless for the reasons discussed above, with an eye on improving automation of its equivalence checking component. We evaluate measure transfer on termination and equivalence checking benchmarks and on student assignments. We find that in most cases where Stainless can prove program equivalence, measure transfer results in a successful termination proof, effectively eliminating the need for manual annotations. In general, one should expect that equivalent programs written by different developers will require a broad selection of different termination measures. Our insight is that, in a practical case study on student assignments, this diversity of measures usually does not arise. This insight leads to a simple automated termination checking approach.

```
def finite(s: Stream): Boolean =
  s match
    case SCons(_, tf, sz) if tf().rank ≥ sz ⇒
      false
    case SCons(_, tf, sz) ⇒ finite(tf())
    case _ ⇒ true
```

(a) Initial implementation. Stainless fails to infer the measure and cannot prove termination.

```
def finite(stream: Stream): Boolean =
  stream match
    case SCons(_, tfun, sz) ⇒
      val tail = tfun()
      tail.rank < sz && finite(tail)
    case SNil() ⇒ true
```

(b) Refactored implementation. Stainless fails to prove termination.

```
def finite(s: Stream): Boolean =
  decreases(s.rank) //given
  s match
    case SCons(_, tf, sz) if tf().rank ≥ sz ⇒
      false
    case SCons(_, tf, sz) ⇒ finite(tf())
    case _ ⇒ true
```

(c) The **decreases** annotation, provided by the user, specifies the measure that decreases in each recursive call. With the help of **decreases** annotation, Stainless succeeds at proving termination.

```
def finite(stream: Stream): Boolean =
  decreases(stream.rank) //inferred
  stream match
    case SCons(_, tfun, sz) ⇒
      val tail = tfun()
      tail.rank < sz && finite(tail)
    case SNil() ⇒ true
```

(d) Automated porting of the **decreases** annotation. Stainless succeeds at proving termination and equivalence to finite from Figure 1c.

Fig. 1. Refactoring and measure transfer. Manually inserted annotations (c) are marked in red; annotations inferred via measure transfer (d) are marked in blue. (Color figure online)

An extended version of this paper is available as a technical report [22] under a CC BY-NC-ND license.

2 Illustrative Example

In this section, we illustrate our approach on an example of program refactoring. We consider functions operating on user-defined streams:

```
sealed abstract class Stream
  def rank = {
    this match
      case SCons(_, _, sz) if (sz > 0) ⇒ sz
      case _ ⇒ BigInt(0)
  } ensuring(_ ≥ 0)
case class SCons(x: BigInt, tailFun: () ⇒ Stream, sz: BigInt) extends Stream
case class SNil() extends Stream
```

Termination analysis of a similar encoding of streams in Stainless was previously discussed in detail [12]. Here, we consider function finite, which defines a sufficient condition that the input stream is finite, according to the provided ranked values.

Figure 1 shows two implementations of function finite: the initial implementation (1a) and the refactored implementation (1b). We run Stainless to prove termination of the initial implementation (1a), and we encounter a timeout. We thus fall back on inserting manual measure annotations (1c). The |decreases| clause specifies that the function terminates because the |rank| of the input stream decreases at each recursive call. To prove the equivalence of the two implementations of finite, Stainless requires that both functions terminate. However, when running Stainless to prove termination of the refactored implementation (1b), once again, we obtain a timeout. Rather than providing another manual measure annotation for the refactored program, we utilize the equivalence checking component to automatically perform measure transfer (1d). As a result, the system is able to prove termination, which completes the equivalence proof.

We found this approach particularly useful for larger programs, to automatically map and transfer measures for inner functions (Appendix A in our technical report [22]). We identify further applications in automated grading of programming assignments, with several reference programs with different termination measures (Appendix B in our technical report [22]).

3 Measure Transfer

In this section, we explain how we use measure transfer from potentially-equivalent programs as a heuristic to speculate termination measures.

Terminology. In our context, a *measure* is a lexicographic combination of function(s) from function arguments to natural numbers. A measure m proves the termination of a recursive function F if there is a decrease of the value of m for each recursive call. In this case, m is also called a *termination measure* for F. In Stainless, measures are provided as annotations for a function using the |decreases| keyword. The annotations consist of (lexicographic combinations of) Scala expressions.

We use the term *measure transfer* to refer to the general process of taking a termination measure m for a function M and conjecturing that m (or a permutation of m) is also a termination measure for a function F. This transfer is guided by a partial equivalence proof of M and F as a heuristic.

Algorithm. We consider a setting with one or more single-function reference programs, annotated with termination measures, and one or more single-function candidate programs, without measure annotations. For each candidate program, our algorithm is as follows:

1. Given: Reference programs $M_1, M_2, \ldots, M_n$ with their respective termination measures $m_1, m_2, \ldots, m_n$, proven terminating, and a candidate program under analysis P.

2. Check whether there exists M_i provably equivalent to P (under the assumption that P is terminating) such that m_i is also a termination measure for P (proving the assumption).

If there are multiple reference programs that are provably equivalent to P (modulo the termination of P), we consider them all until we find a measure m_i that proves the termination of P (or we exhaust all options). If such a measure m_i exists, this concludes the equivalence proof.

The potential equivalence of M_i and P provides the motivation for trying m_i as a candidate termination measure, but there is no guarantee that m_i should be a termination measure for P. However, our experiments (Sect. 4) show that this is often the case in our benchmarks.

Auxiliary Functions. Consider next a setting where programs consist of one or more auxiliary functions. Termination proofs in Stainless are performed separately for each function as entry point [12]. For programs comprising multiple functions, we identify pairs of potentially-equivalent functions for measure transfer. For each such pair, our algorithm is as follows:

1. Given: A reference function M with termination measure m, proven terminating, and a candidate function under analysis P, proven equivalent to M *for some argument permutation* under the assumption that P is terminating,
2. Check whether m is also a termination measure for P, for the same argument permutation (proving the assumption).

Search for potentially-equivalent auxiliary functions and corresponding argument permutations is inherited from the equivalence checking component of Stainless; it is based on type- and test-directed search [21]. For an example of measure transfer for auxiliary functions, see Appendix A of our report [22].

4 Evaluation

We implement measure transfer as a new mode for termination proving as part of equivalence checking in the Stainless verifier, as an alternative to existing measure inference. We evaluate measure transfer on termination and equivalence benchmarks, as well as on programming assignments. For each run, we set a 10 s timeout for Z3 solver queries.

Benchmarks. Table 1 presents our collection of existing and newly written benchmarks for termination and equivalence checking. We consider programs with state, user-defined types, type parameters, as well as helper functions and higher-order functions. Each benchmark contains two equivalent Scala programs: one reference program, annotated with termination measures, and one refactored candidate program, without any measure annotations.

Table 1. Evaluation results. LOC: total number of lines of code. F and D: number of functions and number of measure (decreases) annotations in reference program, respectively. I and T: outcome of equivalence checking when using measure inference and measure transfer, respectively (✓ indicates success and ✗ indicates failure). IT and TT: total time for equivalence checking when using measure inference and measure transfer, respectively.

Name	LOC	F	D	I	IT[s]	T	TT[s]	src
AdjList	32	2	1	✓	26.12	✓	23.74	New
ArrayContent	12	1	1	✓	12.85	✓	13.32	New
ArrayHeap	58	4	1	✓	27.47	✓	26.19	New
ArrayInc	15	2	1	✗	N/A	✓	18.12	New
Boardgame	293	8	3	✗	N/A	✓	1186.6	New
FiniteStreams	28	1	1	✗	N/A	✓	16.07	[17]
MaxHeapify	51	3	1	✗	N/A	✓	15.12	New
Partial	27	4	1	✗	N/A	✓	15.80	[17]
SortedArray	26	2	1	✓	15.18	✓	13.03	New
Valid2DLen	17	1	1	✗	N/A	✓	19.10	New

Table 2. Further evaluation results, on programming assignments. LOC: average number of lines of code per program. F and D: average number of function definitions and average number of measure annotations per program, respectively. R: number of reference programs. S: number of submissions. I and T: number of submissions with successful equivalence proof by measure inference and measure transfer, respectively.

Name	LOC	F	D	R	S	I	T	src
gcd	9	1	1	2	41	0	22	[20]
formula	59	2	1	1	37	0	27	[21]
prime	21	4	2	2	22	0	5	[20]
sigma	10	1	1	3	704	0	678	[21]

Table 2 describes benchmarks from programming courses [20,21]. Each benchmark contains one or more reference solutions annotated with termination measures, and equivalent student submissions with no measure annotations, where automated measure inference fails.

The source code of all our benchmarks is publicly available together with our implementation in Stainless [23].

Results. Measure transfer succeeds for all benchmarks in Table 1, including 6 benchmarks where the type-based measure inference in Stainless [12] fails. Furthermore, for benchmarks where measure inference succeeds, measure transfer typically reduces the processing time. Occasionally, the overhead of measure transfer transformations results in a slight time increase (e.g., in the smallest |ArrayContent| benchmark).

Out of 3 benchmarks with multiple reference programs (Table 2), only |gcd| has different termination measures (shown in Appendix B of our report [22]). In the |sigma| benchmark, measure transfer succeeds for 678 submissions, out of 704 submissions that previously required manual annotations due to limitations of measure inference [21]. The 26 submissions where measure transfer fails are due to either equivalence proof failures (11) or due to introducing inner functions that exist only in the candidate submission (15). In the |formula| benchmark, for 37 submissions where measure inference fails, the evaluation in [21] uses manual annotations to prove termination of 25 submissions (for the remaining submissions, the manual annotator did not find a termination measure). In contrast, measure transfer automatically proves correctness of 27 submissions. In the |prime| benchmark, we encounter a submission that, when manually annotated, passes termination checks and is equivalent to one reference solution. However, the measure transfer fails, because the inner function's measure in the reference solutions gives a negative measure when transferred to the inner function of the submission.

5 Related Work

Our approach is related to ACL2's |defunT| macro [14], which searches for termination measures in a database of already-proved termination theorems. Similarly, we use reference programs to search for termination measures. Both |defunT| and our work are instances of proof transfer [8] between related theorems. In our case, the theorems have the form "function f terminates for all inputs", and we use equivalence as a heuristic in choosing candidate termination measures. More generally, this line of work is in the space of *proof repair* [25], where work on verified programs so far seems to have focused mainly on partial correctness [11, 26], with the above exceptions.

We address the automatic synthesis of |decreases| annotations as termination measures, which are also used in JML-like settings [4]. These termination measures are (lexicographic combinations of) functions to $\mathbb{N}$ and cover an important class of termination proofs by ranking functions. Our work is related to the coupling of the tools COSTA and KeY [1]. Given a Java program, COSTA finds a termination measure, used by KeY to independently verify termination. However, COSTA needs to solve non-trivial constraint problems and considers only specific shapes for the measures. Our approach uses significantly less search and is not restricted to measures of a specific shape.

6 Conclusions

We have presented challenging examples in termination analysis in the context of equivalence proofs, and have shown how we can address them using a technique as simple as measure transfer. Our evaluation showed that measure transfer is effective in practice: it provided significant improvement over the automated measure inference in Stainless (including a speed-up in processing time), and sometimes an improvement over manual annotations. This shows that, for applications such as automated grading, where standard classes of termination measures may fail, measure transfer can lead to improvements for automation and applicability. In the future, we will consider more complex measure transformations, including transfer of termination lemmas.

Acknowledgments. This publication is based on collaboration within the COST Action CA20111 - European Research Network on Formal Proofs (EuroProofNet), supported by COST (European Cooperation in Science and Technology, www.cost.eu), as well as the EPFL Doc.Mobility Grant "Termination Checking for Sound Equivalence

Proofs of Real-World Programs". We thank the anonymous reviewers for their helpful feedback. We thank Ioana Jianu for helping the development of array benchmarks.

Availability of Data and Software. Stainless is under active development and is available at [17]. The complete data set and instructions for reproducing the results from this paper are available in an open access Zenodo repository [23].

Disclosure of Interests. The authors have no competing interests to declare that are relevant to the content of this article.

References

1. Albert, E., Bubel, R., Genaim, S., Hähnle, R., Puebla, G., Román-Díez, G.: A formal verification framework for static analysis - as well as its instantiation to the resource analyzer COSTA and formal verification tool KeY. Softw. Syst. Model. **15**(4), 987–1012 (2016). https://doi.org/10.1007/S10270-015-0476-Y
2. Brockschmidt, M., Cook, B., Ishtiaq, S., Khlaaf, H., Piterman, N.: T2: temporal property verification. In: Chechik, M., Raskin, J. (eds.) TACAS 2016. LNCS, vol. 9636, pp. 387–393. Springer, Cham (2016). https://doi.org/10.1007/978-3-662-49674-9_22
3. Bucev, M., Kunčak, V.: Formally verified quite OK image format. In: Griggio, A., Rungta, N. (eds.) 22nd Formal Methods in Computer-Aided Design, FMCAD 2022, Trento, Italy, October 17–21, 2022. pp. 343–348. IEEE (2022). https://doi.org/10.34727/2022/ISBN.978-3-85448-053-2_41
4. Burdy, L., et al.: An overview of JML tools and applications. Int. J. Softw. Tools Technol. Transf. **7**(3), 212–232 (2005). https://doi.org/10.1007/S10009-004-0167-4
5. Chassot, S., Kunčak, V.: Verifying a realistic mutable hash table - case study (short paper). In: Benzmüller, C., Heule, M.J.H., Schmidt, R.A. (eds.) IJCAR 2024, Part I. LNCS, vol. 14739, pp. 304–314. Springer, Cham (2024). https://doi.org/10.1007/978-3-031-63498-7_18
6. Chen, Y., et al.: Advanced automata-based algorithms for program termination checking. In: Foster, J.S., Grossman, D. (eds.) Proceedings of the 39th ACM SIGPLAN Conference on Programming Language Design and Implementation, PLDI 2018, Philadelphia, PA, USA, June 18-22, 2018, pp. 135–150. ACM (2018). https://doi.org/10.1145/3192366.3192405
7. Claessen, K., Johansson, M., Rosén, D., Smallbone, N.: Hipspec: automating inductive proofs of program properties. In: Fleuriot, J.D., Höfner, P., McIver, A., Smaill, A. (eds.) ATx'12/WInG'12: Joint Proceedings of the Workshops on Automated Theory eXploration and on Invariant Generation, Manchester, UK, June 2012. EPiC Series in Computing, vol. 17, pp. 16–25. EasyChair (2012). https://doi.org/10.29007/3qwr
8. Cohen, C., Crance, E., Mahboubi, A.: TROCQ: proof transfer for free, with or without univalence. In: Weirich, S. (ed.) ESOP 2024, Part I. LNCS, vol. 14576, pp. 239–268. Springer, Cham (2024). https://doi.org/10.1007/978-3-031-57262-3_10
9. Felsing, D., Grebing, S., Klebanov, V., Rümmer, P., Ulbrich, M.: Automating regression verification. In: Proceedings of the 29th ACM/IEEE International Conference on Automated Software Engineering. ASE 2014, New York, NY, USA, pp. 349-360. Association for Computing Machinery (2014). https://doi.org/10.1145/2642937.2642987

10. Giesl, J., et al.: Analyzing program termination and complexity automatically with AProVE. J. Autom. Reason. **58**(1), 3–31 (2017). https://doi.org/10.1007/S10817-016-9388-Y
11. Gopinathan, K., Keoliya, M., Sergey, I.: Mostly automated proof repair for verified libraries. Proc. ACM Program. Lang. **7**(PLDI), 25–49 (2023). https://doi.org/10.1145/3591221
12. Hamza, J., Voirol, N., Kunčak, V.: System FR: formalized foundations for the Stainless verifier. Proc. ACM Program. Lang. **3**(OOPSLA) (2019). https://doi.org/10.1145/3360592
13. INRIA: Functional induction in coq (2021). https://coq.inria.fr/refman/using/libraries/funind.html
14. Kaufmann, M.: DefunT: a tool for automating termination proofs by using the community books (extended abstract). In: Goel, S., Kaufmann, M. (eds.) Proceedings of the 15th International Workshop on the ACL2 Theorem Prover and Its Applications, Austin, Texas, USA, November 5-6, 2018. EPTCS, vol. 280, pp. 161–163 (2018). https://doi.org/10.4204/EPTCS.280.12
15. Kop, C.: WANDA - a higher order termination tool (system description). In: Ariola, Z.M. (ed.) 5th International Conference on Formal Structures for Computation and Deduction, FSCD 2020, June 29-July 6, 2020, Paris, France (Virtual Conference). LIPIcs, vol. 167, pp. 36:1–36:19. Schloss Dagstuhl - Leibniz-Zentrum für Informatik (2020). https://doi.org/10.4230/LIPICS.FSCD.2020.36
16. Kuwahara, T., Terauchi, T., Unno, H., Kobayashi, N.: Automatic termination verification for higher-order functional programs. In: Shao, Z. (ed.) ESOP 2014. LNCS, vol. 8410, pp. 392–411. Springer, Cham (2014). https://doi.org/10.1007/978-3-642-54833-8_21
17. LARA, E.: Stainless (2023). https://github.com/epfl-lara/stainless
18. Leino, K.R.M.: Dafny: an automatic program verifier for functional correctness. In: Clarke, E.M., Voronkov, A. (eds.) Logic for Programming, LPAR-16. LNCS, vol. 6355, pp. 348–370. Springer, Heidelberg (2010). https://doi.org/10.1007/978-3-642-17511-4_20
19. Malík, V., Vojnar, T.: Automatically checking semantic equivalence between versions of large-scale C projects. In: 2021 14th IEEE Conference on Software Testing, Verification and Validation (ICST), pp. 329–339 (2021). https://doi.org/10.1109/ICST49551.2021.00045
20. Milovancevic, D., Bucev, M., Wojnarowski, M., Chassot, S., Kuncak, V.: Formal autograding in a classroom (experience report) (2024). http://infoscience.epfl.ch/record/309386
21. Milovančević, D., Kunčak, V.: Proving and disproving equivalence of functional programming assignments. Proc. ACM Program. Lang. **7**(PLDI) (2023). https://doi.org/10.1145/3591258
22. Milovančević, D., Fuhs, C., Bucev, M., Kuncak, V.: Proving Termination via Measure Transfer in Equivalence Checking (Extended Version). Technical report, EPFL (2024). https://infoscience.epfl.ch/handle/20.500.14299/241339
23. Milovančević, D., Fuhs, C., Bucev, M., Kunčak, V.: Proving Termination via Measure Transfer in Equivalence Checking (Artifact) (2024). https://doi.org/10.5281/zenodo.13787855
24. Nipkow, T., Paulson, L.C., Wenzel, M.: Isabelle/HOL: a proof assistant for higher-order logic, vol. 2283. Springer, Heidelberg (2002). https://doi.org/10.1007/3-540-45949-9
25. Ringer, T.: Proof Repair. Ph.D. thesis, University of Washington, USA (2021). https://hdl.handle.net/1773/47429

26. Ringer, T., Porter, R., Yazdani, N., Leo, J., Grossman, D.: Proof repair across type equivalences. In: Freund, S.N., Yahav, E. (eds.) PLDI '21: 42nd ACM SIGPLAN International Conference on Programming Language Design and Implementation, Virtual Event, Canada, June 20–25, 2021, pp. 112–127. ACM (2021). https://doi.org/10.1145/3453483.3454033, https://doi.org/10.1145/3453483.3454033
27. Sharma, R., Schkufza, E., Churchill, B., Aiken, A.: Data-driven equivalence checking. In: Proceedings of the 2013 ACM SIGPLAN International Conference on Object Oriented Programming Systems Languages & Applications. OOPSLA '13, New York, NY, USA, pp. 391–406. Association for Computing Machinery (2013). https://doi.org/10.1145/2509136.2509509
28. Strichman, O., Godlin, B.: Regression verification - a practical way to verify programs. In: Meyer, B., Woodcock, J. (eds.) VSTTE 2005. LNCS, vol. 4171, pp. 496–501. Springer, Heidelberg (2005). https://doi.org/10.1007/978-3-540-69149-5_54
29. Suter, P., Köksal, A.S., Kuncak, V.: Satisfiability modulo recursive programs. In: Yahav, E. (ed.) SAS 2011, vol. 6887, pp. 298–315. Springer, Heidelberg (2011). https://doi.org/10.1007/978-3-642-23702-7_23
30. Urban, C.: FuncTion: an abstract domain functor for termination - (competition contribution). In: Baier, C., Tinelli, C. (eds.) Tools and Algorithms for the Construction and Analysis of Systems - 21st International Conference, TACAS 2015. LNCS, vol. 9035, pp. 464–466. Springer, Heidelberg (2015). https://doi.org/10.1007/978-3-662-46681-0_46
31. Voirol, N.: Termination Analysis in a Higher-Order Functional Context. Master's thesis, EPFL (2023). http://infoscience.epfl.ch/record/311772

Verification and Refinement

PLACIDUS: Engineering Product Lines of Rigorous Assurance Cases

Logan Murphy[✉], Torin Viger, Alessio Di Sandro, and Marsha Chechik

University of Toronto, Toronto, Canada
{lmurphy,tviger,adisandro,chechik}@cs.toronto.edu

Abstract. In critical software engineering, structured assurance cases (ACs) are used to demonstrate how key properties (e.g., safety, security) are supported by evidence artifacts (e.g., test results, proofs). ACs can also be studied as formal objects in themselves, such that formal methods can be used to establish their correctness. Creating rigorous ACs is particularly challenging in the context of software product lines (SPLs), wherein a family of related software products is engineered simultaneously. Since creating individual ACs for each product is infeasible, AC development must be lifted to the level of product lines. In this work, we propose PLACIDUS, a methodology for integrating formal methods and software product line engineering to develop provably correct ACs for SPLs. To provide rigorous foundations for PLACIDUS, we define a variability-aware AC language and formalize its semantics using the proof assistant Lean. We provide tool support for PLACIDUS as part of an Eclipse-based model management framework. Finally, we demonstrate the feasibility of PLACIDUS by developing an AC for a product line of medical devices.

1 Introduction

In safety-critical software engineering, stakeholders require *assurance* that software products will operate as intended. Several industries (e.g., automotive), have developed safety standards (e.g., ISO 26262 [23]) requiring careful documentation of verification activities via *assurance cases* (ACs) [31]. ACs use structured argumentation to refine system-level requirements into lower-level specifications which can be supported directly by evidence artifacts (e.g., tests, proofs). ACs can also be studied as formal objects in themselves, such that formal methods can be leveraged to verify their correctness [40,42]. Simultaneously, software systems are increasing in scale and complexity. In many cases, companies are not developing individual software products, but a family of related products, i.e., a software product line (SPL) [3]. In such scenarios, sufficient assurance must be obtained for each product in the SPL. Ideally, this should be realized as the creation of a *product line assurance case* (PL AC), from which product ACs can be derived.

Figure 1 illustrates two strategies for producing a verified PL AC. Beginning from an SPL (top left), the naive strategy is to derive the set of all products in the

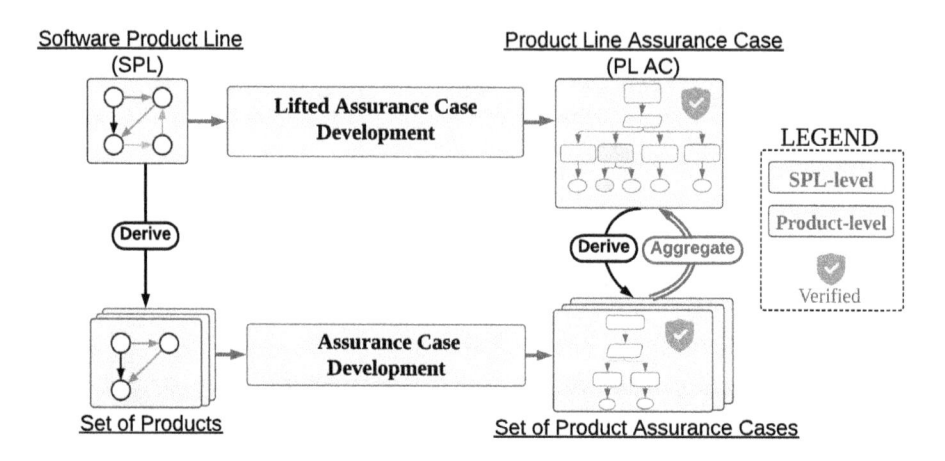

Fig. 1. Brute-force vs. lifted development of rigorous ACs for product lines.

SPL (bottom left) and to develop verified product-level ACs for each product (bottom right) using existing techniques (e.g., [42]). One can then aggregate the product-level ACs into a PL AC (top right) using some kind of variability encoding, such as the GSN patterns extension [21]. This approach, which we refer to as the *brute-force* method, is infeasible in practice, as many SPLs contain a very large number of products.

In SPL engineering (SPLE), *lifting* is the process of redefining a product-level software analysis (e.g., model checking) so that it can be applied directly to product lines [28]. The same idea can be applied to AC development: we need to *lift* the AC development process (Fig. 1, top) such that we can take an SPL (top left) and produce a verified PL AC using SPL-level techniques (top right). However, there are two roadblocks to lifted AC development.

First, there is more to AC development than analysis: it crucially relies on *argumentation*. While lifting software analyses is generally well-understood [28], it is less clear how to lift *arguments*, how these two forms of lifting relate to one another, or how this lifting process should be integrated as part of a broader assurance engineering context. Second, reasoning about PL ACs in a variability-aware fashion requires first formalizing their variational semantics, such that SPL-level data can be treated as first-class citizens. Although languages for PL ACs have been proposed in the past [21], they rely on product-level AC semantics, which inhibits variability-aware reasoning and analysis.

In this paper, we make the following contributions:

1. We propose PLACIDUS, an assurance engineering methodology which integrates formal methods and SPLE to support the lifted development of rigorous ACs.
2. To provide rigorous foundations for PLACIDUS, we formalize variational semantics of PL ACs using the proof assistant Lean [12]. Using this formalization, we show that verified PL ACs can be obtained by (i) lifting

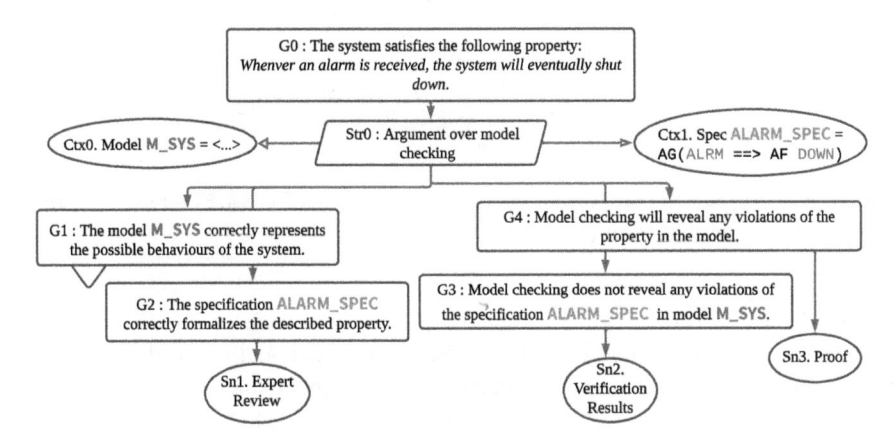

Fig. 2. An AC fragment (in GSN) for a hypothetical system. This AC is obtained by instantiating a generic model checking template with model M_SYS and CTL specification ALARM_SPEC.

product-level argumentation structures and (ii) producing invariance proofs over variability-aware types.
3. We provide tool support for PLACIDUS as part of an Eclipse-based model management framework [33].

To demonstrate the feasibility of PLACIDUS and the features supported by our tooling, we conduct a case study in which we developed a partial AC for a product line of medical devices. The rest of this paper is organized as follows. In Sect. 2, we provide the requisite background on AC development, and SPLE. In Sect. 3, we describe PLACIDUS, our proposed methodology for lifted AC development. In Sect. 4, we present rigorous formal foundations for PLACIDUS, formalized in the proof assistant Lean. In Sect. 5, we present our tooling and the case study. In Sect. 6, we provide an overview of related work. In Sect. 7, we give concluding remarks and discuss future work.

2 Background

In this section, we recall the structure and semantics of assurance cases based on Goal Structuring Notation (GSN [25]), as well as some fundamental concepts from software product line engineering.

2.1 Assurance Cases and GSN

In this work, we focus on assurance cases represented using Goal Structuring Notation (GSN, [25]). In GSN, an AC is modelled as a rooted tree, whose nodes can contain *goals* (i.e., claims to be supported), *evidence* artifacts, assumptions, contextual information (e.g., references to documents or models), and *strategies*. Strategies are used to decompose goals into a finite set of subgoals, with the

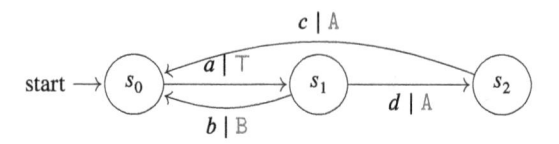

Fig. 3. A Featured Transition System (FTS) over features $\mathbb{F} = \{\texttt{A}, \texttt{B}\}$ and feature model $\Phi = \texttt{A xor B}$ (adapted from [5]).

intended interpretation being a logical refinement: if each of the subgoals hold, then the parent goal should hold. If this refinement is logically sound, the strategy is said to be *deductive*. If all strategies in an AC are deductive, we say the AC itself is deductive. An AC fragment for a hypothetical system is shown in Fig. 2. The root goal G0 asserts a liveness claim about the system. A strategy over model checking (Str0) is performed, decomposing G0 into four subgoals: that there is a representative behavioural model of the system (G1) and a specification which correctly formalizes the given property (G2), that model checking did not reveal any violations (G3), and that the verification procedure itself is actually sound (G4). Each of these subgoals requires either evidence (solution nodes, e.g. Sn.1) or further decomposition. In Fig. 2, goal G1 is left undeveloped.

Ideally, deductive correctness of an AC is checked by formalizing its arguments and verifying the refinements, but this is a costly process. One method for facilitating the creation of sound arguments is the use of *templates* [43]. An argument template is a method for decomposing a goal into a set of subgoals using some predefined construction. We say that a template is *valid* if each argument which can be instantiated from the template is sound. For example, the argument shown in Fig. 2 is an instantiation of a (valid) argument template for model checking. Instantiating this particular template requires providing the model and specification used for verification (i.e., M_SYS and ALARM_SPEC in Fig. 2).

2.2 Software Product Lines

A *software product line* (SPL) is a family of software artifacts (products) with distinct (but often overlapping) structure and behaviours [3]. The variability of an SPL is defined in terms of a set $\mathbb{F}$ of *features*, each of which can be either present or absent in a given product. A product is obtained from the SPL by choosing a *configuration* $\mathfrak{c} \subseteq \mathbb{F}$ of features. Variability in an SPL can be modelled via *feature expressions*,, i.e., propositional expressions whose atomic propositions are (boolean) feature variables. This induces a natural entailment relation $\mathfrak{c} \vDash \phi$ between feature expressions and configurations. Given a feature expression ϕ and configuration $\mathfrak{c}$, we use the notation $\texttt{Conf}(\phi)$ to denote the set of configurations satisfying ϕ. The set of products which are *valid* in an SPL is defined via a *feature model* Φ, also typically given as a feature expression.

Beyond the features and feature model, an SPL must specify a set of domain assets from which products can be configured. In the context of *annotative* product lines, the SPL is given as a collection of domain elements annotated with feature expressions, referred to as *presence conditions*. For example, a product line of transition systems can be represented as a Featured Transition System (FTS, [9]). Figure 3 illustrates an FTS (adapted from [5]) over the feature set $\{A, B\}$ with feature model $\Phi = A \text{ xor } B$. The presence conditions of transitions are written in blue font next to the transition labels. There are two valid configurations of this SPL, as $\text{Conf}(\Phi) = \{\{A\}, \{B\}\}$. A product transition system is *derived* under configuration $\mathfrak{c} \in \text{Conf}(\Phi)$ by removing transitions whose presence conditions are not satisfied by $\mathfrak{c}$. In Fig. 3, the transition labelled by a is present under both configurations, since it is annotated by $\top$, while the transition labelled by b is present only in configuration $\{B\}$. Similar derivation operators can be defined for other types of annotative product lines (e.g., product lines of code, trees, or sets). Given any annotative SPL x and any configuration $\mathfrak{c}$, we can use the notation $x|_\mathfrak{c}$ to denote the product derived from x under $\mathfrak{c}$.

A key problem in SPLE is *lifting*, i.e., the redefinition of an analysis such that it can be applied to SPLs.

Definition 1 (Lifting [28]). Let A and B be types, and let α (resp. β) be the type of "product lines of A" (resp. B). Let $f : A \to B$ be some function. Then a *lift* of f is a function $F : \alpha \to \beta$ such that for all feature models Φ, all $x \in \alpha$ and all $\mathfrak{c} \in \text{Conf}(\Phi)$, we have $F(x)|_\mathfrak{c} = f(x|_\mathfrak{c})$.

In some cases, the correctness criterion for lifting can be relaxed if the "lifted" analysis is at least *sound* with respect to some property of the original analysis. Consider, for instance, a hypothetical verifier V which performs model checking on FTSs. Let M be some FTS we wish to verify against property ϕ, and suppose that there are several products derivable from M with *distinct* counterexamples to ϕ. In order for V to be a lift in the strict sense of Definition 1, V would need to report each of these counterexamples and their respective configurations of M. SNIP [7] is an example of a lifted model checker which performs this kind of analysis. However, there are other SPL-level model checkers (e.g., FTS2VMC [6]) which only report a single counterexample if one exists for *some* product. Such tools are still sound in the sense that a successful verification of the SPL means that all products are verified. We refer to SPL-level analyses which are sound in this sense, but which do not satisfy Definition 1, as *weak lifts*. Both forms of lifting are commonly employed in SPL analysis, and as such we wish to support the use of both as part of lifted AC development.

3 Building Product Lines of Assurance Cases with PLACIDUS

We now describe PLACIDUS[1], a methodology for lifted AC development. PLACIDUS begins from the observation that supporting SPL-level AC development requires lifting the tools used by AC developers to create rigorous product ACs. PLACIDUS focuses on two kinds of development tools: AC templates (for

---
[1] **P**roduct **L**ine **A**ssurance **C**ases v**I**a **D**ed**U**ction and analy**S**is.

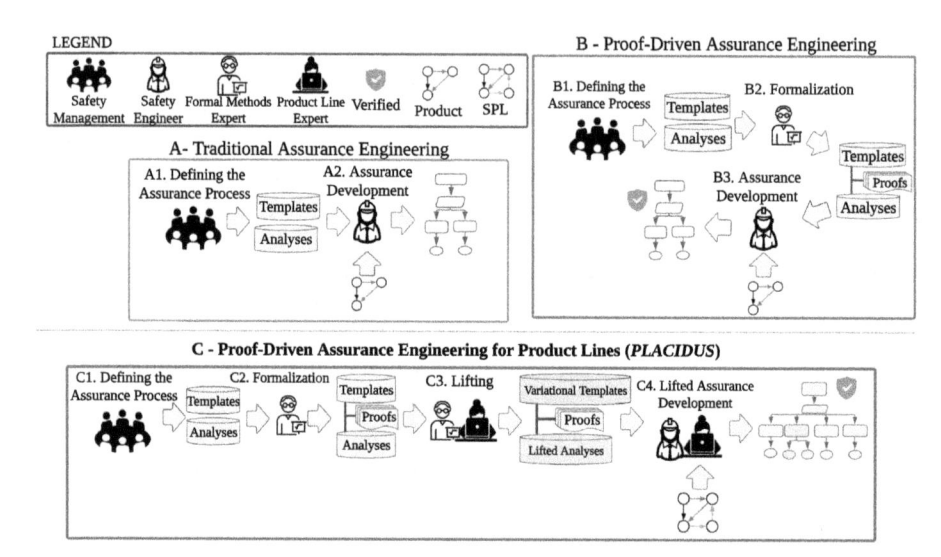

Fig. 4. Three assurance engineering methodologies: traditional assurance engineering (A); proof-driven assurance engineering (B); lifted, proof-driven assurance engineering via **PLACIDUS** (C).

structured argumentation) and software analyses (for evidence production). To maintain the rigor of the assurance process, this lifting must be approached formally. As such, **PLACIDUS** is an interdisciplinary process which integrates expertise in assurance engineering, formal methods and SPLE. We present **PLACIDUS** as an incremental extension of two simpler development methodologies, as illustrated in Fig. 4.

Traditional Assurance Engineering. While there is no single "canonical" assurance engineering methodology, industry standards such as ISO 262626 outline general methodological workflows, of which the "Traditional Assurance Engineering" methodology (labelled A in Fig. 4) is a very simple instance. In this workflow, there are two parties contributing to AC development: safety managers and safety engineers. Before any concrete assurance work is performed for a software product, the safety management team must define the assurance process which is to be followed by the safety engineers (A1). The assurance process is informed by various factors, such as industry standards (e.g., ISO 26262), corporate procedures, and available resources. The process definition includes, in particular, the forms of argumentation (templates) and the analyses engineers can use to develop the AC. The safety engineers can develop an AC for the software product under study by instantiating templates to form structured assurance arguments and running analyses to collect evidence artifacts. The end result is an (informal) AC for the software product.

Proof-driven Assurance Engineering. One of the limitations of the traditional methodology is that the correctness of purely informal ACs needs to be validated manually, which is difficult, expensive and error-prone. If we instead impose formalization as part of AC development, we can use formal methods to verify the correctness of ACs. We refer to this methodology as *proof-driven assurance engineering* (labelled B in Fig. 4). This has been an active research area in assurance engineering, with various formal methods being leveraged to improve the rigor of ACs, including automated theorem provers [16], model checking [36] and proof assistants [19,42]. Like the traditional methodology, the first stage defines the assurance process (B1). Unlike the traditional methodology, a formal methods expert is engaged to *formalize* the assurance process (or parts thereof) (B2). While there are variations in the research literature, most proposals use some version of the following procedure: (i) the semantics of relevant argument structures (templates) is formalized in an appropriate logic; (ii) based on this formalization, argument-level correctness proofs are given; (iii) analyses are provided to produce proofs as assurance evidence. Once the necessary formalization, proofs, and analyses have been developed (B2), the AC developer can use the formalized argument structures and associated proofs to produce a verified (or partially verified) assurance case for the software product under study (B3).

PLACIDUS. We now present PLACIDUS, which is our extension of the proof-driven methodology (B) to support lifted AC development (as per Fig. 1). The first two stages of PLACIDUS (C1, C2) are exactly the same as in the proof-driven methodology (B1, B2), producing a set of formalized argument templates, their correctness proofs, and associated analyses. The core of PLACIDUS is the *lifting* stage (C3) which formally lifts these components to the SPL-level. More concretely: (i) analyses used as part of product-level AC development must be lifted; and (ii) formalized product-level templates must be lifted such that they can be instantiated with SPL-level data. The lifting of software analyses, either as strict lifts or weak lifts, is a very well-studied area of SPLE [28,38], with a wide variety of common analyses having been lifted by researchers. But to the best of our knowledge, the only instance of lifted assurance argument template was proposed by Nešić et al. [29] for a contract-based argumentation template. In PLACIDUS, we expect this lifting to be performed for *all* argument templates. As with the product-level formalization (C2), part of the outcome of C3 is a set of correctness proofs (or proof-producing analyses) associated with the variational templates. But since we are now performing all analysis and reasoning at the SPL-level, the proofs themselves need to become "variational".

As illustrated in Fig. 4, we expect the lifting stage (C3) to require collaboration between experts in formal methods and SPLE. In the lifted development stage (C4), safety engineers will have the verified variational templates and associated analyses at their disposal for AC development. We expect that the lifted development process will also require collaboration between safety engineers and SPLE experts, since SPL-level data will need to be interpreted as part of AC development. Since all AC development tools (templates, analyses) are now variational, they can be applied directly to the SPL under study, avoiding redundant product-level work[2]. The outcome of stage C4 is a *product line of verified ACs*, such that a verified AC can be derived for every valid product in the SPL. Assuming such an object is defined, **PLACIDUS** supports lifted AC development as outlined in Fig. 1.

In the next section, we will show how to define a formal language of PL ACs such that the lifting stage (C3) of **PLACIDUS** – in particular, the lifting and verification of AC templates – becomes well-defined.

4 Formal Foundations of Lifted Assurance Case Development

In Sect. 3, we described a methodology for integrating formal methods and SPLE to support the lifted development of PL ACs. To implement this methodology, rigorous foundations are required. To this end, we have formalized a theory of PL AC semantics using the proof assistant Lean [12]. Lean is a pure dependently-typed functional programming language with inductive types, implementing a version of the Calculus of Inductive Constructions [10]. It also supports Haskell-style typeclasses [22], which will be relevant to our formalization. Due to space limitations, we only showcase a small number of key definitions and statements of theorems in our formalization. The complete formalization, including all proofs of theorems stated in this section, is available in our formalization repository.[3]

This section is structured as follows. First, we provide an overview of how a GSN-like AC language, and its templates, are formalized in Lean. We next introduce our formalization of *variational types* and *variational proofs*, which will form the building blocks of our variational AC language. We then detail a variational extension of our AC language in Lean and discuss the semantic correctness criteria of its ACs. Finally, given our variational AC language, we study the lifting of general classes of argument templates from the product-level to the SPL-level. In particular, we show that lifting and verifying AC templates for SPLs reduces to (i) lifting functions viz. Definition 1, and (ii) creating invariance proofs over sets of products. We thus provide a general formalization of the lifting stage of **PLACIDUS** (C3 in Fig. 4).

Product ACs and Templates. We first define a Lean type GSN as a minimal GSN-like language of ACs, comprising goals, decomposition strategies and evidence. Our language follows the GSN grammar given by Matsuno et al. [27]. The type Goal is a wrapper for propositions of the form $P(x)$, where P is a predicate over some type A and $x \in A$. Evidence for goal g is given by providing a proof of the proposition represented by g. Strategies are tuples of the form (g, {A$_1$, ..., A$_n$}), where g is the parent node and A$_i$ are the children (i.e., GSN subtrees). Since GSN is a Lean type like any other, we can prove theorems about its terms. For instance, we can define the predicate GSN.deductive asserting that a

---
[2] Of course, there may be some product-level work which cannot be avoided; strictly speaking, **PLACIDUS** seeks to eliminate *unnecessary* product-based work.
[3] https://github.com/loganrjmurphy/placs.

strategy (g, {$A_1, ..., A_n$}) satisfies ($\bigwedge_i g_i$) ⇒ g, where g_i is the root goal of A_i. We then define a recursive predicate GSN.deductive_AC asserting that every strategy in the AC satisfies GSN.deductive. Using these predicates, we can formally verify the deductive correctness of ACs formalized in our GSN language.

We next formalize GSN templates. Intuitively, templates are functions which take some existing AC claim as input, and produce a list of sub-ACs as output. In most cases, some auxiliary data is required to perform the instantiation – for instance, decomposing goal G0 in Fig. 2 using a model checking template required providing the model M_SYS and specification ALARM_SPEC as inputs to the template. In our Lean formalization, we define a record type Template which is parameterized over types A and D, where A is the type of the subject in the parent claim and D is the type of the auxiliary instantiation data. The template carries its instantiation function inst : $A \times D \to$ List GSN. We then formalize a predicate valid which asserts that every instantiation of a template results in a sound argument. In practice, many templates are only *conditionally* valid, i.e., the resulting argument is deductive only if the instantiation data $(a, d) : A \times D$ satisfies some precondition.

Example 1. Consider the *domain decomposition* template given by Viger et al. [43] to decompose an invariance claim, i.e., a goal of the form $\forall x \in S. P(x)$ where S is some subset of universe U. The template is instantiated for S by giving a finite family $\mathcal{F} = \{X_1, ..., X_n\}$ of subsets of U, creating n subgoals $\{g_1, ..., g_n\}$ such that goal g_i asserts $\forall x \in X_i. P(x)$. An instantiation of this template is deductive if family $\mathcal{F}$ is *complete* w.r.t. S, i.e. $\bigcup_i X_i \subseteq S$. We have formalized this class of templates in Lean, and proven its (conditional) validity. This process – formalizing and verifying templates – corresponds to step C2 of PLACIDUS (Fig. 4).

Variational Types and Proofs. We next formalize *variational types*, an algebraic generalization of SPLs in terms of *product derivation* operators [44]. To formalize variational types in Lean, we must first formalize features, feature expressions, and the configuration semantics of feature expressions. We formalize features using a typeclass, such that any type 𝔽 can be registered as a "feature type" if it has finitely many elements with decidable equality. Feature expressions over a feature type 𝔽 are encoded as propositional expressions in the natural manner. Presence conditions (PC) and feature models (FeatModel) are defined as type aliases for feature expressions. The semantics of feature expressions in terms of (finite sets of) feature configurations is defined recursively on the structure of the propositional expression. Given any feature model Φ : FeatModel 𝔽, we define the type Conf Φ representing all configurations of 𝔽 allowed under Φ.

Finally, we say that α is a *variational type* if there exists a derivation function under any feature model from α to some (product-level) type A. We refer to such a type α as a *variational extension* of the type A. Intuitively, to say that α is a variational extension of A means that α is the type of "product lines of A". In Lean, we implement variational types using a typeclass Var:

```
class Var (α : Type) (A : Type) where
  derive : α → Conf Φ → A
```

We can then define basic instances of the `Var` typeclass, e.g., lists of elements annotated by presence conditions (`List (A × PC F)`) form a variational extension of lists (`List A`), with derivation under configuration c defined as filtering out elements whose presence conditions are not satisfied by c.

We refer to any term whose type is variational as *variational data*. As we will demonstrate shortly, reasoning about the correctness of PL ACs reduces to reasoning about a specific class of proofs – namely, proofs of invariants over sets of "products" derivable from variational data.

Definition 2 (Variational Proof). Let τ be a variational extension of type T; let P be a predicate over T; let $x \in \tau$, and let Φ be a feature model. Then a proof of $\forall c \in \text{Conf}(\Phi). P(x|_c)$ is referred to as a *variational proof*.

We may not always need a proof for every configuration $c \in \text{Conf}(\Phi)$, but only a subset, i.e., $\text{Conf}(\phi) \subseteq \text{Conf}(\Phi)$, for some feature expression ϕ. In Lean, we use `[Φ] P x` to denote the type of an (unrestricted) variational proofs, and `[Φ| φ] P x` for a proof restricted to $\text{Conf}(\phi)$.

Variational GSN. We now have the components needed to define a variational extension of the type `GSN`, which we call `vGSN`. Following Habli and Kelly [21], our language for PL ACs supports both *structural variability* (i.e., certain fragments of the AC are only relevant for certain products) and *semantic variability* (i.e., the meaning of a claim depends on the choice of feature configuration). We begin by defining the type `vGoal` of variational goals, which is parameterized by a feature model Φ. To model structural variability, each `vGoal` carries a presence condition, as proposed by Shahin [35]. To model semantic variability, we define (predicative) variational goals to consist of product-level predicates (i.e., a predicate over a non-variational type A) and variational data. It follows that the interpretation of a variational goal is no longer a truth-value, but a function from configurations to truth-values. We model evidence in `vGSN` using variational proofs: given a variational goal defined by predicate P, variational data x and annotated by presence condition ϕ, evidence for this goal is a term of type `[Φ| φ] P x`. The inductive definition of `vGSN` in Lean is as follows:

```
inductive vGSN (Φ : FeatModel F)
| evd [Var α A] (φ : PC F) (P : A → Prop) (x : α) (e: [Φ|φ] P x)
| strategy (g : vGoal Φ) (l : List (vGSN Φ))
```

We next define a derivation operator from `vGSN` to `GSN`. Given a configuration c, we recursively descend through the PL AC, checking whether each node's presence condition is satisfied by c. If the presence condition is not satisfied, the node is not present under c, and we abandon its subtree. Otherwise, if we are at an evidence node, we derive the product-level proof of $P(x|_c)$ from the variational proof contained in the evidence node. If we are at a strategy node, we derive the parent goal $g|_c$ and map the derivation operator over the children.

This derivation operator allows us to register vGSN as a variational extension of GSN in Lean.

In addition to their use as evidence for variational goals, variational proofs are also used to demonstrate correctness of the AC itself. For instance, recall that a GSN strategy is referred to as deductive if it corresponds to a sound logical refinement. The analogous criterion for deductive correctness in vGSN is formalized in terms of variational proofs as follows:

```
def vGSN.deductive (g : vGoal Φ) (l : List (vGSN Φ)) : Prop :=
  [Φ| g.pc] GSN.deductive (vGSN.strategy g l)
```

The above definition type-checks since Lean knows that vGoal is a variational extension of Goal and that vGSN is a variational extension of GSN. We can then recursively extend this definition to entire vGSN ACs to define a variational analog (vGSN.deductive_AC) of the GSN predicate GSN.deductive_AC. We can verify that this analog is a correct "lift":

```
theorem vGSN_deductive_AC_iff {A : vGSN Φ} :
  vGSN.deductive_AC A ↔ [Φ| A.root.pc] GSN.deductive_AC A
```

The above theorem allows us to verify deductive correctness for all products (i.e., the variational proof on the RHS) by composing variational proofs for each vGSN strategy individually. In this way, verifying PL ACs reduces to the creation of variational proofs.

Lifting Templates. We now turn to the problem of lifting templates, i.e., step C3 of PLACIDUS (Fig. 4). We begin by defining the type vTemplate of variational decomposition templates. As per the semantics of vGSN, variational templates are defined by product-level predicates, but are instantiated on variational data. The notion of validity for variational templates is defined analogously to that of product-level templates: a variational template is valid if and only if every instantiation of the template (with variational data) produces a deductive strategy. We consider the general case of lifting a conditionally valid product-level template T with instantiation function T.inst : $A \times D \to$ List GSN and precondition T.prec : $A \times D \to$ Prop. If we have variational extensions α and γ of A and D, respectively, the problem of lifting T to a variational Template T' becomes well-defined: we must define an instantiation function T'.inst : $\alpha \times \gamma \to$ List (vGSN Φ) such that Definition 1 holds. If this lifting is correct, then the instantiation of the template is provably sound whenever we have a *variational proof* of the precondition over the set of products under study. The correctness of this process is proved in Lean as the following theorem:

```
theorem lift_sound (T : Template A D) (T' : vTemplate α γ) (φ : PC F) :
    valid T ∧ isLift T.inst T'.inst →
    ∀ x d, [Φ| φ] T.prec (x,d) → deductive (T'.inst (x, d))
```

where $x \in \alpha$, $d \in \gamma$ and ϕ is the presence condition over which the template is instantiated. Intuitively, the above theorem provides a structured approach to "lifting" the correctness of product-level templates, which is established during step C2 of PLACIDUS. We thus reduce lifting and verifying PL AC templates to (i) lifting instantiation functions and (ii) creating variational proofs.

Example 2 (Variational Domain Decomposition). We can lift the domain decomposition template of [42] to the SPL-level and prove the correctness of the lift. In the product setting (i.e., during stage C2), we formalized a predicate complete as the precondition for validity of domain decompositions. We now need to lift the instantiation of domain decompositions to variational data. We define the variational types vSet and vFamily of variational sets and families of sets, respectively. Variational sets are sets of elements annotated with presence conditions [35], and variational families are finite sets of annotated sets, i.e., $\{(X_1, \phi_1), ..., (X_n, \phi_n)\}$. It is straightforward to lift the instantiation of domain decomposition, by setting the presence condition of each (variational) subgoal g_i to be the presence condition ϕ_i. Once we prove the correctness of the lift, we can prove the validity theorem for variational domain decomposition (via lift_sound):

theorem vDomDecompInstLift : isLift DomainDecomp.inst vDomainDecomp.inst

theorem vDomDecompValid (S : vSet α) (F : vFamily α):
[Φ] complete (S,F) $\rightarrow$ deductive (vDomDecomp.inst (S, F))

To produce the needed variational proofs, we can either (i) lift a verifier for product-level completeness, or (ii) define fixed decompositions are complete *a priori*. We give two simple examples of the latter for finite variational sets (vFinset). The first is a function explode which takes a finite set $S = \{(x_1, \phi_1), ..., (x_n, \phi_n)\}$ of annotated elements, and returns the family of annotated singletons $\{(\{x_1\}, \phi_1), ..., (\{x_n\}, \phi_n)\}$. The second is a function aggregate which forms a variational family $\{(X_1, \phi_1), ..., (X_k, \phi_k)\}$, such that elements of each X_i share the same presence condition ϕ_i. We have given reference implementations in Lean for both approaches, and provided variational correctness proofs:

theorem explodeComp   {S : vFinset α} : [Φ] complete (S, explode S)
theorem aggregateComp {S : vFinset α} : [Φ] complete (S, aggregate S)

Lifting Templates for Lifted Analyses. As described in Sect. 3, PLACIDUS uses both lifted templates and lifted software analyses to drive AC development. The lifting of analyses is well-understood in SPLE, and we have formalized the lifting of templates above. But analysis and argumentation are not always decoupled. Consider, for instance, the argument over model checking shown in Fig. 2. The semantics of this argument – and therefore its correctness – is defined against a specific analysis (model checking). In following PLACIDUS, we would like to replace this product-level analysis with a lifted one, without compromising argument soundness. Our formalization makes this process – and its correctness proof – quite straightforward.

We first formalize a general class of argument templates, which we refer to as *analytic templates*, each of which is defined with respect to a fixed analysis

f. Intuitively, an analytic argument makes assertions about the input to the analysis x, the output of the analysis $f(x)$, and the analysis f itself. In general, the input of the analysis should have some relation to the subject of the goal being decomposed. For instance, the subject of G0 in Fig. 2 can be interpreted as a pair (B, P), where B is the set of behaviours executed by the (real) system, and P is the set of behaviours characterized by the informal specification in G0. Doing model checking with model M_SYS and formal specification ALARM_SPEC is only useful if these are correct formalizations of B and P, respectively – hence the subgoals G1 and G2.

Suppose now that we have defined an analytic template T for analysis f, proven its validity as part of stage C2, and implemented a lifted analysis F. Thanks to the variational semantics of vGSN, we can replace f with F during template instantiation, with the only modification to T being the inclusion of an additional subgoal asserting that F is a correct lift of f. It follows very easily that this "lifting" preserves the validity of the template:

```
theorem liftedAnalyticValid (T : AnalyticTemplate f)
  (F : α → β) (h : isLift f F) : T.valid → [Φ] valid (T.lift F)
```

where T.lift F denotes the extension of template T for the lifted analysis F. We also prove an analogous theorem for arguments over weak lifted analyses. Once again, our construction shows how correctness evidence produced for templates at the product level (stage C2) can be systematically lifted to the SPL-level.

In this section, we have provided rigorous foundations for PLACIDUS. Our Lean formalization of variational types was used to implement a generic framework for studying PL ACs, variational templates, and their correctness. In particular, we have shown that the process of lifting and verifying arguments for PL ACs can effectively be reduced to lifting template instantiation functions and creating variational proofs, and shown that for the general class of analytic templates, product-level analyses can be substituted for lifted analyses while preserving argument validity.

5 Tool-Supported Product Line Assurance Case Development

Any integration of formal methods as part of AC development should include extensive tool support, as many AC developers are not formal methods experts. To this end, we have developed tool support for lifted AC development as part of an Eclipse-based model management framework. Our tool aims to support the PLACIDUS methodology and closely follows the formalization outlined in Sect. 4. In this section, we provide a brief overview of our tool (Sect. 5), and demonstrate the feasibility of PLACIDUS and our tooling on a small case study (Sect. 5.2).

5.1 A Model Management Tool for Product Line ACs

MMINT[4] is an Eclipse-based model management framework developed at the University of Toronto. It is a generic framework which can be extended with plugins for specific modeling tasks. One of its extensions, *MMINT-A* [17], is used for model-driven AC development, supporting GSN modeling and model-based analyses. Another extension, *MMINT-PL*, supports product line modelling and lifted model-based analyses [18].

Several functionalities of *MMINT-A* and *MMINT-PL* can be reused directly to support **PLACIDUS**. We combine *MMINT-A*'s GSN metamodel [17], and *MMINT-PL*'s generic variational metamodel (GVM, [18]) to define a metamodel for product lines of GSN ACs. To support **PLACIDUS**, we also needed to implement some new functionalities: (i) we extended *MMINT-A*'s GSN template module to recognize product line models, such that instantiation of GSN templates can be done with either product-level or lifted versions; (ii) users can define product-level analytic templates as formalized in Sect. 4, allowing the results of a specified analysis to be weaved into an AC as part of template instantiation. When these templates are instantiated on variational models, if the analyses associated with the template have been lifted, the lifted analyses are executed, and the lifted template is instantiated instead; (iii): *MMINT-PL*'s GVM is unable to provide appropriate visualizations for arbitrary product line models, so we created a custom visualization module to facilitate the manual inspection of PL ACs.

5.2 Case Study: Assuring a Product Line of Infusion Pumps with **PLACIDUS**

To demonstrate the feasibility of the **PLACIDUS** methodology and the features of our AC development tool, we followed our proposed methodology to create a partial AC for a product line of medical infusion pumps.

System Details. Infusion pumps are devices used to administer medication or other fluids to patients. As different patients may have different medical needs, it is natural to model an SPL of infusion pumps with different optional features. We began from an existing Extended Finite State Machine (EFSM) model of an infusion pump created as part of a multi-institute research project [1]. While this model was not originally defined as an SPL, it was designed to model features and hazards for an infusion pump *in general*, the authors noting that in general "no single device [...] has all of the design features" [45]. We extended the EFSM to an SPL by mapping six optional features to their associated states and transitions and annotating these elements with presence conditions. For example, CHECK_INFUSION_RATE is an optional feature that allows a pump to monitor the current rate of delivery of a drug. The resulting SPL encompasses a family of 36 valid product configurations. In our hypothetical assurance scenario, the top-level assurance obligation (i.e., the root node of the AC) is to show that when

---

[4] https://github.com/adisandro/MMINT.

an alarm is triggered (e.g., due to a dosage limit violation), the system will not administer a dose until the alarm is disabled.

Step C1: Defining the Assurance Process. Before beginning AC development, we need to determine which types of analyses and argumentation are applicable for our assurance task. For simplicity, we considered two kinds of analyses: querying of models (via the Viatra Query Language [41]) and model checking [4]. As part of the assurance process, we require that the use of these analyses be accompanied by sufficient assurance that the models and specifications used for analyses have been validated. We also allow for the use of domain decomposition templates [43] to break down assurance obligations.

Step C2: Formalization. Based on the assurance process defined in Step C1, we can now formalize the associated argument structures. The assurance obligations associated with using queries and model checking can be formalized as analytic templates, analogous to the argument shown in Fig. 2. We can do a (shallow) formalization of the semantics of both analyses in Lean, and verify both analytic templates. The domain decomposition template has been formalized as described in Sect. 4.

Step C3: Lifting. We now lift the analyses and templates formalized in Step C2 so that they can be applied directly to SPLs. For lifted model queries, we reused a lifted query engine developed as part of previous work [18]. For (quasi-)lifted model checking, we used the tool FTS2VMC [6] which verifies featured transition systems (FTSs) against specifications written in an action-based branching time logic (v-ACTL). The templates formalized for both analyses can be lifted automatically via the constructions for lifted and quasi-lifted analytic templates (Sect. 4). We can also employ the lifted constructions for domain decompositions given in Sect. 4.

Having defined, formalized and lifted the analyses and templates for our task, we can perform lifted AC development. We begin with the root goal asserting the primary safety property (not administering drug doses while an alarm is active). Under normal circumstances, we could proceed by running a model query which will return all alarm states in the model, and then assure the property for each alarm scenario. Thanks to our the lifting of the query engine, we can apply the same rationale using our lifted analyses and argument templates, even though different products may be associated with different sets of alarm states. Figure 5 shows the results of instantiating the lifted query template followed by a lifted domain decomposition. When we instantiate the generic model query template, the tool automatically detects that the model is an SPL, and executes the lifted query engine to return a variability-aware set of query results (Ctx0). These results are then woven into the AC using a lifted version of the analytic template. This lifted analytic argument instantiation is sound as per theorem liftedAnalyticValid (Sect. 4) and our original proof that the product-level template was deductive. Returning to the AC, we proceed from goal G4

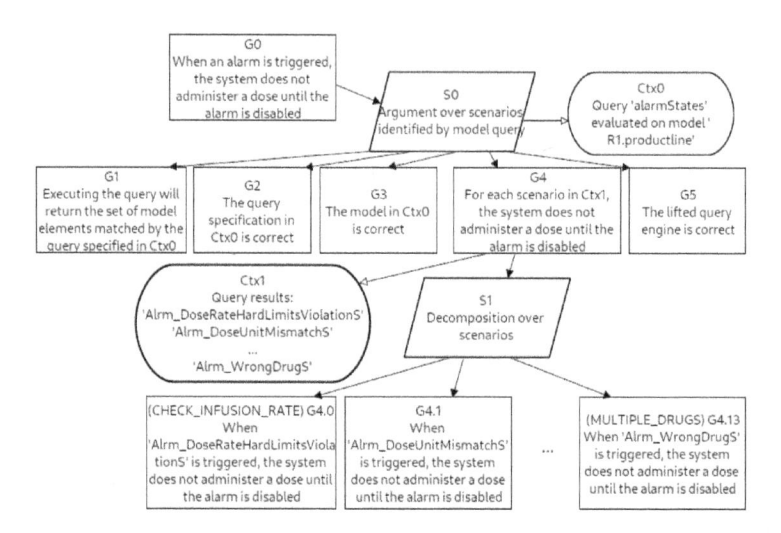

Fig. 5. Instantiations of the lifted query and scenario decomposition templates.

using a variational domain decomposition, assigning each alarm state to its own goal, such that the presence conditions identified by the lifted query result (e.g., CHECK_INFUSION_RATE) are used to annotate each subgoal. The absence of a presence condition (e.g., G3.1) means that the alarm is present in every product. This decomposition corresponds to the verified `explode` construction and is thus also sound by theorem `vDomDecompValid` (Sect. 4).

We can then continue to produce assurance for each identified alarm scenario in a lifted fashion. We focus on goal G4.0, which effectively asserts that every product with feature CHECK_INFUSION_RATE satisfies the given safety property in the context of alarms due to dose rate violations. This can be verified using (lifted) software model checking. As with queries, we can instantiate the model checking template formalized in Step C2 and lifted in Step C3, using the (weak) lifted model checker FTS2VMC for SPL-level verification. We formalize the property in G4.0 as **AG** (Alrm_DoseRateHardLimitsViolationS⇒ **A**[!(Infusion_NormalOperationS) **U** (E_ClearAlarm)]) and run the lifted model checker on the infusion pump FTS model. In this case, the model checker does not reveal any violations, meaning that every product with CHECK_INFUSION_RATE satisfies the given property. This can then be incorporated as variational evidence for this family of products, as shown in Fig. 6. The remaining pieces of evidence (e.g., G7, that the formalization is correct) still need to be produced. Note that in G10, the correctness of the lift is interpreted as the "weak" correctness criterion. Furthermore, evidence for G6 and G10 needs to be produced only once and can be reused in subsequent applications of the template. Once we have provided the required evidence for this argument (and the analogous evidence for the lifted query), we can then repeat this verification process for each alarm scenario until all assurance obligations have been satisfied.

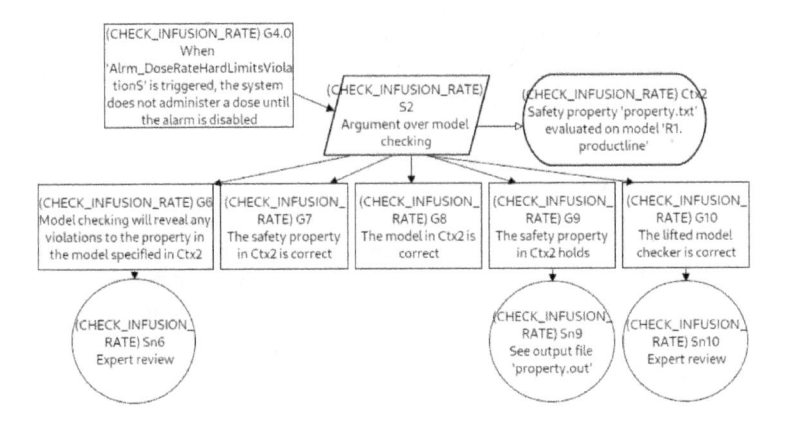

Fig. 6. Tool-generated lifted analytic model checking template instantiation for claim G4.0.

Observations. In developing the above AC fragment for the infusion pump SPL, we demonstrated the feasibility of **PLACIDUS** to support multi-layered AC development in a lifted fashion. We emphasize two specific points. (1) By following **PLACIDUS**, the operational process of AC development becomes essentially the same as in product-level AC development. That is to say, it suffices to know what one would do to assure a single product, and the lifted analyses and templates can correctly generalize this knowledge to the SPL-level. This is due to the particular variational semantics adopted by **PLACIDUS**, as outlined in Sect. 4. (2) Traditionally, the primary use of software analyses in AC development has been to produce evidence artifacts. Lifted analyses can correspondingly produce variational evidence. But they can also be used to *systematically identify variation points in the SPL which are relevant to the design of the AC*. For example, in our case study, the variation points identified by the lifted query led systematically to *structural variability* in the AC (i.e., the subgoals of strategy S1 in Fig. 5).

Limitations and Threats to Validity. One of the limitations of the tooling is that modeling languages and model-based analyses must be defined natively in order to leverage the GVM. For instance, the lifted model checker is not a natively defined model-based analysis, and its verification results are not automatically interpreted as variational data (this contrasts with querying, which is a native model-based analysis). There is also no automated support for template verification; all argument templates are verified manually ahead of time. Part of our future work is integrating the modelling tool with our Lean formalization to provide theorem proving support during AC development.

With respect to the validity of our observations, we note that our partial AC is relatively narrow in scope and was designed by the authors for the purpose of demonstrating **PLACIDUS**. While we believe we have successfully demonstrated the feasibility of our methodology, further empirical validation is required. Ideally, this evaluation can be done as part of a collaboration with industrial assurance engineers, since real-world assurance processes may be more difficult to formalize and lift than those shown here.

6 Related Work

Analysis of Software Product Lines. Implementing scalable analyses of SPLs is one of the central problems in SPLE. Thum et al. [38] divide SPL-level analysis strategies as either *product-based* (e.g., brute-force or sampling-based techniques), *feature-based* (i.e., analyzing feature modules independently and composing the results), or *family-based* (i.e., operating at the level of sets of products). Lifted analyses are a specific form of SPL-level analyses, which can be implemented using any of these three strategies. A wide variety of analyses have been lifted in the SPLE literature, e.g. [8,24,32,34,39]. We have previously proposed a catalogue of *lifting techniques*, i.e., approaches to implementing lifts with various tradeoffs in terms of engineering and validation effort. Our formalization of PL AC semantics in Lean is preceded by various formalizations of SPL analyses and reasoning frameworks in proof assistants. Lifted analyses which have been formally verified include type checking [24] and model-based change impact analyses [35]. Using a similar formalization of configuration semantics, Alves et al. formalized a theory of SPL refinement in Coq [2]. Their formalization uses a lower-level definition of SPLs as compared to variational types, requiring users to explicitly define a particular form of mapping from features to software assets in order to define an SPL instance. By contrast, our formalization of variational types is purely algebraic, only requiring users to define a suitable derivation operator for the variational type.

Assurance Cases for Product Lines. Assurance cases for SPLs were studied by Habli and Kelly [20,21], who argued that safety-relevant variation points in the SPL should be reflected explicitly in the product line AC. Habli and Kelly propose using GSN patterns and the modular GSN extension [21] to represent product line ACs. Habli [20] also provides an SPL safety metamodel which allows for variation points in the SPL to be traced explicitly to a PL AC. This approach was further refined in de Oliveira et al. [13], introducing tool-supported generation of modular PL ACs from feature-based system models and safety analyses. However, this approach does not provide a distinction between product-level and SPL-level semantics or analysis, implicitly assuming that analysis and reasoning are performed at the product. As an alternative to product-based AC development, Habli [20] also considers a primarily feature-based AC development method, in which AC modules are developed independently for each feature, and then the PL AC is obtained by composing these modules. However, this method requires the assurance engineer to either (a) identify and mitigate all potential feature interactions, which can devolves into to the brute-forced assurance engineering, or (b) tolerate an incomplete assessment of potential feature interactions. By contrast, PLACIDUS supports analysis and reasoning over all valid configurations of the SPL, without resorting to product-level work. To the best of our knowledge, the only existing variability-aware AC development process was proposed by Nešić et al. [29], which lifts contract-based templates to PLs of component-based systems [29]. PLACIDUS is effectively an attempt to generalize the approach of Nešić et al. to arbitrary templates and analyses.

Formal Methods for Assurance Case Development. The most obvious use of formal methods for AC development is for the production of evidence; well-established verification techniques such as model checking [4] and deductive verification [26] provide invaluable evidence for formally specified requirements. As we have mentioned above, the integration of formal methods with AC development requires extensive tool support. The AC development tool AdvoCATE [15] uses the AutoCert inference engine [14] to check system software implementations against formal specifications, which are then grafted into the AC following a predefined template. The Evidential Tool Bus (ETB) [11] gathers verification evidence from various external tools, and then creates ACs from the bottom up using compositional rules written in a variant of Datalog. Formal methods can also be used to ensure that instantiations of argument templates actually yield sound arguments. As ACs and proofs are closely related, proof assistants have been used on several occasions to study rigorous AC development. Rushby [30] demonstrated a proof-of-concept of how an AC could be modelled using the proof assistant PVS. The AC editor D-Case was extended with a translation to the Agda programming language, such that an AC could be specified as an Agda program to check for well-formedness [37]. An extension to Isabelle was developed to embed the Structured Assurance Case Metamodel (SACM) as part of its documentation layer [19]. Finally, Viger et al. [42] used Lean to study the correctness of decomposition templates for model-based ACs. To the best of our knowledge, our formalization of ACs in Lean is the first to support the formalization of entire ACs, rather than only individual claims [19] or individual strategies [42].

7 Conclusion

In this work, we proposed PLACIDUS, an assurance engineering methodology supporting lifted assurance case development for software product lines. PLACIDUS extends existing formal approaches to AC development by lifting formal argument templates and software analyses to the SPL-level. We used the proof assistant Lean to formalize rigorous foundations for PLACIDUS. We demonstrated the feasibility and usefulness of our methodology by developing a partial PL AC over a product line of medical devices.

We identify several avenues for future work. One is to further extend our model-based development framework for PLACIDUS with support for additional lifted templates and analyses, and to integrate the modeling layer with the formalization layer, which would enable automated or semi-automated theorem proving to assist in AC development [42]. Another interesting line of work is the problem of efficiently creating and maintaining variational proofs (Sect. 4). While such proofs can be constructed in an *ad hoc* fashion, a systematic approach for defining, certifying, and repairing such objects would be invaluable for proof-driven PL AC development and maintenance. In particular, language-independent techniques for maintaining and repairing variational proofs over evolutions of SPLs could be leveraged to provide assurance engineers with formal guarantees about the maintenance of SPL-level assurance.

References

1. Alur, R., et al.: Formal specifications and analysis of the computer-assisted resuscitation algorithm (CARA) infusion pump control system. Int. J. Softw. Tools Technol. Transfer **5**, 308–319 (2004)
2. Alves, T., Teixeira, L., Alves, V., Castro, T.: Porting the software product line refinement theory to the coq proof assistant. In: Carvalho, G., Stolz, V. (eds.) SBMF 2020. LNCS, vol. 12475, pp. 192–209. Springer, Cham (2020). https://doi.org/10.1007/978-3-030-63882-5_12
3. Apel, S., Batory, D., Kästner, C., Saake, G.: Feature-Oriented Software Product lines. Springer (2016)
4. Baier, C., Katoen, J.P.: Principles of Model Checking. MIT Press (2008)
5. ter Beek, M.H., Damiani, F., Lienhardt, M., Mazzanti, F., Paolini, L.: Static analysis of featured transition systems. In: Proceedings of the 23rd International Systems and Software Product Line Conference-Volume A, pp. 39–51 (2019)
6. ter Beek, M.H., Damiani, F., Lienhardt, M., Mazzanti, F., Paolini, L., Scarso, G.: Fts4vmc: a front-end tool for static analysis and family-based model checking of ftss with vmc. Sci. Comput. Program. **224**, 102879 (2022)
7. Classen, A., Cordy, M., Heymans, P., Legay, A., Schobbens, P.Y.: Model checking software product lines with snip. Int. J. Softw. Tools Technol. Transfer **14**, 589–612 (2012)
8. Classen, A., Cordy, M., Heymans, P., Legay, A., Schobbens, P.Y.: Formal semantics, modular specification, and symbolic verification of product-line behaviour. Sci. Comput. Program. **80**, 416–439 (2014)
9. Classen, A., Heymans, P., Schobbens, P.Y., Legay, A., Raskin, J.F.: Model checking lots of systems: efficient verification of temporal properties in software product lines. In: Proceedings of the 32nd ACM/IEEE International Conference on Software Engineering-Volume 1, pp. 335–344 (2010)
10. Coquand, T., Paulin, C.: Inductively defined types. In: Martin-Löf, P., Mints, G. (eds.) COLOG 1988. LNCS, vol. 417, pp. 50–66. Springer, Heidelberg (1990). https://doi.org/10.1007/3-540-52335-9_47
11. Cruanes, S., Hamon, G., Owre, S., Shankar, N.: Tool integration with the evidential tool bus. In: Giacobazzi, R., Berdine, J., Mastroeni, I. (eds.) VMCAI 2013. LNCS, vol. 7737, pp. 275–294. Springer, Heidelberg (2013). https://doi.org/10.1007/978-3-642-35873-9_18
12. Moura, L., Ullrich, S.: The lean 4 theorem prover and programming language. In: Platzer, A., Sutcliffe, G. (eds.) CADE 2021. LNCS (LNAI), vol. 12699, pp. 625–635. Springer, Cham (2021). https://doi.org/10.1007/978-3-030-79876-5_37
13. de Oliveira, A.L., Braga, R.T.V., Masiero, P.C., Papadopoulos, Y., Habli, I., Kelly, T.: Supporting the automated generation of modular product line safety cases. In:

Zamojski, W., Mazurkiewicz, J., Sugier, J., Walkowiak, T., Kacprzyk, J. (eds.) Theory and Engineering of Complex Systems and Dependability. AISC, vol. 365, pp. 319–330. Springer, Cham (2015). https://doi.org/10.1007/978-3-319-19216-1_30
14. Denney, E., Pai, G.: Automating the assembly of aviation safety cases. IEEE Trans. Reliab. **63**(4), 830–849 (2014)
15. Denney, E., Pai, G.: Tool support for assurance case development. J. Automated Software Eng. **25**(3), 435–499 (2018)
16. Denney, E., Pai, G., Pohl, J.: AdvoCATE: an assurance case automation toolset. In: Ortmeier, F., Daniel, P. (eds.) SAFECOMP 2012. LNCS, vol. 7613, pp. 8–21. Springer, Heidelberg (2012). https://doi.org/10.1007/978-3-642-33675-1_2
17. Di Sandro, A., Selim, G.M.K., Salay, R., Viger, T., Chechik, M., Kokaly, S.: MMINT-A 2.0: tool support for the lifecycle of model-based safety artifacts. In: Proceedings of MODELS'20 Companion, pp. 15:1–15:5. ACM (2020)
18. Di Sandro, A., Shahin, R., Chechik, M.: Adding product-line capabilities to your favourite modeling language. In: Proceedings of the 17th International Working Conference on Variability Modelling of Software-Intensive Systems (VaMoS'23), pp. 3–12 (2023)
19. Foster, S., Nemouchi, Y., Gleirscher, M., Wei, R., Kelly, T.: Integration of formal proof into unified assurance cases with Isabelle/Sacm. Formal Aspects Comput. **33**(6), 855–884 (2021)
20. Habli, I.: Model-based assurance of safety-critical product lines. Ph.D. thesis, University of York (2009)
21. Habli, I., Kelly, T.: A safety case approach to assuring configurable architectures of safety-critical product lines. In: Giese, H. (ed.) ISARCS 2010. LNCS, vol. 6150, pp. 142–160. Springer, Heidelberg (2010). https://doi.org/10.1007/978-3-642-13556-9_9
22. Hall, C.V., Hammond, K., Peyton Jones, S.L., Wadler, P.L.: Type classes in haskell. ACM Trans. Program. Lang. Syst. (TOPLAS) **18**(2), 109–138 (1996)
23. ISO: ISO26262: Road vehicles – Functional safety (2011)
24. Kästner, C., Apel, S., Thüm, T., Saake, G.: Type checking annotation-based product lines. ACM Trans. Software Eng. Methodol. (TOSEM) **21**(3), 1–39 (2012)
25. Kelly, T.P.: Arguing safety: a systematic approach to managing safety cases. Ph.D. thesis, University of York (1999)
26. Leino, K.R.M.: Dafny: an automatic program verifier for functional correctness. In: Clarke, E.M., Voronkov, A. (eds.) LPAR 2010. LNCS (LNAI), vol. 6355, pp. 348–370. Springer, Heidelberg (2010). https://doi.org/10.1007/978-3-642-17511-4_20
27. Matsuno, Y.: A design and implementation of an assurance case language. In: 2014 44th Annual IEEE/IFIP International Conference on Dependable Systems and Networks, pp. 630–641. IEEE (2014)
28. Murphy, L., Di Sandro, A., Shahin, R.I., Chechik, M.: Reusing your favourite analysis framework to handle workflows of product line models. In: Proceedings of the 27th ACM International Systems and Software Product Line Conference - Volume A (2023). https://api.semanticscholar.org/CorpusID:261124727
29. Nešić, D., Nyberg, M., Gallina, B.: Product-line assurance cases from contract-based design. J. Syst. Softw. **176**, 110922 (2021)
30. Rushby, J.: Formalism in safety cases. In: Dale, C., Anderson, T. (eds.) Making Systems Safer, pp. 3–17. Springer, London (2009). https://doi.org/10.1007/978-1-84996-086-1_1
31. Rushby, J.: The interpretation and evaluation of assurance cases. Comp. Science Laboratory, SRI International, Technical report. SRI-CSL-15-01 (2015)

32. Salay, R., Famelis, M., Rubin, J., Di Sandro, A., Chechik, M.: Lifting model transformations to product lines. In: Proceedings of the 36th International Conference on Software Engineering, pp. 117–128 (2014)
33. Sandro, A.D., Salay, R., Famelis, M., Kokaly, S., Chechik, M.: MMINT: a graphical tool for interactive model management. In: Proceedings of the MoDELS 2015 Demo and Poster Session co-located with ACM/IEEE 18th International Conference on Model Driven Engineering Languages and Systems (MoDELS 2015), Ottawa, Canada, September 27, 2015. CEUR Workshop Proceedings, vol. 1554, pp. 16–19. CEUR-WS.org (2015). https://ceur-ws.org/Vol-1554/PD_MoDELS_2015_paper_6.pdf
34. Shahin, R., Chechik, M., Salay, R.: Lifting datalog-based analyses to software product lines. In: Proceedings of the 2019 27th ACM Joint Meeting on European Software Engineering Conference and Symposium on the Foundations of Software Engineering, pp. 39–49 (2019)
35. Shahin, R., Kokaly, S., Chechik, M.: Towards certified analysis of software product line safety cases. In: Habli, I., Sujan, M., Bitsch, F. (eds.) SAFECOMP 2021. LNCS, vol. 12852, pp. 130–145. Springer, Cham (2021). https://doi.org/10.1007/978-3-030-83903-1_9
36. Sljivo, I., Gallina, B., Carlson, J., Hansson, H., Puri, S.: Tool-supported safety-relevant component reuse: from specification to argumentation. In: Casimiro, A., Ferreira, P.M. (eds.) Ada-Europe 2018. LNCS, vol. 10873, pp. 19–33. Springer, Cham (2018). https://doi.org/10.1007/978-3-319-92432-8_2
37. Takeyama, M.: Towards formal assurance case framework in Agda (2014). https://cs.ioc.ee/~tarmo/tsem14/takeyama-slides.pdf
38. Thüm, T., Apel, S., Kästner, C., Schaefer, I., Saake, G.: A classification and survey of analysis strategies for software product lines. ACM Comput. Surv. (CSUR) **47**(1), 1–45 (2014)
39. Thüm, T., Schaefer, I., Apel, S., Hentschel, M.: Family-based deductive verification of software product lines. In: Proceedings of the 11th International Conference on Generative Programming and Component Engineering, pp. 11–20 (2012)
40. Varadarajan, S., et al.: Clarissa: foundations, tools & automation for assurance cases. In: 2023 IEEE/AIAA 42nd Digital Avionics Systems Conference (DASC), pp. 1–10. IEEE (2023)
41. Varró, D., Bergmann, G., Hegedüs, Á., Horváth, Á., Ráth, I., Ujhelyi, Z.: Road to a reactive and incremental model transformation platform: three generations of the VIATRA framework. Software Syst. Model. **15**(3), 609–629 (2016)
42. Viger, T., Murphy, L., Di Sandro, A., Menghi, C., Shahin, R., Chechik, M.: The foremost approach to building valid model-based safety arguments. Softw. Syst. Model. **22**(5), 1473–1494 (2023)
43. Viger, T., Salay, R., Selim, G., Chechik, M.: Just enough formality in assurance argument structures. In: Casimiro, A., Ortmeier, F., Bitsch, F., Ferreira, P. (eds.) SAFECOMP 2020. LNCS, vol. 12234, pp. 34–49. Springer, Cham (2020). https://doi.org/10.1007/978-3-030-54549-9_3
44. Walkingshaw, E., Kästner, C., Erwig, M., Apel, S., Bodden, E.: Variational data structures: exploring tradeoffs in computing with variability. In: Proceedings of the 2014 ACM International Symposium on New Ideas, New Paradigms, and Reflections on Programming & Software, pp. 213–226 (2014)
45. Zhang, Y., Jones, P.L., Jetley, R.: A hazard analysis for a generic insulin infusion pump. J. Diabetes Sci. Technol. **4**(2), 263–283 (2010)

Stateful Functional Modeling with Refinement (a Lean4 Framework)

Frédéric Peschanski[✉]

Sorbonne University, LIP6, CNRS UMR 7606,
Paris, France
`frederic.peschanski@lip6.fr`

Abstract. We present a Lean4 framework for the formal modeling of stateful entities in the context of functional domain modeling. The main objective is to support a step-wise refinement methodology inspired by the Event-B formal method. The implementation provides the main Event-B constructions such as contexts, machines, events and, most importantly, the associated refinement principles. We also experiment with extensions such as event combinators and functional variants of the (relational) refinement principles of Event-B. The embedding is very shallow in that all the constructions are directly based on the Lean4 logic and abstractions, especially dependently-typed structures and type-classes. One benefit is that proof obligations can be discharged using the powerful Lean4 tactic language. Moreover, we enforce the fundamental principle of correctness-by-construction: machine states, events structures and refinement steps cannot be fully constructed without discharging the prescribed proof obligations.

Keywords: State-based formal method · Refinement · Functional domain modeling

1 Introduction

Functional domain modeling advocates the use of functional programming languages as lightweight/semi-formal modeling frameworks [22]. The basic idea is to use algebraic datatypes and functions to develop domain models. In this context, an obvious but important line can be drawn to separate *stateless* from *stateful* entities. While pure functions represent a good fit for stateless modeling, other means are required for the representation and manipulation of state. The article [14] promotes *Mealy machines* to address this problematic. We see a strong connection between such stateful functional thinking and state-based formal methods such as Event-B [2] (among many other: ASM, TLA+, B-classic, etc.). To illustrate this connection, we give below two possible functional types, written using the Lean4 functional programming language, for Mealy machines (on the left) and (a deterministic interpretation) of Event-B events (on the right).

```
structure Mealy                        structure BEvent
    (M : Type) (α β : Type) where          (M : Type) (α : Type) where
  step (m : M) (x : α) : β × M           guard (x : α): Prop
                                         action (m : M) (x : α) : M
```

A Mealy machine is parameterized by a state type M, an input type α and an output type β. Its only functionality is a step function that constructs a pair (output, post-state) from a pre-state m and an input x. The action of a B event is similar to step but without producing an output, and its firing is conditioned by a guard. We find it quite natural to integrate these two definitions. Based on this simple although insightful observation, we present in this paper an experimental formal modeling framework in the context of Lean4 [13]. The choice of Lean4 is motivated first because it is a functional programming language with a very expressive (dependent-)type system – hence a good fit for a type-driven design approach – and second because it is also a proof assistant capable of addressing the mathematical and proof concerns of formal developments.

As a first contribution, we implemented in Lean4 the main Event-B constructions: contexts, machines, events and, most importantly, the associated *refinement* principles. There are important (logical, mathematical) differences with the actual Event-B, although we think that the framework remains "compatible" at the conceptual level. To substantiate this belief, we ported (fully, with proofs) basic but non-trivial Event-B developments, namely the Bridge model from [2] and the tutorial example of [10] (available in the companion repository). In fact, apart from proof obligations, we believe the porting of Event-B models to be rather straightforward. We also propose extensions of the methodology with event combinators and functional variants of the refinement principles.

The second and probably most important contribution of the framework is to enable *step-wise refinement* – according to the Event-B principles – in the context of type-driven, stateful functional modeling. To our knowledge, refinement methodologies have been only scarcely studied in the context of functional programming languages, although Event-B in particular appears to us as particularly interesting from this respect. At the technical level, the framework adopts a shallow approach: all the proposed features are directly based on the Lean4 logic and abstractions, with a prominent role played by dependently-typed *structures* [15] and *typeclasses* [8,21]. One benefit of this approach is that proof obligations can be discharged using the powerful Lean4 tactic language. Moreover, we enforce the fundamental principle of *correctness-by-construction*: machine states, event structures and refinement steps cannot be constructed fully without discharging the prescribed proof obligations.

The outline of the paper is as follows. First, in Sect. 2 we present the embedding of the basic Event-B concepts: contexts, machines and events. We cover both the deterministic and non-deterministic kinds of events, as well as convergence. We also introduce basic event combinators, which illustrates the extensibility of the proposed framework. Section 3 is dedicated to the refinement principles. The basic building block is a relational characterization of refinement, as prescribed by the Event-B methodology. We also introduce variants based on functional abstractions that are proved sound wrt. the relational principles. Section 4 discusses some aspects of the approach from a less technical point of view.

An experimental open source implementation of the proposed framework is available online[1] as a companion to the present paper.

Related Work

The idea of embedding a formal method in a proof assistant is of course not new. These embeddings can be either semantic and "deep", or more syntactic and "shallow". The ProofPower tool [12] is an excellent example of what was initially a shallow approach. It is a suite of tools that allows to write specifications and make proofs based on Higher-order logic (HOL). Most interestingly, it allows users to write specifications using the Z notation, or more precisely a formal realization of the Z notation. Another example of a shallow approach is the embedding of B-classic in PVS [5]. More precisely, it is a translator from the specification of B machines and PVS so-called theories. One interesting aspect is that the translation tries to preserve the functional/deterministic parts of the models in the resulting PVS theory.

An example of a semantic embedding is the one described in the technical report about *the logic of Event-B* [19]. This is an adequate approach for developing the meta-theory underlying the formal method. For example, theorems about the development are established, most notably the *soundness* of the said logic. Note, however, that this is an embedding of the mathematical/logical vernacular of Event-B, and not a formalization of the Event-B artifacts: machines, events, etc. In a way, this is the exact complement of our approach since we reuse the mathematical vernacular of type theory to develop the artifacts of Event-B. A more complete formalization of *an institution for Event-B* in the Coq proof assistant is proposed in [16]. Unfortunately, the Coq development itself is only succinctly described and does not seem to be available. The paper [4] relates the development of a B-tool prototype that allows the modeling based on the Event-B concepts in the context of the Isabelle/HOL proof assistant. The Event-B constructs (events, machines) are translated *via* a semantic embedding, to their corresponding denotational semantics. Another interesting approach is the use of the Event-B logic itself (variants of set theory and first order logic) to extend the method [17]. Other deep embeddings of B-classic – only remotely related to Event-B – have been proposed, most notably in the context of the Isabelle/HOL proof assistant [7,9].

The FoCaLiZe environment [1] proposes a global approach to formal development based on (mostly) functional principles extended with object-oriented features such as inheritance and late binding. While in Event-B abstract machines and their properties cannot be contradicted at the concrete level, in FoCaLiZe the so-called properties and methods of *species* – a kind of class – can be

---

[1] The source code repository of the project can be found at the following address: https://github.com/lean-machines-central/lean-machines. The definitions given in the paper are at times slightly simplified, they are hyperlinked (like this) to their actual implementation.

redefined along inheritance. In such cases, proofs of existing properties at the abstract level are potentially "erased", which means they must be redone at the concrete level. There are also several approaches at formalizing Morgan's *refinement calculus* in proof assistants, e.g. [6,18]. An important aspect is that they provide an imperative view of programming. In comparison, the Event-B refinement principles are, we think, more adapted to the functional perspective.

2 Contexts, Machines and Events

In this section we describe the formalization of the basic concepts of the Event-B method using a simple example of a bounded buffer. We think that most definitions can be understood, at least conceptually, without previous knowledge of the Lean4 syntax[2]. We kept the shorter proof details in the definitions below but these are not intended to be understood directly. This is more to show that, indeed, these are trivial proof steps. Details of more complex proofs are omitted.

2.1 Contexts

The main purpose of a *context* in Event-B is to allow the specification of the static properties – or parameters – of a system[3]. The notion of a record, or a *structure* as it is called in Lean4, can be used to describe the parameters of a machine. Below is the context of the bounded buffer example:

```
structure BufContext where
  maxSize : Nat
  maxSizeProp : maxSize > 0
```

The upper bound for the buffer is maxSize, which is constrained to be strictly positive. Technically speaking, such a structure is simply a kind of a product type, although of a *dependently-typed* nature [15]. We can see, for example, that later fields (e.g. maxSizeProp) may reference former ones (e.g. maxSize). Moreover, structure fields can be of simple types (such as Nat, of type Type) or propositions (of type Prop). It is possible to depend, like in Event-B, on multiple contexts, through *structure inheritance*[4], using the following schema:

```
structure Ctx extends Ctx₁, Ctx₂, ..., Ctxₙ {
  -- specific fields added to the inherited ones
}
```

---

[2] Some definitions are slightly simplified variations of the actual Lean4 development, but this mostly concerns specific annotations to help the type-checker.

[3] In Event-B the contexts are also used to connect the models with auxiliary mathematical libraries. Lean4 provides a dedicated package and module system to cover this aspect.

[4] Note that Lean4 is *not* an object-oriented programming language, in particular there is no subtyping relation involved in structure inheritance, and no notion of dynamic dispatch; this is simply a kind of organized inclusion.

2.2 Machines

Our implementation characterizes the notion of a *machine* via the following typeclass definition:

```
class Machine (CTX : outParam (Type u)) (M) where
  context : CTX
  invariant : M → Prop
  reset : M
```

This construction introduces a type M, namely a *machine type*, parameterized by a *context type* CTX, with the following components:

- a way to access the machine's context,
- a function returning the invariant that must be satisfied by any reachable state of the machine,
- a reset state that corresponds to a pre-state for initialization events[5].

As a side note, the outParam annotation tells the type checker that the context is generally to be inferred. In practice, this means that the user does not have to explicitly deal with the context type in most situations. The type M itself must provide the representation of the machine state. At the most abstract level, the buffer simply corresponds to a kind of a counter, only tracking the number of its elements:

```
structure B0 (ctx : BufContext) where
  size : Nat
```

We remark that the machine type B0 is parameterized by the context defined previously. Technically speaking, this corresponds to a (type-theoretic) functional abstraction, which perfectly characterizes the conceptual relationship between a machine and its context(s) in Event-B. To promote such a definition to the status of a machine type, we need to instantiate the Machine typeclass. For the B0 type, the proposed instantiation is as follows:

```
instance: Machine Context (B0 ctx) where
  context := ctx
  invariant b0 := b0.size ≤ ctx.maxSize
  reset := { size := 0 }
```

2.3 Events

Now equipped with simple yet effective constructions for contexts and machines, we need to formalize the notion of an *event*, which corresponds to a guarded transition from machine states to machine states. While in Event-B events are of a relational and non-deterministic nature, in the context of functional domain modeling it seems appropriate to begin with a functional/deterministic approach (non-deterministic events are considered in Sect. 2.4). As explained previously, our starting point is the definition of deterministic events as kinds of Mealy machines:

---

[5] As a specificity, the reset state is not required to satisfy the machine invariant.

```
-- initialization events
structure InitEventSpec
             (M) [Machine CTX M]
             (α) (β) where
  guard (x : α) : Prop := True
  init (x : α) : β × M

  safety (x : α) :
    guard x
    → Machine.invariant (init x).2
```
```
-- transitional events
structure EventSpec
             (M) [Machine CTX M]
             (α) (β) where
  guard (m : M) (x : α) : Prop := True
  action (m : M) (x : α) : β × M

  safety (m : M) (x : α) :
    Machine.invariant m
    → guard m x
    → Machine.invariant (action m x).2
```

The type M in the two definitions above represents the machine state concerned by the events. The bracket notation [Machine CTX M] indicates that M must be instance of the Machine typeclass discussed previously. The types α and β are respectively the input and output types of the event[6]. The action/init and guard represent the conditional behavior of the event, and the safety field represents the corresponding proof obligation. For transitional events, the m parameter is the pre-state of the action and x is the input. The notation (action m x).2 projects the second element of the pair constructed by the action, corresponding to the post-state. Initialization events are similarly defined, only of course without a pre-state (internally, the reset state is used as a pre-state). These definitions exploit type dependencies (from former fields to later fields) to enforce the fundamental correctness-by-construction criterion. Indeed, an event specification cannot be constructed without discharging (or accepting, axiomatically) the safety requirement.

To illustrate the actual construction of events, we consider the initialization and increment of the B0 machine:

```
def B0.Init := newInitEvent'' {
  init := { size := 0 }
  safety := fun _ => by
    simp [Machine.invariant]
}
```
```
def B0.Put := newEvent'' {
  guard := fun b0 => b0.size < ctx.maxSize
  action := fun b0 => { size := b0.size + 1 }
  safety := fun b0 => fun _ Hgrd => Hgrd
}
```

The newInitEvent'' and newEvent'' functions are *smart constructors* that take an event specification and produce, if correctly type-checked, an actual event. The "double tick" suffix is specialized for events taking no input parameter, and producing no value as output. The fun keyword constructs anonymous functions (a.k.a. *lambda*'s), and for example the action of a Put event simply increments the value of the size field. The safety attribute is specified as a proof that the safety requirement holds. In the safety proof for the initialization event (on the left) we used the powerful Lean4 simplifier, invoked here using the *proof tactic* language. On the right the safety proof is exactly the guard condition Hgrd, which we directly reference as a *proof term*. These direct usages of the Lean4 proof language are made possible mainly thanks to the shallow nature of the proposed embedding.

---

[6] Note that in Event-B events have no explicit output type, although it is a rather straightforward and quite valuable addition.

2.4 Non-deterministic Events

In Event-B events are deterministic/functional only because the relations that define them happen to have deterministic/functional properties. Given our objective of being conceptually compatible with Event-B, and of course also in situations requiring non-determinism, it is important to also support non-deterministic/relational events. In type theory a relation $R \subseteq T \times U$ is commonly represented as a function R : T → U → Prop. The membership $(t, u) \in R$ and its complement $(t, u) \notin R$ are then respectively expressed as: (R t u) and ¬(R t u). This suggests the following formalization of non-deterministic events:

```
structure NDEventSpec (M) [Machine CTX M] (α) (β) where
  guard (m : M) (x : α) : Prop := True
  effect (m : M) (x : α) (_ : β × M) : Prop
```

```
safety (m : M) (x : α):                      feasibility (m : M) (x : α):
  Machine.invariant m                          Machine.invariant m
  → guard m x                                  → guard m x
  → ∀ y, ∀ m', effect m x (y, m')              → ∃ y, ∃ m', effect m x (y, m')
            → Machine.invariant m'
```

The main difference is that now an action is simply a property relating a pre-state m, an input x and a pair (y,m') consisting of an output y and a post-state m'. The safety requirement is modified accordingly, and the prescription of an existential *feasibility* proof obligation is added to the requirements[7]. As an illustration, we formalize below a Batch event that allows to put several elements into the buffer in a single operation:

```
def B0.Batch := newNDEvent'' {
  guard := fun b0 => b0.size < ctx.maxSize
  effect := fun b0 b0' => ∃ n > 0, b0'.size = b0.size + n ∧ b0'.size ≤ ctx.maxSize
  safety := ... proof omitted ...
  feasibility := fun b0 => by
    simp [Machine.invariant]
    intros _ Hgrd
    exists { size := b0.size + 1 }
    exists 1
}
```

Since there is no notion of actual data in this abstract representation of a buffer, the Batch event has no input parameter. The effect of the event is to assert that there exists an unspecified number n of elements that can be added to the buffer. In the feasibility proof, beyond the details, we show that picking n=1 is always possible since the guard ensures that at least one slot is available.

2.5 Convergent Events

Following our compatibility goal, convergence of event behavior must also be discussed in the context of Event-B. A convergent event, in simple terms, should

---

[7] A notion related to feasibility is the verification that types, especially functional ones, are inhabited. Lean4 provides for this a dedicated Inhabited typeclass.

not be enabled infinitely from a given machine state. In terms of proof obligations, the added restrictions[8], if compared to so-called "ordinary" events, can be expressed as follows:

```
structure ConvergentEventSpec
  (v) [Preorder v] [WellFoundedLT v]
  (M) [Machine CTX M] (α) (β)
  extends EventSpec v M α β where

  variant (m : M): v
```

```
convergence (m : M) (x : α):
  Machine.invariant m
  → guard m x
  → variant (action m x).2 < variant m
```

A convergent event must fulfill all the requirements of an ordinary event, with the adjunction of a variant and a proof that the latter is strictly decreasing. To ensure the proper convergence of the event, the codomain type v of the variant must be based on a *well-founded* ordering relation. We build on Lean4 and Mathlib principles for such requirements. In technical terms, the type v must be an instance of the Preorder and WellFoundedLT typeclasses. This means that unlike in Event-B, well-foundedness is not built-in and restricted to specific types such as natural numbers or finite sets. Lean4 provides a range of such well-founded relations (e.g. lexicographic ordering, multiset ordering, etc.), and other relations can be defined by the user if needed.

As an example, we define an event for retrieving an element from a buffer:

```
def B0.Fetch := newConvergentEvent'' {
  guard := fun b0 => b0.size > 0
  action := fun b0 => { size := b0.size - 1}
  safety := ... proof omitted ...
  variant := fun b0 => b0.size
  convergence := fun b0 => by
      simp [Machine.invariant]
      intros _ Hgrd
      omega
}
```

The variant here is simply the size of the buffer, which is decremented each time we fetch an element. While the convergence of this event is conceptually trivial, arithmetic proofs are never simple technically-speaking. The use in the convergence proof of the powerful omega tactic for Presburger arithmetic illustrates once more the interest of having a shallow embedding of the Event-B principles.

2.6 Event Combinators

To illustrate the possibility of extending the framework, we introduce basic *event combinators*, i.e. ways to construct new events from old ones. This is what make events similar to (Mealy) machines, and is thus what differs most in our framework if compared to Event-B *per se*. In this section, by lack of space, we only expose the internal representation of the "data-part" of events, decoupled from

---

[8] A weaker notion of anticipated event is also part of the Event-B vernacular (and our implementation).

the associated proof obligations. In the actual development, the correctness of the combinators below is formally established.

The basic event structure, internally, is as follows:

```
structure _Event (M) [Machine CTX M] (α) (β : Type) where
  guard : M → α → Prop
  action: M → α → (β × M)
```

The sequential composition of events is probably the most obvious combinator one can think of. Interestingly, this can be abstracted as a *category* (from category theory) based on the following formalization:

```
class Category (cat : Type u → Type u → Type v) where
  id : cat α α    -- identity morphisms
  comp : α β γ : Type u → cat β γ → cat α β → cat α γ  -- composition
```

The objects of such a category are types, and the morphisms are of the form cat α β with α, β objects/types. Events appear to be good candidates for such a definition, as the following instantiation illustrates:

```
instance [Machine CTX M]: Category (_Event M) where
  id : _Event M α α
  id := { guard := fun _ _ => True, action := fun m x => (m, x) }

  comp (ev₂ : _Event M β γ) (ev₁ : _Event M α β) : _Event M α γ :=
    { guard := fun m x => ev₁.guard m x ∧ let (y, m') := ev₁.action m x
                                           ev₂.guard m' y
      action := fun m x => let (y, m') := ev₁.action m x
                           ev₂.action m' y
    }
```

The event that "does nothing" and simply returns its input is the obvious categorical identity. The composition operator is sequential composition, i.e. threading the two events ev₁ and ev₂ in sequence. We show in the development that the identity and composition laws of categories are satisfied by the definitions above. Note that the composition laws are not satisfied by convergent events because the composition of two convergent events is not always convergent (e.g. alternatively incrementing and decrementing a counter).

It is also possible to define parallel composition of events, consisting in working with pairs of inputs, outputs and states. The related algebraic notion is that of an *Arrow* [11], defined as follows:

```
class Arrow (arr : Type u → Type u → Type v) extends Category arr where
  arrow : (α → β) → arr α β
  split: arr α β → arr α' β' → arr (α × α') (β × β')
```

The arrow component is simply an encapsulation of a function into the Arrow structure. And the split operator is in essence the parallel combination of arrows. The non-deterministic event structure we propose fits perfectly with this definition:

```
instance [Machine CTX M] [Semigroup M] : Arrow (_NDEvent M) where
  arrow (f : α → β) : _NDEvent M α β := {
    guard := fun _ _ => True
    effect := fun m x (y, m') => y = f x ∧ m' = m
  }
```

```
split (ev₁ : _NDEvent M α β) (ev₂ : _NDEvent M α' β')
      : _NDEvent M (α × α') (β × β') := {
  guard := fun m (x,y) => ev₁.guard m x ∧ ev₂.guard m y
  effect := fun m (x, y) ((x', y'), m') =>
              ∃ m'₁ m'₂, ev₁.effect m x (x', m'₁) ∧ ev₂.effect m y (y', m'₂)
                ∧ m' = m'₁ * m'₂
}
```

The **arrow** definition shows that non-deterministic events can represent plain functions (which is of course also the case of deterministic events). The **split** operator realizes parallel composition[9]. The two events ev_1 and ev_2 are combined into one, producing a pair of parallel output (x',y') from an input x for ev_1 and y for ev_2. The state changes must also be combined, which requires an internal law of composition, hence the **Semigroup** constraint. The Arrow laws are demonstrated for ordinary events in the repository online[10].

The algebraic combinators presented in this section represent only the tip of the iceberg. In the development we define other algebraic constructions such as various functorial and monadic constructions. There exist of course many more ways of combining events (e.g. alternatives with sum input/output types, fixpoint constructions, event merging, etc.).

3 Refinement Model

Probably the most fundamental feature of Event-B is its thorough support for *refinement*. As a starting point, we formalize the refinement proof rules described informally but precisely in [2]. Based on this relational characterization of refinement, we propose two variants of refinement that gradually introduce a functional abstraction.

3.1 Machine Refinement

We propose the following typeclass to represent the basic refinement of a machine of type AM by a (more) concrete machine of type M:

```
class Refinement {ACTX : outParam (Type u₁)} (AM)
                 {CTX : outParam (Type u₂)} (M)
                 [Machine ACTX AM] [Machine CTX M] where
  refine : AM → M → Prop

  refine_safe (am : AM) (m : M):
    Machine.invariant m
    → refine am m
    → Machine.invariant am
```

---

[9] In a functional setting, the **split** operator can be obtained from a more primitive **first** operator but this does not work in a relational setting because the translation involves a form of interleaving which is incompatible with "true" parallelism.

[10] Note that deterministic events also satisfy the Arrow algebra, but the composition operator is then not truly parallel since one has to choose between one event or the other, arbitrarily. Moreover, the semigroup law must be complemented by a safety property: that the composition of two safe states remains safe. The details can be found in the companion repository.

The refine component corresponds to the notion of *gluing invariant* in [2]: a relation between the abstract and the concrete state. This is associated with an important machine-level property named refine_safe: the fact that the concrete invariant together with the refine relation imply the abstract invariant.

```
class FRefinement ...                    class SRefinement   ...
  [Machine ACTX AM] [Machine CTX M]        extends FRefinement AM M where
  where
                                           unlift (m : M) (am' : AM): M
  lift (m : M): AM
                                           lift_unlift (m : M) (am' : AM):
  lift_safe (m : M):                         Machine.invariant m
    Machine.invariant m                      → Machine.invariant am'
    → Machine.invariant (lift m)             → lift (unlift m am') = am'
```

Fig. 1. Variants of refinement: functional (left) and strong refinement (right).

In the context of type theory, which builds on functions rather than sets and relations, a natural extension of these relational refinement requirements is to introduce an explicit *functional abstraction*, namely a FRefinement (Fig. 1, left). This is formalized by a lift function whose purpose is to rebuild, explicitly, an abstract state from a given concrete state. The lift_safe proof obligation ensures, unsurprisingly, that lifting a safe concrete state produces a safe abstract state. It is important to ensure that this functional refinement is compatible with the relational principles. In our development, this is obtained thanks to the following generic instantiation:

```
instance [Machine ACTX AM] [Machine CTX M] [FRefinement AM M] : Refinement AM M
  where
    refine (am : AM) (m : M) := am = lift m

    refine_safe (am : AM) (m : M) := by ... proof details omitted ...
```

This says, almost literally, that any instance of FRefinement is also an instance of Refinement, using the lift function as a glue. This is a good illustration of the important role played by typeclasses in enabling such meta-theoretical reasoning in the context of a shallow embedding.

As an illustration of functional refinement, which is in a way the default approach in our framework, we define below the refinement of the abstract buffer into a more concrete one. This more concrete machine is defined as follows:

```
structure B1 (ctx : BufContext) (α : Type) where
  data : List α

instance: Machine BufContext (B1 ctx α) where
  context := ctx
  invariant b1 := b1.data.length ≤ ctx.maxSize
  reset := { data := [] }
```

There is no context change, hence we reuse BufContext, but now the state contains an explicit list of elements of some type α. It is very simple to lift a concrete B1 state to a corresponding B0 abstract state, as follows:

```
def B1.lift (b1 : B1 ctx α) : B0 ctx := { size := b1.data.length }
```

The instantiation of FRefinement is then easily specified:

```
instance: FRefinement (B0 ctx) (B1 ctx α) where
  lift := B1.lift
  lift_safe := fun b1 => by simp [Machine.invariant]
```

The strong(er) refinement relation SRefinement (Fig. 1, right) introduces a way, namely the unlift function, to reconstruct a concrete post-state from a concrete pre-state and an abstract post-state. In the previous example, the unlift function cannot be specified because one would have to "invent" a new element to insert into a B1 buffer in response to e.g. an increase in the size of the B0 counterpart. Hence, strong refinement is unavailable. To illustrate strong refinement, we consider a further refinement step for the buffer example, based on the following machine state:

```
inductive Priority where
  | Low | Mid | Hi

structure B2 (ctx : BufContext) (α :Type) where
  data : List (Priority × α)
```

Now, the elements of the buffer are associated to a priority: low, middle or high priority. Functional abstraction is of course straightforward: we just have to "forget" about priorities:

```
def B2.lift (b2 : B2 ctx α) : B1 ctx α :=
  { data := List.map Prod.snd b2.data }
```

We apply here the function Prod.snd that extracts the second component of a pair on all the elements of the concrete buffer so that we obtain a simple list of elements – a correct abstract state representation. To implement the stronger form of refinement, the unlift operation must be implemented:

```
def B2.unlift (b2 : B2 ctx α) (b1' : B1 ctx α) : B2 ctx α :=
  -- details omitted
```

From a concrete pre-state b2, the objective is to reconstruct a concrete post-state by analyzing the abstract post-state[11] b1'. One way to obtain this reconstruction is to insert with an (arbitrarily) low priority all the new elements potentially discovered in b1' into the concrete post-state. This relatively non-trivial operation can be programmed comfortably in Lean4 using recursive functions. The details can be found in the companion repository.

Strong refinement is also particularly useful for algorithmic refinement steps, when the abstract state representation is essentially repeated at the concrete level, or in case of so-called *superpositions* [2]. We discuss in the next section

---

[11] If required, the abstract pre-state can be recovered by the expression B2.lift b2.

another interest of strong refinement for the reuse of abstract events at the concrete level.

The proposed typeclass-based formalization of refinement suggests an interesting feature: the possibility for a concrete machine to refine multiple abstract machines. Comparatively, in Event-B a machine can refine at most one abstract machine. We think that removing this limitation increases the potential for the *reuse* of machine specifications. To illustrate this feature, we implemented a toy example of a "push buffer". The idea is to make the buffer controlled by a push button. First, adding an element to the buffer requires the button to be pushed. Conversely, the button cannot be pushed if the buffer is full. Skipping the details (available in the companion repository), the important part is the definition of the two "simultaneous" (strong) refinement instances:

```
instance: SRefinement (B0 ctx) (PushBuffer ctx) where
  -- details omitted

instance: SRefinement Button (PushBuffer ctx) where
  -- defails omitted
```

This says, first, that a `PushBuffer` refines the abstract B0 machine, and is thus "a buffer". But it also refines the `Button` specification, and is thus also controlled by a button. Although the example is very simplistic, it illustrates the fact that such a "multi-refinement" step has the potential to increase the reusability of machine specifications. The push button specification, for instance, is independent from the buffer part, and is thus probably reusable in distinct contexts.

3.2 Event Refinement

The event "zoology" of Event-B is rather complex and covers various different situations. As a kind of "canonical" starting point, we give below the requirement for the specification of a deterministic, transitional event refined from a similar abstract event.

```
structure REventSpec (AM) [Machine ACTX AM]
                     (M) [Machine CTX M]
                     [Refinement AM M]
  (abstract : OrdinaryEvent AM α' β')
  extends EventSpec M α β where

  lift_in : α → α'
  lift_out : β → β'
```

```
strengthening (m : M) (x : α):          simulation (m : M) (x : α):
  Machine.invariant m                     Machine.invariant m
  → guard m x                             → guard m x
  → ∀ am, refine am m                     → ∀ am, refine am m
    → abstract.guard am (lift_in x)       → let (y, m') := action m x
                                            let (z, am') := abstract.action
                                                             am (lift_in x)
                                            lift_out y = z ∧ refine am' m'
```

The parameters of such a refined event specification are the following ones. The types AM and M identify, respectively, the abstract and concrete machine types. These types must be related by the **Refinement** principles presented in the previous section. The **abstract** parameter identifies the event to refine, which has to be deterministic/ordinary (i.e. of type OrdinaryEvent). The lift_in and lift_out functions allow to change, respectively, the input and output types of the refined event. The two proof obligations (added to the **safety** requirement) concern guard strengthening and transition simulation (cf. [2] for more details). In the specific case of functional refinement, these two requirements can be simplified as follows:

```
strengthening (m : M) (x : α):            simulation (m : M) (x : α):
  Machine.invariant m                       Machine.invariant m
  → guard m x                               → guard m x
  → abstract.guard (lift m)                 → let (y, m') := action m x
                   (lift_in x)                let (z, am') := abstract.action
                                                              (lift m)
                                                              (lift_in x)
                                              lift_out y = z ∧ am' = (lift m')
```

We prove in the companion repository that these functional properties satisfy the relational requirements. As an illustration, we give below the definition of a refinement of the B0.Put abstract event defined previously:

```
def B1.Put := newConvergentFREvent' B0.Put {
  guard := fun b1 _ => b1.data.length < ctx.maxSize
  action := fun b1 x => { data := x :: b1.data }
  lift_in := fun _ => ()
    ... proof obligations not shown ...
}
```

The event takes an input element x of type α to add to the buffer data[12]. The lift_in function thus "erases" this parameter to connect to the abstract event. All the proof obligation are easily discharged (as expected).

Note that like in Event-B, the same abstract event can be refined by more than one event at the concrete level. We may consider, for example, a variant of the concrete Put operation that inserts the new element at a distinct position in the buffer, for example at the end:

```
def B1.PutLast := newConvergentFREvent' B0.Put {
  guard := fun b1 _ => b1.data.length < ctx.maxSize
  action := fun b1 x => { data := b1.data ++ [x] }   -- at the end
  lift_in := fun _ => ()
    ... proof obligations not shown ...
}
```

3.3 Other Refinement Situations

Based on definitions similar to the basic case presented previously, all the use cases discussed in [2] are covered by the proposed framework. In this final subsection, we comment on some specific refinement situations, emphasizing the associated simulation requirements.

---

[12] The operation x :: b1.data prepends the element x to the list b1.data.

Refining Non-deterministic Events. There are basically two possibilities for refining non-deterministic events. The first one is to consider the refined event also non-deterministic, which gives the following requirement:

```
simulation (m : M) (x : α):
  Machine.invariant m
  → guard m x
  → ∀ y, ∀ m', effect m x (y, m')
    → abstract.effect (lift m) (lift_in x) (lift_out y, (lift m'))
```

It is also possible to construct a deterministic refined event, in which case the simulation requirement is adapted as follows:

```
simulation (m : M) (x : α):
  Machine.invariant m
  → guard m x
  → let (y, m') := action m x
    abstract.effect (lift m) (lift_in x) (lift_out y, lift m')
```

Concrete Events. It is possible to introduce new events at the concrete level. For this, the only requirement is to refine the skip event that does nothing at the abstract level. In our development the skip event is defined as follows:

```
def skip_NDEvent [Machine CTX M] : _NDEvent M α β :=
{
  guard := fun _ _ => True
  effect := fun m _ (_, m') => m' = m
}
```

Note that skip must be non-deterministic because there is no generic function producing a value of type β from an input of type α. In the non-deterministic case we can express that there is no constraint on the input and output of the event (except for the typing constraints). The simulation proofs obligations we obtain are then the following ones (relational refinement on the left, functional refinement on the right):

```
simulation (m : M) (x : α):          simulation (m : M) (x : α):
  Machine.invariant m                  Machine.invariant m
  → guard m x                          → guard m x
  → ∀ am, refine am m                  → lift m = lift (action m x).2
    → refine am (action m x).2
```

Reusing Abstract Events. While this is to our knowledge not thoroughly investigated in the Event-B literature, the reuse of abstract events appears to us as an important and non-trivial aspect. For example, in case of algorithmic or simple data-refinement steps, it seems interesting to be able to reuse the definitions and proof developments of abstract event at the concrete level. Unfortunately, in the default relational case no dedicated proof rules are provided in e.g. [2]. Thankfully, the functional and strong refinement variants greatly simplify the reuse of abstract events. To illustrate this, below is the only proof obligation remaining to reuse an abstract event in the case of strong refinement:

```
step_inv (m : M) (x : α):
   Machine.invariant m
   → abstract.guard (lift m) x
   → Machine.invariant (unlift m (abstract.action (lift m) x).2)
```

This corresponds to a kind of a "round-trip" requirement, that the abstract action preserves the concrete invariant after being reconstructed concretely thanks to the unlift function. In the actual development, we prove formally that all the functional and (then) relational requirements are fulfilled by this single proof rule.

As an illustration, we show below the second refinement for the Put operation of the buffer extended with priorities.

```
def B2.Put [DecidableEq α] := newAbstractConvergentSREvent' B1.Put {
   step_inv := fun b2 x => by -- proof details not shown
}
```

In this case, the change of representation to introduce priorities is somewhat consequential (cf. the lift and especially the unlift functions), hence the reuse of the abstract event is not trivial, but at least only one proof obligation remains.

4 Discussion

We discuss in this section what we consider important topic related to the approach presented in this paper.

Usability. The framework presented in this paper has been used in the context of a seven weeks graduate course in formal methods and proof assistants at Sorbonne University. Students with a classical computer science background in discrete math and functional programming can learn both the Lean4 fundamentals and the proposed framework in a matter of a few weeks. One important improvement would be the introduction of dedicated syntactic structures for machines, events, etc. In this respect, the powerful metaprogramming features of Lean4 (flexible parsing systems, high-level hygienic macro system, programmable elaborator [20], etc.) open up a broad range of possibilities. Another axis related to usability is the support for more proof automation based on dedicated tools such as Duper[13].

Correctness. The emphasis we put (as in Event-B) on correctness-by-construction is achieved in the proposed implementation largely thanks to typeclasses and dependently-typed structures with inheritance. The approach is heavily inspired by the Mathlib4 project, and especially the formalization of algebraic structures such as groups or categories [3]. The framework being developed as a Lean4 library, its own soundness is checked by the proof assistant. Last but not least, type theory provides an ideal framework for automatic *proof checking*. While proofs can be checked by the Lean4 prover, there also exists external proof checkers, thus achieving a high level of confidence regarding the correctness of the formal developments.

---

[13] https://github.com/leanprover-community/duper.

Extensibility. One interesting aspect of developing a formal method tool within a generic proof assistant is the opportunity of creating variations and/or extensions of the framework. In the paper, we illustrated this aspect by defining event combinators, and also by extending the basic refinement model with more constrained extensions. We also think that the possibility of refining *multiple* abstract machines in a single refinement step can be quite interesting in practice. For instance, the separate development of the environment part and control part of a system could benefit from this feature.

Executable Specifications. While B-classic comes with a precise notion of what is an executable specification, this is not the case of most other formal methods. Indeed, it is very difficult to address both the high-level and abstract specification needs, as well as the more mundane problematic of program execution. Beyond its use a as proof assistant, Lean4 is also (and perhaps, before all) a dependently-typed functional programming environment. Its compiler is able to separate (and remove) the mathematical contents so that only the executable parts of the program remain after code generation. This is a powerful feature of the calculus of inductive constructions, based on proof irrelevance and type-erasure. Ultimately, it is possible to develop software applications that can be run on most computer platforms. While the resulting program is not *certified* (since the compiler and runtime are not certified themselves), this is a very good way to develop partially or fully executable specifications.

5 Conclusion and Future Work

This paper presented a framework for the Lean4 functional programming language and proof assistant that helps at modeling stateful entities by stepwise refinement, according to the Event-B methodology. While still experimental, we believe the framework – developed as an open source software – to be usable in its present form. There are two main directions the project is aimed for. One direction is to exploit the powerful metaprogramming facilities of Lean4 to provide dedicated constructions and interactive tools to support the modeling activity. We also intend to experiment more with the various extensions we briefly introduced in the paper: event combinators, combined refinement steps and alternative refinement principles.

Acknowledgement. The author wishes to thank the IFM24 reviewers for their particularly deep and insightful comments and suggestions. This work also benefited from the (mostly, but not always, positive) feedback from students following the SVP (specification and validation of programs) second-year master's course given at Sorbonne University.

References

1. The focalize project. https://focalize.ensta-paris.fr/
2. Abrial, J.: Modeling in Event-B - System and Software Engineering. Cambridge University Press (2010)
3. Baanen, A.: Use and abuse of instance parameters in the lean mathematical library. CoRR abs/2202.01629 (2022). https://arxiv.org/abs/2202.01629
4. Ballenghien, B., Wolff, B.: Event-b as DSL in Isabelle and HOL experiences from a prototype. In: Bonfanti, S., Gargantini, A., Leuschel, M., Riccobene, E., Scandurra, P. (eds.) ABZ 2024. LNCS, vol. 14759, pp. 241–247. Springer, Cham (2024). https://doi.org/10.1007/978-3-031-63790-2_18
5. Bodeveix, J.-P., Filali, M.: Type synthesis in B and the translation of B to PVS. In: Bert, D., Bowen, J.P., Henson, M.C., Robinson, K. (eds.) ZB 2002. LNCS, vol. 2272, pp. 350–369. Springer, Heidelberg (2002). https://doi.org/10.1007/3-540-45648-1_18
6. Boulmé, S.: Intuitionistic refinement calculus. In: Della Rocca, S.R. (ed.) TLCA 2007. LNCS, vol. 4583, pp. 54–69. Springer, Heidelberg (2007). https://doi.org/10.1007/978-3-540-73228-0_6
7. Chartier, P.: Formalisation of B in Isabelle/HOL. In: Bert, D. (ed.) B 1998. LNCS, vol. 1393, pp. 66–82. Springer, Heidelberg (1998). https://doi.org/10.1007/BFb0053356
8. Dapoigny, R., Barlatier, P.: Modeling ontological structures with type classes in Coq. In: Pfeiffer, H.D., Ignatov, D.I., Poelmans, J., Gadiraju, N. (eds.) ICCS-ConceptStruct 2013. LNCS (LNAI), vol. 7735, pp. 135–152. Springer, Heidelberg (2013). https://doi.org/10.1007/978-3-642-35786-2_11
9. Déharbe, D., Merz, S.: Software component design with the b method—a formalization in Isabelle/HOL. In: Braga, C., Ölveczky, P.C. (eds.) FACS 2015. LNCS, vol. 9539, pp. 31–47. Springer, Cham (2016). https://doi.org/10.1007/978-3-319-28934-2_2
10. Hoang, T.S.: An introduction to the event-B modelling method. In: Hoang, T.S. (ed.) Industrial Deployment of System Engineering Methods, pp. 211–236. Springer, Heidelberg (2013). https://doi.org/10.1007/978-3-642-33170-1
11. Hughes, J.: Generalising monads to arrows. Sci. Comput. Program. **37**(1–3), 67–111 (2000)
12. Jones, R.B.: Methods and tools for the verification of critical properties. In: Jones, C.B., Shaw, R.C., Denvir, T. (eds.) 5th Refinement Workshop, pp. 88–118. Springer, London (1992). https://doi.org/10.1007/978-1-4471-3550-0_6
13. Moura, L., Ullrich, S.: The lean 4 theorem prover and programming language. In: Platzer, A., Sutcliffe, G. (eds.) CADE 2021. LNCS (LNAI), vol. 12699, pp. 625–635. Springer, Cham (2021). https://doi.org/10.1007/978-3-030-79876-5_37
14. Perone, M., Karachalias, G.: Crème de la crem: composable representable executable machines. In: Proceedings of the 1st ACM SIGPLAN International Workshop on Functional Software Architecture, pp. 11–19. Association for Computing Machinery (2023)
15. Pollack, R.: Dependently typed records for representing mathematical structure. In: Aagaard, M., Harrison, J. (eds.) TPHOLs 2000. LNCS, vol. 1869, pp. 462–479. Springer, Heidelberg (2000). https://doi.org/10.1007/3-540-44659-1_29
16. Reynolds, C.: Formalizing the institution for event-B in the Coq proof assistant. In: Raschke, A., Méry, D. (eds.) ABZ 2021. LNCS, vol. 12709, pp. 162–166. Springer, Cham (2021). https://doi.org/10.1007/978-3-030-77543-8_17

17. Rivière, P., Singh, N.K., Aït-Ameur, Y.: Eb4eb: a framework for reflexive event-b. In: 26th International Conference on Engineering of Complex Computer Systems (ICECCS), pp. 71–80 (2022)
18. Sall, B.D., Peschanski, F., Chailloux, E.: A mechanized theory of program refinement. In: Ait-Ameur, Y., Qin, S. (eds.) ICFEM 2019. LNCS, vol. 11852, pp. 305–321. Springer, Cham (2019). https://doi.org/10.1007/978-3-030-32409-4_19
19. Schmalz, M.: The logic of event-b. Technical report 698, ETH Zürich (2011)
20. Ullrich, S., de Moura, L.: Beyond notations: hygienic macro expansion for theorem proving languages. Log. Methods Comput. Sci. **18**(2) (2022)
21. Wadler, P., Blott, S.: How to make ad-hoc polymorphism less ad-hoc. In: Conference Record of the 16th ACM Symposium on Principles of Programming Languages, pp. 60–76. ACM Press (1989)
22. Wlaschin, S.: Domain Modeling Made Functional. The Pragmatic Programmers (2018)

Modeling Register Pairs in CompCert

Alexander Loitzl[✉] and Florian Zuleger[✉]

TU Wien, Vienna, Austria
alexander.loitzl@student.tuwien.ac.at, florian.zuleger@tuwien.ac.at

Abstract. The CompCert C compiler is a moderately optimizing, formally verified compiler that ensures the preservation of the input program's semantics through a machine-checkable correctness proof. We introduce CompCert^p, an extension of the CompCert compiler, which incorporates the modeling of register pairs. This enhancement targets 32-bit architectures, such as the 32-bit Arm, which combine two registers to support 64-bit operands. So far, CompCert abstracts register pairs as 64-bit registers and allocates the entire pair when operating on 32-bit values, effectively cutting the number of available registers for 32-bit computations in half. This creates a harder register allocation problem and the emitted code requires post-processing outside of the formally verified compiler to comply with calling conventions. Our enhancement models all of Arm's registers, improving register allocation and the generated code's size. Additionally, it models the correct calling conventions for floating-point arguments within the formal semantics, eliminating the need for unverified modifications and therefore decreasing the trusted computing base (TCB). We adapt the proofs for all CompCert-supported architectures and demonstrate that, despite a slight increase in compile time, CompCert^p generates code that is either smaller or comparable in size to that produced by the original CompCert.

Keywords: program verification · compilers · semantics · register allocation · CompCert · Coq

1 Introduction

CompCert has gained traction in both academia [1,2,4,5,18] and industry, where it is used for the development of safety-critical systems [6,10]. The CompCert toolchain supports a large subset of C99 and several target architectures. Its correctness proof covers the translation from CompCert C, the C semantics formalized in Coq, to the target's formalized assembly language. It ensures the correctness of all optimizations and therefore rules out a common source of bugs in compilers [19].

This work was conducted as part of the author's master's thesis project in cooperation with AbsInt.

© The Author(s), under exclusive license to Springer Nature Switzerland AG 2025
N. Kosmatov and L. Kovács (Eds.): IFM 2024, LNCS 15234, pp. 128–147, 2025.
https://doi.org/10.1007/978-3-031-76554-4_8

Both the formal C semantics and that of the target machine are part of the TCB. The latter contains a model of memory, instruction semantics and the register file. Discrepancies between the model and the instruction set architecture (ISA) decrease the trust in the proof and may require unverified post-processing, as is the case for the Arm target.

The floating-point register file of 32-bit Arm (VFPv2, VFPv3-D16) is split into thirty-two 32-bit registers S0-S31, grouped into aligned *register pairs* D0-D15, as depicted in Fig. 1. Similarly, for the currently unsupported TriCore architecture, two aligned registers may be used to hold any 64-bit value.

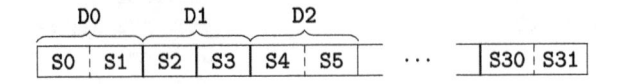

Fig. 1. Arm's register layout

Since CompCert models the register file as a simple map from registers to values, it models only the view of the combined 64-bit registers and the two halves of a pair are not addressable. This makes it possible to generate code for the Arm target, but requires additional, unverified post-processing to adhere to calling conventions. This workaround is not feasible for TriCore, as, unlike Arm, it does not have distinct floating-point registers and registers are more scarce.

Our contributions address this shortcomings by introducing register pairs in the compiler backend. While our contributions are tightly integrated into the CompCert development, we refer to the adapted version as CompCert^p for sake of clarity. Below, we highlight CompCert's shortcomings for Arm by example.

Example. Consider the C code on the left of Fig. 2. It calls the function sum, which sums up three floating-point numbers. The parameters a and c are single-

```
1 double sum(single a, double b, single c){
2    double d = (double) (a + c);
3    return d + b;
4 }
5
6 int main(){
7    sum (0.f, 1.0, 2.f);
8    return 0;
9 }
```

```
1 sum(x5, x4, x6){
2    x2 = x5 +fs x6;
3    x1 = doubleofsingle(x2);
4    x3 = x1 +f x4;
5    return x3;
6 }
7
8 main() {
9    x2 = 0.f;x3 = 1.;x4 = 2.f;
10   x5 = "sum"(x2, x3, x4);
11   x1 = 0;
12   return x1;
13 }
```

Fig. 2. Simple program summing up floating-point numbers

```
1  sum:
2  ...
3  vadd.f32 s0, s0, s1
4  vcvt.f64.f32 d0, s0
5  vadd.f64 d0, d0, d1
6  ...
7  main:
8  ...
9  vmov.f32 s0, #1.
10 vmov.f64 d1, #2.
11 vmov.f32 s1, #2.
12 bl   sum
13 mov  r0, #0
14 ...
```

```
1  sum:
2  vmov.f32 s4, s1
3  ...
4  vadd.f32 s0, s0, s4
5  vcvt.f64.f32 d0, s0
6  vadd.f64 d0, d0, d1
7  ...
8  main:
9  ...
10 vmov.f32 s0, #1.
11 vmov.f64 d1, #2.
12 vmov.f32 s4, #3.
13 vmov.f32 s1, s4
14 bl   sum
15 mov  r0, #0
16 ...
```

Fig. 3. Assembly output of CompCert^p (left) and CompCert (right)

precision (we write *single* instead of *float* to make the distinction clear) and their sum is explicitly cast to a double-precision value before adding b.

The corresponding code on the right of Fig. 2 is in the RTL intermediate language of the compiler and closely resembles the original C code. RTL is the last intermediate language before register allocation, during which temporaries x1-x6 are replaced by hardware registers. Up to this point, there is no difference between CompCert^p and CompCert.

In Fig. 3 we show excerpts of the assembly output of both CompCert^p and CompCert. The output of CompCert^p on the left directly corresponds to the instructions of the RTL code except that it uses hardware registers instead of temporaries. In the output of CompCert on the right, two additional move instructions are highlighted (line 2 and line 13), which are inserted by the aforementioned unverified post-processing step implemented in OCaml.

The additional moves are inserted to fix the discrepancies in CompCert's internal calling conventions for the Arm hard-float target. CompCert simply passes the arguments in order, using a 64-bit register for each. In Fig. 4, we depict CompCert's allocation for the sum function where the two 32-bit parameters a and c block an entire 64-bit register. Arm's actual hard-float calling conventions for non-variadic functions, however, pass each argument in the first available register that fits its size. In particular, arguments are not necessarily passed in order, if, due to alignment of a double-precision argument, a single-precision register is left free.

This discrepancy is fixed by the inserted move instructions, putting each argument into the correct register: For the sum function, the third parameter c is moved from register S4 to S1. We note that this strategy potentially requires more registers than Arm's calling conventions, as is the case for the sum function. If CompCert prematurely runs out of the eight reserved registers for passing arguments, it may not follow the calling conventions at all and pass additional arguments on the stack instead [12]. We finally note that CompCert^p directly passes the arguments as required by Arm's calling conventions, compare Fig. 4, eliminating the need for an (unverified) post-processing step.

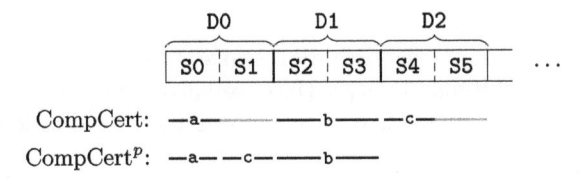

```
        D0        D1        D2
     ┌───────┐ ┌───────┐ ┌───────┐
     │ S0 S1 │ │ S2 S3 │ │ S4 S5 │  ...
     └───────┘ └───────┘ └───────┘
CompCert:   —a——    ——b—— —c—
CompCert$^p$: —a— —c— ——b——
```

Fig. 4. Argument locations of CompCert and CompCert^p for sum

Contributions. We present CompCert^p, an extension of the CompCert compiler which

- improves on CompCert's Arm semantics by modeling all registers and reduces the TCB by implementing the correct calling conventions in the formal semantics,
- extends the backend to handle register pairs allowing for future support of the TriCore architecture,
- generates identical code for all other architectures and keeps their semantics unchanged,
- either improves on or performs similarly to CompCert in terms of generated code size, and
- is scheduled to be integrated into the commercially available version of CompCert distributed by AbsInt[1].

Structure. In Sect. 2, we give a brief overview of CompCert and its register allocator. In Sect. 3, we motivate our design choices and discuss their impact on the semantics and the associated proof effort in Sect. 4. We evaluate CompCert^p on selected benchmarks in Sect. 5 and conclude the paper in Sect. 6.

2   Overview of the CompCert Compiler

CompCert is a formally verified, optimizing C compiler supporting several target architectures (Arm, PowerPC, x86, RISC-V). It is implemented using the Coq proof assistant so that the correctness proof can be carried out directly on its source code. The proof spans the translation from CompCert's C semantics through 8 intermediate languages down to the modeled semantics of the target machine. It connects the input program's behavior to that of the assembly output via the notion of *semantic preservation*.

---
[1] https://www.absint.com.

Definition 1 (Semantic Preservation [12]).
*For all source programs S and compiler-generated code C,
if the compiler, applied to the source S, produces the code C,
without reporting a compile-time error,
then the observable behavior of C improves one of the allowed observable behaviors of S.*

Note that, according to the definition above, CompCert may abort, e.g., on malformed input, and it may *improve* the observable behavior by giving meaning to undefined programs, which is necessary to perform dead code elimination.

2.1 Architecture of CompCert

CompCert is split into eight intermediate languages: three in the C-specific frontend [7], five in the backend [11]. To reduce the proof burden, large parts of the backend are designed to support all target architectures and the architecture specific components are plugged in. All languages share a common memory model [13] and value representation, and those languages operating on machine registers adopt a similar view of the register file.

Values. All of CompCert's languages manipulate *values*:

$$\mathtt{val} \ni v := \mathtt{int}(n) \mid \mathtt{long}(n) \mid \mathtt{single}(n) \mid \mathtt{double}(n) \mid \mathtt{ptr}(b, ofs) \mid \mathtt{undef}.$$

Only the arithmetic values capture their bit representation. Pointers consist of a memory block b and an offset ofs into that block. This allows pointer arithmetic within a block, while keeping pointers abstract is a requirement for reasoning about CompCert's complex memory transformations. Arithmetic values are typed naturally as $\mathtt{int}$, $\mathtt{long}$, $\mathtt{single}$, and $\mathtt{double}$, pointers are typed either as $\mathtt{int}$ or $\mathtt{long}$, depending on the target architecture, and $\mathtt{undef}$ is of any type.

Register File and Register Allocation. CompCert adopts a simple view of the register file for its intermediate languages. It assumes a map from general purpose registers (GPRs) to values, therefore satisfying two useful properties about their read/write behavior:

$$\forall p, v : rs[p \leftarrow v](p) = v, \text{ and} \tag{1}$$

$$\forall r, r', v : \text{If } r \neq r', \text{ then } rs[r' \leftarrow v](r) = rs(r). \tag{2}$$

The two properties are used extensively in CompCert's correctness proofs to reason about the state of the register map throughout the execution of the program.

The simple model of the register file also allows CompCert to use a textbook implementation of IRC [9]. IRC is a graph-coloring register allocator and connects the two intermediate languages RTL and LTL. The source language RTL operates on *temporaries*, of which, similar to local variables in C, an unbounded number is available. The target language LTL operates on the limited number of available machine registers. The task of the allocator is to map the temporaries used in RTL to machine registers such that the semantics of the original program is preserved. The allocator reduces the problem of register allocation to that of graph coloring, and tries to color the *interference graph* with the available machine registers using a heuristic approach. The interference graph connects any two temporaries that have overlapping live ranges and therefore cannot be mapped to the same register. If no coloring can be found, the allocator *spills* a temporary by storing it on the stack and inserting appropriate loads and stores. Additionally, the allocator tries to delete move instructions between two temporaries by *coalescing* the source and destination temporary, making the move redundant.

3 Detailed Design Overview

The CompCert development is quite mature and proposed additions need to be carefully assessed. We focused on four key aspects: (1) the impact on the semantics of CompCert C and supported architectures other than Arm, (2) maintainability and ease of integration into the CompCert development, (3) the proof effort required to establish its correctness, and (4) its similarity to the actual machine semantics.

Figure 5 highlights those components of CompCert that have been adapted in CompCert^p. Most importantly, we do not require any additional translation passes or intermediate languages and only three of the existing intermediate languages are affected. By keeping the interface to the machine operations (datatype Op), the memory model, and value representation the same, we do not change the CompCert C semantics or any of the assembly semantics other than Arm. In the following, we discuss how we achieved this by working our way backwards starting at the assembly semantics.

3.1 Assembly Semantics

Previously, in CompCert, the simple register model required all registers to be disjoint and therefore only the view of the double-precision registers was modeled. This effectively cuts the number of available registers for single-precision computations in half and the (hard-float) calling conventions could not be modeled correctly in the Arm semantics.

CompCert^p models all 32 single-precision registers rather than the 16 double-precision registers. Register pairs are explicitly modeled as pairs of their two subregisters and the register D<n> is refered to as (S<2n+1>, S<2n>). Every access to a register pair splits and combines the value when storing and loading from the register file, respectively. Therefore, all registers are available during register allocation and we can model the correct calling conventions in the formal semantics, allowing us to omit the unverified post-processing step that inserts moves for the Arm hard-float target.

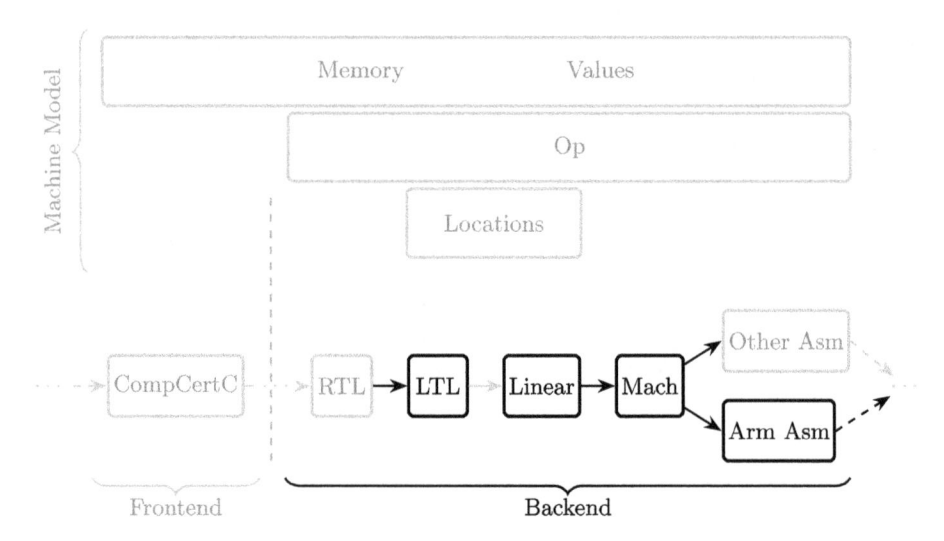

Fig. 5. Overview of CompCert with affected components highlighted

3.2 Shared Backend

To support generating code for the revised Arm target using register pairs, we need to adapt all intermediate languages after register allocation. We change the semantics of LTL, Linear, and Mach to operate on the type `rpair mreg` rather than machine registers `mreg`.

$$\texttt{rpair mreg} \ni p := \texttt{Two}\ (r1 : \texttt{mreg}, r2 : \texttt{mreg}) \mid \texttt{One}\ (r : \texttt{mreg}).$$

The semantics are adapted such that when encountering a register pair Two $(r1, r2)$, the value contained in the pair is constructed from the values contained in the individual halves $r1$, and $r2$. Registers wrapped by the constructor One are treated as before and the register allocator, when assigning a single register to a temporary, wraps it's result with the One constructor. This ensures that the affected intermediate languages are downwards compatible in the sense that for those architectures using no pairs, CompCert^p generates the same code. The architecture-specific translation from the Mach intermediate language rejects any code using pairs for all architectures except Arm, allowing us to keep the semantics of all other architectures unchanged.

Since we adapt the semantics of all languages similarly, adapting the translations between them is straightforward. The translation between LTL and Linear only affects the code structure and requires no changes, indicated in Fig. 5. For the translation between Linear and Mach, the main effort lies in changing the way callee-save registers are preserved.

3.3 Register Allocation

Existing Register Allocator. CompCert's allocator, IRC, uses a heuristic approach to color the interference graph using the degree of nodes in the graph. If a node has degree less than K, the number of available machine registers, it is guaranteed to be colorable and therefore picking a color can be delayed. The node is removed from the graph and the process is repeated for the remaining graph. This simplification is interleaved with *conservative coalescing* [8], which combines two non-interfering nodes that are the source and destination of a move instruction. These two simplifications are repeated until the graph is either empty or a register has to be spilled.

Figure 6, on the right, contains IRC's interference graph of Fig. 2's sum function after coalescing, hence, several nodes with no interference edge between them have already been combined. The graph contains the temporaries $x1$-$x6$ and some *pre-colored* nodes D0-D2 to enforce the calling conventions. At this stage, IRC would now continue with its simplification phase, removing one low-degree node after the other until the graph is empty and then assign registers to the remaining temporaries.

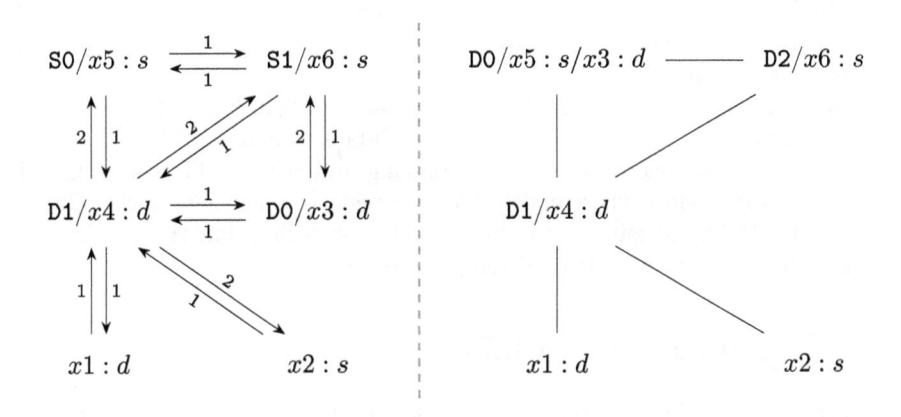

Fig. 6. Interference Graphs of sum. The interference graph of CompCert (right) is undirected, while that of CompCert^p (left) is a directed weighted graph. We illustrate the effect of coalescing by listing all individual nodes separated by a "/". The type of a temporary is indicated by s for single-precision and d for double-precision.

Extended IRC. The register allocator of CompCert^p is built on top of the existing implementation of IRC and closely follows the approaches presented in [16,17]. Unlike in the formal semantics, all named registers are modeled, i.e., both D<n> and its subregisters S<2n> and S<2n+1> are available to the allocator.

Our register allocator keeps the principal phases of IRC but captures the interactions of aliasing registers by dividing registers into classes. For Arm, we give the allocator access to the class of integer GPRs R, the class of single-precision GPRs S, and the class of double-precision GPRs D. We define the measure $worst(C, C')$ between any two classes C and C'. The measure captures how many candidates for a register in class C can be blocked if it interferes with a register of class C'. For Arm, we get $worst(S, D) = 2$ and $worst(D, S) = 1$.

A single-precision register can only block one double-precision register, while a double-precision register blocks two single-precision register candidates. If registers of two classes cannot interfere, e.g., an integer register with a floating-point register, we leave *worst* undefined. All architectures except Arm have two classes, floating-point and integer GPRs, and we define $worst(C, C') = 1$ if $C = C'$, and otherwise leave it undefined.

We can capture the new interactions by using a weighted directed graph. For any edge $e = (u, v)$, the associated weight $\omega(e) = worst(V, U)$ where U and V are the classes of u and v respectively. Hence, the weight of an edge $e = (u, v)$ captures the number of v' register candidates blocked by the source u. The degree $d(v)$ of a node v is the sum of the incoming edge weights:

$$d(v) = \sum_{e=(u,v)\in E} \omega(e). \tag{3}$$

Since IRC caches the degree of all nodes and updates them whenever the graph is transformed, we keep the internal representation of the non-directed graph, but use *worst* to update the cached degrees.

Consider CompCert[p]'s interference graph on the left of Fig. 6. The edge from D1/$x4$ to $x2$ has weight 2 as it blocks two candidates (S2 and S3) for a potential coloring of $x2$. The principal idea of coalescing and the simplification phase is then the same as before where nodes of low degree can be safely removed. During the actual coloring, aliasing has to be respected, ensuring that two neighboring nodes are not colored with two overlapping registers.

4 Semantics and Proof Effort

Our extensions are built on top of CompCert and therefore all proofs have been carried out using the Coq proof assistant. We make the development available as an artifact [14] and only comment on the most interesting problems. As illustrated in Fig. 5, the changes are limited to a handful of intermediate languages and the Arm assembly semantics. Adapting the semantics of all languages similarly, splitting and recombining at the level of values, allows for a straightforward adaptation of CompCert's proofs of semantics preservation. Rather than CompCert[p] being a standalone addition, the changes are tightly integrated into the entire compiler. In total, the development grew by around 3k lines of code and amounts to about 3 person-months of effort. Below we discuss the consequences of value splitting on the semantics, the verification of the register allocation, and the preservation of callee-save registers.

4.1 Pairs in the Verified Backend

To facilitate the correctness proofs of the translation passes, the components shared by multiple intermediate languages, like machine operations and memory, operate on values. The specifics of a language may then be captured as part of its state. Below we show a simplified version of the RTL transition rule for an arithmetic operation, only listing those parts of the state that change as part of the transition. For a more detailed description, we refer to [11].

$$\frac{c(pc) = \lfloor \mathtt{op}_{RTL}(op, \boldsymbol{r}, r, pc') \rfloor \quad \mathtt{eval\_op}(\_, \_, op, R(\boldsymbol{r})) = \lfloor v \rfloor}{\_ \vdash S(\_, \_, \_, pc, R, \_) \xrightarrow{\epsilon} S(\_, \_, \_, pc', R[r \leftarrow v], \_)}$$

An RTL execution state contains the current program counter pc and a map R from temporaries to values. The rule defines the conditions in order to take a step in the RTL semantics, if the current program counter pc is pointing to an $\mathtt{op}_{RTL}$ instruction. If performing operation op on the values contained in the registers of the arguments $\boldsymbol{r}$ evaluates to v, we can take a step, updating the result temporary r with value v.

We have a similar rule for LTL where the instruction $\mathtt{op}_{LTL}$ operates on optional register pairs (**rpair mreg**) and the state contains a map L from locations (Stack slots and registers) to values. We extend the location map in a straightforward fashion by defining three operations: **combine**, **loword**, and **hiword** to perform splitting and combining on the level of values.

$$L((r1, r2)) \stackrel{def}{=} \mathtt{combine}(L(r1), L(r2)), \text{ and}$$

$$L[(r1, r2) \leftarrow v] \stackrel{def}{=} L[r1 \leftarrow \mathtt{hiword}(v)][r2 \leftarrow \mathtt{loword}(v)].$$

Below, we show the transition rule for $\mathtt{op}_{LTL}$, which is similar to that of RTL, but captures the execution in a basic block, and therefore does not increase the program counter. Note however, that the arguments $\boldsymbol{p}$ and result location p are either single registers or pairs and are evaluated as given above.

$$\frac{\mathtt{eval\_op}(\_, \_, op, L(\boldsymbol{p})) = \lfloor v \rfloor}{\_ \vdash B(\_, \_, \_, \mathtt{op}_{LTL}(op, \boldsymbol{p}, p) :: bb, L, \_) \xrightarrow{\epsilon} B(\_, \_, \_, bb, L[p \leftarrow v], \_)}$$

Proving that an execution of the $\mathtt{op}_{LTL}$ instruction preserves the semantics of an associated $\mathtt{op}_{RTL}$ instruction breaks down to showing that we pass the same values to the operation op, i.e., $R(\boldsymbol{r}) = L(\boldsymbol{p})$. Hence, we need to show that we can correctly use the operations **combine**, **hiword**, and **loword** to split and reconstruct values. While splitting and combining the bit-representation of data is intuitive, we cannot directly model it with CompCert's value representation.

Splitting Values. We cannot give meaning to the splitting and combining of arbitrary values. We define **hiword** and **loword** only on **long** and **double** values and the **combine** operation is only defined for two **int** or two **single** values. We use the constructor **single** to be able to differentiate between split halves of **double** and **long** values. The three operations allow us to split and recombine values of type **double**, captured by Lemma 1.

Lemma 1. $\forall v, \vdash v : \mathtt{double} \Rightarrow v = \mathtt{combine}(\mathtt{hiword}(v), \mathtt{loword}(v))$.

We can state a similar lemma for long with the additional requirement, that for the current target machine, pointers do not have type long. Since pointers do not expose their bit representation, we cannot split them.

Lemma 1 lets us reason about recombining a value that has been previously split, hence allowing us to reason about loading from the register file after a store. The converse is not possible, i.e., we cannot guarantee anything about a value that has been combined with another and then split again. Even if type information is available, since undef is of any type, combining arbitrary values might destroy any information.

4.2 Validating the Allocation Result

The register allocation is performed by untrusted OCaml code. Only the resulting LTL code is checked for semantic preservation of the original RTL code by the formally verified validation algorithm described in [15].

CompCert^p's LTL semantics is the first that allows pairs as operands and the new validator needs to be able to relate the original RTL code, which stores double-precision values in temporaries, to the LTL code, which splits and combines the values stored in pairs. The updated validation algorithm retains the two phases of the original algorithm, first performing structural checks relating the two programs syntactically and then a data-flow analysis relating live temporaries with their allocated register or stack slot.

Our validation algorithm restricts accepted LTL programs to those in which pairs are only used to hold values that can be correctly split and recombined. During the structural checks, we additionally check that the subregisters of a pair are distinct and ensure that, if the operands of a move are pairs, they are disjoint. The data-flow analysis relates temporaries to the machine registers they have been mapped to. If mapped to a pair, we ensure that it contains a value of type long or double. This allows us to make use of Lemma 1, or the corresponding lemma for long, to reason about the result of loading the pair from the location map, relating it to the original value in the RTL code. Going back to the op instructions above, we can then prove that, if the two sets of arguments, r and p, are related by the data-flow analysis, we load the same values from the respective maps.

4.3 Preservation of Callee-Save Registers

Up to the Mach intermediate language the automatic preservation of callee-save registers is built into the semantics of function calls. This is resolved during Stacking, the translation pass from Linear to Mach. It determines the used callee-save registers of a function and inserts instructions into the function prologue and epilogue that ensure their preservation across function calls. The new instructions do not have any corresponding ones in the previous translation passes, setting the Stacking pass apart from other translation passes affected by our changes.

When reasoning about the preservation of callee-save registers, there is no information about their contained values at compile time. This prevents us from storing and loading pairs as we cannot establish correct splitting and recombining of values. The naive solution of just storing each single-precision register individually might double the required load and store instructions.

```
Definition save_callee_rpair m sp ofs p rs :=
  match p with
  | Two r1 r2 => let rhi:= if big_endian then r2 else r1 in
                 let rlo := if big_endian then r1 else r2 in
                 let κ := type_of rlo in
                 let κ' := type_of rhi in
                 if m[(sp,ofs) ←κ rs(rlo)] = ⌊m'⌋
                 then m'[(sp,ofs + |κ|) ←κ' rs(rhi)]
                 else ⊤
  | ...
  end.
```

Fig. 7. Pseudocode of save_callee_rpair for pairs

To resolve this issue, we introduce two new instructions to the Mach intermediate language to perform stack accesses. Unlike the other instructions, Msavecallee and Mrestorecallee do not combine and split values but rather treat the two halves individually. Figure 7 showcases the semantics of Msavecallee for a register pair. We write $m[(sp, ofs) ←_κ v]$ to denote storing a value v of type $κ$ at the location (sp, ofs) in memory m.

Conceptually easy, it also highlights the special care required if we do not perform the splitting and combining at the level of values. The instruction needs to be endian-aware, storing each half at its correct address. In addition, we need to explicitly compute the offset to store the second register.

For the correctness proof we need to show that we can save the register contents onto the stack using Msavecallee instructions and later reload the correct value using Mrestorecallee instructions. We define a separating conjunction contains_rpair depicted in Fig. 8. It is quite similar to save_callee_rpair and has a matching contains predicate for each store. Intuitively, the contains predicate states that the memory m at the given block sp and offset ofs contains a value v of a certain type $κ$. The ** is the star operator from separation logic ensuring disjoint memory regions.

Equipped with the contains_rpair predicate, Fig. 9 states the lemma capturing the use of save_callee_rpair to save a register pair to the stack. As expected, the lemma allows us to establish that, after saving a register to the stack using callee_save_rpair, the memory satisfies the contains_rpair predicate, which states that the memory contains the two values stored in the register pair. The first two assumptions ensure that the registers have the same

```
Definition contains_rpair sp ofs p rs :=
  match p with
  | Two r1 r2 => let rhi := if Archi.big_endian then r2 else r1 in
                 let rlo := if Archi.big_endian then r1 else r2 in
                 let κ := type_of rlo in
                 let κ' := type_of rhi in
                 contains κ sp pos (rs rlo)
                 ** contains κ' sp (pos + |κ|) (rs rhi)
  | ...
  end.
```

Fig. 8. Simplified separating conjunction `contains_rpair`

size and that the size of the pair divides the offset being stored to. This is a requirement to satisfy alignment constraints of the stack. The third assumption states that the memory has a disjoint range from `ofs` to `(ofs + size_of p)` in block `sp` with write access.

```
Lemma contains_rpair_save_callee_rpair:
  forall m sp ofs P p rs,
    wf_pair p ->
    size_of p | ofs ->
    m |= range b ofs (ofs + size_of p) ** P ->
    exists m',
      save_callee_rpair m sp ofs p rs = Some m'
      /\ m' |= contains_rpair sp ofs p rs ** P.
```

Fig. 9. Lemma establishing the correct saving of callee-save registers

When proving the correct preservation of the callee-save registers we rely on the properties and functions showcased above. We can state and prove a similar lemma that allows us to correctly reload the values from the stack given it satisfies the separating conjunction.

The changes to the Mach semantics are also reflected in the Arm assembly semantics. We adapt the semantics of the `Pfldd_a` and `Pfstd_a` instructions, corresponding to the Arm instructions `vldr` and `vstr`, respectively. The instructions have already been introduced to CompCert to handle the loading and storing of callee-save registers. They reflect the semantics of `Msavecallee` and `Mrestorecallee`, now similarly storing the individual registers and explicitly computing the offset. This is defined in accordance with the Arm semantics [3].

5 Experimental Evaluation

The development of CompCert^p builds on CompCert (Release 23.10) distributed by AbsInt and we compare CompCert^p against this release. For a fair comparison, we additionally include a small fix in the unverified post-processing[2], which we discovered during the development of CompCert^p. The artifact [14] published online contains all proofs on the public version of CompCert.

We compare generated code size, compile time, and allocation statistics of CompCert and CompCert^p. We take several benchmarks from the SPEC CPU 2000[3] benchmark suite and three sets of 100 generated C code files: *fuzz1*, *fuzz2*, and *fuzz3*. They contain increasingly complex floating-point expressions and function calls using floating-point parameters. We use them as a stress test of our register allocator to highlight the changes in the code generation of CompCert^p and include them in the artifact.

We run all tests on the RISC-V target as a representative for the architectures that do not support register pairs. For Arm, we run all tests on the two supported Arm ABIs. The hard float ABI uses D0 - D7 (S0 - S15) to pass floating point parameters as described previously. The soft float ABI uses the standard calling conventions to pass arguments in the registers R0-R3 and only uses the floating-point registers for computations. All tests were run on a notebook with an AMD Ryzen 7 Pro 5850U CPU (8 Cores, 16 hardware threads, 1.9/4.4GHz clock) and 32GB of DDR4 RAM running Debian *trixie* (kernel 6.6.15). In an attempt to decrease system noise, we ran all tests in recovery mode, set up a shielded set of cores and set the CPU scaling governor to *performance*. Below we highlight the most interesting changes and include the complete data in the appendix.

5.1 Compile Time

Figure 10 shows the compile times of CompCert^p in relation to CompCert. The measurements for the SPEC benchmarks were repeated 10 times, the others 5 times. We show the standard deviation with error bars. We used `perf`[4] to get timings of the different phases during compilation, giving us an insight into the various tests and how hard their allocation problems are. In most cases, we see an increased time for both register allocation and allocation validation.

In Table 1, we capture the average change in compile time across all benchmark suites for all tested targets. We see a slight increase in total compile time and for Arm a significant increase in the time it takes to validate the allocation result. Since allocation validation is usually short, this does not contribute a big increase to the total compile time.

---

[2] https://github.com/AbsInt/CompCert/commit/ccb88a8.
[3] https://www.spec.org/cpu2000.
[4] https://perf.wiki.kernel.org.

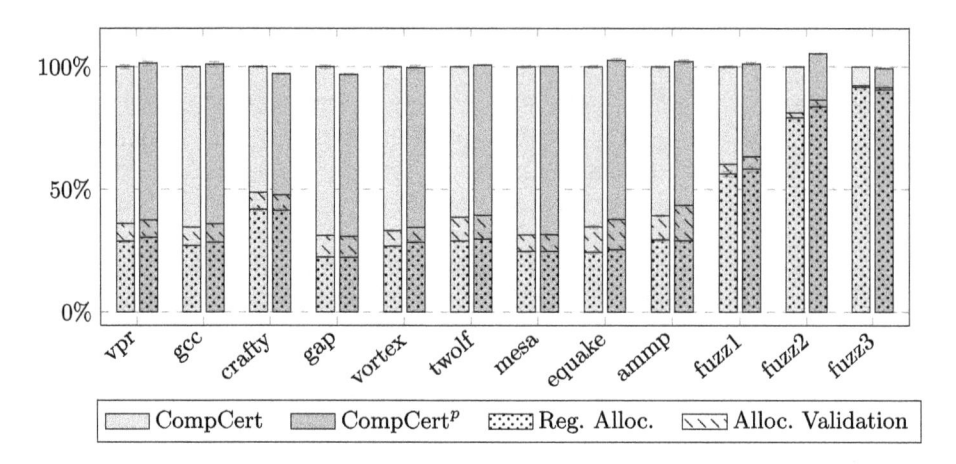

Fig. 10. Relative compile times for Arm (hard float).

Table 1. Relative change in compile times split into phases

Phase	arm_hard	arm_soft	riscv
Register Allocation	+2.41%	+2.0%	+4.00%
Allocation Validation	+10.94%	+11.66%	+1.17%
Remaining Translations	−1.43%	−0.55%	+0.59%
Total compile time	+0.59%	+0.54%	+1.91%

5.2 Code Size

Since many of the SPEC benchmarks do not operate on floating-point values, code size does not change significantly for most of the contained test suites. Hence, we only report on the *vpr* and *mesa* benchmarks, which contain a significant number of floating point operations, and our generated *fuzz* benchmarks.

Table 2 contains the change in the generated code size of CompCert[p] in relation to CompCert. We see the biggest improvements in our generated test cases for the Arm hard float target. Omitting the unverified pass that inserts moves around function calls significantly decreases code size. For the soft float target, we see a smaller impact and even a slight increase in code size for some benchmarks. The soft float ABI only uses four 32-bit registers to pass arguments and we suspect this bottleneck to decrease the positive effects of the additional available registers. Since it does not use the previously unmodeled single-precision registers to pass arguments, it does not benefit from the omission of move instructions.

Table 2. Relative change in generated code size for Arm

ABI	vpr	mesa	fuzz1	fuzz2	fuzz3
hard float	−0.83%	−1.77%	−4.78%	−4.7%	−4.7%
soft float	−0.2%	−0.71%	−0.2%	+0.19%	+0.27%

5.3 Allocation Statistics

We list detailed allocator statistics for those benchmarks for which we recorded the code size in Sect. 5.2. We capture the moves remaining in the program after register allocation and the moves inserted by the unverified pass for the hard float ABI. Additionally, we record the number of reloads and spills inserted by the allocator. For the fuzzed suites we take the average of all contained test cases.

Table 3 contains the statistics for the hard float ABI. We can see that the post-processing phase of CompCert, necessary to comply with Arm's calling conventions, inserts a considerable amount of moves, whereas this is not necessary in CompCert^p. In all benchmarks, except for *vpr*, we recorded a considerable reduction in spills or reloads. Note, that we do not count reloads that happen as part of enforcing the calling conventions.

Table 3. Selected register allocation statistics for Arm (hard float)

Instance	Remaining C	Remaining C^p	Inserted C	Inserted C^p	Spills C	Spills C^p	Reloads C	Reloads C^p
vpr	4557	4557	165	0	275	275	298	297
mesa	13414	13420	939	0	1401	1276	2265	2133
fuzz1	119	118	40	0	17	17	17	15
fuzz2	404	404	148	0	115	115	74	65
fuzz3	1515	1515	533	0	456	461	267	226

For the soft float ABI, the difference between CompCert and CompCert^p is less significant. For the *vpr* benchmark, their output is similar and for the other affected benchmarks, the improvements are smaller. For details we refer to the appendix.

5.4 Summary

To sum up, CompCert^p generally improves on CompCert in terms of code generation. It either generates similar or smaller code if floating-point calculations are performed by the input program. The improvement comes from the omission of move instructions inserted by CompCert's unverified post-processing and a decrease in spill code. This comes at the cost of a slightly increased compile time for all architectures.

6 Conclusion

CompCert^p's adapted backend supports register pairs such that the semantics of architectures with no pair support are not affected. We revise the Arm semantics of CompCert to include register pairs, allowing us to correctly implement the calling conventions for floating-point arguments in the proven part of CompCert^p. We can therefore omit a previously required, unverified post-processing step of CompCert, thereby increasing the trust in the correctness proof. With support for register pairs in the backend of the compiler, we are now able to support a TriCore backend which is under development.

We perform extensive tests on well-known benchmarks and generated test cases showing that CompCert^p either generates smaller or similar code with a slightly increased compile time.

Acknowledgments. We thank Bernhard Schommer, Michael Schmidt, and Christoph Mallon at AbsInt for valuable discussions about CompCert and register allocation.

Disclosure of Interests. The authors have no competing interests to declare that are relevant to the content of this article.

Appendix

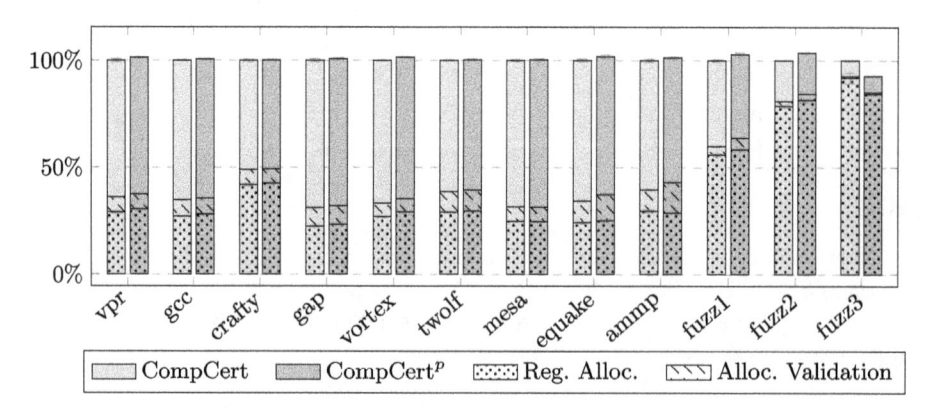

Fig. 11. Relative compile time: Arm (soft float).

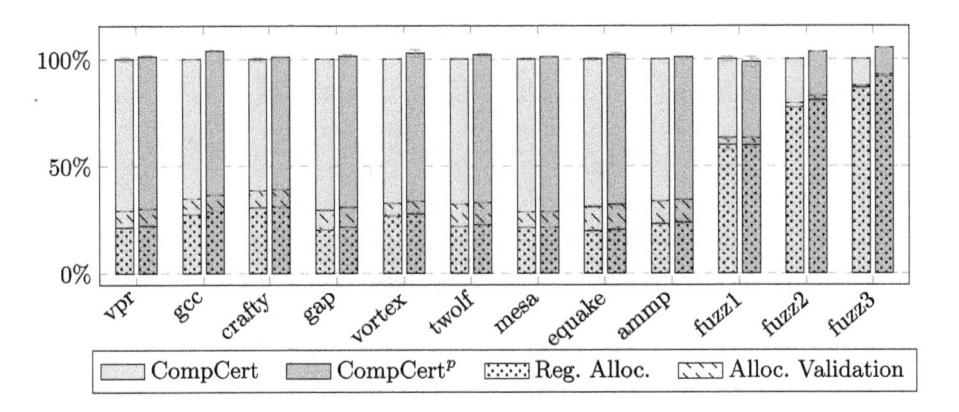

Fig. 12. Relative compile time: RISC-V.

Table 4. Register allocation statistics for Arm (hard float)

Instance	Remaining		Inserted		Spills		Reloads	
	C	C^p	C	C^p	C	C^p	C	C^p
vpr	4557	4557	165	0	275	275	298	297
gcc	52810	52810	0	0	1125	1125	2006	2006
crafty	19501	19501	0	0	512	512	240	241
gap	20145	20145	0	0	390	390	869	869
vortex	19542	19542	0	0	266	266	324	324
twolf	8888	8888	0	0	342	342	506	506
mesa	13414	13420	939	0	1401	1276	2265	2133
equake	631	631	0	0	1	1	2	2
ammp	3995	3995	0	0	114	114	333	333
fuzz1	119	118	40	0	17	17	17	15
fuzz2	404	404	148	0	115	115	74	65
fuzz3	1515	1515	533	0	456	461	267	226

Table 5. Register allocation statistics for Arm (soft float)

Instance	Remaining		Spills		Reloads	
	C	C^p	C	C^p	C	C^p
vpr	4557	4557	275	275	298	297
gcc	52810	52810	1125	1125	2006	2006
crafty	19501	19501	512	512	240	241
gap	20145	20145	390	390	869	869
vortex	19542	19542	266	266	324	324
twolf	8888	8888	342	342	506	506
mesa	13415	13420	1398	1276	2260	2133
equake	631	631	1	1	2	2
ammp	3995	3995	114	114	333	333
fuzz1	119	119	17	17	17	16
fuzz2	403	404	115	116	75	68
fuzz3	1515	1562	456	472	268	242

References

1. Anand, A., et al.: CertiCoq: a verified compiler for Coq. In: The Third International Workshop on Coq for Programming Languages (CoqPL) (2017)
2. Appel, A.W.: Verified software toolchain. In: Barthe, G. (ed.) ESOP 2011. LNCS, vol. 6602, pp. 1–17. Springer, Heidelberg (2011). https://doi.org/10.1007/978-3-642-19718-5_1
3. Arm Limited: Arm architecture reference manual for a-profile architecture. https://developer.arm.com/documentation/ddi0487
4. Barthe, G., et al.: Formal verification of a constant-time preserving c compiler. Proc. ACM Program. Lang. **4**(POPL) (2019). https://doi.org/10.1145/3371075
5. Barthe, G., Demange, D., Pichardie, D.: Formal verification of an SSA-based middle-end for CompCert. ACM Trans. Program. Lang. Syst. **36**(1) (2014). https://doi.org/10.1145/2579080
6. Bedin França, R., Blazy, S., Favre-Felix, D., Leroy, X., Pantel, M., Souyris, J.: Formally verified optimizing compilation in ACG-based flight control software. In: ERTS2 2012: Embedded Real Time Software and Systems. AAAF, SEE, Toulouse, France (2012)
7. Blazy, S., Dargaye, Z., Leroy, X.: Formal verification of a C compiler front-end. In: Misra, J., Nipkow, T., Sekerinski, E. (eds.) FM 2006. LNCS, vol. 4085, pp. 460–475. Springer, Heidelberg (2006). https://doi.org/10.1007/11813040_31
8. Briggs, P., Cooper, K.D., Torczon, L.: Improvements to graph coloring register allocation. ACM Trans. Program. Lang. Syst. **16**(3), 428–455 (1994). https://doi.org/10.1145/177492.177575
9. George, L., Appel, A.W.: Iterated register coalescing. ACM Trans. Program. Lang. Syst. **18**(3), 300–324 (1996). https://doi.org/10.1145/229542.229546

10. Kästner, D., et al.: CompCert: practical experience on integrating and qualifying a formally verified optimizing compiler. In: ERTS2 2018 - 9th European Congress Embedded Real-Time Software and Systems, pp. 1–9. 3AF, SEE, SIE, Toulouse, France (2018)
11. Leroy, X.: A formally verified compiler back-end. J. Autom. Reason. **43**(4), 363–446 (2009). https://doi.org/10.1007/s10817-009-9155-4
12. Leroy, X.: The compcert C verified compiler: documentation and user's manual (2023)
13. Leroy, X., Appel, A.W., Blazy, S., Stewart, G.: The CompCert memory model. In: Appel, A.W. (ed.) Program Logics for Certified Compilers. Cambridge University Press, Cambridge (2014). https://doi.org/10.1017/CBO9781107256552.037
14. Loitzl, A.: Artifact for "Modeling Register Pairs in CompCert". https://doi.org/10.5281/zenodo.12010656
15. Rideau, S., Leroy, X.: Validating register allocation and spilling. In: Gupta, R. (ed.) CC 2010. LNCS, vol. 6011, pp. 224–243. Springer, Heidelberg (2010). https://doi.org/10.1007/978-3-642-11970-5_13
16. Runeson, J., Nyström, S.-O.: Retargetable graph-coloring register allocation for irregular architectures. In: Krall, A. (ed.) SCOPES 2003. LNCS, vol. 2826, pp. 240–254. Springer, Heidelberg (2003). https://doi.org/10.1007/978-3-540-39920-9_17
17. Smith, M.D., Ramsey, N., Holloway, G.: A generalized algorithm for graph-coloring register allocation. SIGPLAN Not. **39**(6), 277–288 (2004). https://doi.org/10.1145/996893.996875
18. Song, Y., Cho, M., Kim, D., Kim, Y., Kang, J., Hur, C.K.: Compcertm: Compcert with c-assembly linking and lightweight modular verification. Proc. ACM Program. Lang. **4**(POPL) (2019). https://doi.org/10.1145/3371091
19. Yang, X., Chen, Y., Eide, E., Regehr, J.: Finding and understanding bugs in c compilers. In: Proceedings of the 32nd ACM SIGPLAN Conference on Programming Language Design and Implementation, PLDI 2011, pp. 283–294. Association for Computing Machinery, New York (2011). https://doi.org/10.1145/1993498.1993532

Quantitative Analysis

Monitoring Extended Hypernode Logic

Marek Chalupa[✉], Thomas A. Henzinger, and Ana Oliveira da Costa

Institute of Science and Technology Austria (ISTA),
Klosterneuburg, Austria
{mchalupa,tah,ana.costa}@ista.ac.at

Abstract. *Hypernode logic* can reason about the prefix relation on stutter-reduced finite traces through the *stutter-reduced prefix predicate*. We increase the expressiveness of hypernode logic in two ways. First, we split the stutter-reduced prefix predicate into an explicit stutter-reduction operator and the classical prefix predicate on words. This change gives hypernode logic the ability to combine synchronous and asynchronous reasoning by explicitly stating which parts of traces can stutter. Second, we allow the use of regular expressions in formulas to reason about the structure of traces. This change enables hypernode logic to describe a mixture of trace properties and hyperproperties.

We show how to translate extended hypernode logic formulas into multi-track automata, which are automata that read multiple input words. Then we describe a fully online monitoring algorithm for monitoring k-safety hyperproperties specified in the logic. We have implemented the monitoring algorithm, and evaluated it on monitoring synchronous and asynchronous versions of observational determinism, and on checking the privacy preservation by compiler optimizations.

1 Introduction

Runtime Verification (RV) is the act of formally analyzing traces obtained from a running system. The analyzer is called *monitor* and runs either *online* alongside the system, or *offline* if it analyzes traces from log files. Initially, the domain of RV was verifying (*monitoring*) *trace properties* [1], i.e., properties of individual traces. Recently, motivated mainly by software security, lots of attention is paid to RV of *hyperproperties* [23] that describe *relations* between traces.

In this paper, we are concerned with online RV of hyperproperties specified in an extended version of *hypernode logic* [9]. The main feature of hypernode logic is the *stutter-reduced prefix predicate* $\precsim$ that is satisfied for two finite traces iff the first one is a prefix of the other after removing stuttering from both of them. For example, $aabccc \precsim abbbca$ holds because after removing stuttering from both sides, we get that abc is a prefix of $abca$.

This work was supported in part by the ERC-2020-AdG 101020093, and by the Austrian Science Fund (FWF) SFB project SpyCoDe F8502.

$$\forall \pi, \pi' : (\mathbf{i_1}(\pi) \precsim \mathbf{i_1}(\pi') \land \mathbf{i_2}(\pi) \precsim \mathbf{i_2}(\pi'))$$
$$\implies (\mathbf{o_1}(\pi) \precsim \mathbf{o_1}(\pi') \land \mathbf{o_2}(\pi) \precsim \mathbf{o_2}(\pi'))$$

Fig. 1. A hypernode logic formula describing asynchronous version of observational determinism for two input and two output variables (left), and a hypernode automaton checking for observational determinism with declassification of the second set of variables (right).

The stutter-reduced prefix predicate, together with boolean operations and quantification over traces, makes hypernode logic suitable for describing important security properties like asynchronous *observational determinism (OD)* [28, 37] and *generalized non-interference (GNI)* [34]. The synchronous version of OD states that, whenever two execution traces agree on publicly visible inputs, they must agree on publicly visible outputs. The asynchronous version adds that this requirement must hold up to stuttering and prefixing of the traces. For example, if we have two public input variables $\mathbf{i_1}$ and $\mathbf{i_2}$, and two public output variables $\mathbf{o_1}$ and $\mathbf{o_2}$, asynchronous OD can be specified by the formula on the left in Fig. 1. In the formula, the expression $\mathbf{i}(\pi)$ is the projection of trace π to values of variable $\mathbf{i}$. This projection is another standard part of hypernode logic, because traces are sequences of valuations of variables (i.e., snapshots of states).

Although hypernode logic can be used as a stand-alone specification language, it was introduced to label the states of *hypernode automata* [9]. Hypernode automata are finite-state automata with actions over edges that enable to switch between specifications in the states. Intuitively, the semantics of a hypernode automaton is such that the input set of traces must satisfy the formula in the initial state of the automaton *until* an *action* is seen, at which point the state of the automaton is changed according to the action; the continuation of the traces after the seen action must satisfy the formula from the new state until next action is seen, and so on. For example, consider the hypernode automaton on the right in Fig. 1. In its initial state, the automaton checks OD for all variables. At the moment when the action `declassify_2` comes (as a special event on the trace), the automaton changes state and checks OD only for variables $\mathbf{i_1}$ and $\mathbf{o_1}$. The declassification is reverted if the action `classify_2` occurs.

In this paper, we extend hypernode logic in two directions. First, we add regular expressions to the logic, which allows to reason about the structure of traces. Second, we split the $\precsim$ predicate into an explicit *stutter-reduction operator* $\lfloor \cdot \rfloor$, and the classical prefix relation $\leq$. In the *extended hypernode logic (eHL)*, we can write the following formulas:

$$\lfloor \mathbf{x}(\pi) \rfloor \leq \lfloor \mathbf{y}(\pi') \rfloor \qquad \lfloor \mathbf{x}(\pi) \rfloor \leq (a.b)^* \qquad aa.\lfloor \mathbf{x}(\pi) \rfloor.aa = \mathbf{y}(\pi)$$

The formula on the left is equivalent to the formula $\mathbf{x}(\pi) \precsim \mathbf{y}(\pi')$ in the original hypernode logic. The middle formula expresses a trace property that the values of $\mathbf{x}$ on trace π after removing stuttering must follow the pattern *ababab*.... The last formula says that values of variable **y** on trace π start and end with two *a*s, and the rest coincides with the stutter-reduced values of **x** on the same trace.

Using quantification, we can express a mix of synchronous and asynchronous hyperproperties and trace properties. For example, consider the formula below

$$\forall \pi : 0^*.1 \leq \mathbf{flag}(\pi) \implies \exists \pi' : (\mathbf{flag}(\pi') \leq 0^* \land \lfloor \mathbf{x}(\pi) \rfloor = \lfloor \mathbf{x}(\pi') \rfloor).$$

This formula specifies that for any program execution π where **flag** is set to *true*, there must exist another execution where this flag is never set, and these executions coincide on values of **x** modulo stuttering.

Beyond obtaining a more expressive version of hypernode automata, our main motivation for extending hypernode logic is its RV. The logic eHL is expressive enough to describe many interesting asynchronous hyperproperties, while it admits an RV algorithm that is efficient for many such hyperproperties. In the main part of this paper, we show how to translate eHL formulas into *2-track automata with priorities* on edges, and we formulate a fully online monitoring algorithm that instantiates these automata to monitor $\forall^*$-quantified eHL formulas. These formulas define a subset of *k-safety* hyperproperties [23], which can be monitored for violations, and include many relevant security policies.

Contributions

- We define the logic eHL by extending hypernode logic with *regular expressions* and the *stutter-reduction operator* that allows to selectively specify what parts of traces are allowed to stutter. As a result, we get an asynchronous hyperlogic that can describe relations between traces that are partially synchronous and partially asynchronous, but also regular trace properties of finite traces.
- We define a translation of the eHL into multi-track automata that allow to evaluate a formula of eHL on a tuple of fixed traces.
- We define a monitoring algorithm for monitoring the eHL that uses the multi-track automata from the previous point.
- We implemented the translation and the monitoring algorithm to monitor universally quantified eHL formulas, and evaluated it on monitoring various versions of observational determinism.

2 Preliminaries

An *alphabet* is a finite set of letters (symbols). *Words* are finite sequences of letters from an alphabet, and a *language* is a set of finite words. A *regular expression (RE)* describes a language using the syntax $\alpha ::= \emptyset \mid \epsilon \mid a \mid \alpha.\alpha \mid \alpha + \alpha \mid \alpha^*$ where a's are symbols from an alphabet. The language of a regular expression is defined recursively as

$$\mathcal{L}(\emptyset) = \emptyset \qquad \mathcal{L}(\epsilon) = \{\epsilon\} \qquad \mathcal{L}(a) = \{a\}$$
$$\mathcal{L}(\alpha.\alpha') = \mathcal{L}(\alpha).\mathcal{L}(\alpha') \quad \mathcal{L}(\alpha + \alpha') = \mathcal{L}(\alpha) \cup \mathcal{L}(\alpha') \quad \mathcal{L}(\alpha^*) = \bigcup_{n \in \mathbb{N}} \mathcal{L}(\alpha)^n$$

where $L.L' = \{w.w' \mid w \in L \text{ and } w' \in L'\}$, and $L^n = L.L^{n-1}$ with $L^0 = \{\epsilon\}$. We use the standard shortcut $\alpha^+ \stackrel{\text{def}}{=} \alpha.\alpha^*$. For a word $w = uv$, we say that u is a *prefix of* w, denoted $u \leq w$. For sets of words U, V we define that $U \leq V$ if for any $u \in U$ there exists $v \in V$ s.t. $u \leq v$.

Let X be a finite set of *program variables* over a finite domain $\mathcal{D}$. A *valuation* $v: X \to \mathcal{D}$ is a mapping from program variables X to their domain $\mathcal{D}$, with the set of all valuations denoted $\mathcal{D}^X$. A *trace* is a word over $\mathcal{D}^X$ and, in this context, a valuation is called *event*.

A *hyperproperty* **H** defines a set of sets of traces[1]. A set of traces S satisfies a hyperproperty if $S \in \mathbf{H}$. The *hyperproperty monitoring problem* asks whether a *finite* set of traces implies the satisfaction or violation of a given hyperproperty. Finally, a hyperproperty **H** is k-*safety hyperproperty* if for every $S \notin \mathbf{H}$, there exist $O \leq S$ with $|O| \leq k$, s.t. O implies the violation of **H**. In other words, if the violation of **H** can be witnessed by at most k traces.

3 Hypernode Logic

Bartocci et al. [9] introduced hypernode logic to compare prefixing of traces while ignoring stuttering of letters.

The formulas of hypernode logic are defined by the grammar $\varphi ::= \exists \pi \, \varphi \mid \neg \varphi \mid \varphi \wedge \varphi \mid x(\pi) \precsim x(\pi)$, where the first-order variable π ranges over a set $\mathcal{V}$ of trace variables and the unary function symbol x ranges over the set X of program variables.

Hypernode logic refers to time only through the binary *stutter-reduced prefix* predicate $\precsim$. Intuitively, $x(\pi) \precsim y(\pi')$ is true if the sequence of values of x in trace π is a prefix of the sequence of values of y in π' given that we ignore stuttering. For example, $aabaabbb \precsim ababab$, because when we remove stuttering on both sides, we get that $abab$ (the left side) is a prefix of $ababab$ (the right side).

3.1 Extended Hypernode Logic

We extend hypernode logic by adding an explicit *stutter-reduction operator* $\lfloor \cdot \rfloor$, which marks parts of formula that should ignore stuttering. With this operator, we do not need the special stutter-reduced prefix predicate $\precsim$ if we have the classical prefix relation on words $\leq$, because we can define $\varphi_1 \precsim \varphi_2$ as $\lfloor \varphi_1 \rfloor \leq \lfloor \varphi_2 \rfloor$. These changes have the effect that we can select which parts of traces are allowed to stutter and which not, allowing to combine synchronicity and asynchronicity in a single logic. In valuation-based traces like those used in hypernode logic, stuttering arises in situations when some asynchronous components progress while the others may be stalling or waiting.

Additionally, we extend the logic by allowing formulas to contain regular expressions over constants. They are useful to describe prefixes and suffixes of

---

[1] Hypernode logic is meant for finite traces and so we work with finite traces only. Usually, traces can be also infinite (and hypernode logic extends to infinite traces through hypernode automata [9]).

traces. For example, we can use regular expressions to check that the **x** component of a trace π starts with a or b with the formula $(a+b) \leq \mathbf{x}(\pi)$. By adding regular expressions, we can describe many finite regular trace properties.

Syntax. The formulas of extended hypernode logic are defined by the grammar:

$$\psi ::= \epsilon \mid c \mid \mathbf{x}(\pi) \mid \psi.\psi \mid \psi+\psi \mid \psi^* \mid \lfloor\psi\rfloor$$
$$\varphi ::= \exists \pi \, \varphi \mid \neg\varphi \mid \varphi \wedge \varphi \mid \psi \leq \psi$$

where c are constant symbols from a finite alphabet disjoint with $\mathcal{V}$ and X. As usual, we drop the dot symbol from $\psi.\psi$ and write only $\psi\psi$ where the meaning is clear (with the usual operator binding precedence). Formulas generated by the non-terminal ψ are called *trace formulas* and formulas of the form $\psi \leq \psi$ are called *atomic comparisons* or simply *atoms*.

Semantics. We first define the semantics of trace formulas. We interpret them over a trace assignment $\Pi : \mathcal{V} \to (\mathcal{D}^X)^*$ that assigns trace variables to traces:

$$\Pi[\![c]\!] = \{c\} \qquad\qquad \Pi[\![\psi.\psi']\!] = \Pi[\![\psi]\!].\Pi[\![\psi']\!]$$
$$\Pi[\![\epsilon]\!] = \{\epsilon\} \qquad\qquad \Pi[\![\psi+\psi']\!] = \Pi[\![\psi]\!] \cup \Pi[\![\psi']\!]$$
$$\Pi[\![\mathbf{x}(\pi)]\!] = \{(\Pi(\pi))(\mathbf{x})\} \qquad\qquad \Pi[\![\psi^*]\!] = \bigcup_{n \in \mathbb{N}} \Pi[\![\psi]\!]^n$$

$$\Pi[\![\lfloor\psi\rfloor]\!] = \{<_1 <_2 \cdots <_k \mid <_1^+ <_2^+ \cdots <_k^+ \in \Pi[\![\psi]\!], <_i \neq <_{i+1} \text{ for } 1 \leq i < k\}$$

The semantics of trace formulas corresponds precisely to regular expressions apart from the interpretation of trace variables and the stutter-reduction operation, which have no counter-parts in regular expressions.

The satisfaction relation $\models$ for a formula of eHL over a trace assignment Π is standard apart for the prefix operator. Because we allow choice and iteration, their evaluation defines a set of words. Therefore, the semantics for the prefix predicate must be extended to sets of words. Our semantics quantifies existentially over all the possible words defined by the trace formulas we are comparing. Altogether, the satisfaction relation is defined as:

$$\Pi \models \exists \pi \varphi \text{ iff there exists } \tau \in T : \Pi[\pi \mapsto \tau] \models \varphi;$$
$$\Pi \models \neg\varphi_1 \text{ iff } \Pi \not\models \varphi_1;$$
$$\Pi \models \varphi_1 \wedge \varphi_2 \text{ iff } \Pi \models \varphi_1 \text{ and } \Pi \models \varphi_2;$$
$$\Pi \models \psi_1 \leq \psi_2 \text{ iff } \exists w_1 \in \Pi[\![\psi_1]\!], \exists w_2 \in \Pi[\![\psi_2]\!] : w_1 \leq w_2$$

Simple eHL Formulas. An important restriction that we make for this paper is that we restrict ourselves only to *simple* eHL formulas.

Definition 1 (Simple eHL formula). *A formula of eHL is called* simple *if any trace sub-formula contains at most one symbol $\mathbf{x}(\pi)$ and this symbol is not inside iteration.*

Atomic	Partial derivatives	Multi-track	Multi-track automaton
comparison	automaton	automaton	with priorities
(over alphabet Σ)	(over alphabet $\Sigma_x^\oplus$)	(over alphabet $\Sigma_x^\oplus$)	(over alphabet Σ)

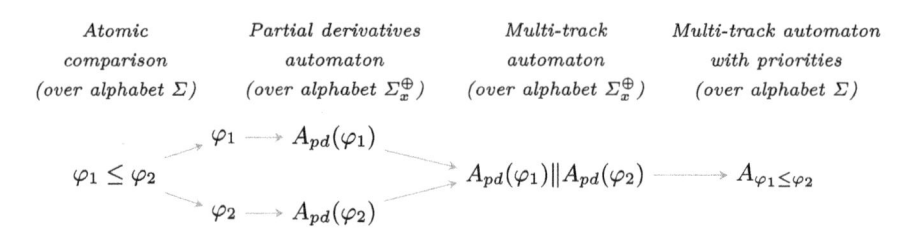

$$\varphi_1 \leq \varphi_2 \quad \begin{array}{c} \varphi_1 \longrightarrow A_{pd}(\varphi_1) \\ \varphi_2 \longrightarrow A_{pd}(\varphi_2) \end{array} \quad A_{pd}(\varphi_1) \| A_{pd}(\varphi_2) \longrightarrow A_{\varphi_1 \leq \varphi_2}$$

Fig. 2. A scheme of the translation of an atom to a multi-track automaton.

For example, $a\lfloor b\mathbf{x}(\pi)\rfloor \leq \mathbf{y}(\pi)$ or $\mathbf{x}(\pi) \leq \mathbf{y}(\pi)$ are simple, while $\mathbf{y}(\pi)\mathbf{x}(\pi) \leq ab$ or $\mathbf{y}(\pi)\mathbf{x}(\pi) \leq \mathbf{y}(\pi)$ or $(a + \mathbf{x}(\pi))^* \leq (ab)^*$ are not simple. In general, trace formulas are of the form α or $\alpha.\mathbf{x}(\pi).\beta$ where α and β are regular expressions, and some sub-formulas are possibly wrapped in the stutter-reduction operator.

The goal of the restriction to simple formulas is to forbid the concatenation of two traces, which would not allow translating the formulas into automata as described in Sect. 4. The class of simple eHL formulas is rich enough to describe all properties that we are interested in. In the rest of the paper, we work only with simple formulas and call them only *formulas*.

4 Translating eHL to Automata

In this section, we show a construction of *finite 2-track automata with priorities* that evaluate atomic comparisons over two input words. We do not cover the boolean structure and quantification by the translation, because they will be handled separately by our monitoring algorithm in the next section.

The process of translating an atomic comparison is pictured in Fig. 2. During the translation, we first generate finite automata for each trace formula in the comparison using *partial derivatives* [8] of regular expressions that we have extended to work with eHL formulas. These automata are over an extended alphabet where symbols carry information whether they have been read from a trace variable or/and from a stutter-reduced part of a formula. Then we compose these automata using a form of synchronous product into a 2-track automaton. Finally, we translate this 2-track automaton (which is still over the extended alphabet) into a 2-track automaton over the original alphabet, but with priorities on edges. The final automaton is over the original alphabet.

4.1 Trace Formula Derivatives

Trace formulas in eHL can be viewed as REs extended with the stutter-reduction operator and program variables. We begin this section with reviewing partial derivatives of REs and the construction of partial derivative automata.

Partial Derivatives of Regular Expressions. The construction procedure of the automaton for atomic comparisons is based on *partial derivatives* [8,36] of regular expressions. Given a regular expression α over the alphabet Σ, the *set of partial derivatives* $D_a(\alpha)$ w.r.t. letter a is defined recursively as

$$D_a(\emptyset) = D_a(\epsilon) = \emptyset \tag{1}$$

$$D_a(a') = \begin{cases} \{\epsilon\} & \text{if } a = a' \\ \emptyset & \text{otherwise} \end{cases} \tag{2}$$

$$D_a(\alpha_1 + \alpha_2) = D_a(\alpha_1) \cup D_a(\alpha_2) \tag{3}$$

$$D_a(\alpha_1.\alpha_2) = D_a(\alpha_1).\{\alpha_2\} \cup D_a(\nu(\alpha_1)\alpha_2) \tag{4}$$

$$D_a(\alpha^*) = D_a(\alpha).\{\alpha^*\} \tag{5}$$

where ν is the *nullability* predicate defined as $\nu(\alpha) = \epsilon$ if $\epsilon \in \mathcal{L}(\alpha)$ and $\emptyset$ otherwise. We can compute this predicate from the structure of α [18,36]. We also define derivatives w.r.t. words, languages, and derivatives of sets of expressions as usual:

$$D_\epsilon(\alpha) = \{\alpha\} \qquad D_{aw}(\alpha) = D_w(D_a(\alpha))$$
$$D_L(\alpha) = \bigcup_{w \in L} D_w(\alpha) \qquad D_w(A) = \bigcup_{\alpha \in A} D_w(\alpha).$$

Antimirov has proven that the set of partial derivatives of a regular expression w.r.t. an arbitrary word is finite.

Theorem 1 ([8, Corollary 3.5]). *For any regular expression α over an alphabet Σ and any word $w \in \Sigma^*$ it holds that $D_w(\alpha)$ is finite.*

A consequence of this theorem is that we can build a non-deterministic finite automaton $A_{pd}(\alpha)$ that recognizes $\mathcal{L}(\alpha)$ for an RE α [8, Theorem 4.1].

Definition 2 (Partial derivative automaton A_{pd}). *Given an RE α over an alphabet Σ, the* partial derivative automaton $A_{pd}(\alpha)$ *is the non-deterministic automaton*

$$A_{pd}(\alpha) = (D_{\Sigma^*}(\alpha), \Sigma, \delta_\alpha, \alpha, F_\alpha)$$

where $D_{\Sigma^*}(\alpha)$ is the set of states with α being the initial state and $F_\alpha = \{\alpha' \in D_{\Sigma^*}(\alpha) \mid \nu(\alpha') = \epsilon\}$ being the final states. For any $\alpha' \in D_{\Sigma^*}(\alpha)$ and $a \in \Sigma$, the partial transition function δ_α is defined as $\delta_\alpha(\alpha', a) = D_a(\alpha')$ if $D_a(\alpha') \neq \emptyset$.

If it is clear or not important from the context what is α, we write just A_{pd} instead of $A_{pd}(\alpha)$.

Derivatives of Trace Formulas. Our goal is to extend partial derivatives of regular expressions to trace formulas. For formulas that coincide with regular expressions, their derivative is the partial derivative as if the formula is taken as regular expression; we abuse the notation and use such formulas and regular expressions interchangeably.

Let us introduce some preliminaries first. For a regular expression α, function *first*(α) gives the set of letters that are at the beginning of some word in $\mathcal{L}(\alpha)$: *first*$(\alpha) = \{a \mid au \in \mathcal{L}(\alpha), a \in \Sigma\}$. It can be computed from the structure of α [16]. Derivatives of stutter-reduced formulas will be defined w.r.t.. letters $a^{\oplus}$, and derivatives of values of program variables w.r.t.. letters a_x for $a \in \Sigma$. Altogether, we are going to work with the alphabet

$$\Sigma_x^{\oplus} = \bigcup_{a \in \Sigma} \{a, a_x, a^{\oplus}, a_x^{\oplus}\}.$$

Note that Eqs. (1)–(5) work for marked letters without any change. Taking derivatives of the rest of formulas w.r.t. marked letters is the subject of the subsequent text. Unless stated otherwise, from now on if we write letter a without any marks, we mean a letter from the original alphabet Σ.

Finally, we define the function $rm : \Sigma_x^{\oplus} \to \Sigma$ as $rm(y) = a$ iff $y \in \{a, a_x, a^{\oplus}, a_x^{\oplus}\}$. This function removes marks from any letter $a \in \Sigma_x^{\oplus}$. We extend it to words as $rm(a.w) = rm(a).rm(w)$ and $rm(\epsilon) = \epsilon$.

Formulas with Lookahead and Their Derivatives. For defining the derivatives of stutter-reduced formulas, we extend formulas with a single-letter lookahead. The syntax we use is $\varphi \mid A$ for the formula φ, where the lookahead set of letters $A \subseteq \Sigma$ define the letters that may be consumed from the formula as the next letter. We always use lookahead sets $\bar{a}$ for some letter $a \in \Sigma$, which represents the set $\Sigma \setminus \{a\}$. For example, $((a + b).\mathbf{x}(t)) \mid \bar{b}$ means that the next letter that can be consumed from the formula $(a+b).\mathbf{x}(t)$ is not b, and therefore the whole formula is equivalent to $a.\mathbf{x}(t)$. The *first* of formulas with lookahead is empty if the (unmarked) lookahead letter is mismatched, *first*$(\alpha \mid A) =$ *first*$(\alpha) \cap A$, while the nullability predicate ignores the lookahead, $\nu(\alpha \mid A) = \nu(\alpha)$. The derivative of formulas with lookahead is defined as

$$D_m(\alpha \mid A) = \begin{cases} D_m(\alpha) & \text{if } rm(m) \in A \text{ for } m \in \Sigma_x^{\oplus} \\ \emptyset & \text{otherwise} \end{cases} \quad (6)$$

Derivatives of Stutter-Reduced Formulas. To distinguish the cases when we ignore stuttering and when not, we define the derivatives of stutter-reduced formulas only w.r.t. letters marked with symbol $^{\oplus}$. Intuitively, deriving a word w.r.t. $a^{\oplus}$ removes the *longest (non-empty) repetition of a* from its beginning. The nullability predicate and function *first* for stutter-reduced formulas are defined by the equations $\nu(\lfloor \alpha \rfloor) = \nu(\alpha)$ and *first*$(\lfloor \alpha \rfloor) =$ *first*(α), resp., and the derivatives involving stutter-reduction operator are defined as:

$$D_a(\lfloor \alpha \rfloor) = D_{a_x}(\lfloor \alpha \rfloor) = \emptyset \quad (7)$$

$$D_{a^\oplus}(\lfloor\alpha\rfloor) = \{(\lfloor\alpha'\rfloor \mid \bar{a}) \mid \alpha' \in D_{a^+}(\tilde\alpha)\} \tag{8}$$
$$D_{a_x^\oplus}(\lfloor\alpha\rfloor) = \{(\lfloor\alpha'\rfloor \mid \bar{a})) \mid \alpha' \in D_{a^* a_x^+ a^*}(\tilde\alpha)\} \tag{9}$$

The expression $\tilde\alpha$ is α with every stutter-reduced sub-formula $\lfloor\beta\rfloor$ replaced with β. In other words, $\tilde\alpha$ removes all stutter-reduction operators from α. The justification for using $\tilde\alpha$ is that removing stuttering from a stutter-reduced word yields the same word, and therefore $\mathcal{L}(\lfloor\alpha\rfloor) = \mathcal{L}(\lfloor\tilde\alpha\rfloor)$. Removing the nested stutter-reduction operators is important in order to avoid complications with recursion in Eqs. (8) and (9).

Equation (7) guarantees that we have (non-empty) derivatives of stutter-reduced formulas only w.r.t. $^\oplus$-marked letters. Equation (8) computes derivatives of $\tilde\alpha$ w.r.t. language a^+, that is, w.r.t. any non-empty string of a's. The maximality is achieved by wrapping the resulting derivatives with the lookahead that forbids a being the next letter in the resulting formulas.

Equation (9) is similar to Eq. (8), but it computes derivatives w.r.t. the language $a^* a_x^+ a^*$. To see why it is the case and it is not enough to take derivatives w.r.t. the language a_x^+, consider, for example, the formula $\lfloor aa\mathbf{x}(\pi)a^*\rfloor$. We want the derivative of this formula w.r.t. $a_x^\oplus$ to correspond to consuming the longest possible prefix of a's from any word represented by the formula $aa\mathbf{x}(\pi)a^*$, and some of the a's must belong to $\mathbf{x}(\pi)$. Therefore, we must first consume all a's until we get to $\mathbf{x}(\pi)$, then we must consume as many a's from $\mathbf{x}(\pi)$, but at least one, and then, because we may have consumed all letters from $\mathbf{x}(\pi)$, we must consume as many a's as possible from the rest of the formula. To be more concrete, consider the case when $\mathbf{x}(\pi) = aab$. Then $aa\mathbf{x}(\pi)a^*$ is the language $aaaaba^*$ (where the blue letters are letters from $\mathbf{x}$). Consuming the longest prefix of as s.t., at least one is from $\mathbf{x}$ leaves us with ba^*a, which is exactly the model of $\mathbf{x}(\pi)a^*$ for $\mathbf{x}(\pi) = b$ (i.e., for $\mathbf{x}\pi$ with the prefix of a's removed). Now, if $\mathbf{x}(\pi) = aaa$, all as are consumed by the derivative, which yields ϵ in the result.

Given $a \in \Sigma$, the set of derivatives $D_{l^+}(\tilde\alpha)$ for $l \in \{a, a_x\}$ can be computed as the least fixpoint of the following monotonic function:

$$F(X) = D_l(\tilde\alpha) \cup D_l(X)$$

The set of derivatives $D_{a^* a_x^+ a^*}(\tilde\alpha)$ can be computed similarly, but with multiple consecutive fixpoint computations. If we use the equality $a^* a_x^+ a^* = (\epsilon + a^+)a_x^+(\epsilon + a^+)$, we see that we can compute the result in these three steps that use only previously introduced computations:

$$D_{a^* a_x^+ a^*}(\tilde\alpha) = d_2 \cup D_{a^+}(d_2) \qquad d_2 = D_{a_x^+}(d_1) \qquad d_1 = D_{a^+}(\tilde\alpha) \cup \{\tilde\alpha\}$$

Derivatives of Program Variables. Without any prior knowledge, the term $\mathbf{x}(\pi)$ can represent any word over Σ, and therefore its derivative and accompanying functions are defined to simulate the derivatives of Σ^*. To capture the information that a letter has been consumed from a trace (this information is going to be important later), we define the derivatives only w.r.t. x-marked letters.

$$D_a(\mathbf{x}(\pi)) = \emptyset \qquad\qquad \nu(\mathbf{x}(\pi)) = \epsilon$$
$$D_{a_x}(\mathbf{x}(\pi)) = \{\mathbf{x}(\pi)\} \qquad\qquad \mathit{first}(\mathbf{x}(\pi)) = \Sigma$$

Notice that derivatives of program variables are not defined w.r.t.. $^\oplus$-marked letters. This is because we never compute such derivatives.

Basic Optimizations. Although not important for the termination of the computation of derivatives, and the language represented by the derivatives, we work modulo these simple equations that reduce the size of derivatives:

$$\epsilon \mid L = \epsilon \qquad \emptyset \mid L = \emptyset \qquad \lfloor \epsilon \rfloor = \epsilon \qquad \lfloor a \rfloor = a \text{ for any } a \in \Sigma$$

Also, in Eqs. (8) and (9), we can consider only those formulas α' for which it holds that $\mathit{first}(\alpha') \neq \{a\}$.

Proposition 1. *The set of derivatives $D_{(\Sigma_x^\oplus)^*}(\varphi)$ is finite for any trace formula φ.*

Proof. (Sketch) Showing that the set of derivatives is finite for formulas without the stutter-reduced operator is straightforward. The size of the set of derivatives of $\lfloor \alpha \rfloor$ defined in Eqs. (8) and (9) is finite, because the set of derivatives of $\tilde{\alpha}$ is finite as it does not contain sub-formulas with the stutter-reduced operator. □

4.2 Automata for Trace Formulas

As stated at the beginning of this section, for a regular expression α, one can use derivatives to build the automaton $A_{pd}(\alpha)$ that recognizes $\mathcal{L}(\alpha)$ (Definition 2). Because derivatives of trace formulas extend (partial) derivatives of regular expressions while retaining the finiteness property (Proposition 1), we can use the very same construction to build an automaton for a trace formula. Abusing a notation, we denote this automaton also A_{pd}. Examples of A_{pd}s for some formulas can be found later in this section in Fig. 3.

Given a formula φ over an alphabet Σ, we denote by $\|\varphi\|$ the *alphabetic size* of the formula, which is the number of symbols from Σ plus the number of program variables in φ^2. The following proposition states a rough worst-case bound on the size of the automata for trace formulas.

Proposition 2. *Let $A_{pd}(\varphi)$ be the automaton for an eHL formula φ over an alphabet Σ. Then, $A_{pd}(\varphi)$ has $O(|\Sigma| \cdot \|\varphi\|)$ states.*

Proof. The number of states is the size of the set $D_{(\Sigma_x^\oplus)^*}(\varphi)$. First, let us bound the size of $D_{\Sigma^*}(\tilde{\varphi})$. Because $\tilde{\varphi}$ does not contain any stutter reduction operator, we can write $\tilde{\varphi} = \alpha \mathbf{x}(\pi)\beta$. The set $D_{\Sigma^*}(\tilde{\varphi})$ can be divided into three sets:

$$D_{\Sigma^*}(\tilde{\varphi}) = \{\alpha' \mathbf{x}(\pi)\beta \mid \alpha' \in D_{\Sigma^*}(\alpha)\} \cup \{\mathbf{x}(\pi)\beta\} \cup D_{\Sigma^*}(\beta)$$

---

[2] This is a direct extension of the alphabetic size (or *alphabetic width*) of a regular expression which is the number of symbols in the expression [8,16].

From [8, Corollary 3.5], we know that $|D_{\Sigma^*}(\alpha)| \leq \|\alpha\| + 1$ and $|D_{\Sigma^*}(\beta)| \leq \|\beta\| + 1$, and therefore $|D_{\Sigma^*}(\tilde{\varphi})| \leq \|\alpha\| + \|\beta\| + 3$.

Now, if φ contains a stutter reduction operator, the set $D_{(\Sigma_x^\oplus)^*}(\varphi)$ has extra derivatives $\lfloor \gamma \rfloor \mid \bar{a}$, in the worst case for any $a \in \Sigma$ and $\gamma \in D_{\Sigma^*}(\tilde{\varphi})$ (see Eqs. (8) and (9)). Therefore, the upper bound on the size of $D_{(\Sigma_x^\oplus)^*}(\varphi)$ (and therefore the number of states) is $|\Sigma| \cdot (\|\alpha\| + \|\beta\| + 3) + \|\alpha\| + \|\beta\| + 3 = O(|\Sigma| \cdot (\|\alpha\| + \|\beta\|)) = O(|\Sigma| \cdot \|\varphi\|)$. □

Corollary 1. *Let $A_{pd}(\varphi)$ be the automaton for an eHL formula φ over an alphabet Σ. Then, $|A_{pd}(\varphi)| = O(|\Sigma|^3 \cdot \|\varphi\|^2)$.*

Proof. There are $O(|\Sigma| \cdot \|\varphi\|)$ states in the automaton (Proposition 2). In the worst case, each state in the automaton contains a transition under every symbol from $\Sigma_x^\oplus$ to every other state (the automaton is non-deterministic). Because $|\Sigma_x^\oplus| = 4 \cdot |\Sigma|$, this gives the final size $O(4|\Sigma| \cdot (|\Sigma| \cdot \|\varphi\|)^2) = O(|\Sigma|^3 \cdot \|\varphi\|^2)$. □

4.3 Multi-track Automata for Atomic Comparisons

In this subsection, we show how to translate A_{pd} automata for trace formulas in an atom into a 2-track finite automaton with priorities on edges. This automaton is over the alphabet Σ, and therefore can be directly evaluated over concrete input traces. We start with defining the composition of A_{pd} automata.

Definition 3 (Automaton for atomic comparison). *Given an atomic comparison $\psi = \varphi_1 \leq \varphi_2$, the atom automaton (AA) $A_\psi = (Q_\psi, q_{0\psi}, \Sigma_x^\oplus, \delta_\psi, F_\psi)$ is the composition of $A_{pd}(\varphi_1) = (Q, q_0, \Sigma_x^\oplus, \delta, F)$ and $A_{pd}(\varphi_2) = (Q', q_0', \Sigma_x^\oplus, \delta', F')$ defined as:*

- *$Q_\psi = Q \times Q'$ are the states,*
- *$q_\psi = (q_0, q_0')$ is the initial state,*
- *$F_\psi = \{(\alpha, \beta) \mid \alpha \in F\}$ are the accepting states,*
- *$\Sigma_x^\oplus$ is the marked alphabet, and*
- *δ_ψ is the transition function where $(\alpha, \alpha') \xrightarrow{(x,x')} (\beta, \beta') \in \delta_\psi$ iff $\alpha \xrightarrow{x} \beta \in \delta$, $\alpha' \xrightarrow{x'} \beta' \in \delta'$, and $rm(x) = rm(x')$.*

Worth a remark is that the accepting states of A_ψ are the states where the *first* component of the state is accepting. This makes the automaton accept when, after successfully reading the left trace, it finds two words w_1 and w_2 in the models of φ_1 and φ_2, resp., such that $w_1 \leq w_2$. For the space limitations, we do not give a formal definition of the run of AA, as we use it only as an intermediate step in the translation. An example of an AA is shown in Fig. 3.

Having an AA, we translate it into a *finite 2-track automaton with priorities on edges*. We need the priorities to encode lookahead in order to read the longest repetition of a letter stemming from stutter-reduced terms.

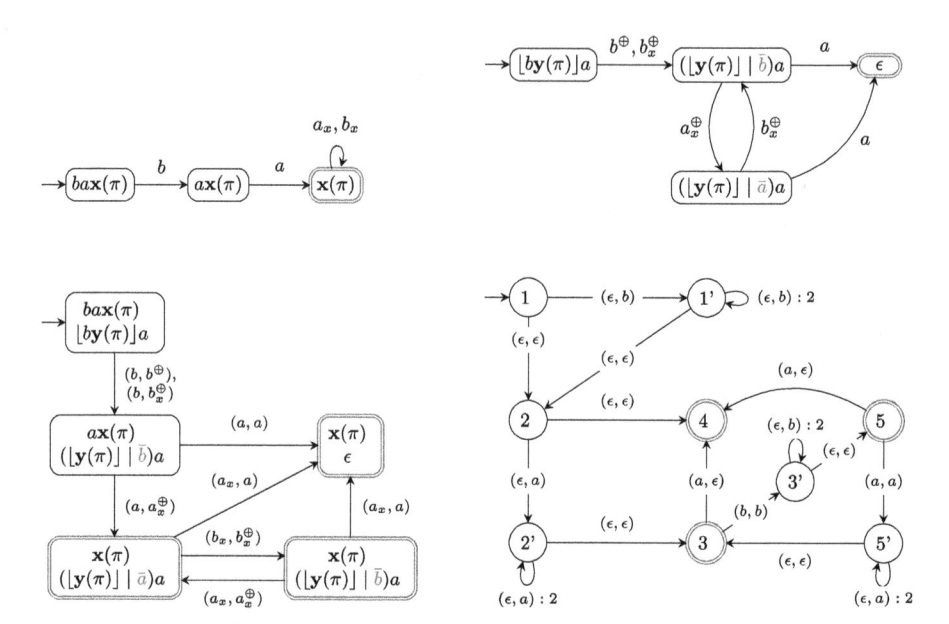

Fig. 3. The automata on top are automata for trace formulas $bax(\pi)$ (left) and $\lfloor by(\pi) \rfloor a$ (right) over the alphabet $\Sigma = \{a, b\}$. Bottom left is their composition, i.e., the AA for the atom $\psi = bax(\pi) \leq \lfloor by(\pi) \rfloor a$, and on the bottom right is the resulting AAP. All automata are stripped off of redundant states.

Definition 4 (Atom automaton with priorities (AAP)). *Given an alphabet Σ, and an AA $A_\psi = (Q_\psi, q_0, \Sigma_x^\oplus, \delta_\psi, F_\psi)$, an atom automaton with priorities (AAP) is a tuple $(Q, q_0, \Sigma_2, \Delta, F)$ where*

- $Q = Q_\psi \cup \{q^a \mid q \in Q_\psi, a \in \Sigma\}$ *is the set of states,*
- $q_0 \in Q$ *is the initial state,*
- $\Sigma_2 = (\Sigma \cup \{\epsilon\})^2$ *is the alphabet consisting of pairs of letters and ϵ,*
- $F \subseteq Q$ *are the final states s.t. , $q, q^a \in F$ iff $q \in F_\psi$,*
- $\Delta \subseteq Q \times \Sigma_2 \times \mathbb{N} \times Q$ *is the transition relation defined below.*

Given an AAP transition (q, l, p, q') between states q and q' over the letter l and with priority p, we write it as $q \xrightarrow{l:p} q'$, and we write just $q \xrightarrow{l} q'$ if p is 0. The transition relation Δ is defined by the translation scheme in Fig. 4. The translation replaces letters without the x-mark with ϵ, because these letters are not read from any input trace. For x-marked letters, the translation applies the rm function (to obtain a letter from Σ) and if the letter was also marked with $\oplus$, it turns the edge with this letter into a new state with self-loop edges that consume as many repetitions of the letter as possible before leaving the state. An example of the translation is shown in Fig. 3.

A run of an AAP on a pair of words (w_1, w_2) is a sequence of states and transitions $q_0 \xrightarrow{l_1:p_1} q_1 \xrightarrow{l_2:p_2} \cdots \xrightarrow{l_n:p_n} q_n$ such that $l_1.l_2 \cdots l_n = (w_1, w_2')$ where

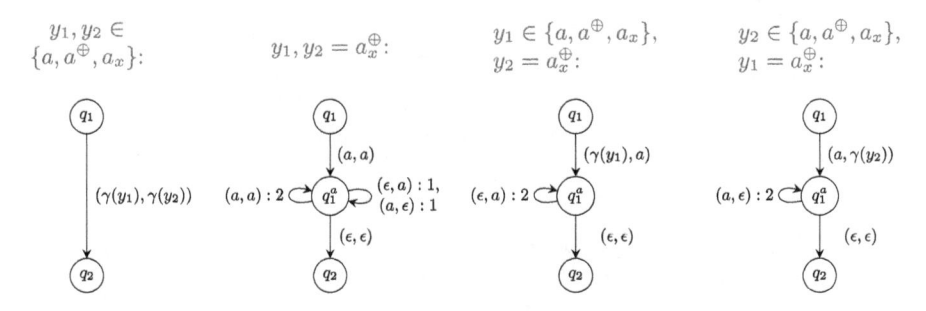

Fig. 4. The scheme of translating an edge $q_1 \xrightarrow{(y_1, y_2)} q_2$ during the translation of AA to AAP. The function γ is defined as $\gamma(a_x) = a$, and $\gamma(y) = \epsilon$ otherwise.

$l_i.l_j$ is the piece-wise concatenation, q_0 is the initial state, and for every transition $t = q_{i-1} \xrightarrow{(a_i, b_i) : p_i} q_i$ it holds that $t \in \Delta$ and if there exists a transition $t' = q_{i-1} \xrightarrow{(a'_i, b'_i) : p'_i} q'_i$, $t' \in \Delta$, with $a'_i \leq a_i \wedge b'_i \leq b_i$, then $p'_i \leq p_i$. In words, the last condition states that among the transitions that the AAP could have taken in the particular place of the run, t was among those with the highest priority. Notice that the run requires only w_1 to be read entirely. The run is *accepting* if it ends with an accepting state, and the AAP *accepts* iff there exists an accepting run. We conclude this section with giving a bound on the size of AAPs.

Proposition 3. *Let $\psi = \varphi_1 \leq \varphi_2$ be an atom of eHL over an alphabet Σ, A_ψ the AA for ψ and A the AAP for A_ψ. Then $|A| = |A_\psi| = O(\|\varphi_1\| \cdot \|\varphi_2\| \cdot |\Sigma|^3)$.*

Proof. From Proposition 2, we know that $A_{pd}(\varphi_1)$ has $O(|\Sigma| \cdot \|\varphi_1\|)$ states, and $A_{pd}(\varphi_2)$ has $O(|\Sigma| \cdot \|\varphi_2\|)$ states. Therefore, A_ψ has $O(|\Sigma|^2 \cdot \|\varphi_1\| \cdot \|\varphi_2\|)$ states. Now, in $A_{pd}(\varphi_1)$ ($A_{pd}(\varphi_2)$, resp.) every state s_1 (s_2) has $O(|\Sigma| \cdot \|\varphi_1\|)$ ($O(|\Sigma| \cdot \|\varphi_2\|)$) transitions under a letter $a \in \Sigma_x^\oplus$, and therefore the state (s_1, s_2) in A_ψ can have $O(|\Sigma|^2 \|\varphi_1\| \cdot \|\varphi_2\|)$ transitions under (a_1, a_2) with $rm(a_1) = rm(a_2) = rm(a)$. That gives us $O(|\Sigma|^3 \|\varphi_1\| \cdot \|\varphi_2\|)$ transitions in total. In summary, $|A_\psi| = O(|\Sigma|^3 \|\varphi_1\| \cdot \|\varphi_2\| + |\Sigma|^2 \|\varphi_1\| \cdot \|\varphi_2\|) = O(|\Sigma|^3 \|\varphi_1\| \cdot \|\varphi_2\|)$.

From Definition 4, A has $O(|\Sigma| \cdot (|\Sigma|^2 \|\varphi_1\| \cdot \|\varphi_2\|))$ states and for each transition from A_ψ, it can add at most 3 new transitions. Therefore, it has $O(|\Sigma|^3 \|\varphi_1\| \cdot \|\varphi_2\|)$ states and likewise transitions. □

5 Monitoring eHL

In this section, we give a monitoring algorithm for universally quantified eHL formulas. In the following, we assume a formula $\psi = \forall \pi_1 ... \pi_k : \psi_{qf}$ where ψ_{qf} is quantifier-free *body* of the formula.

The monitoring algorithm is combinatorial [30], that is, it instantiates quantifiers with every k-tuple of input traces and then evaluates ψ_{qf} on these traces. The formula ψ_{qf} is a boolean combination of atomic comparisons. To evaluate it

Fig. 5. The BDD for the formula on the left in Fig. 1.

Algorithm 1: The monitoring algorithm.

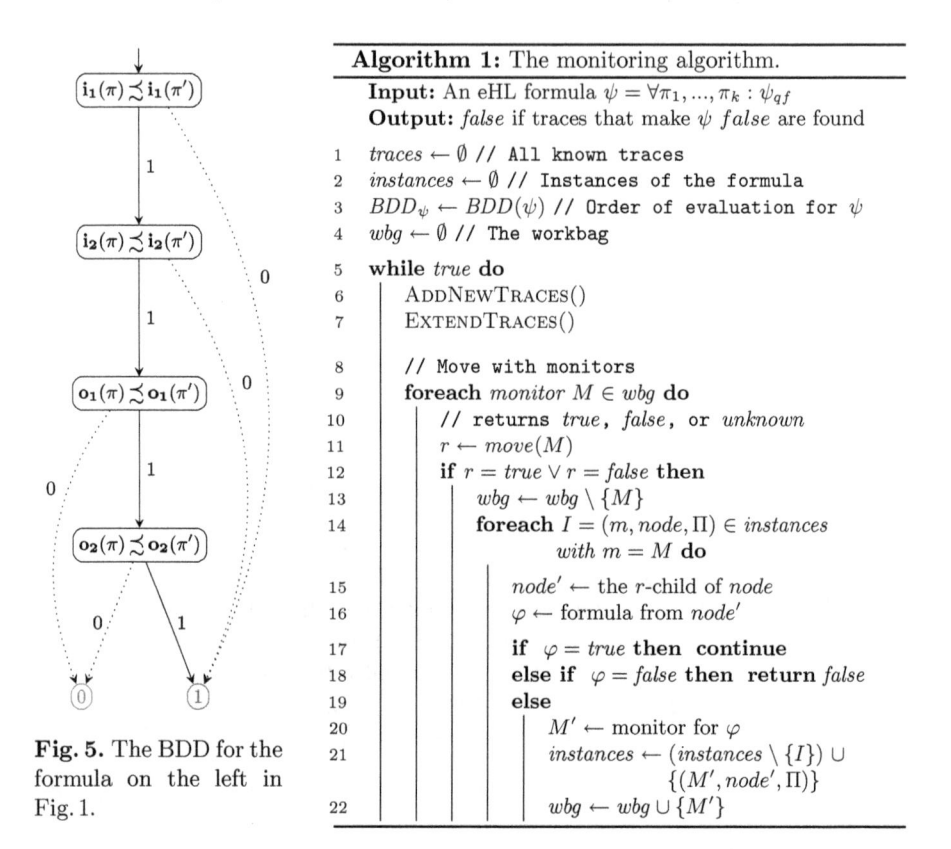

Input: An eHL formula $\psi = \forall \pi_1, ..., \pi_k : \psi_{qf}$
Output: *false* if traces that make ψ *false* are found

1 *traces* $\leftarrow \emptyset$ // All known traces
2 *instances* $\leftarrow \emptyset$ // Instances of the formula
3 $BDD_\psi \leftarrow BDD(\psi)$ // Order of evaluation for ψ
4 *wbg* $\leftarrow \emptyset$ // The workbag
5 **while** *true* **do**
6   ADDNEWTRACES()
7   EXTENDTRACES()
8   // Move with monitors
9   **foreach** *monitor* $M \in wbg$ **do**
10   // returns *true*, *false*, or *unknown*
11        $r \leftarrow move(M)$
12   **if** $r = true \vee r = false$ **then**
13           $wbg \leftarrow wbg \setminus \{M\}$
14   **foreach** $I = (m, node, \Pi) \in instances$ with $m = M$ **do**
15             $node' \leftarrow$ the r-child of $node$
16             $\varphi \leftarrow$ formula from $node'$
17   **if** $\varphi = true$ **then continue**
18   **else if** $\varphi = false$ **then return** *false*
19   **else**
20                $M' \leftarrow$ monitor for φ
21   *instances* $\leftarrow (instances \setminus \{I\}) \cup \{(M', node', \Pi)\}$
22                $wbg \leftarrow wbg \cup \{M'\}$

on a k-tuple of traces, the algorithm first fixes the order of evaluation of atomic comparisons using a *binary decision diagram (BDD)* [17]. A BDD is built from ψ_{qf} where atomic comparisons are taken as boolean variables. The monitoring algorithm starts the evaluation of ψ_{qf} by evaluating the atom from the root of the BDD. Once the atom evaluates to $r \in \{true, false\}$ (the underlying AAP accepts or rejects), the algorithm starts evaluating the r-successor atom from the BDD. This repeats until *true* (1) or *false* (0) node from the BDD is reached, which is the final result of the evaluation of ψ_{qf} on the k-tuple of traces. An example of such a BDD is shown in Fig. 5. In the example, the evaluation starts in the very top node with the formula $\mathbf{i_1}(\pi) \precsim \mathbf{i_1}(\pi')$ (with concrete traces substitued for π and π'). If the formula evaluates to *true* (1), then the algorithm starts evaluating $\mathbf{i_2}(\pi) \precsim \mathbf{i_2}(\pi')$. If this formula evaluates to *false* (0), the whole evaluation ends with 1. Otherwise, the evaluation continues with the next formula, and so on.

Internally, the algorithm keeps a set of formula *instances* that consist of a trace assignment, the node of the BDD (the atom that is being evaluated), and a monitor for the atom, which is simply a set of states of the atom's AAP. These data structures are updated incrementally as new traces and events come.

In a greater detail, the algorithm, whose main part is shown in Algorithm 1, repeats 3 major steps in a loop:

1) adding new traces and instances of the formula (line 6),
2) extending existing traces (line 7), and
3) moving with monitors (AAPs) for atoms and updating instances (lines 9–22)

The first two steps update observations (traces), and create new formula instances and atom monitors. We assume that new traces can be announced at any time and that they are opaque objects that can only be queried for next events. Whenever a new trace t is announced, the algorithm generates all possible trace assignments that include t. For each of these assignments, the algorithm creates an instance of ψ that is associated with this trace assignment and the monitor that evaluates the atom from the root of the BDD on the assigned traces. This step of the algorithm is done by line 6 of Algorithm 1. New incoming events are appended to the traces on line 7.

The third step of the algorithm moves with all the AAPs for atoms that the algorithm currently has (line 11). That is, the algorithm tries to take a transition in any monitor (AAP) M that has unprocessed events on its input traces. If M still needs to read more events, *move* returns *unknown*. Otherwise, if M can take no transition, it rejects and *false* is returned. If M accepts, *move* returns *true*.

When M accepted or rejected its traces, it is removed from the workbag (line 13) and every instance that was waiting for the result of this monitor is updated: based on the result of the monitor, next node of the BDD is taken and if it is not *true* or *false*, the next monitor is created for this node. If node was *true* or *false*, it is the final result of evaluating the instance of the formula.

Based on the description of the algorithm so far, the loop on line 14 is unnecessary, because we have only a single instance waiting for the result of a monitor. However, we need that loop because we use an important optimization to avoid creating duplicate atom monitors: once we create a monitor that evaluates an atom on traces t_1 and t_2, we re-use this monitor in all instances of ψ that evaluate the same atom on t_1 and t_2 too. Also, after the monitor has finished its computation, we remember the result and directly use it instead of evaluating the atom on t_1 and t_2 again.

This optimization is not shown in the code for the sake of space and simplicity, but it has a huge impact on the algorithm. It makes the algorithm to evaluate at most n^2 monitors of an atom for n traces. Notice that the algorithm iterates over monitors and not over instances (line 9), which means that if the formula contains A different atoms, we can evaluate all its instances by evaluating $A \cdot n^2$ atoms. Thus, the number of atoms evaluated by the algorithm does not depend on the number of formula instances, which is n^q for q quantifiers. However, the algorithm still must process all of these instances at least once on line 14.

The algorithm runs in an infinite loop, but if the set of input traces is finite, we can add a condition at the end of the loop that if no new updates to the traces are to come and all monitors for atoms have been processed (at which point all formula instances must have been evaluated), the algorithm can terminate with the conclusion that the formula holds for the input set of traces.

6 Implementation and Evaluation

We have implemented the monitoring algorithm from Sect. 5 and made it available on GitHub [2]. The implementation consists of Python scripts that parse an input formula and generate a C++ project that implements the monitor. The generated project includes a build system configuration with a set of compile time options to adjust the compiled monitor. The code generation is built on the framework VAMOS [21].

We conducted a set of experiments (available in an online artifact [5]) to see how our algorithm performs and to compare it to other monitors. All experiments ran on machines with *AMD EPYC* CPU with the frequency 3.1 GHz. Time limit was set to 120 s per one execution of a monitor.

6.1 Monitoring Observational Determinism

We experimented with monitoring different variants of OD. In the first set of experiments, we monitor the synchronous version of OD on random traces over alphabets being n-bit numbers (n atomic propositions), where n is a parameter. Synchronous OD can be specified by the eHL formula $\forall t_1, t_2 : \mathbf{in}(t_1) \neq \mathbf{in}(t_2) \vee \mathbf{out}(t_1) = \mathbf{out}(t_2)$[3]. We compared eHL monitor to *multi-trace prefix transducers (MPT)* [20] and *RVHyper* [26], both of which can monitor synchronous OD. We ran the monitor with the reflexivity and symmetry reductions[4] of instances of the formula [27], because the other two tools also do. As shown in Fig. 6 in the first two plots from left, the eHL monitor scales rather well with the length and number of traces, but worse with the size of the alphabet (number of bits). The cause of this is that AAPs use the alphabet explicitly, and therefore for n bits, there can be nodes that have 2^{2n} outgoing transitions. MPTs use symbolic equality between letters, so they are agnostic to the size of the alphabet – on contrary, they perform better for bigger alphabets, which is caused simply by the fact that for smaller alphabets, random traces are more likely to be OD for "longer time" and monitors must analyze longer prefixes. Although the size of the alphabet does matter to RVHyper (whose specification language is HyperLTL [22]), it generates monitor automata that break the input alphabet into separate bits (atomic propositions) and in our experiments it performs the best. However, it crashes when given approx. 1000 or more traces.

In the other part of experiments with OD, we wanted to see the price of having stutter reduction. Because neither MPTs nor RVHyper can handle stuttering, we experimented only with eHL monitors. We generated a single trace with *no stuttering* and used its multiple copies as the input "set" of traces. This case is hard for monitors as they must analyze all combinations of traces to their very end. We checked the performance difference when these traces are analyzed by the monitor for synchronous OD and by the monitor for asynchronous OD, which was

---

[3] $\mathbf{v}(t_1) = \mathbf{v}(t_2)$ is a shortcut for $\mathbf{v}(t_1) \leq \mathbf{v}(t_2) \wedge \mathbf{v}(t_2) \leq \mathbf{v}(t_1)$.

[4] With the reductions, we check only a subset of tuples of traces, because OD holds trivially for any tuple (t, t), and it holds for (t_1, t_2) iff it holds for (t_2, t_1).

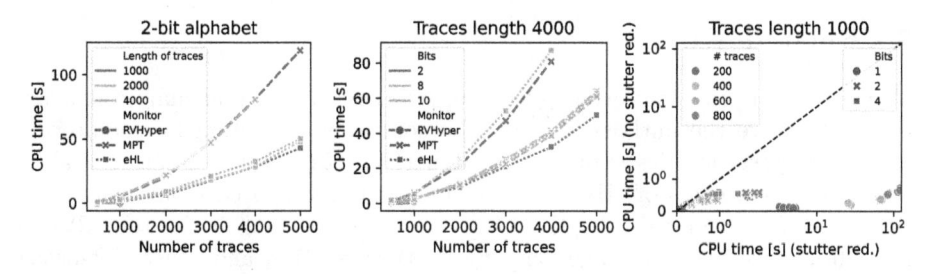

Fig. 6. The two left plots compare different monitors on synchronous OD and the rightmost plot compares monitoring synchronous vs. asynchronous OD by eHL monitors.

Table 1. Monitoring asynchronous OD of a hashing procedure on 500, 1000, and 1500 random n-byte inputs. The columns *atoms* and *atom monitors* contain the number of atoms in the formula and the number of evaluated atom instances.

		Atom monitors (10^6)			CPU time [s]			Memory [MB]		
n	atoms	500	1000	1500	500	1000	1500	500	1000	1500
4	72	0.50	2.00	4.50	0.3	0.8	1.5	13.6	23.4	33.0
8	80	1.19	4.64	10.36	8.7	39.7	93.3	18.9	37.1	60.2
16	96	1.32	5.10	11.53	13.8	57.3	107.6	20.7	40.7	65.7

specified by the eHL formula $\forall t_1, t_2 : \lfloor \mathbf{in}(t_1) \rfloor \neq \lfloor \mathbf{in}(t_2) \rfloor \vee \lfloor \mathbf{out}(t_1) \rfloor = \lfloor \mathbf{out}(t_2) \rfloor$. The scatter plot on the right of Fig. 6 shows that using stutter reduction can increase the runtime significantly. The increase is expected as the stutter reduction operator makes AAPs bigger by adding copies of states with different lookahead sets and, most importantly, transitions with epsilon steps.

6.2 Monitoring Compiler Optimizations

In the next part of experiments, we took the hashing procedure of the cryptographic library *LibHydrogen* [3] and checked that compiler optimizations preserve privacy. We created a binary that computes a 32-byte hash from n input bytes (n is a parameter), and generated traces from optimized and non-optimized versions of the binary. We used the standard -*O3* optimizations provided by *Clang* [4].

On the traces, we checked asynchronous OD over 7-bit input alphabet (the size of ASCII characters). For n input bytes, the formula has $2 * n$ atoms (each equality is broken into two inequalities) and 64 atoms for output bytes. The AAP for each atom had 16513 states (129 accepting) and 81920 transitions (all the AAPs are isomorphic). We tested 500, 1000, and 1500 inputs, which means 1000, 2000, and 3000 traces (one trace from the optimized and one from the non-optimized binary for each input). The results are summarized in Table 1.

7 Related Work

The first work on monitoring hyperproperties is by Agrawal and Bonakdarpour [7], where the authors introduce a monitoring algorithm for monitoring k-safety hyperproperties expressed in HyperLTL [22]. Other monitoring algorithms for (fragments of) HyperLTL include automata-based monitoring algorithms by Finkbeiner et al. [25,27,30] (now implemented in the tool RVHyper [26]), rewriting-based algorithm by Brett et al. [15], and constraint-based algorithms by Hahn et al. [30,31] and Aceto et al. [6].

HyperLTL (and thus all hitherto mentioned algorithms) assumes synchronized traces. eHL can also handle synchronized traces, but is incomparable to HyperLTL as eHL cannot refer to specific points in time. Other synchronous formalisms relevant to this work are *finite-word hyperautomata* of Borzoo and Sarai [13] that define *regular hyperlanguages*, and canonical automata of Finkbeiner et al. [24] for representing k-safety hyperproperties.

The first work on RV of asynchronous hyperproperties is by Chalupa and Henzinger [20] where the authors use *multi-trace prefix-expression transducers (MPTs)*. MPTs can handle asynchronicity caused by "padding" events, but cannot handle stuttering as eHL. The only other work on RV of asynchronous hyperproperties is by Beutner et al. [12] about RV of second-order hyperproperties.

Recently, many formalisms were proposed in the literature to specify asynchronous hyperproperties extending well-known synchronous approaches: from μ-calculus [29] to HyperLTL [10,11,14]. These approaches aim at a broader expressivity power at the expense of costly or even undecidable model-checking, and there has been no focus so far on their runtime verification.

Regular expressions [32] are a standard formalism for describing languages. Their derivatives [18] and partial derivatives [8,35] are at the core of our translation of trace formulas into automata. REs can be translated into finite-state (single-trace) automata [32], while we translate pairs of formulas into multi-track automata. Regular hyperlanguages [13] are specified by *regular hyperexpressions*.

Multi-track automata [19] have been previously used for analyzing relations among strings. Prioritized edges were used with timed automata [33].

8 Conclusion and Future Work

We have defined eHL, an extended version of hypernode logic that allows a mixture of synchronous and asynchronous specifications of hyperproperties as well as a mixture of trace properties and hyperproperties. We show how to translate atomic comparisons of eHL into 2-track automata and how to use these automata to build a monitoring algorithm for $\forall^*$ eHL formulas. We have implemented the monitoring algorithm and conducted a set of experiments which have shown that eHL monitors can analyze relations between thousands of traces with thousands of events, provided the data domain is small.

Future work includes optimizing the monitors for large alphabets. We believe that this work will also serve as the first step to creating a monitoring algorithm for hypernode automata.

References

1. Bartocci, E., Falcone, Y. (eds.): Lectures on Runtime Verification. LNCS, vol. 10457. Springer, Cham (2018). https://doi.org/10.1007/978-3-319-75632-5
2. HNA repository. https://github.com/ista-vamos/hna. Accessed 19 June 2024
3. LibHydrogen. https://libhydrogen.org. Accessed 19 June 2024
4. LLVM project. https://llvm.org. Accessed 20 June 2024
5. Monitoring extended hypernode logic (artifact). https://doi.org/10.5281/zenodo.13294507. Accessed 17 Sept 2024
6. Aceto, L., Achilleos, A., Anastasiadi, E., Francalanza, A.: Monitoring hyperproperties with circuits. In: Mousavi, M.R., Philippou, A. (eds.) FORTE 2022. LNCS, vol. 13273, pp. 1–10. Springer, Cham (2022). https://doi.org/10.1007/978-3-031-08679-3_1
7. Agrawal, S., Bonakdarpour, B.: Runtime verification of k-safety hyperproperties in HyperLTL. In: IEEE 29th Computer Security Foundations Symposium (CSF), pp. 239–252 (2016). https://doi.org/10.1109/CSF.2016.24
8. Antimirov, V.M.: Partial derivatives of regular expressions and finite automaton constructions. Theor. Comput. Sci. **155**(2), 291–319 (1996). https://doi.org/10.1016/0304-3975(95)00182-4
9. Bartocci, E., Henzinger, T.A., Nickovic, D., da Costa, A.O.: Hypernode automata. In: 34th International Conference on Concurrency Theory, CONCUR 2023, 18–23 September 2023, Antwerp, Belgium. LIPIcs, vol. 279, pp. 21:1–21:16. Schloss Dagstuhl - Leibniz-Zentrum für Informatik (2023). https://doi.org/10.4230/LIPICS.CONCUR.2023.21
10. Baumeister, J., Coenen, N., Bonakdarpour, B., Finkbeiner, B., Sánchez, C.: A temporal logic for asynchronous hyperproperties. In: Silva, A., Leino, K.R.M. (eds.) CAV 2021. LNCS, vol. 12759, pp. 694–717. Springer, Cham (2021). https://doi.org/10.1007/978-3-030-81685-8_33
11. Beutner, R., Finkbeiner, B., Frenkel, H., Metzger, N.: Second-order hyperproperties. In: Enea, C., Lal, A. (eds.) CAV 2023. LNCS, vol. 13965, pp. 309–332. Springer, Cham (2023). https://doi.org/10.1007/978-3-031-37703-7_15
12. Beutner, R., Finkbeiner, B., Frenkel, H., Metzger, N.: Monitoring second-order hyperproperties. In: 23rd International Conference on Autonomous Agents and Multiagent Systems. AAMAS '24, pp. 180–188 (2024)
13. Bonakdarpour, B., Sheinvald, S.: Finite-word hyperlanguages. In: Leporati, A., Martín-Vide, C., Shapira, D., Zandron, C. (eds.) LATA 2021. LNCS, vol. 12638, pp. 173–186. Springer, Cham (2021). https://doi.org/10.1007/978-3-030-68195-1_17
14. Bozzelli, L., Peron, A., Sánchez, C.: Asynchronous extensions of HyperLTL. In: 2021 36th Annual ACM/IEEE Symposium on Logic in Computer Science (LICS), pp. 1–13 (2021). https://doi.org/10.1109/LICS52264.2021.9470583
15. Brett, N., Siddique, U., Bonakdarpour, B.: Rewriting-based runtime verification for alternation-free HyperLTL. In: Legay, A., Margaria, T. (eds.) TACAS 2017. LNCS, vol. 10206, pp. 77–93. Springer, Heidelberg (2017). https://doi.org/10.1007/978-3-662-54580-5_5
16. Broda, S., Machiavelo, A., Moreira, N., Reis, R.: The average transition complexity of Glushkov and partial derivative automata. In: Mauri, G., Leporati, A. (eds.) DLT 2011. LNCS, vol. 6795, pp. 93–104. Springer, Heidelberg (2011). https://doi.org/10.1007/978-3-642-22321-1_9
17. Bryant, R.E.: Graph-based algorithms for Boolean function manipulation. IEEE Trans. Comput. **35**(8), 677–691 (1986). https://doi.org/10.1109/TC.1986.1676819

18. Brzozowski, J.A.: Derivatives of regular expressions. J. ACM **11**(4), 481–494 (1964). https://doi.org/10.1145/321239.321249
19. Bultan, T., Yu, F., Alkhalaf, M., Aydin, A.: Relational string analysis. In: String Analysis for Software Verification and Security, pp. 57–68. Springer, Cham (2017). https://doi.org/10.1007/978-3-319-68670-7_5
20. Chalupa, M., Henzinger, T.A.: Monitoring hyperproperties with prefix transducers. In: Katsaros, P., Nenzi, L. (eds.) RV 2023. LNCS, vol. 14245, pp. 168–190. Springer, Cham (2023). https://doi.org/10.1007/978-3-031-44267-4_9
21. Chalupa, M., Muehlboeck, F., Lei, S.M., Henzinger, T.A.: Vamos: middleware for best-effort third-party monitoring. In: Lambers, L., Uchitel, S. (eds.) FASE 2023. LNCS, vol. 13991, pp. 260–281. Springer, Cham (2023). https://doi.org/10.1007/978-3-031-30826-0_15
22. Clarkson, M.R., Finkbeiner, B., Koleini, M., Micinski, K.K., Rabe, M.N., Sánchez, C.: Temporal logics for hyperproperties. In: Abadi, M., Kremer, S. (eds.) POST 2014. LNCS, vol. 8414, pp. 265–284. Springer, Heidelberg (2014). https://doi.org/10.1007/978-3-642-54792-8_15
23. Clarkson, M.R., Schneider, F.B.: Hyperproperties. J. Comput. Secur. **18**(6), 1157–1210 (2010). https://doi.org/10.3233/JCS-2009-0393
24. Finkbeiner, B., Haas, L., Torfah, H.: Canonical representations of k-safety hyperproperties. In: 2019 IEEE 32nd Computer Security Foundations Symposium (CSF), pp. 17–1714 (2019). https://doi.org/10.1109/CSF.2019.00009
25. Finkbeiner, B., Hahn, C., Stenger, M., Tentrup, L.: Monitoring hyperproperties. In: Lahiri, S., Reger, G. (eds.) RV 2017. LNCS, vol. 10548, pp. 190–207. Springer, Cham (2017). https://doi.org/10.1007/978-3-319-67531-2_12
26. Finkbeiner, B., Hahn, C., Stenger, M., Tentrup, L.: RVHyper: a runtime verification tool for temporal hyperproperties. In: Beyer, D., Huisman, M. (eds.) TACAS 2018. LNCS, vol. 10806, pp. 194–200. Springer, Cham (2018). https://doi.org/10.1007/978-3-319-89963-3_11
27. Finkbeiner, B., Hahn, C., Stenger, M., Tentrup, L.: Monitoring hyperproperties. Formal Methods Syst. Des. **54**(3), 336–363 (2019). https://doi.org/10.1007/s10703-019-00334-z
28. Goguen, J.A., Meseguer, J.: Security policies and security models. In: 1982 IEEE Symposium on Security and Privacy, pp. 11–11 (1982). https://doi.org/10.1109/SP.1982.10014
29. Gutsfeld, J.O., Müller-Olm, M., Ohrem, C.: Automata and fixpoints for asynchronous hyperproperties. Proc. ACM Program. Lang. **5**(POPL), 1–29 (2021). https://doi.org/10.1145/3434319
30. Hahn, C.: Algorithms for monitoring hyperproperties. In: Finkbeiner, B., Mariani, L. (eds.) RV 2019. LNCS, vol. 11757, pp. 70–90. Springer, Cham (2019). https://doi.org/10.1007/978-3-030-32079-9_5
31. Hahn, C., Stenger, M., Tentrup, L.: Constraint-based monitoring of hyperproperties. In: Vojnar, T., Zhang, L. (eds.) TACAS 2019. LNCS, vol. 11428, pp. 115–131. Springer, Cham (2019). https://doi.org/10.1007/978-3-030-17465-1_7
32. Hopcroft, J.E., Ullman, J.D.: Introduction to Automata Theory, Languages and Computation. Addison-Wesley, Boston (1979)
33. Lin, S.-W., Hsiung, P.-A., Huang, C.-H., Chen, Y.-R.: Model checking prioritized timed automata. In: Peled, D.A., Tsay, Y.-K. (eds.) ATVA 2005. LNCS, vol. 3707, pp. 370–384. Springer, Heidelberg (2005). https://doi.org/10.1007/11562948_28
34. McCullough, D.: Specifications for multi-level security and a hook-up. In: 1987 IEEE Symposium on Security and Privacy, pp. 161–161 (1987). https://doi.org/10.1109/SP.1987.10009

35. Mirkin, B.G.: An algorithm for constructing a base in a language of regular expressions. J. Symb. Log. **36**(4), 694–694 (1971). https://doi.org/10.2307/2272532
36. Moreira, N., Reis, R.: Manipulation of regular expressions using derivatives: An overview. In: Caron, P., Mignot, L. (eds.) CIAA 2022. LNCS, vol. 13266, pp. 19–33. Springer, Cham (2022). https://doi.org/10.1007/978-3-031-07469-1_2
37. Zdancewic, S., Myers, A.: Observational determinism for concurrent program security. In: 16th IEEE Computer Security Foundations Workshop (CSF), pp. 29–43 (2003). https://doi.org/10.1109/CSFW.2003.1212703

Towards Quantitative Analysis of Simulink Models Using Stochastic Hybrid Automata

Pauline Blohm[✉], Paula Herber, and Anne Remke

University of Münster, Münster, Germany
{pauline.blohm,paula.herber,anne.remke}@uni-muenster.de

Abstract. Model-driven development frameworks such as MATLAB Simulink are widely used in industrial design processes to conquer the increasing complexity of embedded control systems such as self-driving cars or critical infrastructures. As these systems are often safety-critical, formal methods to ensure safety, performance and resilience are highly desirable, in particular also in the presence of unknown and uncertain environments. The semantics of Simulink is, however, only informally defined. In this paper, we present a modular approach to transform stochastic Simulink models to stochastic hybrid automata (SHA). Our key idea is threefold: 1) We provide transformation rules that map Simulink blocks to SHA templates, 2) we map distributed signal flow to a discrete event synchronization mechanism, and 3) we present a parallel composition algorithm. Our transformation gives us access to established quantitative analysis techniques such as reachability analysis and statistical model checking. We show the feasibility of our approach using a temperature control system with a stochastic failure and repair model.

Keywords: Simulink · Hybrid Automata · Quantitative Analysis

1 Introduction

The demand for functionality and flexibility of embedded control systems is steadily increasing. At the same time, they are increasingly used in critical infrastructures, for example, controlling energy or water supply, and in safety-critical systems such as self-driving cars and other autonomous vehicles. With that, we increasingly use embedded control systems not only for our convenience or for profit, but also trust our lives and personal well-being to these systems. This makes it crucial to ensure the safety, performance, and resilience of these systems under all circumstances. Formal methods have the potential to a) ensure that embedded systems function correctly for all possible system parameters and all possible input scenarios, and b) to provide statistical guarantees in the presence of uncertainty and probabilistic behavior. However, the integration of existing formal verification techniques and stochastic analysis techniques for embedded control systems that combine discrete and continuous behavior with feedback loops, is a major challenge. Model-driven development frameworks such as MATLAB Simulink enable the designer to model complex differential equations together with sophisticated control architectures. As a consequence, it is widely adopted for embedded control systems that combine discrete and continuous behavior, i.e. hybrid systems. The MATLAB Simulink framework enables graphical modeling and simulation of the models under development. However, the semantics of Simulink is only informally defined in [34]. Several approaches have been proposed to define formal semantics for Simulink. However, they typically target a qualitative formal verification of safety properties. To the best of our knowledge, there exists no formally founded approach for a quantitative analysis of stochastic Simulink models besides statistical model checking.

In this paper, we present a modular approach to transform Simulink models with stochastic extensions into a subclass of stochastic hybrid automata (SHA). Our key idea is threefold: First, we define transformation rules that provide a mapping from a subset of Simulink blocks into SHA templates. Second, we map the signal flow of the data-flow oriented Simulink model to a discrete-event synchronization mechanisms, which helps us to preserve the execution order of the original model in the control-flow oriented SHA formalism. Third, we define a composition algorithm that composes the SHA templates using the synchronization mechanism and creates one monolithic SHA that represents the behavior of the overall Simulink model. Our transformation preserves the informally defined semantics of Simulink for a clearly defined subset of the Simulink language, which comprises discrete control, continuous blocks as well as stochastic components. Stochastic behavior can either be modeled in Simulink or added to the resulting SHA. Using our transformation, we gain access to sophisticated state-of-the-art quantitative analysis tools such as MODESTTOOLSET [10] or REALYST [18]. With the quantitative analysis techniques provided by these tools, we can ensure that hybrid systems that are modeled in Simulink remain operational even in unexpected situations, under external disruptions, and in the presence of uncertainties with statistical guarantees. We demonstrate the applicability of our approach using a temperature control system where the heating and cooling units are subject to stochastic failures and repair times and provide statistical guarantees that the temperature is kept in a predefined range.

The rest of this paper is structured as follows: In Sect. 2, we introduce the necessary background, namely Simulink and SHA. In Sect. 3, we introduce our transformation from Simulink into SHA. We present experimental results in Sect. 4, summarize related work in Sect. 5 and conclude in Sect. 6.

2 Background

Simulink [34] is an industrially well established graphical modeling language for hybrid systems. It comes with a tool suite for simulation and automated code generation. Simulink models consist of blocks that are connected by discrete or continuous signals. The Simulink block library provides a large set of predefined

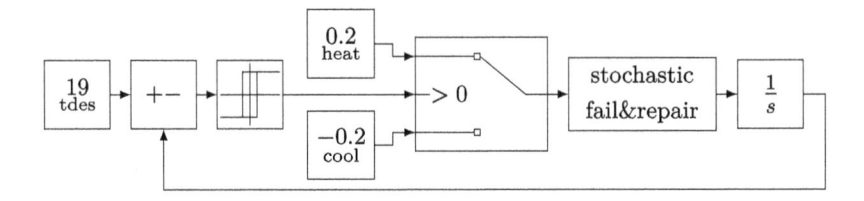

Fig. 1. Simulink model of a temperature control with stochastic failure and repair.

blocks, from arithmetics over control flow blocks to integrators and complex transformations. Together with the MATLAB library, linear and non-linear differential equations can be modeled and simulated. Furthermore, the Simulink library provides random blocks to sample values from a random distribution.

Example. Figure 1 shows a stochastic Simulink model of a temperature control system, which aims to keep the temperature in the room close to the desired temperature *tdes*. Heating and cooling rates are modeled as constant blocks *heat*, *cool* and similarly the desired temperature as *tdes*. The system switches between heating and cooling if the temperature is lower resp. higher than desired. A *relay* block is used to prevent rapid switching, i.e. the system only switches if the temperature deviation is above a given tolerance. The *stochastic fail subsystem* models the control unit failing and being repaired after a random delay. Both, failure and repair times are sampled from a uniform distribution, *fail* $\sim \mathcal{U}(10, 20)$ and *repair* $\sim \mathcal{U}(2, 6)$. After failure the system is stuck in heating mode and after repair the system resumes normal operation, i.e., it immediately switches to cooling or heating according to the current temperature. Failure and repair times are sampled using a uniform random number generator block.

Stochastic Hybrid Automata. We define linear hybrid automata with random clocks (*LHAC*) based on the definition of linear terms and linear hybrid automata [4]. A *linear term* over the set *Var* of variables is a linear combination of $v \in Var$ with integer coefficients. A *linear formula* over *Var* is a boolean combination of inequalities between linear terms over *Var*. Extending existing models by introducing stochasticity, e.g. as presented in [36] is not trivial, as one needs to ensure that the probability space is sound. Thus, to extend linear hybrid automata with stochastic behavior, we apply the concept of *random clocks* as introduced by [17], from which we inherit the syntactical restrictions that ensure that stochasticity is integrated in a sound way. We assume the *LHAC* to be *non-blocking*, i.e. that every path can be extended with another jump or time step. This does not restrict the transformation presented, as the Simulink models we consider are inherently deadlock-free.

Definition 1. *Linear Hybrid Automaton with Random Clocks. A linear hybrid automaton with random clocks (LHAC) is a tuple* $\mathcal{L} = (Loc, Var, Inv, Init, Flow, Jump, Dist, Event)$ *where*

– *Loc is a nonempty, finite set of locations.*

- $Var = Var_{rand} \cup Var_{cont}$ is a finite, ordered set consisting of (continuous) variables Var_{cont} (with $|Var_{cont}| = n$) as well as random clocks Var_{rand} (with $|Var_{rand}| = d$). A valuation v is a function that assigns a real-value $v(x) \in \mathbb{R}$ to each variable $x \in Var$. We write $\mathcal{V}$ for the set of valuations.
- Inv is a labeling function that assigns to each location $l \in Loc$ an invariant $Inv(l)$ that is defined by a linear formula Ψ over Var.
- Init is a function that assigns initial states to each $l \in Loc$ where the initial states are defined by a linear term Φ over Var for each variable $v \in Var$.
- Flow is a labeling function that assigns to each location $l \in Loc$ a set of flows where for all locations $l \in Loc$ the flow $Flow(l)$ is defined by a set of linear ordinary differential equations (ODEs) of the form $\dot{x} = Ax + Bu$ where $x = (x_1, \ldots, x_{n+d})^T$ are the variables $x_i \in Var, i \in \mathbb{N}$, A is a matrix of dimension $(n+d) \times (n+d)$, $u = (u_1, \ldots, u_m)^T$ are control variables with rectangular domain U and B is a matrix of dimension $(n+d) \times m$.
- Jump is a finite set of edges called jumps. Each jump $j = (l, g, r, l') \in Jump$ has source location $source(j) = l$, target location $target(j) = l'$, guard $guard(j) = g$ and reset $reset(j) = r$, where the guard is a linear formula and the reset assigns a linear term for each variable $x \in Var$. We distinguish between stochastic and non-stochastic jumps, where stochastic jumps are always non-guarded.
- Dist is a function that assigns a continuous distribution to each random clock $c \in Var_{rand}$.
- Event : Jump $\to Var_{rand}$ assigns a random clock to each stochastic jump.

Random clocks are used to model that a jump is executed after a randomly-distributed time delay. For each random clock $c \in Var_{rand}$, an expiration time s_c is sampled from the distribution $distr = Dist(c)$. A random clock c evolves with a rate of 1 in locations where a stochastic jump j with $Event(j) = c$ exists and with a rate of 0 otherwise. Once the random clock reaches s_c a stochastic jump j with $Event(j) = c$ is immediately executed. Thus, a state $\sigma = (l, v, s)$ contains the current location l, the valuation v of all variables including the random clocks and the sampled expiration times $s = (s_1, \ldots s_d)$ of the random clocks. We assume the random clocks to be ordered. The operational semantics for $LHAC$ is given in Fig. 2. The rules for nonstochastic jumps (Rule_{Jump_N}) and time elapse (Rule_{Flow}) are based on the semantics provided by [4], the rule for stochastic jumps (Rule_{Jump_S}) is adapted from the semantics for rectangular automata with random clocks as defined in [16,17].

Jumps describe discrete state changes in the automaton. A nonstochastic jump $j = (l, g, r, l') \in Jump$ can be taken as soon as it is *enabled* in a state $\sigma = (l, v, s)$, i.e. when the invariant $Inv(l)$ of the source location l as well as the guard g are fulfilled and the valuation of the variables after the reset are applied v' fulfills the invariant of the target location l'. Additionally, nonstochastic jumps can only be taken if no stochastic jump is enabled in the current state. A stochastic jump $j = (l, g, r, l') \in Jump$ with $Event(j) = c$ is enabled if the valuation of c equals their expiration time s_c, the invariant $Inv(l)$ of the source location l is fulfilled and the valuation of the variables after the reset are applied v' fulfills the

$$\text{Rule}_{Jump_N} \frac{(l, g, r, l') \in Jump \quad v \in Inv(l) \cap g \quad v' \in r(v) \cap Inv(l')}{(l, v, s) \to_{\mathcal{L}} (l, v', s)}$$

$$\text{Rule}_{Jump_S} \frac{\begin{array}{c} j = (l, g, r, l') \in Jump \quad v \in Inv(l) \quad v' \in r(v) \cap Inv(l') \\ Event(j) = c \quad v_c = s_c \quad v'_c = 0 \quad s'_c \in supp(Dist(c)) \\ \forall c_i \in Var_{rand} \setminus \{c\} : v'_{c_i} = v_{c_i} \wedge s'_i = s_i \end{array}}{(l, v, s) \xrightarrow{c}_{\mathcal{L}} (l, v', s')}$$

$$\text{Rule}_{Flow} \frac{\begin{array}{c} f \in Flow(l) \quad f(0) = v \quad v' = f(t) \quad \forall 0 \leq t' \leq t : f(t') \in Inv(l) \\ \forall c_i \in Var_{rand}, 0 \leq i \leq d : v_{c_i} < s_i \end{array}}{(l, v, s) \xrightarrow{t}_{\mathcal{L}} (l, v', s)}$$

Fig. 2. Operational semantics for the $LHAC$ $\mathcal{L}$.

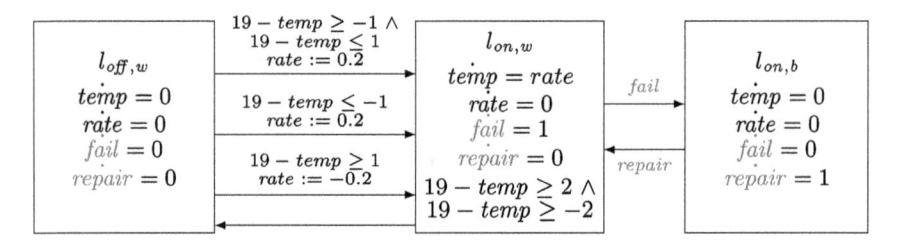

Fig. 3. $LHAC$ modeling a temperature control with stochastic failure and repair. $Init(l_{off,w}) = \{temp = 19, rate = fail = repair = 0\}, Init(l_{on,w}) = Init(l_{on,b}) = \emptyset$.

invariant of the target location l'. Note that stochastic jumps are assumed to be non-guarded [17] and executed as soon as they are enabled. During the jump, c will be reset to zero and a new expiration time is sampled from the corresponding distribution $distr = Dist(c)$. We use $supp(Dist(c)) = \{s \in \mathbb{R}_{\geq 0} | distr(s) > 0\}$ to denote the set a new expiration time is sampled from.

During a time step in a location l, the valuations of the variables evolve according to the linear ODE defined in $Flow(l)$ while the valuation fulfills the invariant $Inv(l)$. Each random clock c evolves with a rate of 1 in a location l iff a stochastic jump $j_c = (l, g, r, l')$, $Event_{j_c} = c$ exists and with rate 0 otherwise.

Example. An example $LHAC$ is shown in Fig. 3, which is a simplified version of the Simulink example shown in Fig. 1. The temperature is modeled by $temp$, $rate$ models the cooling or heating rate. The random clocks $fail$ and $repair$ are highlighted. Initially, the control is off, the temperature of the room is constant and the system cannot fail. Control may be turned on, which brings the LHAC to the middle state and sets $rate$ to cooling (-0.2) or heating (0.2) depending on the current temperature. Then $temp$ evolves with derivative $rate$ and the random clock $fail$ with rate 1. The control stays on until either the expiration

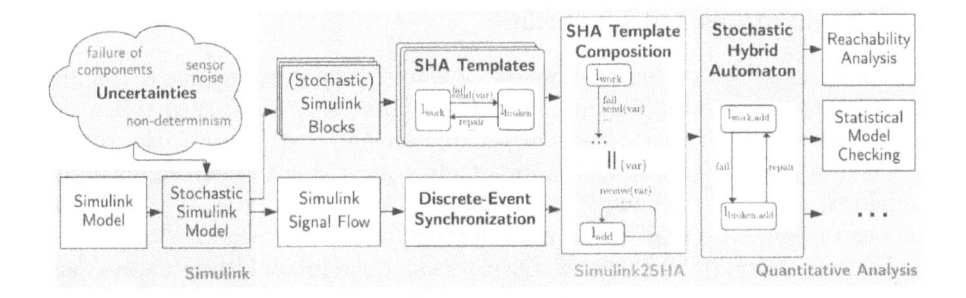

Fig. 4. Modular transformation of stochastic Simulink models to SHA.

time s_{fail} is reached or the temperature of the room gets too warm or too cold. If the control fails *fail* is reset to zero and the random clock *repair* now evolves with rate 1. Control stays broken until the expiration time s_{repair} is reached.

3 Formalization of Stochastic Simulink Models

To enable quantitative analysis of stochastic Simulink models, we present a modular approach to transform such models into stochastic hybrid automata (SHA). Our overall approach is shown in Fig. 4. We assume that a given Simulink model has been extended with stochastic components, which model uncertainties about the environment or the system itself, for example, failures of components, sensor noise, or non-deterministic choices within algorithmic implementations. A key challenge when transforming stochastic Simulink models into SHA is that Simulink is data-flow oriented, while SHA are control-flow oriented. In Simulink, computations are performed in each block based on input signals, with an underlying execution order determined by data dependencies to ensure correct simulation. In contrast, SHA models execute sequentially, with the control flow explicitly defined by discrete events that trigger state transitions.

To overcome this problem, we define transformation rules that map Simulink blocks into *SHA Templates*. These templates precisely capture the execution semantics of the blocks as an input/output relation, where the inputs of the block are left unknown and the evolution of the output is modeled explicitly. To translate the *Simulink Signal Flow*, we introduce a *Discrete-Event Synchronization*, i.e. we introduce synchronization labels to capture the relationship between input and output ports that are connected by signals in the Simulink model and preserve the correct execution order via a parallel *composition* of the SHA templates. The result of the composition is a monolithic SHA that can be analyzed with established quantitative analysis techniques such as reachability analysis or statistical model checking.

In the following, we first outline assumptions and limitations. Then, we present the transformation of Simulink blocks to SHA templates. Finally, we define the discrete-event synchronization mechanism, and present an algorithm for the composition of the SHA templates.

3.1 Assumptions and Limitations

The language subset currently supported by our transformation already contains key representatives from Simulink block classes necessary for the signal-flow oriented construction of hybrid systems, i.e., discrete and continuous blocks, control flow and arithmetic blocks. This allows us to reason about crucial quantitative properties, such as time-bounded reachability of safety properties, e.g., that continuous variables are kept within a given range by a discrete controller.

In the current state of our work, we focus on representatives of the most important block classes, i.e. sum blocks, switch blocks, unit delay and relay blocks, continuous integrators and a custom Simulink subsystem that models stochastic failure and repair. We assume a flattened model without hierarchy. The Simulink model may contain feedback loops, but no algebraic loops.

The transformation is currently manual. We have not yet investigated whether non-linear ODEs will require additional transformation rules, and the complexity of the underlying ODEs is conceptually limited by the class of systems that can be expressed as *LHAC*. In our experiments, we consider a linear first-order ODE, addressing more complex models is subject to future work.

3.2 From Simulink Blocks to Automata Templates

In the following, SHA templates are defined as *LHAC*sync, which extend *LHAC* with synchronization labels. Note that, *LHAC*sync do not have a full execution semantics, which is later provided by the synchronization mechanism and the parallel composition.

Definition 2. *A LHACsync is a tuple* $\mathcal{L}_{sync} = (Loc, Var, Inv, Init, Flow, Jump, Dist, Sync)$ *where*

- *Loc, Inv, Jump, and Dist are defined as for LHAC.*
- $Var = Var_{output} \cup Var_{input} \cup Var_{rand}$ *is the set of variables.*
- *Init assigns a pair of initial state and condition to each location* $l \in Loc$ *for each* $v \in Var_{output}$. *A condition is a linear formula.*
- *Flow assigns a flow to each location* $l \in Loc$ *for each variable* $v \in Var_{output}$.
- $Sync = Sync_{send} \cup Sync_{receive}$ *is a labeling function assigning a set of sending and receiving variables to each jump* $j \in Jump$.

We distinguish between *input* and *output* variables in the *LHAC*sync $\mathcal{L}_{sync}$, where input variables $v \in Var_{input}$ have an unknown evolution and initial state. They can thus be considered as parameters of the automaton $\mathcal{L}_{sync}$, whereas the output variables $v \in Var_{output}$ are regular continuous variables with predefined evolution and initial value. The labeling function *Sync* is used to indicate that variables x are changed in a discrete manner. The function $Sync_{receive}$ is used to catch discrete changes of input variables $y \in Var_{input}$.

(a) Constant block with parameter val.

(b) SHA template modeling the Constant block with $Init(l_0) = (\{out = \texttt{val}\}, \texttt{true})$.

Fig. 5. Transformation rule for Constant block.

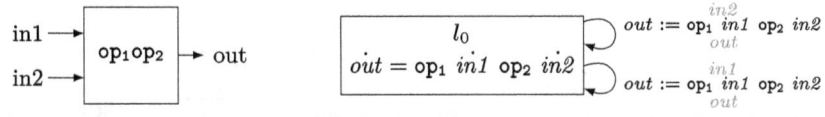

(a) Sum block with parameter $\texttt{op}_1$ and $\texttt{op}_2$.

(b) SHA template modeling the Sum block with $Init(l_0) = (\{out = \texttt{op}_1\ in1\ \texttt{op}_2\ in2\}, \texttt{true})$.

Fig. 6. Transformation rule for sum block.

Transformation Rules. To precisely capture the semantics of a subset of Simulink blocks, we define transformation rules that map each Simulink block into an SHA template. The transformation rules are shown in Fig. 5, 6, 7, 8, 9, 10 and 11. For each Simulink block that is considered in this paper, we show the corresponding SHA template, which is expressed as a *LHAC*sync. Parameters of the original Simulink block, e.g. switch conditions or initial values, are defined as **parameters** and are replaced by the actual value during the transformation of a block. Variables that are sent or received are highlighted accordingly.

Constant Block. The transformation rule for the Constant block is given in Fig. 5. The Constant block drives a signal *out* with a constant value **val**. The corresponding SHA template has of a single location l_0, with $Init(l_0) = (\{out = \texttt{val}\}, \texttt{true})$, and a single output variable *out* which does not evolve.

Sum Block. The transformation rule for the Sum block is given in Fig. 6. The Sum block adds or subtracts values of $n \in \mathbb{N}^{\geq 2}$ input signals. Each input signal i has a corresponding operator $\texttt{op}_i \in \{+, -\}$ and the outgoing signal is calculated as $out = \sum_{i=1}^{n}(\texttt{op}_i in_i)$. Exemplary, we provide the transformation rule for two inputs. The SHA template consists of a single location l_0, the input variables *in1* and *in2*, and a single output variable *out*. After initialization, the variable *out* evolves with *in1* and *in2*. Two jumps are used to receive discrete updates of *in1* and *in2*, where the value of *out* is changed accordingly and *out* is sent.

Integrator Block. The transformation rule for the Integrator block, which integrates over an incoming signal **in**, is given in Fig. 7. The single output variable *out* is initialized with **init** (a block parameter) and evolves with *in*.

Relay Block. The transformation rule for the Relay block is shown in Fig. 8. The Relay blocks output signal switches between two values **on_val** and **off_val**

(a) Integrator block with parameter init.

(b) SHA template modeling the Integrator block with $Init(l_0) = (\{out = \texttt{init}\}, \texttt{true})$.

Fig. 7. Transformation rule for Integrator block.

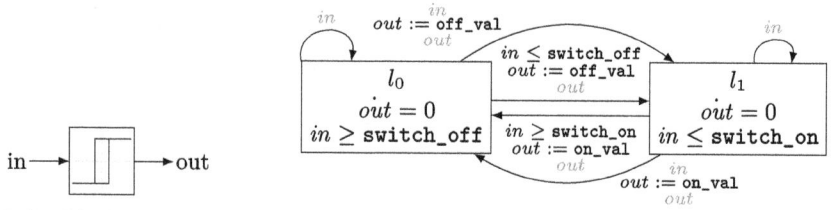

(a) Relay block with parameters switch_on, switch_off, on_val and off_val.

(b) SHA template modeling the Relay block with $Init(l_0) = (\{out = \texttt{on\_val}\}, in \geq \texttt{switch\_on})$ and $Init(l_1) = (\{out = \texttt{off\_val}\}, in < \texttt{switch\_on})$.

Fig. 8. Transformation rule for Relay block.

depending on the value of the input signal. The relay stays in its current state, on or off, until the input signal exceeds the corresponding threshold, i.e. below switch_off or above switch_on. If the initial value of the input signal falls between switch_on and switch_off the relay is off. The SHA template modeling this behavior has two location l_0 and l_1, one output variable out, which is only set during the jumps, and one input variable in. The jumps from l_0 to l_1 and vice versa is taken once in reaches switch_off, respectively switch_on, which can result from continuous evolution or via a discrete reset of in. Depending on in, the initial state is either $out = \texttt{on\_val}$ in l_0 or $out = \texttt{off\_val}$ in l_1.

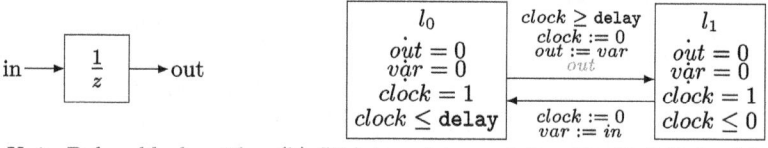

(a) Unit Delay block with parameters delay and init.

(b) SHA template modeling the Unit Delay block with $Init(l_0) = (\{out = \texttt{init}, clock = 0, var = in\}, \texttt{true})$.

Fig. 9. Transformation rule for Unit Delay block.

Unit Delay Block. The transformation rule for the Unit Delay block is given in Fig. 9. It holds and delays an incoming signal in for one sample period of length delay. The initial value init of the outgoing signal is a block parameter.

The SHA template has two locations l_0 and l_1, the output variables *out*, *var* modeling the current value of *in*, and *clock* modeling the current time passed in l_0 as well as the input variable *in*. After **delay** time periods in location l_0 have passed, a jump to l_1 is taken where *clock* is reset to zero, the value of *var* is written to *out* and the discrete change of *out* is sent. l_1 is left immediately and the current value of *in* is written to *var*.

(a) Switch block with parameters **cond**.

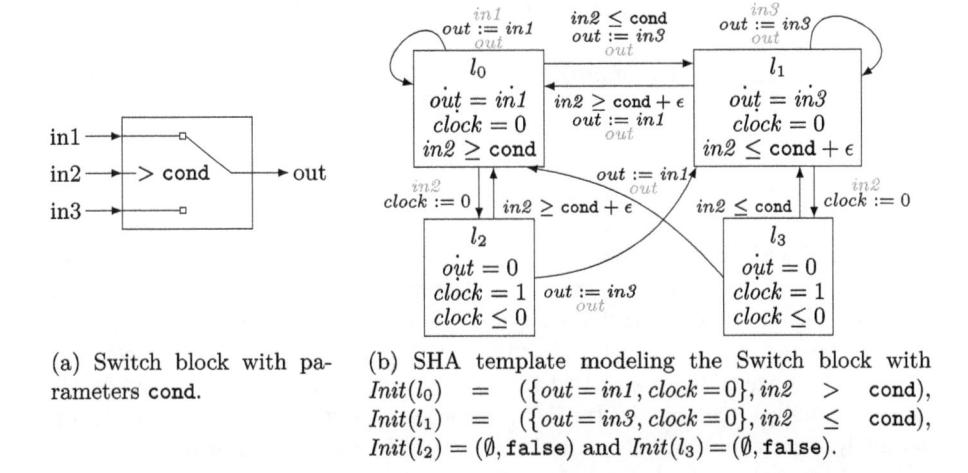

(b) SHA template modeling the Switch block with
$Init(l_0) = (\{out = in1, clock = 0\}, in2 > \text{cond})$,
$Init(l_1) = (\{out = in3, clock = 0\}, in2 \leq \text{cond})$,
$Init(l_2) = (\emptyset, \texttt{false})$ and $Init(l_3) = (\emptyset, \texttt{false})$.

Fig. 10. Transformation rule for Switch block.

Switch Block. The transformation rule for the Switch blocks is shown in Fig. 10. The output signal switches between two input signals *in1* and *in3* depending on whether the value of *in2* fulfills a condition op **cond** with op $\in \{>, \geq, =\}$. Exemplary, we only show the SHA template for the > **cond** case. The SHA template consists of four location l_0 to l_3, the output variables *out* and *clock*, which is used to model urgency in l_2 and l_3, as well as the three input variables *in1*, *in2* and *in3*. The initial state depends on whether *in2* initially fulfills the condition. Once the condition is no longer met, the automaton switches from l_0 to l_1, or vice versa, and updates *out*. As this switch depends on *in2*, the switch can either happen continuously or discretely. To account for discrete changes, we first switch to l_2, respectively l_3, to evaluate whether a discrete change of *in2* affects the condition. Note that we cannot define an invariant and guard that together model the immediate switch back to l_0 as soon as *in2* > **cond** holds, as the invariant and guard may not be disjoint. To overcome this problem, we introduce an $\epsilon \in \mathbb{R}^+$, and use **cond** $+ \epsilon$ in the guard resp. invariant. Choosing a value for ϵ that is less or equal to the step size used in the Simulink model maintains the behavior of the model.

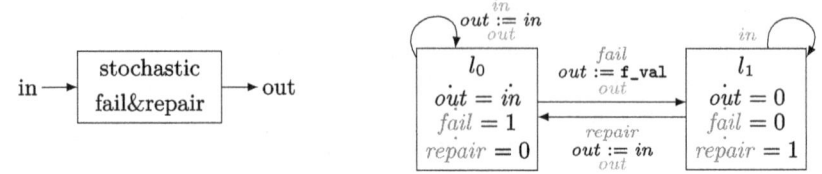

Fig. 11. Transformation rule for stochastic subsystem.

(a) Stochastic subsystem with parameters `f_val`, $f \sim \mathcal{U}(a_f, b_f)$, $r \sim \mathcal{U}(a_r, b_r)$.

(b) SHA template modeling the stochastic subsystems with $Init(l_0) = (\{out = in, fail = 0, repair = 0\}, \text{true})$, $Dist(fail) = \mathcal{U}(a_f, b_f)$ and $Dist(repair) = \mathcal{U}(a_r, b_r)$.

Stochastic Failure and Repair Block. We introduce a custom Simulink subsystem that models stochastic failure and repair of a signal, i.e. while the signal is working the value of the inport is written to the outport and while its broken a fixed `fail_val` is written to the outport. For now, we consider the `fail_val` to be constant and the fail and repair times to be sampled from a uniform distribution. We show the transformation rule for this subsystem in Fig. 11. The SHA template for this subsystem has two locations l_0 and l_1, an output variable *out*, an input variable *in* and two random clocks *fail* and *repair* modeling the stochastic failure and repair. Initially, the system is working, i.e. it is in l_0 and *out* evolves with *in*. Once the sampled expiration time s_{fail} is reached, the jump to l_1 is executed, updates the value of *out* to `fail_val` and sends this change. Once the sampled expiration time s_{repair} is reached, the jump to l_0 is executed, updates the value of *out* to *in* and sends this change.

3.3 From Signal Flow to Discrete Event Synchronization

After transforming the individual Simulink blocks to SHA templates, we derive the synchronization mapping from the signal flow of the Simulink model. The synchronization mapping ensures that the control flow from the data-flow oriented Simulink model is correctly implemented within the composed SHAs discrete-event synchronization. The synchronization mapping is defined as follows: For each signal line in the Simulink model: 1) We identify the blocks that are connected by this signal and fetch the corresponding SHA templates. 2) We identify the *sending* template, i.e. the template that corresponds to the block that drives the signal line. 3) We identify the variables that are used in the SHA templates to read from the signal. We define a synchronization mapping as:

Definition 3. *Synchronization Mapping. A synchronization mapping for a signal line of the Simulink model is a tuple $m = (s, snd, Rcv)$, where*

- *s is the label that synchronizes on the signal line,*
- *$snd = (\mathcal{L}_{sync}, v) \in LHAC sync \times Var$ is a tuple of an SHA template $\mathcal{L}_{sync}$ and the variable v that writes to the signal line in the sending SHA template,*
- *$Rcv \subseteq LHAC sync \times Var$ is a set of tuples of a receiving SHA template and the variable reading from the signal line in that SHA template.*

We say a variable $v \in snd \cup Rcv$ iff the variable is contained in any of the tuples, i.e. iff $\bigvee_{(\mathcal{L}_{sync}, var) \in snd \cup Rcv}(v = var)$.

Example. Consider the Simulink example from Fig. 1. The transformation of the Sum and Relay block with the rules provided in Fig. 5, 6, 7, 8, 9, 10 and 11 results in the SHA templates $\mathcal{L}_{sync,S}$ for the Sum block, and $\mathcal{L}_{sync,R}$ for the Relay block. The signal connection between these two blocks can be described by the mapping $m_{StoR} = (\text{sum}, (\mathcal{L}_{sync,S}, out), \{(\mathcal{L}_{sync,R}, in)\})$.

3.4 SHA Template Composition

We present a composition of SHA templates based on the discrete-event synchronization mechanism presented above. This yields a monolithic stochastic hybrid automaton following the *LHAC* formalism as presented in Sect. 2. Parallel composition of the SHA templates is performed iteratively resolving one synchronization mapping and merging the jumps that synchronize over $v \in snd \cup Rcv$. We show how an individual synchronization mapping is resolved. After all synchronization mappings are resolved, we show how the monolithic SHA, called *composed automaton*, is extracted from the final intermediate automaton.

Let us first introduce some notation: Let $\mathbf{L} = \{\mathcal{L}_{sync,i} \mid 0 \leq i \leq n\}$ be the set of all SHA templates derived from transforming the Simulink blocks of the model with $\mathcal{L}_{sync,i} = (Loc_i, Var_i, Inv_i, Init_i, Flow_i, Jump_i, Dist_i, Sync_i)$. $\mathcal{M} = \{m_j \mid 0 \leq j \leq l\}$ is the set of all synchronization mappings derived from the signal lines of the Simulink model and $m_{comp} = (name, snd, Rcv) \in \mathcal{M}$ is the synchronization mapping that is currently resolved. We refer to the set of SHA templates that is considered in this synchronization mapping as $\mathbf{L}_{comp}$.

The intermediate automaton considered in this step of the composition is denoted $\mathcal{L}_{sync,\mathcal{I}}$. We refer to the set of SHA templates that are already composed in $\mathcal{L}_{sync,\mathcal{I}}$ as $\mathbf{L}_{\mathcal{I}}$ and to the set of all SHA templates that are added in this composition step as $\mathbf{L}_{new} = \mathbf{L}_{comp} \setminus \mathbf{L}_{\mathcal{I}}$.

Renaming of Variables. Since SHA templates may use the same variable names, e.g. *out* or *in*, we maintain information contained in the synchronization mapping m_{comp} about variable dependencies by renaming variables as follows.

1. For each variable v in a newly added automaton $\mathcal{L}_{sync,s} \in \mathbf{L}_{new}$ that is not synchronized, i.e. $v \in Var_s$, $Var_s \in \mathcal{L}_{sync,s}$ with $v \notin snd \cup Rcv$, we add a subscript indicating the origin $\mathcal{L}_{sync,s}$, i.e. $v \rightsquigarrow v_s$.
2. For each variable y in a newly added automaton $\mathcal{L}_{sync,s} \in \mathbf{L}_{new}$ that is synchronized, i.e. $y \in Var_s$, $Var_s \in \mathcal{L}_{sync,s}$, with $y \in snd \cup Rcv$, we rename to the label *name* given by the synchronization mapping m_{comp}, i.e. $y \rightsquigarrow name$.
3. For each variable z_s in an already composed automaton $\mathcal{L}_{sync,s} \in \mathbf{L}_{\mathcal{I}}$ that is synchronized, i.e. $z_s \in Var_s$, $Var_s \in \mathcal{L}_{sync,s}$ with $z \in snd \cup Rcv$, we rename z_s in the intermediate automaton $\mathcal{L}_{sync,\mathcal{I}}$ to the label *name*, i.e. $z_s \rightsquigarrow name$.

Example. Consider the Simulink example from Fig. 1 and the synchronization mapping m_{StoR} describing the connection between Sum and Relay block. Assume that the SHA templates of the Constant and Sum blocks have already been composed to the intermediate automaton $\mathcal{L}_{sync,\mathcal{I}}$. During renaming, the non-synchronized variable out of the Relay automaton $\mathcal{L}_{sync,R}$ is renamed to out_R. As the blocks synchronize over the in variable of the Relay block and the out_S variable of the Sum block, we rename these variables to sum, i.e., $in \rightsquigarrow$ sum in $\mathcal{L}_{sync,R}$ and $out_S \rightsquigarrow$ sum in $\mathcal{L}_{sync,\mathcal{I}}$.

Creating the Composed Intermediate Automaton. We parallely compose the intermediate automaton $\mathcal{L}_{sync,\mathcal{I}}$ with the set of SHA templates $\mathbf{L}_{new}$ via the synchronization mapping m_{comp}, i.e. $\mathcal{L}_{sync,new} = \mathcal{L}_{sync,\mathcal{I}} \|_{m_{comp}} \mathbf{L}_{new}$. The intermediate automaton is empty if no composition step has been performed yet.

Syntactically, the composition over a synchronization mapping m_{comp} is a parallel composition of all considered automata. A location in the composed intermediate automaton $\mathcal{L}_{sync,new}$ is a tuple that consists of one location for each composed automaton. The invariant and flow for a location are derived by conjoining the invariants and disjoining flows of all sub-locations. Similarly, the set of variables is now a union of all variable sets of the considered automata. The function $Dist$ assigning a distribution to a random clock is also a union of the functions $Dist_i$ in the single automata. The function $Init$ assigning a conditional initial state to each location disjoins the initial states and conjoins their respective conditions for each $Init_i$ of the sub-location. The jumps in the $\mathcal{L}_{sync,new}$ resolve the synchronization mapping m_{comp} in our SHA templates by merging the jumps of the SHA templates that send or receive the synchronized variable. Our definition extends a CSP-style synchronous, symmetric synchronization [24] with a mechanism to distinguish between sending and receiving that preserves correct execution order in the resets. For the semantic definition of jumps we distinguish between *non-synchronized jumps* and *synchronized jumps*.

A Non-synchronized Jump. $j = (\mathbf{l}, g, r, \mathbf{l}')$ from source location $\mathbf{l} = (l_1, ..., l_n)$ to target location $\mathbf{l}' = (l'_1, ..., l'_n)$ with $l_i, l'_i \in Loc_i, Loc_i \in \mathcal{L}_{sync,i}$ exists in the automaton $\mathcal{L}_{sync,new} = \mathcal{L}_{sync,\mathcal{I}} \|_{m_{comp}} \mathbf{L}_{new}$ where $s = name$ iff

1. $\exists l_i \in \mathbf{l} \wedge l'_i \in \mathbf{l}' : \exists j_i \in Jump_i : j_i = (l_i, g, r, l'_i) \wedge name \notin Sync_i(j_i)$, i.e. there exists a jump in one SHA template and that does not send or receive the variable $name$ that is synchronized.
2. $\forall j \neq i : l_j = l'_j$, i.e. no change happens in all other SHA templates.
3. If $Event_i(j_i) = c$ we assign $Event_{new}(j) = c$, i.e. if the jump j_i in the SHA template is stochastic the jump j in $\mathcal{L}_{sync,new}$ will also be stochastic.
4. We assign $Sync_{new}(j) = Sync_i(j_i)$.

A Synchronized Jump. $j = (\mathbf{l}, g, r, \mathbf{l}')$ from a source location $\mathbf{l} = (l_1, ..., l_n)$ to a target location $\mathbf{l}' = (l'_1, ..., l'_n)$ with $l_i, l'_i \in Loc_i, Loc_i \in \mathcal{L}_{sync,i}$ exists in the automaton $\mathcal{L}_{sync,new} = \mathcal{L}_{sync,\mathcal{I}} \|_{m_{comp}} \mathbf{L}_{new}$ where $s = name$ iff

1. $\forall\, l_i \in \mathbf{l},\, l'_i \in \mathbf{l}',\, \mathcal{L}_{sync,i} \in \mathbf{L}_{comp} : \exists j_i \in Jump_i,\, j_i = (l_i, g_i, r_i, l'_i) \wedge name \in Sync(j_i)$, i.e. in all $\mathcal{L}_{sync,i} \in \mathbf{L}_{comp}$ exists a jump from l_i to l'_i where $name$ is either sent or received.

2. $\forall l_i \in \mathbf{l}, l'_i \in \mathbf{l'}, \mathcal{L}_{sync,i} \notin \mathbf{L}_{comp} : l_j = l'_j$, i.e. no change happens in all $\mathcal{L}_{sync,i} \notin \mathbf{L}_{comp}$.
3. $g = \bigwedge_{\substack{1 \le i \le n \\ \mathcal{L}_{sync,i} \in \mathbf{L}_{comp}}} g_i$, for $g_i \in j_i$, i.e. the guard of j conjoins the guards of j_i in $\mathcal{L}_{sync,i} \in \mathbf{L}_{comp}$.
4. $r = apply_{r_{snd}(name)} \left(\bigcup_{\substack{1 \le i \le n \\ \mathcal{L}_{sync,i} \in \mathbf{L}_{comp}}} r_i \right)$ where $apply$ is a function replacing each occurrence of $name$ in the reset r_i of the jump j_i in all receiving SHA templates with the linear term a, where $\mathcal{L}_{sync,snd}$ is the sending SHA template and $r_{snd}(name) = (name = a)$.
5. $Sync_{new}(j) = \bigcup_{\substack{1 \le i \le n \\ \mathcal{L}_{sync,i} \in \mathbf{L}_{comp}}} Sync_i(j_i) \setminus name$, i.e. we keep all synchronization labels except from the one that is being resolved.
6. If $Event_{snd}(j_{snd}) = c$ then we assign $Event_{new}(j) = Event_{snd}(j_{snd})$ i.e. if j_{snd} is stochastic in $\mathcal{L}_{sync,snd}$ the jump j is stochastic in $\mathcal{L}_{sync,new}$.

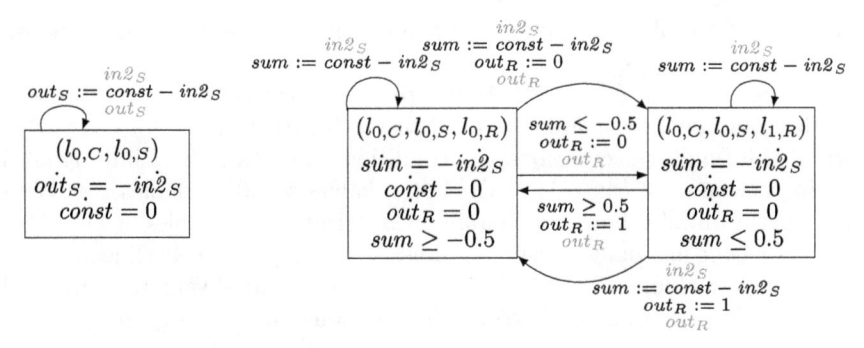

(a) $\mathcal{L}_{sync,\mathcal{I}}$ after resolving m_{CtoS}.

(b) $\mathcal{L}_{sync,new}$ after resolving m_{StoR}.

Fig. 12. Intermediate automaton after different composition stages of the Simulink temperature control system (Fig. 1).

Example. Consider $\mathcal{L}_{sync,\mathcal{I}}$ resulting from the resolution of m_{CtoS}, as shown in Fig. 12a. Exemplary, we show how to construct a synchronized and a non-synchronized jump of $\mathcal{L}_{sync,new} = \mathcal{L}_{sync,\mathcal{I}} \|_{m_{StoR}} \mathcal{L}_{sync,R}$. The final result $\mathcal{L}_{sync,new}$ is shown in Fig. 12b. There exists a non-synchronized jump $j_N = (1, g_N, r_N, \mathbf{l'})$ from source location $\mathbf{1} = (l_{0,C}, l_{0,S}, l_{0,R})$ to $\mathbf{l'} = (l_{0,C}, l_{0,S}, l_{1,R})$ with guard $g_n = sum \le -0.5$, reset $r_N = out_R := 0$ and synchronization label out_R because (1) there exists a jump j_R in $\mathcal{L}_{sync,R}$ with $j_R = (l_{0,R}, sum \le -0.5, out_R := 0, l_{1,R})$ and $sum \notin \{out_R\} = Sync_R(j_R)$ and (2) no other change happens in $\mathcal{L}_{sync,\mathcal{I}}$. We preserve the synchronization label out_R from j_R, i.e. $Sync_{new}(j_N) = Sync_R(j_R)$. There exists a synchronized jump $j_S = (1, g_S, r_S, \mathbf{l'})$ from $\mathbf{1}$ to $\mathbf{l'}$ with guard $g_S = true$, reset $r_S = sum := const - in2_S \cup out_R := 0$ and synchronization labels out_R and $in2_S$ because (1) there exists a jump j'_R in

$\mathcal{L}_{sync,R}$ with $j'_R = (l_{0,R}, true, out_R := 0, l_{1,R})$ and $sum \in Sync_R(j_R)$ and a jump $j_\mathcal{I}$ in $\mathcal{L}_{sync,\mathcal{I}}$ with $j_\mathcal{I} = ((l_{0,C}, l_{0,S}), true, sum := const - in2_S, (l_{0,C}, l_{0,S}))$ and $sum \in Sync_\mathcal{I}(j_\mathcal{I})$, (2) no other automata are synchronized, (3) the guards are disjoined, i.e. $g_S = true \wedge true$ and (4) the resets are joined, i.e. $r_S = out_R := 0 \cup sum := const - in2_S$. As sum is not used in the resets, the *apply* function does not need to replace its occurrence. If the value of sum would be used, e.g. as $out_R := sum$, this variable would need to be replaced by its reset, i.e. $out_R := const - in2_S$. Additionally, all synchronization labels except sum are kept, i.e. $Sync_{new}(j_N) = (\{out_R, sum\} \cup \{sum\}) \setminus sum$.

Extracting the Composed Automaton. We need a final transformation to obtain the composed automaton $\mathcal{L}$ following the *LHAC* syntax. This requires to resolve the relaxations of flows and initial states of the *LHAC*sync. Function *Sync* is omitted, as it is not part of the *LHAC* syntax. The conjoined flow in the composed automaton assigns a flow for every variable in *Var*. Similarly, for the initial state each location is assigned a pair $(\sigma, cond)$ where σ is the initial state for all variables in *Var*. Thus, we only need to resolve the conditions.

Initial State of the Composed Automaton. To identify the unique initial state of the composed automaton we need to resolve each initial state σ and check whether it fulfills the corresponding condition *cond*. As all Simulink signals have an initial state, we can resolve the initial values for all variables $v \in Var$ even though the initial values may contain linear terms over variables in *Var*. This can either be done manually or using established techniques to solve linear equations, e.g. Gaussian elimination [33]. Once we obtain the initial valuation v_σ, we check whether the condition *cond* holds. The function *Init* is then given by:

$$Init(l) = \begin{cases} \sigma_l \text{ where } (\sigma_l, cond_l) = Init_{new}(l) & v_{\sigma_l} \models cond_l \\ \emptyset & v_{\sigma_l} \not\models cond_l \end{cases}$$

The initial state of the Simulink model is unique. Thus, the initial state of the composed automaton $\mathcal{L}$ is given by l_{init}, the corresponding valuation v_σ and the sampled expiration times for the random clocks with $Init(l_{init}) = v_\sigma$.

Reducing the Composed Automaton. The composed automaton resulting from the transformation can be reduced by removing unused variables and jumps.

  For constants, we can remove the variable and replace each occurrence with the value assigned in the initial state.
- For purely discrete variables, i.e. variables that evolve with rate 0 in each location, we can remove all jumps that are used to catch that the continuous evolution of the variable results in a discrete change. For example, consider the transformation rule for the relay in Fig. 8. The jump from l_0 to l_1 with guard $in \leq \text{switch\_off}$ is only executed when in continuously evolves. If in is purely discrete this jump can be eliminated.

- Similarly, for purely continuous variables we can remove all edges where the discrete update for this variable is received as this will never be sent.
- Variables that are only changed discretely and have a fixed value for each location can be replaced with the corresponding value in each location.

Example. The result of our transformation for the Simulink model of the temperature control unit (Fig. 1) is shown in Fig. 13. The locations l_{heat} and l_{cool} model the working system, where the temperature tmp evolves with the rate r and failed rate fr. The locations l_{turn_off} and l_{turn_on} are used to switch from *heat* to *cool* and vice-versa. All these locations also exist if the system is broken.

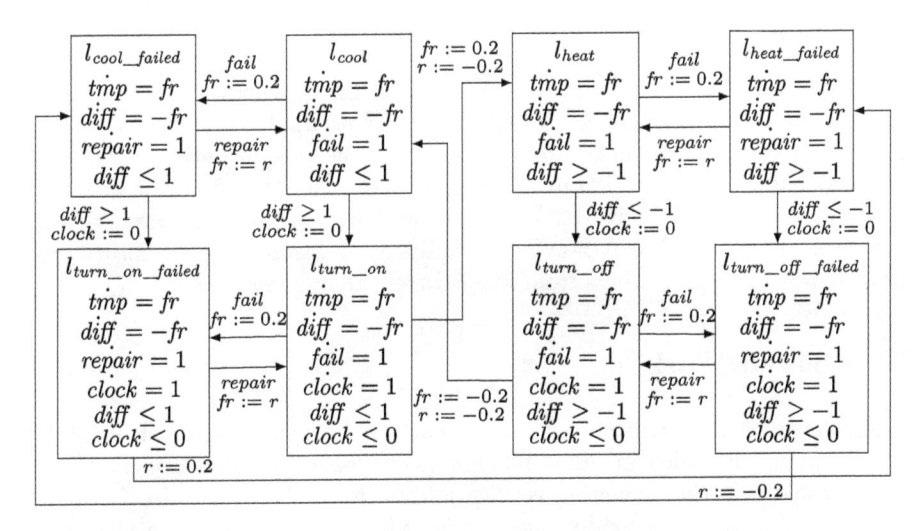

Fig. 13. SHA resulting from the transformation of the Simulink temperature control system (Fig. 1).

Table 1. Results of the quantitative analysis with Simulink and REALYST. All results and errors were rounded to the fourth decimal.

Tool		$P(\Diamond\ tmp \geq 20)$	$P(\Diamond\ tmp \geq 20.5)$	$P(\Diamond\ tmp \geq 21)$	$P(\Diamond\ tmp \geq 21.5)$
Simulink	CI	[0.9992, 1]	[0.2900, 0.3155]	[0.0196, 0.0280]	[0, 0.008]
	midpoint	0.9996	0.3028	0.0238	0.0004
	comp. time [s]	6855	6855	6855	6855
REALYST	reachability	0.9997	0.3052	0.0251	0
	error	0.0008	0.0004	0.0001	0
	comp. time [s]	642	624	604	597

4 Evaluation

Our transformation provides access to established tools for quantitative analysis such as REALYST [18], which allows the computation of optimal time-bounded reachability probabilities for subclasses of hybrid automata extended with random clocks. To demonstrate the feasibility of our overall approach, we used REALYST to perform time-bounded reachability analysis for the monolithic SHA of the temperature control system shown in Fig. 13. With that, we can provide statistical guarantees that the temperature stays below a given threshold, even if the system fails. We use a PCTL-like notation to express these properties, e.g., $P(\Diamond\ tmp \geq 20)$ gives the probability that tmp eventually reaches or exceeds 20. We compare the REALYST results with a simulation-based evaluation of the Simulink model. As Simulink does not provide confidence intervals, we compute confidence intervals with $\lambda = 0.95$ based on the Wilson score [37], as implemented in [1]. We simulate the model for 5 000 runs and track whether predefined temperature thresholds are reached or exceeded. We used a fixed-step solver with a step size $s = 0.001$. For both tools we observed the system until $t = 24$, which ensures that at least one failure occurs. As shown in Table 1, the reachability probabilities computed with REALYST are within the confidence intervals computed in Simulink while REALYST is significantly faster. The statistical error provided by REALYST stems from multi-dimensional integration.

5 Related Work

There have been quite some efforts to enable the formal verification of systems that are modeled in Simulink. For example, in [5], Simulink models are transformed into the deductive verification platform Why3 [20]. In [23], safety properties for Simulink models are verified via the UCLID verification system [25]. In [32], Simulink models are transformed into Boogie [7] and verified with the Z3 solver [15]. However, all of these approaches, including the Simulink Design Verifier [35], are limited to discrete subsets of Simulink. Formal verification methods that support hybrid systems modeled in Simulink are, e.g., proposed in [12,13,27–29,38]. In [13], the authors propose the tool CheckMate for modeling hybrid automata in Simulink, which can then be formally verified by exploring the state space via reachability analysis. A similar approach is followed in [29], where the authors present a transformation from a subset of Simulink to the hybrid automata dialect SpaceEx. However, they focus on techniques for a special class of systems and do not provide general transformation rules for a broader set of blocks. In [12,38], the authors transform Simulink models with Stateflow parts into Hybrid CSP and enable the verification in the Hybrid Hoare Logic Prover. Finally, in our own previous work [3,27,28], we have presented a transformation from Simulink into the differential dynamic logic [31], which enables deductive verification using the interactive theorem prover KeYmaera X [21]. However, all of these methods focus on the qualitative analysis of safety properties, and none of them takes stochastic components into consideration.

There has been a number of works on statistical model checking (SMC) for Simulink. In [39], the authors present an SMC approach based on Bayesian statistics and show that it is feasible for hybrid systems with stochastic transitions, a generalization of Simulink/Stateflow models. In [26], the authors propose an extension of Plasma Lab [9] for Simulink. They use custom C-code blocks that generate independent sequences of random draws to model failure probabilities and check bounded linear temporal logic properties over sequences of states and time stamps. As the random draws are not part of the model, they do not provide a stochastic model with formal semantics, and thus the approach is generally not amenable to sophisticated reachability analysis and more advanced quantitative analysis techniques as they are provided by state-of-the-art quantitative analysis tools such as MODESTTOOLSET [10] or REALYST [17].

A railway signaling system modeled in Simulink was manually translated and analyzed using UPPAAL SMC in [8]. However, the authors do not propose systematic transformation rules but rather focus on analyzing this specific case study. In [19], the authors propose a transformation from Simulink into stochastic timed automata (STA) and perform SMC with UPPAAL SMC on the resulting network of STA. However, they do not consider stochastic blocks and transform a given Simulink model into a deterministic STA model where all probabilities are one. UPPAAL SMC has been integrated into UPPAAL Stratego [14], which uses priced timed automata to model stochastic behavior and also provides tooling for timed games [11] and learning-based strategy synthesis [6]. However, while UPPAAL Stratego comes with a graphical interface and is designed for usability, the underlying formalisms are less expressive than stochastic hybrid automata, in particular w.r.t. continuous system behavior governed by differential equations and controlled by continuous and stochastic variables.

We presented an approach for learning with a formally verified shield in [1,2], where statistical model checking is used to optimize the probability that a Simulink model satisfies certain measures of interest. However, the focus there is on SMC-based learning, c.f. [30], and no transformation from Simulink into a formal representation is provided.

In summary, to the best of our knowledge, existing approaches for the analysis of Simulink either focus on qualitative properties or on SMC and do not provide the means for quantitative reachability analyses.

6 Conclusion

We have presented a transformation for stochastic Simulink models to SHA using compositional transformation rules and a discrete-event synchronization. We have presented transformation rules for a subset of Simulink blocks as well as a synchronization mechanism that retains the signal flow of the Simulink model in the transformed SHA templates. To compose the SHA templates that represent the individual blocks, we give a dedicated parallel composition algorithm that preserves the execution order of the Simulink model. We evaluated our approach using a temperature control system with stochastic failure and repair.

Using REALYST we performed time-bounded reachability analysis to get statistical guarantees that the temperature is kept below a threshold. The results lie inside the confidence intervals calculated from a simulation-based evaluation in Simulink. At the same time, the computation times in REALYST were significantly faster. However, please note that the class of hybrid systems supported by REALYST has limitations and that models with more complex continuous behavior will suffer in terms of computation time. In future work, we plan to automate our transformation, and to increase the supported subset of Simulink blocks, e.g., to different failure and repair strategies [22]. Furthermore, we plan to provide better support for the integration of stochasticity into Simulink models and into our transformation.

Acknowledgement. We thank Joanna Delicaris and Jonas Stübbe for the fruitful discussions and their valuable help using REALYST.

References

1. Adelt, J., Bruch, S., Herber, P., Niehage, M., Remke, A.: Shielded learning for resilience and performance based on statistical model checking in simulink. In: Steffen, B. (ed.) AISoLA 2023. LNCS, vol. 14380, pp. 94–118. Springer, Cham (2024). https://doi.org/10.1007/978-3-031-46002-9_6
2. Adelt, J., Herber, P., Niehage, M., Remke, A.: Towards safe and resilient hybrid systems in the presence of learning and uncertainty. In: In: Margaria, T., Steffen, B. (eds.) ISoLA 2022. LNCS, vol. 13701, pp. 299–319. Springer, Cham (2022). https://doi.org/10.1007/978-3-031-19849-6_18
3. Adelt, J., Liebrenz, T., Herber, P.: Formal verification of intelligent hybrid systems that are modeled with simulink and the reinforcement learning toolbox. In: Huisman, M., Păsăreanu, C., Zhan, N. (eds.) FM 2021. LNCS, vol. 13047, pp. 349–366. Springer, Cham (2021). https://doi.org/10.1007/978-3-030-90870-6_19
4. Alur, R., et al.: The algorithmic analysis of hybrid systems. Theoret. Comput. Sci. **138**, 3–34 (1995). https://doi.org/10.1016/0304-3975(94)00202-T
5. Araiza-Illan, D., Eder, K., Richards, A.: Formal verification of control systems' properties with theorem proving. In: UKACC International Conference on Control, pp. 244–249. IEEE (2014). https://doi.org/10.1109/CONTROL.2014.6915147
6. Ashok, P., Křetínský, J., Larsen, K.G., Le Coënt, A., Taankvist, J.H., Weininger, M.: SOS: safe, optimal and small strategies for hybrid markov decision processes. In: Parker, D., Wolf, V. (eds.) QEST 2019. LNCS, vol. 11785, pp. 147–164. Springer, Cham (2019). https://doi.org/10.1007/978-3-030-30281-8_9
7. Barnett, M., Chang, B.-Y.E., DeLine, R., Jacobs, B., Leino, K.R.M.: Boogie: a modular reusable verifier for object-oriented programs. In: de Boer, F.S., Bonsangue, M.M., Graf, S., de Roever, W.-P. (eds.) FMCO 2005. LNCS, vol. 4111, pp. 364–387. Springer, Heidelberg (2006). https://doi.org/10.1007/11804192_17
8. Basile, D., ter Beek, M.H., Ferrari, A., Legay, A.: Modelling and analysing ERTMS L3 moving block railway signalling with Simulink and UPPAAL SMC. In: Larsen, K.G., Willemse, T. (eds.) FMICS 2019. LNCS, vol. 11687, pp. 1–21. Springer, Cham (2019). https://doi.org/10.1007/978-3-030-27008-7_1

9. Boyer, B., Corre, K., Legay, A., Sedwards, S.: PLASMA-lab: a flexible, distributable statistical model checking library. In: Joshi, K., Siegle, M., Stoelinga, M., D'Argenio, P.R. (eds.) QEST 2013. LNCS, vol. 8054, pp. 160–164. Springer, Heidelberg (2013). https://doi.org/10.1007/978-3-642-40196-1_12
10. Budde, C.E., D'Argenio, P.R., Hartmanns, A., Sedwards, S.: A statistical model checker for nondeterminism and rare events. In: Beyer, D., Huisman, M. (eds.) TACAS 2018. LNCS, vol. 10806, pp. 340–358. Springer, Cham (2018). https://doi.org/10.1007/978-3-319-89963-3_20
11. Cassez, F., David, A., Fleury, E., Larsen, K.G., Lime, D.: Efficient on-the-fly algorithms for the analysis of timed games. In: Abadi, M., de Alfaro, L. (eds.) CONCUR 2005. LNCS, vol. 3653, pp. 66–80. Springer, Heidelberg (2005). https://doi.org/10.1007/11539452_9
12. Chen, M., et al.: MARS: a toolchain for modelling, analysis and verification of hybrid systems. In: Hinchey, M.G., Bowen, J.P., Olderog, E.-R. (eds.) Provably Correct Systems. NMSSE, pp. 39–58. Springer, Cham (2017). https://doi.org/10.1007/978-3-319-48628-4_3
13. Chutinan, A., Krogh, B.H.: Computational techniques for hybrid system verification. IEEE Trans. Automatic Control. 48(1), 64–75 (2003). https://doi.org/10.1109/TAC.2002.806655
14. David, A., Larsen, K.G., Legay, A., Mikučionis, M., Poulsen, D.B.: UPPAAL SMC tutorial. Int. J. Softw. Tools Technol. Transfer 17(4), 397–415 (2015). https://doi.org/10.1007/s10009-014-0361-y
15. de Moura, L., Bjørner, N.: Z3: an efficient SMT solver. In: Ramakrishnan, C.R., Rehof, J. (eds.) TACAS 2008. LNCS, vol. 4963, pp. 337–340. Springer, Heidelberg (2008). https://doi.org/10.1007/978-3-540-78800-3_24
16. Delicaris, J., Remke, A., Ábrahám, E., Schupp, S., Stübbe, J.: Maximizing Reachability Probabilities in Rectangular Automata with Random Events. Science of Computer Programming (2024). https://doi.org/10.1016/j.scico.2024.103213
17. Delicaris, J., Schupp, S., Ábrahám, E., Remke, A.: Maximizing reachability probabilities in rectangular automata with random clocks. In: David, C., Sun, M. (eds.) TASE 2023. LNCS, vol. 13931, pp. 164–182. Springer, Cham (2023). https://doi.org/10.1007/978-3-031-35257-7_10
18. Delicaris, J., Stübbe, J., Schupp, S., Remke, A.: Realyst: A C++ tool for optimizing reachability probabilities in stochastic hybrid systems. In: Kalyvianaki, E., Paolieri, M. (eds.) VALUETOOLS 2023. LNICS, vol. 539, pp. 170–182. Springer, Cham (2023). https://doi.org/10.1007/978-3-031-48885-6_11
19. Filipovikj, P., Mahmud, N., Marinescu, R., Seceleanu, C., Ljungkrantz, O., Lönn, H.: Simulink to UPPAAL statistical model checker: analyzing automotive industrial systems. In: Fitzgerald, J., Heitmeyer, C., Gnesi, S., Philippou, A. (eds.) FM 2016. LNCS, vol. 9995, pp. 748–756. Springer, Cham (2016). https://doi.org/10.1007/978-3-319-48989-6_46
20. Filliâtre, J.-C., Paskevich, A.: Why3 — where programs meet provers. In: Felleisen, M., Gardner, P. (eds.) ESOP 2013. LNCS, vol. 7792, pp. 125–128. Springer, Heidelberg (2013). https://doi.org/10.1007/978-3-642-37036-6_8
21. Fulton, N., Mitsch, S., Quesel, J.-D., Völp, M., Platzer, A.: KeYmaera X: an axiomatic tactical theorem prover for hybrid systems. In: Felty, A.P., Middeldorp, A. (eds.) CADE 2015. LNCS (LNAI), vol. 9195, pp. 527–538. Springer, Cham (2015). https://doi.org/10.1007/978-3-319-21401-6_36

22. Haverkort, B.R., Kuntz, M., Remke, A., Roolvink, S., Stoelinga, M.I.A.: Evaluating repair strategies for a water-treatment facility using arcade. In: IEEE/IFIP International Conference on Dependable Systems & Network,. pp. 419–424 (2010). https://doi.org/10.1109/DSN.2010.5544290
23. Herber, P., Reicherdt, R., Bittner, P.: Bit-precise formal verification of discrete-time MATLAB/Simulink models using SMT solving. In: International Conference on Embedded Software, pp. 1–10. IEEE (2013). https://doi.org/10.1109/EMSOFT.2013.6658586
24. Hoare, C.A.R.: Communicating sequential processes. Commun. ACM **21**(8), 666–677 (1978). https://doi.org/10.1145/359576.359585
25. Lahiri, S.K., Seshia, S.A.: The UCLID decision procedure. In: Alur, R., Peled, D.A. (eds.) CAV 2004. LNCS, vol. 3114, pp. 475–478. Springer, Heidelberg (2004). https://doi.org/10.1007/978-3-540-27813-9_40
26. Legay, A., Traonouez, L.-M.: Statistical model checking of Simulink models with plasma lab. In: Artho, C., Ölveczky, P.C. (eds.) FTSCS 2015. CCIS, vol. 596, pp. 259–264. Springer, Cham (2016). https://doi.org/10.1007/978-3-319-29510-7_15
27. Liebrenz, T., Herber, P., Glesner, S.: Deductive verification of hybrid control systems modeled in Simulink with KeYmaera X. In: Sun, J., Sun, M. (eds.) ICFEM 2018. LNCS, vol. 11232, pp. 89–105. Springer, Cham (2018). https://doi.org/10.1007/978-3-030-02450-5_6
28. Liebrenz, T., Herber, P., Glesner, S.: A service-oriented approach for decomposing and verifying hybrid system models. In: Arbab, F., Jongmans, S.-S. (eds.) FACS 2019. LNCS, vol. 12018, pp. 127–146. Springer, Cham (2020). https://doi.org/10.1007/978-3-030-40914-2_7
29. Minopoli, S., Frehse, G.: SL2SX translator: from Simulink to SpaceEx models. In: International Conference on Hybrid Systems: Computation and Control, pp. 93–98. ACM (2016). https://doi.org/10.1145/2883817.2883826
30. Niehage, M., Hartmanns, A., Remke, A.: Learning optimal decisions for stochastic hybrid systems. In: ACM-IEEE International Conference on Formal Methods and Models for System Design, pp. 44–55. ACM (2021)
31. Platzer, A.: Differential dynamic logic for hybrid systems. J. Autom. Reason. **41**(2), 143–189 (2008). https://doi.org/10.1007/s10817-008-9103-8
32. Reicherdt, R., Glesner, S.: Formal verification of discrete-time MATLAB/Simulink models using boogie. In: Giannakopoulou, D., Salaün, G. (eds.) SEFM 2014. LNCS, vol. 8702, pp. 190–204. Springer, Cham (2014). https://doi.org/10.1007/978-3-319-10431-7_14
33. Stoer, J., Bulirsch, R.: Systems of linear equations. In: Introduction to Numerical Analysis. Texts in Applied Mathematics, vol. 12, pp. 190–288. Springer, New York (2002). https://doi.org/10.1007/978-0-387-21738-3_4
34. The MathWorks: Simulink. https://de.mathworks.com/products/simulink.html
35. The MathWorks: Simulink Design Verifier. https://de.mathworks.com/products/simulink-design-verifier.html
36. Willemsen, L., Remke, A., Ábrahám, E.: Comparing two approaches to include stochasticity in hybrid automata. In: Jansen, N., Tribastone, M. (eds.) QEST 2023. LNCS, vol. 14287, pp. 238–254. Springer, Cham (2023). https://doi.org/10.1007/978-3-031-43835-6_17
37. Wilson, E.: Probable inference, the law of succession, and statistical inference. J. Am. Stat. Assoc. **22**(158), 209–212 (1927). https://doi.org/10.2307/2276774

38. Zou, L., Zhan, N., Wang, S., Fränzle, M.: Formal verification of Simulink/Stateflow diagrams. In: Finkbeiner, B., Pu, G., Zhang, L. (eds.) ATVA 2015. LNCS, vol. 9364, pp. 464–481. Springer, Cham (2015). https://doi.org/10.1007/978-3-319-24953-7_33
39. Zuliani, P., Platzer, A., Clarke, E.M.: Bayesian statistical model checking with application to stateflow/simulink verification. Formal Meth. Syst. Des. **43**, 338–367 (2013). https://doi.org/10.1007/s10703-013-0195-3

Monitoring Real-Time Systems Under Parametric Delay

Martin Fränzle[1], Thomas M. Grosen[2(✉)], Kim G. Larsen[2], and Martin Zimmermann[2]

[1] Carl von Ossietzky Universität, Oldenburg, Germany
martin.fraenzle@uol.de
[2] Aalborg University, Aalborg, Denmark
{tmgr,kgl,mzi}@cs.aau.dk

Abstract. Timed Büchi automata provide a very expressive formalism for expressing requirements of real-time systems. Online monitoring of embedded real-time systems can then be achieved by symbolic execution of such automata on the trace observed from the system. This direct construction however only is faithful if observation of the trace is immediate in the sense that the monitor can assign exact time stamps to the actions it observes, which is rarely true in practice due to the substantial and fluctuating parametric delays introduced by the circuitry connecting the observed system to its monitoring device. We present a purely zone-based online monitoring algorithm, which handles such parametric delays exactly without recurrence to costly verification procedures for parametric timed automata. We have implemented our monitoring algorithm on top of the real-time model checking tool UPPAAL, and report on encouraging initial results.

Keywords: Monitoring · Timing uncertainty · Timed Büchi Automata

1 Introduction

Online monitoring is an important tool to ensure functional correctness of safety-critical systems. It analyses the execution traces observed from the system during its runtime by determining in real-time whether the observed traces satisfy the system's specification. Continuous online monitoring consequently is concerned with unbounded time horizons, unlike offline monitoring where a fixed finite trace is analysed after the execution has terminated. Hence, specifications for online monitoring are typically defined over infinite traces, with the most significant

---

M. Fränzle has been funded by the State of Lower Saxony, Zukunftslabor Mobilität, and by Deutsche Forschungsgemeinschaft, grants FR 2715/5-1 and FR 2715/6-1.
T. M. Grosen and K. G. Larsen have been funded by the VILLUM Investigator grant S4OS, and together with M. Zimmermann they have been supported by DIREC - Digital Research Centre Denmark.

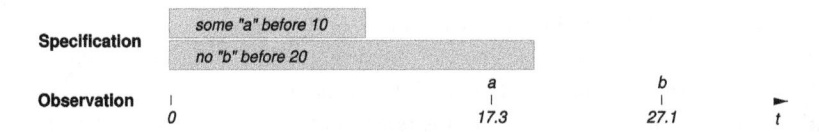

```
                   ┌─────────────────────────┐
   Specification   │  some "a" before 10     │
                   │  no "b" before 20       │
                   └─────────────────────────┘
                                    a              b
   Observation     |                |              |              ▶
                   0               17.3           27.1            t
```

Fig. 1. Monitoring under observation delay: at time $t = 27.1$ we can conclusively decide that the MITL property $F_{[0,10]}a \wedge G_{[0,20]}\neg b$ is violated irrespective of the latency of the observation channel, provided the jitter is less than 0.2.

approach being temporal logics. As specifications often include real-time requirements, e.g., "every request is answered within 10 milliseconds (ms)", we focus here on metric-time temporal logics over timed words. More precisely, we consider Metric Interval Temporal Logic (MITL) [2], which offers a good balance between expressiveness and algorithmic properties. For example, the request-response specification above is expressed by the MITL formula $G_{\geq 0}(\texttt{req} \to F_{\leq 10}\texttt{resp})$.

While the specifications classify infinite traces, the traces observed online and to be checked against the specification remain finite. Nevertheless, one can still return verdicts [7]: for example, *every* infinite extension of a finite trace with some request that is not answered within 10 ms violates the request-response specification above. Hence, violation of the specification is already witnessed by such a finite trace. Dually, consider the specification "system calibration is completed within 500 ms", expressed by the formula $F_{\leq 500}\texttt{cc}$ with the proposition $\texttt{cc}$ representing the completion of calibration. Every infinite extension of a finite trace on which the calibration is completed within 400 ms satisfies the specification. Hence, satisfaction of the specification is already witnessed by such a finite trace. However, there are also traces and specifications for which no verdict can currently be drawn, like in the situation where no calibration has been observed yet at current time of 350 ms. As usual, we capture these three situations with the three verdicts $\top$ (satisfaction for every extension), $\bot$ (violation for every extension), and $?$ (inconclusive).

Online monitoring can be achieved by compiling the MITL specification into an equivalent timed Büchi automaton and then symbolically executing the automaton on the observed trace of the system [7,15]. However, this approach is correct only if the actions of the monitored system can be observed immediately by the monitor. In practice, there is usually a communication delay between the system and the monitor. This delay is induced by various types of circuitry at their interfaces, like technical sensors, conversion between analog and digital signals, and communication networks forwarding signals to the monitor. We follow the approach described in McGraw-Hill's Encyclopedia of Networking and Telecommunications [24] where a communication delay consists of a constant part (latency) and varying part (jitter).

Consequently, the monitored system and the symbolic execution are no longer synchronized but deviate by a delay, for which only bounds, yet not exact values tend to be known. But even then, one can still provide meaningful verdicts, see Fig. 1: The specification $F_{\leq 10}a \wedge G_{\leq 20}\neg b$ expresses that an a occurs within 10 ms and no b occurs within 20 ms. The observed trace shows the first a at 17.3 ms and the first b at 27.1 ms. This observation is only consistent with satisfaction of the constraint $F_{\leq 10}a$ if a's observation delay exceeds 7.3 ms, while satisfaction of $G_{\leq 20}\neg b$ requires a delay of at most 7.1 ms for b. Thus, if the jitter is strictly smaller than 0.2 ms, the specification is definitely violated. Note that the verdict "violated" is true independently of the actual value of the unknown, parametric communication latency.

On the other hand, if the parametric latency is known to be in the range $[4.5, 8]$ ms and the jitter is in $[0, 0.3]$ ms, then we cannot give a definitive verdict: The a may have occurred at 10 ms and then has been observed with 7 ms latency plus 0.3 ms jitter at $17.3 = 10 + 7 + 0.3$ ms, and the b may have occurred at 20.1 ms and then observed with the same latency (yet independent jitter) at $27.1 = 20.1 + 7 + 0$ ms. In this case, the property would be satisfied. But the a may also have occurred at 10.3 ms, violating the property, and still be observed with the same latency at $17.3 = 10.3 + 7 + 0$ ms. From the observations, we can nevertheless derive bounds on the parametric latency, as the property definitely is violated irrespective of the actual (unknown) value of the jitter whenever the actual latency is smaller than 7 ms or larger than 7.1 ms. It however cannot be guaranteed to be satisfied when the latency is in the range of $[7, 7.1]$ ms, as satisfaction then depends on the exact value of the jitter, which is not detectable. Thus, one can determine information beyond the verdicts $\top$, $\bot$, and $?$ in terms of bounds on the delay that imply definitive verdicts.

Our Contribution. Based on previous work by Grosen et al. [15] on online monitoring of MITL specifications without delay via timed Büchi automata, we present a symbolic MITL monitoring algorithm that provides exact verdicts under unknown delay consisting of parametric (i.e. unknown within bounds) latency and jitter. While an unknown delay is a timing parameter, our construction avoids the semidecidability [3] of analysis for parameterized timed automata, and instead uses only classical clock zones [9].

In addition, our approach has the advantage that it is even more informative than typical monitoring algorithms, which only return a verdict in $\{\top, \bot, ?\}$. Recall the example specification $F_{\leq 10}a \wedge G_{\leq 20}\neg b$ in the case where the jitter is constrained to $[0, 0.3]$ ms. As argued above, this specification can, given this bound on the jitter, only be satisfied if $7 \leq l \leq 7.1$, where l denotes the actual latency. Our algorithm, for which we also provide a prototype implementation and experimental evaluation, computes such parametric constraints on the set of potential latencies under which the specification can be satisfied as well as on the set of potential latencies under which the specification can be violated.

The implementation is built on top of the real-time model checking tool UPPAAL [19] using the difference-bounded matrix (DBM) data structure allowing for representation of convex polytopes called zones. Most importantly, the DBM data structure can be used for efficient implementation of various geometrical operations over zones needed for the symbolic analysis of timed automata, such as testing for emptiness, inclusion, equality, and computing projection and intersection of zones [9]. Our experiments show encouraging initial results on an industrial gear controller model from [20].

All proofs omitted due to space restrictions can be found in the full version [14].

Related Work. Our automata-based monitoring of finite traces against specifications over infinite words using the three verdicts $\{\top, \bot, ?\}$ follows the seminal work of Bauer et al. [7], who presented monitoring algorithms for LTL and timed LTL. Their algorithm for timed LTL is based on clock regions [1], while we follow the approach of Grosen et al. [15] and use clock zones [9], whose performance is an order of magnitude faster. Also, they translated timed LTL into event-clock automata, which are less expressive than the timed Büchi automata (TBA) used both by Grosen et al. [15] and here. More recently, the same approach has been used to monitor real-time properties under assumptions [11].

As our algorithms work with TBA, we also support MITL specifications, as these can be compiled into TBA. The monitoring problem for MITL (without delay) has been investigated before. Baldor et al. showed how to construct a monitor for dense-time MITL formulas by constructing a tree of timed transducers [5]. Ho et al. split unbounded and bounded parts of MITL formulas for monitoring, using traditional LTL monitoring for the unbounded parts and permitting a simpler construction for the (finite-word) bounded parts [16]. Bulychev et al. apply a technique of rewriting a given WMTL formula during monitoring as part of performing statistical model checking. None of the above works makes use of the efficient DBM datastructure or extends to the setting of TBA that provides the basis of our approach. Here we note, that as a specification formalism TBA exceeds the expressive power of MITL, which might be useful in certain applications (e.g. in the presence of counting properties).

There is also a large body of work on monitoring with finite-word semantics. Roşu et al. focussed on discrete-time finite-word MTL [25], while Basin et al. proposed algorithms for monitoring real-time finite-word properties [6] and compared the differences between different time models. André et al. consider monitoring finite logs of parameterized timed and hybrid systems [29]. Finally, Ulus et al. described monitoring timed regular expressions over finite words using unions of two-dimensional zones [26,27].

The problem of monitoring trace properties under uncertain observation has been addressed before [12,13,17,23,28], most notably based on Signal Temporal Logic (STL), exploiting STL's quantitative semantics [22] that characterizes robustness against variation in state variables. These approaches are mostly orthogonal to ours, as they tend to address uncertainty in the state observed at a time instant rather than uncertainty in the time stamps associated to state observations. It would consequently be interesting to combine the two approaches, thus permitting both state uncertainty due to inexact measurements and time uncertainty due to inexact clocks and fluctuating communication latencies. It should also be noted that robust STL monitoring comes in diverse variants representing different error models, starting from monitors that exploit the compositional real-valued robustness semantics [12,23]. This semantics however underapproximates the factual robustness of the verdict against state shifts in the observed trace such that monitoring algorithms based on this compositional semantics are sound and computationally efficient, yet incomplete. Due to the safe approximation, they may yield inconclusive verdicts in actually determined situations. Complete and thus optimally informed STL monitoring under uncertainty, which guarantees a verdict whenever the property is determined, has only recently been investigated. Visconti et al. in [28] developed sound and complete monitoring wrt. an interval model of state measurement error, where each single measurement features an independent displacement ranging over a bounded interval. Finkbeiner et al. in [13] address a refined model distinguishing between a constant, yet unknown up to bounds, offset and a time-varying, interval-bounded noise, as suggested by the pertinent ISO norm 5725 on measurement accuracy (there called "trueness" and "precision" of a measurement). We here adopt the latter, more refined model of measurement error and transfer it into the time domain, thus implementing sound and complete monitoring for the case when timestamps are affected by a parametric (unknown, yet constant) observation latency plus a fluctuating jitter that differs between observations. Closest to our approach is [18], which addresses a more confined model of observation delay comprising a fixed known (non-parametric) latency plus a varying jitter. It also covers clock drift, which is an additional source of (relative) jitter that we have excluded to simplify the exposition.

2 Preliminaries

The set of natural numbers (excluding zero) is $\mathbb{N}$, we define $\mathbb{N}_0 = \mathbb{N} \cup \{0\}$, the set of rational numbers is $\mathbb{Q}$, the set of non-negative rational numbers is $\mathbb{Q}_{\geq 0}$. the set of real numbers is $\mathbb{R}$, and the set of non-negative real numbers is $\mathbb{R}_{\geq 0}$. The powerset of a set S is denoted by 2^S.

Timed Words. A timed word over a finite alphabet Σ is a pair $\rho = (\sigma, \tau)$ where σ is a nonempty word over Σ and τ is a sequence of non-decreasing non-negative real numbers of the same length as σ. Timed words may be finite or infinite; in the latter case, we require $\limsup \tau = \infty$, i.e., time diverges. The set of finite timed words is denoted by $T\Sigma^*$ and the set of infinite timed words by $T\Sigma^\omega$. We also represent a timed word as a sequence of pairs $(\sigma_1, \tau_1), (\sigma_2, \tau_2), \ldots$. If $\rho = (\sigma_1, \tau_1), (\sigma_2, \tau_2), \ldots, (\sigma_n, \tau_n)$ is a finite timed word, we denote by $\tau(\rho)$ the total time duration of ρ, i.e., τ_n.

If $\rho_1 = (\sigma_1^1, \tau_1^1), \ldots, (\sigma_n^1, \tau_n^1)$ is a finite timed word, $\rho_2 = (\sigma_1^2, \tau_1^2), (\sigma_2^2, \tau_2^2), \ldots$ is a finite or infinite timed word, and $t \in \mathbb{Q}_{\geq 0}$ then the timed word concatenation $\rho_1 \cdot_t \rho_2$ is defined iff $\tau(\rho_1) \leq t$. Then, $\rho_1 \cdot_t \rho_2 = (\sigma_1, \tau_1), (\sigma_2, \tau_2), \ldots$ such that

$$\sigma_i = \begin{cases} \sigma_i^1 & \text{iff } i \leq n \\ \sigma_{i-n}^2 & \text{else} \end{cases} \text{ and } \tau_i = \begin{cases} \tau_i^1 & \text{iff } i \leq n \\ \tau_{i-n}^2 + t & \text{else.} \end{cases}$$

Timed Automata. A timed Büchi automaton (TBA) $\mathcal{A} = (Q, Q_0, \Sigma, C, \Delta, \mathcal{F})$ consists of a finite alphabet Σ, a finite set Q of locations, a set $Q_0 \subseteq Q$ of initial locations, a finite set C of clocks, a finite set $\Delta \subseteq Q \times Q \times \Sigma \times 2^C \times G(C)$ of transitions with $G(C)$ being the set of clock constraints over C, and a set $\mathcal{F} \subseteq Q$

of accepting locations. A transition (q, q', a, λ, g) is an edge from q to q' on input symbol a, where λ is the set of clocks to reset and g is a clock constraint over C. A clock constraint is a conjunction of atomic constraints of the form $x \sim n$, where x is a clock, $n \in \mathbb{N}_0$, and $\sim \in \{<, \leq, =, \geq, >\}$. A state of $\mathcal{A}$ is a pair (q, v) where q is a location in Q and $v \colon C \to \mathbb{R}_{\geq 0}$ is a valuation mapping clocks to their values. For any $d \in \mathbb{R}_{\geq 0}$, $v + d$ is the valuation $x \mapsto v(x) + d$.

A run of $\mathcal{A}$ from a state (q_0, v_0) over a timed word $(\sigma_1, \tau_1)(\sigma_2, \tau_2) \cdots$ is a sequence of steps $(q_0, v_0) \xrightarrow{(\sigma_1, \tau_1)} (q_1, v_1) \xrightarrow{(\sigma_2, \tau_2)} (q_2, v_2) \xrightarrow{(\sigma_3, \tau_3)} \cdots$ where for all $i \geq 1$ there is a transition $(q_{i-1}, q_i, \sigma_i, \lambda_i, g_i)$ such that $v_i(x) = 0$ for all x in λ_i and $v_i(x) = v_{i-1}(x) + (\tau_i - \tau_{i-1})$ otherwise, and g_i is satisfied by the valuation $v_{i-1} + (\tau_i - \tau_{i-1})$. Here, we use $\tau_0 = 0$. Given a run r, we denote the set of locations visited infinitely many times by r as $\text{Inf}(r)$. A run r of $\mathcal{A}$ is accepting if $\text{Inf}(r) \cap \mathcal{F} \neq \emptyset$. The language of $\mathcal{A}$ from a starting state (q, v), denoted $L(\mathcal{A}, (q, v))$, is the set of all infinite timed words with an accepting run in $\mathcal{A}$ starting from (q, v). We define the language of $\mathcal{A}$, written $L(\mathcal{A})$, to be $\bigcup_q L(\mathcal{A}, (q, v_0))$, where q ranges over Q_0 and where $v_0(x) = 0$ for all $x \in C$.

Logic. We use Metric Interval Temporal Logic (MITL) to express properties to be monitored; these are subsequently translated into equivalent TBA which we use in our monitoring algorithm. The syntax of MITL formulas over a finite alphabet Σ is defined as

$$\varphi ::= p \mid \neg \varphi \mid \varphi \vee \varphi \mid X_I \varphi \mid \varphi \, U_I \varphi$$

where $p \in \Sigma$ and I ranges over non-singular intervals over $\mathbb{R}_{\geq 0}$ with endpoints in $\mathbb{N}_0 \cup \{\infty\}$. We write $\sim n$ for $I = \{d \in \mathbb{R}_{\geq 0} \mid d \sim n\}$ for $\sim \in \{<, \leq, \geq, >\}$ and $n \in \mathbb{N}$. We also define the standard syntactic sugar: $\mathbf{true} = p \vee \neg p$, $\varphi \wedge \psi = \neg(\neg \varphi \vee \neg \psi)$, $F_I \varphi = \mathbf{true} \, U_I \varphi$, and $G_I \varphi = \neg F_I \neg \varphi$.

The satisfaction relation $\rho, i \models \varphi$ is defined for infinite timed words $\rho = (\sigma_1, \tau_1), (\sigma_2, \tau_2), \ldots$, positions $i \geq 1$, and an MITL formulas φ:

- $\rho, i \models p$ iff $p = \sigma_i$.
- $\rho, i \models \neg \varphi$ iff $\rho, i \not\models \varphi$.
- $\rho, i \models \varphi \vee \psi$ if $\rho, i \models \varphi$ or $\rho, i \models \psi$.
- $\rho, i \models X_I \varphi$ iff $\rho, (i+1) \models \varphi$ and $\tau_{i+1} - \tau_i \in I$.
- $\rho, i \models \varphi \, U_I \psi$ iff there exists $k \geq i$ s.t. $\rho, k \models \psi$, $\tau_k - \tau_i \in I$, and $\rho, j \models \varphi$ for all $i \leq j < k$.

We write $\rho \models \varphi$ whenever $\rho, 1 \models \varphi$. The language $L(\varphi)$ of an MITL formula φ is the set of all $\rho \in T\Sigma^\omega$ such that $\rho \models \varphi$.

Theorem 1 ([2,10]). *For each MITL formula φ there exists a TBA $\mathcal{A}$ with $L(\varphi) = L(\mathcal{A})$.*

Figure 2 illustrates Theorem 1 by providing TBA's for the formula $F_{[0,10]} a \wedge G_{[0,20]} \neg b$ from the introduction and its negation.

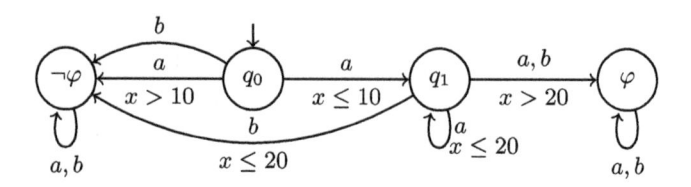

Fig. 2. An automaton for the language of the property $\varphi = F_{[0,10]}a \wedge G_{[0,20]}\neg b$ and its negation: If location φ is accepting then it accepts $L(\varphi)$, if location $\neg\varphi$ is accepting then it accepts $L(\neg\varphi)$.

3 Monitoring Under Delayed Observation

According to McGraw-Hill's Encyclopedia of Networking and Telecommunications [24], a communication delay consists of a constant part (latency) and varying part (jitter). We describe the delay as a pair $(\delta, \varepsilon) \in \mathbb{R}^2_{\geq 0}$ where δ is the constant latency for all signals and ε is the bound on the jitter. Thus, all signals from the system are delayed within $[\delta, \delta + \varepsilon]$ before they arrive at the monitor.

In the simplest case, our obligation is to monitor violation of an MITL specification φ by a system while observing the events through a channel *Chan* featuring a constant, yet unknown (up to a given, but maybe trivial, lower bound $l \in \mathbb{R}_{\geq 0}$ and upper bound $u \in \mathbb{R}_{\geq 0}$) transportation latency $\delta \in [l, u]$ and a varying jitter bounded by $\varepsilon \in \mathbb{R}_{\geq 0}$. Figure 1 shows an example of a property and an observation that conclusively violates the specification at time 27.1, even if the channel latency $\delta \in [0, \infty[$ is unknown, as long as the jitter is bounded by 0.2.

Thus, we need to distinguish between observations (the timed word corresponding to the events as they are observed by the monitoring device, subject to delay) and the possible ground-truths, as they may have been emitted by the monitored system. We begin by formalizing the concept of observation, where the occurrence of observed events is constrained by a set $\mathcal{D}$ capturing known bounds on the delay. Obviously, under latency δ (and arbitrary jitter), the first observation can only be made after at least δ units of time.

Definition 1. *A delay set $\mathcal{D}$ is a nonempty subset of $\mathbb{R}^2_{\geq 0}$ containing pairs of latencies and jitters. A $\mathcal{D}$-observation, i.e. an observation that can in principle be made under delay in $\mathcal{D}$, is a finite timed word* $\rho^* = (\sigma_1^*, \tau_1^*), \ldots, (\sigma_m^*, \tau_m^*)$ *with* $\tau_1^* \geq \delta$ *for some* $(\delta, \varepsilon) \in \mathcal{D}$.

As the ground-truth occurrence times of events in the system cannot be determined exactly from their delayed copies that the monitor receives through the communication channel, we have to consider all ground-truth timed words that the particular observation is consistent with, as follows.[1]

---

[1] Note that we simplify our definitions by assuming that jitter does not change the order of observations. Under the additional assumption that only a (uniformly) bounded number of events can be generated by the system in each unit of time, it is possible to take "overtaking" of events into account, by looking at all consistent permutations. However, this would lead to a severe overhead in the implementation.

Definition 2 (Consistency). Let $\rho^* = (\sigma_1^*, \tau_1^*), \ldots, (\sigma_m^*, \tau_m^*)$ be a $\{(\delta, \varepsilon)\}$-observation and let $\rho = (\sigma_1, \tau_1), \ldots, (\sigma_n, \tau_n)$ be a finite timed word. We say that ρ is consistent with ρ^* at observation time $t \in \mathbb{R}_{\geq 0}$ under latency δ and jitter ε iff

1. $\tau_n \leq t$ and $\tau_m^* \leq t$,
2. $n \geq m$, and $\sigma_i = \sigma_i^*$ and $\tau_i + \delta - \tau_i^* \in [0, \varepsilon]$ for all $i \in \{1, \ldots, m\}$, and
3. if $n > m$ then $\tau_{m+1} \geq t - (\delta + \varepsilon)$.

We denote the set of timed words ρ that are consistent with a $\{(\delta, \varepsilon)\}$-observation ρ^* at observation time t under latency δ and jitter ε by $GT_{\delta,\varepsilon}(\rho^*, t)$. Then, we define $GT_\mathcal{D}(\rho^*, t) = \bigcup_{(\delta,\varepsilon) \in \mathcal{D}} GT_{\delta,\varepsilon}(\rho^*, t)$.

$GT_\mathcal{D}(\rho^*, t)$ thus collects the possible ground-truths that are consistent with the observation ρ^* when the time elapsed since the system has started is t, and the delay (δ, ε) is within the set $\mathcal{D}$. Note that $GT_\mathcal{D}(\rho^*, t)$ is always nonempty, if ρ^* is a $\mathcal{D}$-observation and $t \geq \tau(\rho^*)$ (recall that $\tau(\rho^*)$ denotes the last time point of ρ^*).

Example 1. Figure 3 shows a $\{(\delta, \varepsilon)\}$-observation and a consistent ground-truth and illustrates how the delay shifts the timestamps of the events. The length of ρ is $n = 9$ and the length of ρ^* is $m = 4$. Recall that t is the time of observation.

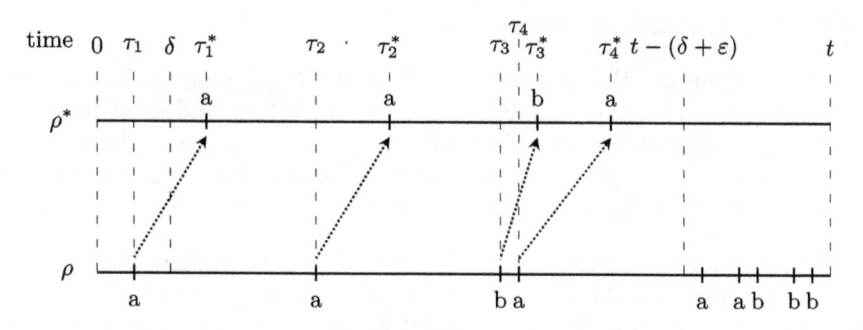

Fig. 3. A $\{(\delta, \varepsilon)\}$-observation ρ^* and a consistent ground-truth ρ.

In particular, notice the following:

- No event can occur in the observation ρ^* with a timestamp smaller than δ, as it takes at least δ units of time for an event to reach to be send from the system through the communication channel to the monitor. Obviously, at the system side (i.e., in the ground-truth ρ) events can happen at any timestamp, also before δ (e.g., the first a).
- The difference $\tau_i^* - \tau_i$ for $i \leq 4$ (i.e., the difference between the observation time and the time the event was emitted) must be in the interval $[\delta, \delta + \varepsilon]$.
- The time elapsed between the b and the last a in the observation ρ^* is larger than the time elapsed between the corresponding events in the ground-truth ρ. This means the jitter for the a is larger than the jitter for the b.

- The last five events in ρ have not yet been observed in ρ^*. Such events can only have timestamps in the interval $[t-(\delta+\varepsilon),t]$, as all earlier events must necessarily have been observed. Said differently, there cannot be any events between timestamp τ_4 (corresponding to the last observed event in ρ^* with timestamp τ_4^*) and timestamp $t-(\delta+\varepsilon)$, as any such event would have arrived at the monitor, even under the maximal possible delay of $\delta+\varepsilon$.
However, there can be an arbitrary number of events in ρ between timestamps $t-(\delta+\varepsilon)$ and t.

A monitor obviously ought to supply a verdict iff that verdict applies across *all possible* ground-truth timed words that the observed word explains. To define our definition of monitor, we use the set $\mathbb{B}_3 = \{\top, ?, \bot\}$ of verdicts, as usual.

Definition 3 (Monitor verdicts under delay). *Given a language $L \subseteq T\Sigma^\omega$, a set of possible observation delays $\mathcal{D}$, a $\mathcal{D}$-observation $\rho^* \in T\Sigma^*$, and an observation time $t \geq \tau(\rho^*)$, the function $\mathcal{V}_\mathcal{D} \colon 2^{T\Sigma^\omega} \to T\Sigma^* \times \mathbb{R}_{\geq 0} \to \mathbb{B}_3$ evaluates to the verdict*

$$\mathcal{V}_\mathcal{D}(L)(\rho^*,t) = \begin{cases} \top & \text{if } \rho \cdot_t \mu \in L \text{ for all } \rho \in GT_\mathcal{D}(\rho^*,t) \text{ and all } \mu \in T\Sigma^\omega, \\ \bot & \text{if } \rho \cdot_t \mu \notin L \text{ for all } \rho \in GT_\mathcal{D}(\rho^*,t) \text{ and all } \mu \in T\Sigma^\omega, \\ ? & \text{otherwise.} \end{cases}$$

$\mathcal{V}_\mathcal{D}(L)(\rho^*,t)$ *is undefined when $t < \tau(\rho^*)$.*

Example 2. Consider the property $\varphi = F_{[0,10]} a \wedge G_{[0,20]} \neg b$ and observed word $\rho^* = (a, 17.3), (b, 27.1)$ shown in Fig. 1, time point $t = 27.1$, and set of delays $\mathcal{D} = \{(\delta, \varepsilon) \mid \varepsilon = 0.2\}$. As the jitter is bounded by 0.2, in all ground truths either a occurred after time point 10, or b occurred before time point 20. Thus, all extensions of all possible ground truths satisfy $\neg \varphi$, i.e., $\mathcal{V}_\mathcal{D}(L(\varphi)))(\rho^*,t) = \bot$.

Note that for the special case of $\mathcal{D} = \{(0,0)\}$ we cover classical (i.e., delay-free) monitoring [15]. Before we turn our attention to computing $\mathcal{V}$ we study some properties of our definition. First, let us note that the ability to make firm verdicts increases with increased certainty of the observation channel delay.

Lemma 1. *Let $L \subseteq T\Sigma^\omega$, $\rho^* \in T\Sigma^*$, let $\mathcal{D} \subseteq \mathcal{D}'$ be delay sets, let ρ^* be a $\mathcal{D}$-observation, and let $t \geq \tau(\rho^*)$. Then, $\mathcal{V}_{\mathcal{D}'}(L)(\rho^*,t) = \top$ implies $\mathcal{V}_\mathcal{D}(L)(\rho^*,t) = \top$ and $\mathcal{V}_{\mathcal{D}'}(L)(\rho^*,t) = \bot$ implies $\mathcal{V}_\mathcal{D}(L)(\rho^*,t) = \bot$.*

As a refinement of the verdict function in Definition 3, one may provide information about the delay parameters (δ,ε) that can explain an observation. Given $L \subseteq T\Sigma^\omega$, a finite timed word $\rho^* \in T\Sigma^*$, and $t \geq \tau(\rho^*)$, the set of delays $\Delta(L,\rho^*,t)$ that are consistent with the observation ρ^* at t is defined as

$$\Delta(L,\rho^*,t) = \{(\delta,\varepsilon) \mid \exists \rho \in GT_{\delta,\varepsilon}(\rho^*,t) \exists \mu \in T\Sigma^\omega \text{ s.t. } \rho \cdot_t \mu \in L\}.$$

We denote by $\Delta_\mathcal{D}(L,\rho^*,t)$ the set $\Delta(L,\rho^*,t) \cap \mathcal{D}$. Now we can characterize the conclusive monitoring verdicts via these delay sets.

Lemma 2. *Given $L \subseteq T\Sigma^\omega$, a set $\mathcal{D}$ of delays, a $\mathcal{D}$-observation $\rho^* \in T\Sigma^*$, and $t \geq \tau(\rho^*)$, we have*

1. $\Delta_\mathcal{D}(L, \rho^*, t) = \emptyset$ *iff* $\mathcal{V}_\mathcal{D}(L)(\rho^*, t) = \bot$, *and*
2. $\Delta_\mathcal{D}(\overline{L}, \rho^*, t) = \emptyset$ *iff* $\mathcal{V}_\mathcal{D}(L)(\rho^*, t) = \top$.

But even in the case when both delay-sets are nonempty (i.e., the verdict is ?), we can still provide useful information in terms of the sets $\Delta(L, \rho^*, t)$ and $\Delta(\overline{L}, \rho^*, t)$ of consistent delays. In particular, the set of consistent delays is non-increasing during observations. To explain this, we first define a notion of extensions for finite timed words (w.r.t. current time instants t, t'). Formally, let $\rho = (\sigma_1, \tau_1), \ldots, (\sigma_n, \tau_n)$ and $\rho' = (\sigma'_1, \tau'_1), \ldots, (\sigma'_{n'}, \tau'_{n'})$ be two finite timed words. Also let $t, t' \in \mathbb{R}_{\geq 0}$. Then, we define $(\rho, t) \sqsubseteq (\rho', t')$, if $n \leq n'$, $\sigma_i = \sigma'_i$ and $\tau_i = \tau'_i$ for all $i \leq n$, and either $n = n'$ and $t \leq t'$ or $n < n'$ and $t \leq \tau'_{n+1}$. By extending the observations, we (potentially) reduce the set of consistent delays.

Lemma 3. *Let $(\rho_1^*, t_1) \sqsubseteq (\rho_2^*, t_2)$ for finite timed words ρ_1^*, ρ_2^* and $t_1 \geq \tau(\rho_1^*)$ and $t_2 \geq \tau(\rho_2^*)$. Then, $\Delta(L, \rho_1^*, t_1) \supseteq \Delta(L, \rho_2^*, t_2)$.*

Another interesting point is that in some cases, no extension of the observed word will provide a definitive verdict.

Example 3. Consider the language $L(F_{\leq 10} a)$, the observation $\rho^* = (a, 15)$, and the set $\mathcal{D} = \{(\delta, 0) \mid \delta \in [0, 10]\}$ of delays. For any given $t \geq \tau(\rho^*)$ the sets of consistent delays are $\Delta_\mathcal{D}(L, \rho^*, t) = \{(\delta, 0) \mid \delta \in [5, 10]\}$ and $\Delta_\mathcal{D}(\overline{L}, \rho^*, t) = \{(\delta, 0) \mid \delta \in [0, 5)\}$, i.e., both sets of consistent delays are a strict subset of $\mathcal{D}$. Further, due to Lemma 3, this will be the case, no matter what observations occur in the future, as the set of consistent delays can only shrink when further observations are made. So, the verdict is ?, even if additional observations occur.

The following lemma formalizes this: as soon as the set of consistent delays w.r.t. L ($\overline{L}$) is no longer equal to $\mathcal{D}$, then the verdict can never become $\top$ ($\bot$).

Lemma 4. *Let $L \subseteq T\Sigma^\omega$, $\mathcal{D}$ be a set of delays, and $\rho^* = (\sigma_1^*, \tau_1^*), \ldots, (\sigma_m^*, \tau_m^*)$ a nonempty $\mathcal{D}$-observation. Then, for all $t > \tau(\rho^*)$*

1. $\Delta_\mathcal{D}(L, \rho^*, t) \subsetneq \mathcal{D} \cap \{(\delta, \varepsilon) \mid \delta \leq \tau_1^*\}$ *implies there is no $\rho_1^* \in T\Sigma^*$ such that $\mathcal{V}_\mathcal{D}(L)(\rho^* \cdot_t \rho_1^*, t') = \top$ for any $t' \geq t + \tau(\rho_1^*)$, and*
2. $\Delta_\mathcal{D}(\overline{L}, \rho^*, t) \subsetneq \mathcal{D} \cap \{(\delta, \varepsilon) \mid \delta \leq \tau_1^*\}$ *implies there is no $\rho_1^* \in T\Sigma^*$ such that $\mathcal{V}_\mathcal{D}(L)(\rho^* \cdot_t \rho_1^*, t') = \bot$ for any $t' \geq t + \tau(\rho_1^*)$.*

Note that $\Delta_\mathcal{D}(L, \rho^*, t) \subsetneq \mathcal{D} \cap \{(\delta, \varepsilon) \mid \delta \leq \tau_1^*\}$ and $\Delta_\mathcal{D}(\overline{L}, \rho^*, t) \subsetneq \mathcal{D} \cap \{(\delta, \varepsilon) \mid \delta \leq \tau_1^*\}$ can both be true simultaneously (as in Example 3). In this situation, we will under no future observation reach a conclusive verdict.

4 Towards an Algorithm

Typically, monitoring algorithms rely on automata-based techniques. To this end, first the specification and its complement are translated into suitable automata. Then one computes the set of states reachable by processing the observation and then checks whether from one of these states the automaton can still accept an infinite continuation. If this is the case for both automata, then the verdict is ?, if it is only the case for the automaton for the specification, then the verdict is ⊤, and vice versa for the complement automaton and ⊥.

We want to follow the same blueprint, but we need to make adjustments to handle delay. Intuitively, we need to compute all states that are reachable by possible ground-truths of a given observation. However, a ground-truth may contain more events than the observation, as some events may not yet have been observed due to delay. This complicates the construction of the set of reachable states, as an unbounded number of events may not yet have been observed.

In the definition of $GT_\mathcal{D}$ (Definition 2) there is an implicit universal quantification over all possible sequences of such events that have not yet been observed (e.g., the last five events in ρ in Fig. 3). We exploit the fact that the verdicts are defined with respect to all possible extensions μ of a possible ground-truth (i.e., also a universal quantification over the μ's) to "merge" the universal quantification over events that have not yet been observed into the universal quantification of the extension μ. Then, a possible ground-truth has exactly the same number of events as the observation (i.e., ground-truth and observation have Equal Length). We begin defining this restricted notion of possible ground-truth by strengthening Definition 2.

Definition 4 (EL-Consistency). *Let $\rho^* = (\sigma_1^*, \tau_1^*), \ldots, (\sigma_m^*, \tau_m^*)$ be a $\{(\delta, \varepsilon)\}$-observation and let $\rho = (\sigma_1, \tau_1), \ldots, (\sigma_n, \tau_n)$ be a finite timed word. We say that ρ is EL-consistent with ρ^* at observation time $t \in \mathbb{R}_{\geq 0}$ under latency δ and jitter ε iff ρ is consistent with ρ^* at t under δ and ε and $m = n$. We denote the set of timed words ρ that are EL-consistent with an $\{(\delta, \varepsilon)\}$-observation ρ^* at observation time t under latency δ and jitter ε by $GT^{el}_{\delta,\varepsilon}(\rho^*, t)$ and define $GT^{el}_\mathcal{D}(\rho^*, t) = \bigcup_{(\delta,\varepsilon) \in \mathcal{D}} GT^{el}_{\delta,\varepsilon}(\rho^*, t)$.*

Example 4. Continuing Example 1, an EL-consistent ground-truth of the observation ρ^* in Fig. 3 has exactly four events corresponding to the four events in the observation. Thus, there cannot be any unobserved events between $t - (\delta + \varepsilon)$ and t in an EL-consistent ground-truth (e.g., the last five events of ρ in Fig. 3).

Now, we present the revised verdict function using only EL ground-truths. Note that merging the unobserved events from the possible ground-truth ρ into the extension μ requires changing the time instant at which we concatenate the ground-truth and the extension: $t - (\delta + \varepsilon)$ is the earliest time point at which an event can occur that may not yet have been observed at time t. Due to jitter however, there might also be events after $t - (\delta + \varepsilon)$ that have been observed, which are in the possible ground-truth ρ: the last such event happened at time $\tau(\rho)$. Hence, we need to concatenate at time point $\max(\tau(\rho), t - (\delta + \varepsilon))$.

Definition 5 (Monitor verdicts under delay – EL version). *Given $L \subseteq T\Sigma^\omega$, a set $\mathcal{D}$ of delays, a $\mathcal{D}$-observation $\rho^* \in T\Sigma^*$, and $t \geq \tau(\rho^*)$, the function $\mathcal{V}_\mathcal{D}^{el}: 2^{T\Sigma^\omega} \to T\Sigma^* \times \mathbb{R}_{\geq 0} \to \mathbb{B}_3$ evaluates to the verdict*

$$\mathcal{V}_\mathcal{D}^{el}(L)(\rho^*, t) = \begin{cases} \top & \text{if } \rho \cdot_{\max(\tau(\rho), t-(\delta+\varepsilon))} \mu \in L \text{ for all } (\delta, \varepsilon) \in \mathcal{D}, \\ & \text{all } \rho \in GT_{\delta,\varepsilon}^{el}(\rho^*, t) \text{ and all } \mu \in T\Sigma^\omega, \\ \bot & \text{if } \rho \cdot_{\max(\tau(\rho), t-(\delta+\varepsilon))} \mu \notin L \text{ for all } (\delta, \varepsilon) \in \mathcal{D}, \\ & \text{all } \rho \in GT_{\delta,\varepsilon}^{el}(\rho^*, t) \text{ and all } \mu \in T\Sigma^\omega, \\ ? & \text{otherwise.} \end{cases}$$

$\mathcal{V}_\mathcal{D}^{el}(L)(\rho^*, t)$ is undefined when $t < \tau(\rho^*)$.

Next, we show that both verdict functions coincide.

Lemma 5. $\mathcal{V}_\mathcal{D}^{el}(L)(\rho^*, t) = \mathcal{V}_\mathcal{D}(L)(\rho^*, t)$ *for all $L \subseteq T\Sigma^\omega$, all sets $\mathcal{D}$ of delays, all $\mathcal{D}$-observations ρ^*, and all $t \geq \tau(\rho^*)$.*

Next, we show that we can indeed make the definition of $\mathcal{V}^{el}$ effective using automata-theoretic constructions. First, we formally capture the set of states that can be reached by processing the possible EL ground-truths of an observation. Let $\mathcal{A}$ be a TBA. We write $(q_0, v_0) \xrightarrow{\rho}_\mathcal{A} (q_n, v_n)$ for a finite timed word $\rho = (\sigma, \tau) \in T\Sigma^*$ to denote the existence of a finite sequence of states $(q_0, v_0) \xrightarrow{(\sigma_1, \tau_1)} (q_1, v_1) \xrightarrow{(\sigma_2, \tau_2)} \cdots \xrightarrow{(\sigma_n, \tau_n)} (q_n, v_n)$ of $\mathcal{A}$ where for all $1 \leq i \leq n$ there is a transition $(q_{i-1}, q_i, \sigma_i, \lambda_i, g_i)$ of $\mathcal{A}$ such that $v_i(x) = 0$ for all x in λ_i and $v_{i-1}(x) + (t_i - t_{i-1})$ otherwise, and g is satisfied by the valuation $v_{i-1} + (t_i - t_{i-1})$, where we use $t_0 = 0$. Given a TBA $\mathcal{A}$, a set $\mathcal{D}$ of delays, a finite observed timed word $\rho^* \in T\Sigma^*$, and $t \geq \tau(\rho^*)$, we define

$$\mathcal{R}_\mathcal{A}^\mathcal{D}(\rho^*, t) = \{(q, v + \max(0, (t - (\tau(\rho) + \delta + \varepsilon)))) \mid (q_0, v_0) \xrightarrow{\rho}_\mathcal{A} (q, v) \text{ where}$$
$$(q_0, v_0) \text{ with } q_0 \in Q_0, v_0(x) = 0 \text{ for all } x \in C, \text{ and}$$
$$\rho \in GT_{\delta,\varepsilon}^{el}(\rho^*, t) \text{ for some } (\delta, \varepsilon) \in \mathcal{D}\}.$$

We call this the reach-set of ρ in $\mathcal{A}$ at t w.r.t. $\mathcal{D}$.

Next, we define the set of states of a TBA from where it is possible to reach an accepting location infinitely many times in the future, i.e., those states from which an accepting run is possible. This is useful, because if processing a finite timed word leads to such a state, then the timed word can be extended to an infinite one in the language of the automaton, a notion that underlies the definitions of the verdict functions. Given a TBA $\mathcal{A} = (Q, Q_0, \Sigma, C, \Delta, \mathcal{F})$, the set of states with nonempty language is

$$S_\mathcal{A}^{ne} = \{(q, v) \mid q \in Q, v \in C \to \mathbb{R}_{\geq 0} \text{ s.t. } \mathcal{L}(\mathcal{A}, (q, v)) \neq \emptyset\}.$$

The set $S_\mathcal{A}^{ne}$ can be computed using a zone-based fixpoint algorithm [15]. Using these definitions, we can give an *effective* definition of the verdict functions, which we show to be equivalent to the previous definitions and implementable.

In the following definition, $\mathbb{A}$ denotes the set of all TBA.

Definition 6 (Monitoring TBA). *Given a TBA $\mathcal{A}$, a complement automaton $\overline{\mathcal{A}}$ (i.e., with $L(\overline{\mathcal{A}}) = T\Sigma^\omega \setminus L(\mathcal{A})$), a set $\mathcal{D}$ of delays, a $\mathcal{D}$-observation $\rho^* \in T\Sigma^*$, and $t \geq \tau(\rho)$, $\mathcal{M}_\mathcal{D}: \mathbb{A} \times \mathbb{A} \to T\Sigma^* \times \mathbb{R}_{\geq 0} \to \mathbb{B}_3$ computes the verdict*

$$\mathcal{M}_\mathcal{D}(\mathcal{A}, \overline{\mathcal{A}})(\rho^*, t) = \begin{cases} \top & \text{if } \mathcal{R}^\mathcal{D}_{\overline{\mathcal{A}}}(\rho^*, t) \cap S^{ne}_{\overline{\mathcal{A}}} = \emptyset, \\ \bot & \text{if } \mathcal{R}^\mathcal{D}_\mathcal{A}(\rho^*, t) \cap S^{ne}_\mathcal{A} = \emptyset, \\ ? & \text{otherwise.} \end{cases}$$

$\mathcal{M}_\mathcal{D}(\mathcal{A}, \overline{\mathcal{A}})(\rho^*, t)$ is undefined if $t < \tau(\rho)$.

Next we show that this automata-based definition of monitoring is equal to the verdict functions defined above.

Theorem 2. $\mathcal{M}_\mathcal{D}(\mathcal{A}, \overline{\mathcal{A}})(\rho^*, t) = \mathcal{V}^{el}_\mathcal{D}(L(\mathcal{A}))(\rho^*, t)$ *for all sets $\mathcal{D}$ of delays, all TBA $\mathcal{A}$ (and complement automata $\overline{\mathcal{A}}$), all $\mathcal{D}$-observations ρ^*, and all $t \geq \tau(\rho^*)$.*

Recall that $S^{ne}_\mathcal{A}$ can be computed for any given TBA $\mathcal{A}$. Therefore, in the next section, we show how to calculate $\mathcal{R}^\mathcal{D}_\mathcal{A}(\rho^*, t)$ for a given TBA $\mathcal{A}$, set $\mathcal{D}$ of delays, observation ρ^*, and time point t using a zone-based algorithm. This will then allow us to compute verdicts effectively.

5 A Zone-Based Online Monitoring Algorithm

In this section, we demonstrate how to compute the reach-set of ρ^* in $\mathcal{A}$ at t w.r.t. $\mathcal{D}$. So far we have developed the theory with observations, latency, and jitter being reals. Now, we are concerned with algorithms and thus assume all these quantities to be rationals. For the monitoring algorithm, we use – as standard in analysing timed automata models – symbolic states being pairs (q, Z) of locations and zones. A zone is a finite conjunction of constraints of the form $x \sim t$ and $x - x' \sim t$ for clocks x, x', constants $t \in \mathbb{Q}_{\geq 0}$, and $\sim \in \{<, \leq, =, \geq, >\}$. Given two zones Z and Z' over a set C of clocks, and a set of clocks $\lambda \subseteq C$, we define the following operations on zones (which can be efficiently implemented using the DBM data-structure [9]):

- $Z[\lambda] = \{v \mid \exists v' \models Z \text{ s.t. } v(x) = 0 \text{ if } x \in \lambda, \text{ otherwise } v(x) = v'(x)\}$
- $Z^\nearrow = \{v \mid \exists v' \models Z \text{ s.t. } v = v' + d \text{ for some } d \in \mathbb{R}_{\geq 0}\}$
- $Z \wedge Z' = \{v \mid v \models Z \text{ and } v \models Z'\}$

We can use these functions to compute the successor states after an input. Given a TBA $\mathcal{A} = (Q, Q_0, \Sigma, C, \Delta, \mathcal{F})$, a symbolic state (q, Z), and a letter $a \in \Sigma$, we define

$$\text{Post}((q, Z), a) = \{(q', Z') \mid (q, q', a, \lambda, g) \in \Delta, Z' = (Z^\nearrow \wedge g)[\lambda]\},$$

as the set of states one can reach by taking an a-transition at some point in the future from (q, Z). Using Post we can compute the successor states of a timed input $(a, \tau) \in \Sigma \times \mathbb{Q}_{\geq 0}$ by extending the zones with an additional clock *time* just recording time since system start. The successors of a symbolic state is

$$\operatorname{Succ}((q, Z), (a, \tau)) = \{(q', Z') \mid (q', Z'') \in \operatorname{Post}((q, Z), a), Z' = Z'' \wedge time = \tau\}$$

and the successors of a set of symbolic states S is

$$\operatorname{Succ}(S, (a, \tau)) = \bigcup\nolimits_{(q', Z') \in S} \operatorname{Succ}((q', Z'), (a, \tau)).$$

In handling delayed observations, we assume that the delay set $\mathcal{D}$ consists of pairs (δ, ε) where the latency δ is bounded by an interval $[l, u] \subseteq \mathbb{R}_{\geq 0}$ for given $l, u \in \mathbb{Q}_{\geq 0}$, and that the jitter is bounded by a given $\varepsilon \in \mathbb{Q}_{\geq 0}$.

To represent the latency and thereby be able to reason about and indirectly store the latency bounds, we add a clock *etime* representing the "expected" real time that an event generated just now could be observed by the monitor after having been delayed according to the latency. This allows us

1. to represent the actual latency as $etime - time$,
2. to represent the initial knowledge about latencies by initializing $etime - time$ to the initially known bounds on latency, namely $etime - time \in [l, u]$ by setting *time* to 0 and constraining *etime* to $[l, u]$, and
3. to refine our knowledge about the actual latency after having observed an event (σ^*, τ^*) by then setting *etime* to a value in $[\tau^* - \varepsilon, \tau^*]$.

Consequently, we change the initial zones to include the latency bounds l and u as the differences between the clocks *etime* and *time*. This way, *etime* represents the expected time an event is observed at the monitor, given l and u, and *time* represents the actual time the event happened (at the system). The aforementioned refinement (see Item 3 above and Fig. 4) then permits to deduce actual latency ranges consistent with the specification (or its negation) from observation times of events.

In detail, this refinement of the $etime - time$ relation works as follows. Given a TBA $\mathcal{A}$ extended with the clocks *time* and *etime*, and an observation $(\sigma, \tau^*) \in \Sigma \times \mathbb{Q}_{\geq 0}$, the successors of (q, Z) are

$$\operatorname{Succ}_d((q, Z), (\sigma, \tau^*)) = \{(q', Z') \mid (q', Z'') \in \operatorname{Post}((q, Z), \sigma),$$
$$Z' = Z'' \wedge etime \leq \tau^* \wedge etime \geq \tau^* - \varepsilon\}$$

and the successors $\operatorname{Succ}_d(S, (\sigma, \tau^*))$ of a set of symbolic states S is equal to $\cup_{(q,Z) \in S} \operatorname{Succ}_d((q, Z), (\sigma, \tau^*))$.

The online monitoring algorithm will essentially apply Succ_d repeatedly to update the reach-set, once for each new observation. Note that there is a slight mismatch, as Succ_d is computed with the two auxiliary clocks *time* and *etime*, which are not clocks of $\mathcal{A}$.

The initial reach-set is given by the following zone Z_0^d requiring all ordinary clocks of the TBA $\mathcal{A}$ to be zero and with *time* and *etime* satisfying $etime - time \in [l, u]$. That is

$$Z_0^d \equiv \underbrace{etime - time \leq u \wedge time - etime \leq -l}_{etime-time \in [l,u]} \wedge \underbrace{\bigwedge_{x \in C \cup \{time\}} x = 0}_{x_1, \ldots, x_{|C|} = 0,\ time = 0}.$$

Given a fixed jitter bound ε, we can now compute the reach-set after a sequence of observations under delay, where the latency is bounded in $[l, u]$.

Theorem 3. *Given a TBA $\mathcal{A}$, a delay set $\mathcal{D} = \{(\delta, \varepsilon) \mid \delta \in [l, u]\}$ with $l, u, \varepsilon \in \mathbb{Q}_{\geq 0}$, a $\mathcal{D}$-observation $\rho^* = (\sigma_1, \tau_1^*), \ldots, (\sigma_n, \tau_n^*)$, and $t \in \mathbb{Q}_{\geq 0}$ with $t \geq \tau_n^*$, let $S_0 = \{(q_0, Z_0^d) \mid q_0 \in Q_0\}$ and $S_i = \text{Succ}_d(S_{i-1}, (\sigma_i, \tau_i^*))$ for $i \in \{1, \ldots, n\}$. Then, the reach-set $\mathcal{R}_{\mathcal{A}}^{\mathcal{D}}(\rho^*, t)$ is the projection of*

$$\{(q', Z') \mid (q', Z'') \in S_n, Z' = Z''^{\nearrow} \wedge etime = t - \varepsilon\}$$

to the clocks of $\mathcal{A}$ (obtained by removing all constraints on time and etime).

This theorem allows us to implement a monitoring algorithm by computing the reach-sets and intersecting them with the set of nonempty language states.

The observation of events may lead to refinement of the difference between *time* and *etime* as depicted in Fig. 4.

Lemma 6. *Given $\mathcal{A}$, $\mathcal{D}$, ρ^*, t, and S_n as in Theorem 3, we can compute the set of consistent delays by looking at the bounds on etime $-$ time:*
$$\Delta_{\mathcal{D}}(L(\mathcal{A}), \rho^*, t) = \{(\delta, \varepsilon) \in \mathcal{D} \mid S_n \models etime - time = \delta\}.$$

This information can be used to decorate the $?$ verdict, so that we can report a set of bounds on the latency for which we would provide a $\top$ or $\bot$ verdict.

Example 5. Let us show an example of our algorithm for monitoring under delayed observation. Note that, for the sake of readability, we use sets of clock constraints instead of conjunction of clock constraints when specifying zones.

Consider the property $\varphi = F_{[0,10]} a \wedge G_{[0,20]} \neg b$ from Fig. 1. The TBA's accepting $L(\varphi)$ and $L(\neg \varphi)$ are shown in Fig. 2. The nonempty language states for $\mathcal{A}_\varphi$ and $\mathcal{A}_{\neg\varphi}$ are $S_{\mathcal{A}_\varphi}^{ne} = \{(q_0, \{x \leq 10\}), (q_1, \text{true}), (\varphi, \text{true})\}$ and $S_{\mathcal{A}_{\neg\varphi}}^{ne} = \{(q_0, \text{true}), (q_1, \{x \leq 20\}), (\neg\varphi, \text{true})\}$. Let us assume the latency is between 0 and 10, and the jitter is bounded by 0.2. Now we compute the reach-sets S_0 (initial), S_1 (after $(a, 17.3)$), and S_2 (after $(b, 27.5)$) as

$$S_0 = \{(q_0, \{x = 0,\ etime \leq 10,\ (etime - x) \in [0, 10]\})\},$$
$$S_1 = \{(q_1, \{x \in [7.1, 10],\ etime \in [17.1, 17.3],\ (etime - x) \in [7.1, 10]\}),$$
$$\quad (\neg\varphi, \{x \in [10, 17.3],\ etime \in [17.1, 17.3],\ (etime - x) \leq 7.3\})\},\text{ and}$$
$$S_2 = \{(\varphi, \{x \in]20, 20.4],\ etime \in [27.3, 27.5[,\ (etime - x) \in [7.1, 7.5]\}),$$
$$\quad (\neg\varphi, \{x \in [17.3, 27.5],\ etime \in [27.3, 27.5],\ (etime - x) \in [0, 10]\})\}.$$

Note that we omit the clock *time* and only look at x and *etime* since *time* and x always have the same constraints.

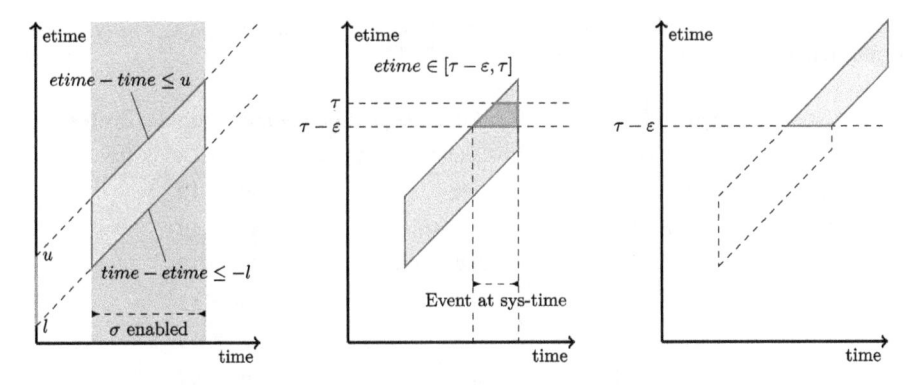

Fig. 4. Illustration of a single zone in the Succ_d computation (only *time-etime* plane depicted). Left: initial zone (in green) is diagonally extrapolated for time passage and then intersected with the guard of an edge. Middle: observing event σ at time τ. By restricting *etime* to $[\tau - \varepsilon, \tau]$, the clock *time* is restricted to when the event could have occurred at the system. Right: computing the future zone we see that the bound on $time - etime$ is now stricter and thus the bounds for the consistent latencies are refined.

All reach-sets intersect with both sets of nonempty language states; thus, the verdict is ?. However, we can refine this verdict with knowledge about the consistent delays that change after each observation. The jitter bound is fixed at 0.2, but the bounds on the latency can be found in the clock constraints on the difference between *etime* and x. For $\bot$, the latency range remains $[0, 10]$ in all reach-sets. For $\top$, the consistent latency range is $[0, 10]$ in S_0, $[7.1, 10]$ in S_1, and it is $[7.1, 7.5[$ in S_2. This means that if the latency is outside $[7.1, 7.5[$, then the verdict is $\bot$.

On the other hand, for the observation $\rho^* = (a, 17.3), (b, 27.1)$ from Example 2 (and using the same latency and jitter bounds as above), we compute the reach-sets S_0, S_1, and S_2' where

$$S_2' = \{(\neg\varphi, \{x \in [16.9, 27.1], etime \in [26.9, 27.1], (etime - x) \in [0, 10]\})\}.$$

As S_2' has an empty intersection with $S_{\mathcal{A}_\varphi}^{ne}$, the verdict is $\bot$.

6 Prototype Implementation

We implemented the methods described in this paper in the tool MONITAAL[2] written in C++. This includes the difference-bounded matrix data structure to handle clock-zones, parsing property automata modelled in UPPAAL, computing the set of nonempty language states, computing the reach-sets in an online fashion over an observed word based on latency and jitter bounds in $[0, \infty[$, providing verdicts $\top, \bot$ or ? and latency bounds consistent with $\top$ and $\bot$.

---
[2] https://github.com/DEIS-Tools/MoniTAal.

Table 1. Results for simultaneously monitoring six response properties over a trace generated by the gear controller model from [21].

# Observ.	$\tau(\rho)$	Time (ms) Delay	Time (ms) Delay-free	Max. resp. time (μs) Delay	Max. resp. time (μs) Delay-free	# Symbolic States Delay	# Symbolic States Delay-free
1000	63112	76	42	182	143	39	12
2000	124028	223	84	228	188	57	12
3000	184743	418	116	382	86	78	12
4000	244717	691	154	410	81	109	12
5000	306015	1037	198	571	281	135	12
6000	366814	1463	237	680	163	167	12
7000	438799	1973	278	767	175	192	12
8000	501070	2554	314	986	193	215	12
9000	563296	3212	357	1159	175	238	12
10000	624530	3929	384	1099	109	266	12

We demonstrate MONITAAL on a trace generated by simulating the gear controller model from [21] in UPPAAL [8]. The model, along with formal requirements, was created by the company Mecel. For the monitored properties, we replaced six error locations in the model with response properties on the form $G_{[0,\infty]} a \to F_{[0,b]} c$ expressing that some signal a is followed by a response c within some bound b. For such a property, it is not possible to give a $\top$ verdict, since it will always possible to violate it in the future. The six properties are all satisfied by the model, which means that we will never terminate with a verdict, no matter how long the trace observed. This allows us to test how arbitrarily long traces can affect the performance of our algorithm.

We show results with and without delay consisting of a latency in [0, 100], and a jitter bounded by 5. The results in Table 1 show the number of observations, length (in time) of the observed word, the overall running time, the maximal response time (the time it takes to process a single observation and return the next verdict), and the maximal number of stored symbolic states. The running time, maximal response time and number of symbolic states over the number of observations are plotted in Fig. 5. Under delay we see that the state storage grows linearly with the number of observations, which in turn results in a growing response time. The reason for this is that the uncertainty of the delay increases the size of the reach-set. Nevertheless, the maximal response time is in all cases less than 1.2 ms. In the delay-free case, the memory usage is constant, thus the response time is also constant, although with tiny fluctuations. The total time in the delayed case has approximately a quadratic growth. This is not surprising, since it is the running sum of the response time which seems to grow linearly, but we do not have enough experiments here to conclude a precise relation between the state storage and response time. In general, the results show us that the tool in this case is able to handle multiple properties and long traces in terms of time horizon as well as number of observations.

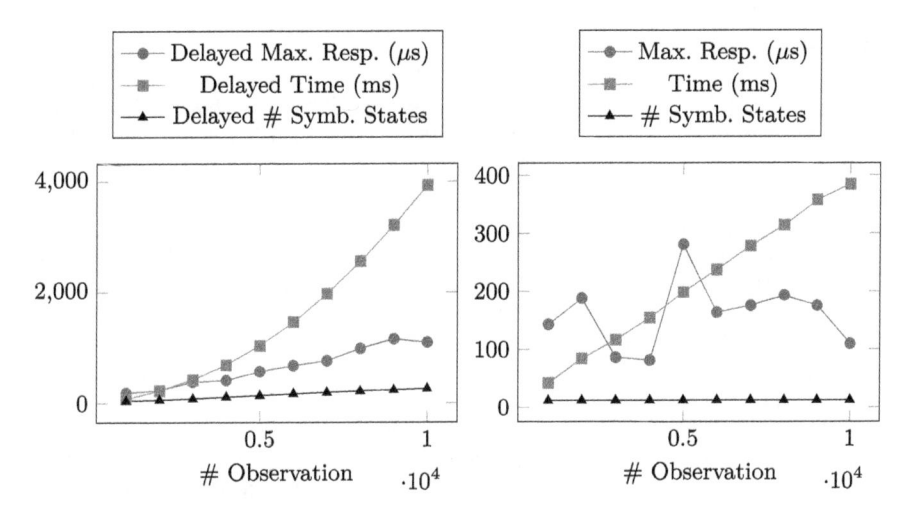

Fig. 5. Graph plotting the total time, maximal response time and number of symbolic states over the trace length (number of observations) from Table 1 of the delayed (left) and delay-free (right) case.

7 Conclusion

We have introduced a zone-based algorithm realizing optimal (in the sense of being anticipating [7]) online operational monitoring of embedded real-time systems when the communication between the monitor and the system is subject to unknown (up to bounds) delay. This situation is rather typical in practice as observations are mediated by sensors, may involve conversion between analog and digital, or pass communication networks and consequently are indirect in general, leading to delays and inexact time-stamping. Our constructions thus fill a gap in the pre-existing theories for monitoring hard real-time systems, which tend to assume full and exact temporal observability by immediate coupling or, equivalently, perfect synchrony between systems and their monitors.

A notable point of our construction is that it applies a reduction to simple timed automata and is purely zone-based despite the unknown communication delay being a timing parameter. The construction thus not only avoids the complexities of property analysis for parameterized timed automata [4], but also provides an instance of monitoring under uncertainty where the underlying arithmetic constraint systems remain of fixed dimensionality (namely the number of clocks in the property automata plus two for monitoring) despite their history dependence. This is in stark contrast to direct constraint encodings growing linearly over history length as in [13].

In further research, we study the question of monitorability [7]: some properties will never give definitive verdicts (e.g., "infinitely often a") and are therefore not useful for monitoring. We conjecture that our zone-based approach can be exploited to decide monitorability of real-time properties.

References

1. Alur, R., Dill, D.L.: A theory of timed automata. Theoret. Comput. Sci. **126**(2), 183–235 (1994). https://doi.org/10.1016/0304-3975(94)90010-8
2. Alur, R., Feder, T., Henzinger, T.A.: The benefits of relaxing punctuality. J. ACM **43**(1) (1996)
3. Alur, R., Henzinger, T.A., Vardi, M.Y.: Parametric real-time reasoning. In: Kosaraju, S.R., Johnson, D.S., Aggarwal, A. (eds.) Proceedings of the Twenty-Fifth Annual ACM Symposium on Theory of Computing, May 16–18, 1993, San Diego, CA, USA, pp. 592–601. ACM (1993). https://doi.org/10.1145/167088.167242
4. André, É., Lime, D., Roux, O.H.: Reachability and liveness in parametric timed automata. Log. Methods Comput. Sci. **18**(1) (2022). https://doi.org/10.46298/lmcs-18(1:31)2022
5. Baldor, K., Niu, J.: Monitoring dense-time, continuous-semantics, metric temporal logic. In: Qadeer, S., Tasiran, S. (eds.) RV 2012. LNCS, vol. 7687, pp. 245–259. Springer, Heidelberg (2013). https://doi.org/10.1007/978-3-642-35632-2_24
6. Basin, D., Klaedtke, F., Zălinescu, E.: Algorithms for monitoring real-time properties. In: Khurshid, S., Sen, K. (eds.) RV 2011. LNCS, vol. 7186, pp. 260–275. Springer, Heidelberg (2012). https://doi.org/10.1007/978-3-642-29860-8_20
7. Bauer, A., Leucker, M., Schallhart, C.: Monitoring of real-time properties. In: Arun-Kumar, S., Garg, N. (eds.) FSTTCS 2006. LNCS, vol. 4337, pp. 260–272. Springer, Heidelberg (2006). https://doi.org/10.1007/11944836_25
8. Behrmann, G., David, A., Larsen, K.G.: A tutorial on UPPAAL. In: Bernardo, M., Corradini, F. (eds.) SFM-RT 2004. LNCS, vol. 3185, pp. 200–236. Springer, Heidelberg (2004). https://doi.org/10.1007/978-3-540-30080-9_7
9. Bengtsson, J., Yi, W.: Timed automata: semantics, algorithms and tools. In: Desel, J., Reisig, W., Rozenberg, G. (eds.) ACPN 2003. LNCS, vol. 3098, pp. 87–124. Springer, Heidelberg (2004). https://doi.org/10.1007/978-3-540-27755-2_3
10. Brihaye, T., Geeraerts, G., Ho, H.-M., Monmege, B.: MIGHTYL: a compositional translation from MITL to timed automata. In: Majumdar, R., Kunčak, V. (eds.) CAV 2017. LNCS, vol. 10426, pp. 421–440. Springer, Cham (2017). https://doi.org/10.1007/978-3-319-63387-9_21
11. Cimatti, A., Grosen, T.M., Larsen, K.G., Tonetta, S., Zimmermann, M.: Exploiting assumptions for effective monitoring of real-time properties under partial observability. arXiv:2409.05456 (2024). https://doi.org/10.48550/arXiv.2409.05456
12. Donzé, A., Ferrère, T., Maler, O.: Efficient robust monitoring for STL. In: Sharygina, N., Veith, H. (eds.) CAV 2013. LNCS, vol. 8044, pp. 264–279. Springer, Heidelberg (2013). https://doi.org/10.1007/978-3-642-39799-8_19
13. Finkbeiner, B., Fränzle, M., Kohn, F., Kröger, P.: A truly robust signal temporal logic: monitoring safety properties of interacting cyber-physical systems under uncertain observation. Algorithms **15**(4), 126 (2022). https://doi.org/10.3390/a15040126
14. Fränzle, M., Grosen, T.M., Larsen, K.G., Zimmermann, M.: Monitoring real-time systems under parametric delay. arXiv:2404.18282 (2024). https://doi.org/10.48550/ARXIV.2404.18282
15. Grosen, T.M., Kauffman, S., Larsen, K.G., Zimmermann, M.: Monitoring timed properties (revisited). In: Bogomolov, S., Parker, D. (eds.) FORMATS 2022. LNCS, vol. 13465, pp. 43–62. Springer, Cham (2022). https://doi.org/10.1007/978-3-031-15839-1_3

16. Ho, H.-M., Ouaknine, J., Worrell, J.: Online monitoring of metric temporal logic. In: Bonakdarpour, B., Smolka, S.A. (eds.) RV 2014. LNCS, vol. 8734, pp. 178–192. Springer, Cham (2014). https://doi.org/10.1007/978-3-319-11164-3_15
17. Kallwies, H., Leucker, M., Sánchez, C.: Symbolic runtime verification for monitoring under uncertainties and assumptions. In: Bouajjani, A., Holík, L., Wu, Z. (eds.) ATVA 2022. LNCS, vol. 13505, pp. 117–134. Springer, Cham (2022). https://doi.org/10.1007/978-3-031-19992-9_8
18. Köhl, M.A., Hermanns, H.: Model-based diagnosis of real-time systems: Robustness against varying latency, clock drift, and out-of-order observations. ACM Trans. Embed. Comput. Syst. **22**(4), 68:1–68:48 (2023). https://doi.org/10.1145/3597209
19. Larsen, K.G., Pettersson, P., Yi, W.: UPPAAL in a nutshell. Int. J. Softw. Tools Technol. Transf. **1**(1-2), 134–152 (1997). https://doi.org/10.1007/S100090050010
20. Lindahl, M., Pettersson, P., Yi, W.: Formal design and analysis of a gear controller. In: Steffen, B. (ed.) Tools and Algorithms for Construction and Analysis of Systems (TACAS). LNCS, vol. 1384, pp. 281–297. Springer, Heidelberg (1998). https://doi.org/10.1007/BFb0054178
21. Lindahl, M., Pettersson, P., Yi, W.: Formal design and analysis of a gearbox controller. Springer Int. J. Software Tools Technol. Transfer (STTT) **3**(3), 353–368 (2001)
22. Maler, O., Nickovic, D.: Monitoring temporal properties of continuous signals. In: Lakhnech, Y., Yovine, S. (eds.) FORMATS/FTRTFT -2004. LNCS, vol. 3253, pp. 152–166. Springer, Heidelberg (2004). https://doi.org/10.1007/978-3-540-30206-3_12
23. Ničković, D., Yamaguchi, T.: RTAMT: online robustness monitors from STL. In: Hung, D.V., Sokolsky, O. (eds.) ATVA 2020. LNCS, vol. 12302, pp. 564–571. Springer, Cham (2020). https://doi.org/10.1007/978-3-030-59152-6_34
24. Sheldon, T.: McGraw-Hill's Encyclopedia of Networking and Telecommunications. McGraw-Hill Professional (2001)
25. Thati, P., Rosu, G.: Monitoring algorithms for metric temporal logic specifications. In: Havelund, K., Rosu, G. (eds.) Proceedings of the Fourth Workshop on Runtime Verification, RV@ETAPS 2004, Barcelona, Spain, April 3, 2004. Electronic Notes in Theoretical Computer Science, vol. 113, pp. 145–162. Elsevier (2004). https://doi.org/10.1016/J.ENTCS.2004.01.029
26. Ulus, D., Ferrère, T., Asarin, E., Maler, O.: Timed pattern matching. In: Legay, A., Bozga, M. (eds.) FORMATS 2014. LNCS, vol. 8711, pp. 222–236. Springer, Cham (2014). https://doi.org/10.1007/978-3-319-10512-3_16
27. Ulus, D., Ferrère, T., Asarin, E., Maler, O.: Online timed pattern matching using derivatives. In: Chechik, M., Raskin, J.-F. (eds.) TACAS 2016. LNCS, vol. 9636, pp. 736–751. Springer, Heidelberg (2016). https://doi.org/10.1007/978-3-662-49674-9_47
28. Visconti, E., Bartocci, E., Loreti, M., Nenzi, L.: Online monitoring of spatio-temporal properties for imprecise signals. In: Arun-Kumar, S., Méry, D., Saha, I., Zhang, L. (eds.) MEMOCODE '21: 19th ACM-IEEE International Conference on Formal Methods and Models for System Design, Virtual Event, China, November 20 - 22, 2021. pp. 78–88. ACM (2021). https://doi.org/10.1145/3487212.3487344
29. Waga, M., André, É., Hasuo, I.: Model-bounded monitoring of hybrid systems. ACM Trans. Cyber Phys. Syst. **6**(4), 30:1–30:26 (2022). https://doi.org/10.1145/3529095

System Analysis and Security

VeyMont: Choreography-Based Generation of Correct Concurrent Programs with Shared Memory

Robert Rubbens[(✉)], Petra van den Bos, and Marieke Huisman

Formal Methods and Tools, University of Twente, Enschede, The Netherlands
{r.b.rubbens,p.vandenbos,m.huisman}@utwente.nl

Abstract. In the VeyMont tool, choreographies can be used to specify concurrent programs using a sequential format. To support choreography-based development, VeyMont verifies a given choreography for functional correctness and memory safety, and subsequently generates a correct concurrent program. However, the initial version of VeyMont did not support programs with shared memory. This paper shows how we overcome this limitation, by adding support for ownership annotations to VeyMont. Moreover, we also adapted the concurrent program generation, so that it does not only generate code, but also annotations. As a result, further changes and optimizations of the concurrent program can directly be verified. We demonstrate the extended capabilities of VeyMont on illustrative case studies.

Keywords: Deductive verification · Choreographies · Concurrent programs

1 Introduction

In program verification, auto-active verifiers prove correctness of programs automatically, with respect to a given specification. Writing specifications is non-trivial already in a sequential setting, and concurrency makes it even more challenging, as a concurrent program has a combinatorial number of interleavings to be considered. VeyMont [7] addressed this problem by combining choreographies [18], for specifying (concurrent) protocols, with deductive verification. VeyMont generates implementations for choreographies, which can be verified by using the VerCors verifier for concurrent software [3] as back-end. The choreographies of VeyMont allow specifying a concurrent program in a sequential format to ease verification, and then to generate the correct concurrent program.

In its purest form, a choreography [18] describes a sequence of message exchanges between participants of the choreography, called endpoints. The ordering of messages is partially fixed: an endpoint skips exchanges it does not participate in. Choreographies are deadlock free on the message level, meaning no

---

Supported by the NWO VICI 639.023.710 Mercedes project.

```
1  choreography incrField() {
2    endpoint a = Role();
3    endpoint b = Role();
4
5    requires a.x > 0;
6    ensures a.x == b.x;
7    ensures a.x > 2;
8    run {
9      a.x := a.x + 1;
10     communicate a.x -> b.x;
11     b.x := b.x + 1;
12     communicate b.x -> a.x;
13   }
14 }
```

(a) A shared field is simulated by broadcasting intermediate results between a and b.

```
1  choreography incrStore(Store s) {
2    endpoint a = Role(s);
3    endpoint b = Role(null);
4
5    requires a.s.x > 0;
6    ensures a.s.x > 2;
7    run {
8      a.s.x := a.s.x + 1;
9      // Store reference sent to b
10     communicate a.s -> b.s;
11     b.s.x := b.s.x + 1;
12     // Store reference sent to a
13     communicate b.s -> a.s;
14   }
15 }
```

(b) A shared field is incremented by both a and b. The messages function as barriers.

Fig. 1. Two choreographies where endpoints a and b each increment a value.

endpoint will be stuck waiting for a message that will never be sent. Note that in choreographies with shared memory and local actions, as presented in this work, deadlock in general is still possible. This is because endpoints can take local actions, such as acquiring locks, which might deadlock. Choreographies also guarantee that messages are well typed, meaning an endpoint will never receive an int when they are expecting a float. Finally, for each endpoint a specialized implementation can be generated. When these implementations are executed in parallel, messages are exchanged between processes as specified in the choreography. While similar, choreographies differ from session types [13]: a session type can only be used to type check implementations that are written by a user, choreographies allow automatic derivation of an implementation for each of its endpoints.

In VeyMont [7], a choreography specifies a concurrent program, such that its implementation can be generated. VeyMont supports verification of memory safety and functional correctness of these choreographies, which allows reasoning about e.g. program state properties. Such reasoning is not supported for the messages of traditional choreographies, which do not have local actions and shared memory. To support this verification, VeyMont requires users to annotate choreographies with contracts for functional correctness, e.g. pre- and postconditions. Additionally, it generates verification annotations for memory safety: in particular permissions to specify ownership of heap elements, like objects and their fields. The reasoning happens on the level of the choreography, and is preserved in the generated implementation [15]. VerCors [1] is used as the back-end verification engine for VeyMont.

An example VeyMont choreography is given in Fig. 1a. It defines two endpoints a and b of class Role (lines 2 and 3). The class Role has a field x of type int. The run declaration defines actions (line 8): a increments a.x, and then sends the value stored in a.x to b. Then b increments b.x, and sends it back to a. The precondition of run (line 5) is that a.x is more than 0. This is an example of a constraint on input data, and necessary to prove the postconditions: that a.x and b.x are equal (line 6), and that the value of a.x is more than 2 (line 7).

In this paper we extend VeyMont to address two limitations of the original implementation. The first limitation is the single-owner policy, where each endpoint owns all the fields reachable from it. For example, in Fig. 1a, a owns its only field a.x, while b owns b.x, in any program state, and sharing is only supported via duplicated values. This choice allowed to automatically generate permission annotations for verifying memory safety with the VerCors back-end.

Unfortunately, the single-owner policy excludes concurrent programs that share memory between threads. This is problematic, because sharing memory is an important pattern in many concurrent programs. Also, choreographies with a single-owner policy do not scale well for more endpoints, and for large data structures the overhead of duplication is large. Finally, the single-owner policy disallows sharing read-only data structures. What we instead wish to have is shared memory as used in Fig. 1b. The choreography is the same as Fig. 1a, except that endpoint a is initialized with a reference to a store s, which is used to update the field x within. This reference is then communicated between a and b, instead of the literal integer. While the choreography still includes `communicate` statements to prevent data races, access to x is now shared. In this paper, we extend VeyMont with transfer of ownership using `communicate` statements, i.e. at line 10 of Fig. 1b, ownership of s should be transferred from a to b. It is safe to transfer ownership here, because the receiver waits for the message of the sender. This implied synchronization points justifies permission transfers.

A second limitation of the original VeyMont [7] is that the verification annotations of a choreography are not preserved in the generated implementation. Consequently, the verification properties cannot be directly verified on the implementation. Since the properties have not been proven to hold for any variant of the program, an adapted and verified implementation can only be obtained by adapting and verifying the choreography, and then generating the implementation. From an engineering viewpoint, and especially for small changes, this may cause unnecessary overhead. Also, it is risky to change the generated implementation, e.g. for performance, as this might introduce bugs that cannot be detected by verification. Additionally, the lack of annotations in the generated implementation also prevents application of tools that further process & leverage annotations. One example of such a tool is Alpinist [22], which is a GPU program optimizer that uses annotations to check applicability of optimizations and preserves annotations in the output program.

Furthermore, because a generated implementation without annotations cannot be verified, bugs in the code generator of VeyMont are not spotted. In this work, we increase confidence in the generated implementation by making it verifiable with VerCors. This allows the user to establish correctness of the generated implementation without depending on the implementation details of VeyMont.

Contributions. In this work we present an extension of VeyMont that supports choreographies with shared memory and preserves verification annotations in the generated implementations. VeyMont supports fine-grained and dynamic ownership via endpoint annotations. In particular, access to shared memory can be exchanged between endpoints by annotating a `communicate` statement with permissions. By extending this approach to expressions and statements, VeyMont can generate implementations with verification annotations. We demonstrate the extended VeyMont through three consecutive improvements of the Tic-Tac-Toe case study, as presented in the original VeyMont tool paper [7]. These case studies show that even in simple programs, complicated properties can emerge. We provide the full annotated programs and tool implementation in the artifact [21].

Paper Structure. After preliminaries (Sect. 2), we describe the workflow and choreographic language of VeyMont, and introduce our approach with an example (Sect. 3). Then, we elaborate how choreographies are verified (Sect. 4), and how the concurrent program with verification annotations is generated (Sect. 5). After, we discuss our case studies (Sect. 6), and related work (Sect. 7). Finally, we conclude and discuss future work (Sect. 8).

2 Deductive Verification with VerCors

We introduce Prototypical Verification Language (PVL), the internal language of VerCors, because we used it to define the choreographic language of VeyMont. Also we introduce permission-based separation logic (PBSL), which is part of PVL, and is leveraged to verify choreographies. VerCors can also verify other languages, such as Java and C. We refer to [1] for more information about VerCors.

PVL is an object-oriented language. It supports OOP concepts like classes, methods and fields. PVL programs are imperative, with mutable local variables, `if` and `while` statements. Additionally, PVL programs may have contracts and assertions. Method contracts have pre- and postconditions, specified using `requires` and `ensures`. Assertions on expressions can be placed in a method body using the `assert` keyword. For examples, see lines 5, 6 and 11 of Fig. 4. More information on PVL is available at [1,25].

Permission-Based Separation Logic. VerCors is able to verify functional correctness, e.g. via pre- and postconditions and loop invariants. It also verifies memory safety and data-race freedom using permission-based separation logic [6]. Permissions specify which fields are writable or readable using the following syntax: `Perm(o.x, f)`. Here, o is an object, x a field, and f a fractional permission amount $0 < f \leq 1$. Fraction $f = 1$ specifies read and write access. Fraction $0 < f < 1$ specifies only read access. Fields that are not specified with `Perm` are inaccessible. Permissions can be combined in an expression using the separating conjunction `**` operator, such that the sum of fractions never exceeds 1 for a field. Permissions can be split and combined, e.g. `Perm(o.f, 1)` can be split into `Perm(o.f, 1\2) ** Perm(o.f, 1\2)`. Note the use of "\" to indicate fractional division, as opposed to integer division using "/". Expressions in PBSL are "self-framing", which means that an expression must specify a permission for a field before reading it. For example, `Perm(x.f, 1) ** x.f == 0` is self-framing.

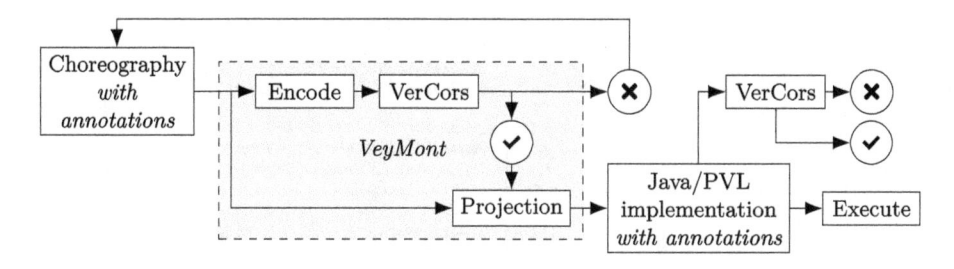

Fig. 2. Workflow for using VeyMont choreographies

VerCors also supports predicates, which allow grouping expressions, including permissions, under an opaque name. They are defined using the syntax: `resource` $P(\overline{Ta})$ = A, where P is the predicate name, $\overline{Ta}$ is a sequence of typed parameters, and A is the predicate body. As predicates are opaque, VerCors requires annotations that specify when a predicate body should be exchanged for a predicate name and its arguments, and vice versa. This is done with the `fold` and `unfold` statements. More specifically, if the expression A holds in the current verification state, then `fold` $P(\overline{e})$ will cause all permissions in A to be removed from the verification state. Then, the predicate $P(\overline{e})$ is added to the verification state. The `unfold` statement does the inverse: it removes $P(\overline{e})$, and adds A. See for example lines 7 and 8 of Fig. 5b. There is also \unfolding, which is for use in expressions. It unfolds a predicate temporarily while evaluating an expression, and folds it directly afterwards.

To mediate access to shared resources, PVL supports lock invariants, which defines assertions only available by acquiring a lock [11]. A lock invariant is declared on a class. By locking an object, the lock invariant is acquired, after which the lock invariant of the object is added to the current verification state. When unlocking the object, the lock invariant needs to be true in the current verification state, and if so its assertions are removed from the state. A lock invariant is declared at lines 1 to 5 of Fig. 8b.

3 VeyMont Workflow and Choreography Language

We now discuss the workflow and choreography language of VeyMont, including the new features that we added to support shared memory.

3.1 VeyMont Workflow

The workflow for using VeyMont is shown in Fig. 2, and consists of 3 steps:

Step 1: Verify. When a choreography with annotations is input into VeyMont, the semantics of the choreography is encoded (see Sect. 4), such that VerCors can verify it. If verification fails, there is a problem with the choreography: either it has a bug, or the contracts are not properly specified.

```
⟨GlobalDecl⟩ ::=  ⟨Class⟩                    ⟨ChorStmt⟩ ::= ···
              |   ⟨Procedure⟩                            | [⟨Name⟩:] ⟨Expr⟩ . ⟨Name⟩ := ⟨Expr⟩;
              |   [⟨Contract⟩]                           | channel_invariant ⟨Expr⟩;
                  choreography ⟨Name⟩ (⟨Params⟩) {       | communicate [⟨Name⟩:] ⟨Expr⟩ -> [⟨Name⟩:] ⟨Expr⟩;
                     ⟨ChorDecl⟩*
                  }                           ⟨Expr⟩ ::= ···
                                                       | Perm[⟨Name⟩](⟨Expr⟩, ⟨Expr⟩)
⟨ChorDecl⟩ ::=                                         | (\endpoint ⟨Name⟩; ⟨Expr⟩)
           |  endpoint ⟨Name⟩ = ⟨Name⟩(⟨Args⟩);         | (\chor ⟨Expr⟩)
           |  [⟨Contract⟩] run { ⟨ChorStmt⟩* }          | \msg
           |  ⟨Method⟩                                  | \receiver
                                                       | \sender
```

Fig. 3. VeyMont syntax in EBNF.

Step 2: Endpoint Projection. If verification succeeds, VeyMont applies endpoint projection on the choreography to generate an implementation for each choreography endpoint, with annotations. Section 5 discusses the endpoint projection. VeyMont can generate both PVL and Java code.

Step 3: Use. The generated implementation can be used in two ways. First, if Java code was generated, it can be executed. Second, for PVL code, it can be verified with standalone VerCors. If standalone verification fails, there was either a bug in the projection step, the choreography contains annotations that cannot be projected (using \chor, see Sect. 3.2), or the user made changes to the generated implementation that are incompatible with the current annotations.

3.2 Choreography Language

VeyMont extends the PVL language with syntax for defining choreographies. This syntax extension is summarized informally in Fig. 3.

Global Declarations. VeyMont definitions coexist with other PVL definitions such as classes. This way VeyMont programs can use procedures and types from PVL. VeyMont adds a type of global declaration, the **choreography**. This is the root definition for a VeyMont choreography. It consists of an optional contract, a name, parameters, and zero or more choreography declarations. In a VeyMont program, multiple choreographies can co-exist simultaneously.

Choreographic Declarations. A choreographic declaration is either an **endpoint** declaration, a **run** declaration, or a method declaration. An **endpoint** declaration defines an endpoint that participates in the choreography. Semantically this corresponds to an object created with a constructor. An endpoint has a name, a name of a PVL class, and a list of expressions as arguments for the constructor. The **run** declaration consists of an optional contract, and a body consisting of choreographic statements. Lastly, a regular PVL method definition is also a *ChorDecl*, when its body consists of choreographic statements.

Choreographic Statements. There are two choreographic statements: choreographic assignment and the **communicate** statement. Choreographic assignment

(:=) is similar to regular assignment, with the restriction that the value can only be computed using state from one endpoint. It consist of an expression of the object being assigned to, the target field, and an expression. Moreover, the choreographic assignment can optionally be labeled with an endpoint name to enable using a shared field from a different endpoint. The following verifies if a has permission for both b.f and a.f: "a: b.f := a.f;".

The communicate statement sends a value from one endpoint to another. It requires a receiving endpoint and field, and a sending endpoint and expression. When endpoints are omitted, they are derived from the expressions, e.g. a.x has a as the implicit endpoint. communicate statements are semi-synchronous: sending is non-blocking, receiving is blocking. Annotations for ownership transfer of a communicate statement, as well as functional constraints over the message, can be specified in a channel_invariant annotation. For example, the annotation "channel_invariant \msg > 2; communicate a.x -> b.x;" can be added to verify that the message sent from a.x to b.x is bigger than 2. Currently, only the choreographic expressions (explained in the next paragraph) \msg, \sender, \receiver as well as global functions, are allowed within channel_invariant. This is purely a limitation of the current implementation, as channels can straightforwardly be extended with extra context.

Within a choreography declaration, also selected PVL statements are allowed, such as assert, assume, if, while and blocks of statements.

Choreographic Expressions. There are six choreographic expressions. An endpoint name can be denoted within brackets at a permission annotation, to specify ownership by the endpoint of the stated permission. The keyword \endpoint requires the name of an endpoint and an expression. This indicates that, in the encoding (Sect. 4), the expression should only be evaluated for the endpoint, and only included in the implementation of the endpoint (Sect. 5). Within a channel_invariant, three additional expressions are available. These are \msg, \sender and \receiver. They are used to indirectly refer to the sender, receiver, and message of the next communicate statement.

Finally, the \chor keyword wraps an expression. This expression can access memory of all endpoints in the choreography. Specifically, within \chor *endpoint ownership annotations* are ignored. Because of this, it cannot be included in the generated implementation. Consequently, if a choreography contains a \chor expression, the generated implementation might not verify. More formally, we believe that if a correct choreography does not contain \chor, the generated implementation also verifies. We have not proven this, and leave it for future work. The \chor keyword is included because it makes the workflow of the original VeyMont [7] possible. It is also useful for prototyping contracts of a choreography, as endpoint ownership annotations prevent asserting expressions that ignore endpoint ownership, which limits the user when debugging annotations. Finally, \chor serves a similar role as the assume statement. Once a choreography is proven correct, the \chor should be removed. An example of \chor is in the TTT case study on page 14.

```
1  choreography increment(Store s) {
2    endpoint a = Role(s);
3    endpoint b = Role(null);
4
5    requires Perm[a](a.s, 1\2) ** Perm[a](a.s.x, 1) ** a.s.x > 0;
6    ensures Perm[a](a.s, 1\2) ** Perm[a](a.s.x, 1) ** a.s.x > 2;
7    run {
8      a: a.s.x := a.s.x + 1;
9      channel_invariant Perm(a.s, 1\2) ** Perm(a.s.x, 1) ** a.s.x > 1;
10     communicate a: a.s -> b: b.s;
11     assert Perm[b](a.s, 1\2) ** Perm[b](a.s.x, 1);
12     b: a.s.x := a.s.x + 1;
13     channel_invariant Perm(a.s, 1\2) ** Perm(a.s.x, 1\2) ** a.s.x > 2;
14     communicate b: b.s -> a: a.s;
15   } }
```

Fig. 4. A choreography where the endpoints increment a shared field with ownership annotations. Adapted from Fig. 1b. Note that some endpoint ownership annotations that can be inferred by VeyMont are included for clarity.

3.3 New Features of VeyMont

This paper introduces two extensions for VeyMont choreographies: endpoint ownership annotations, and channel invariants.

Endpoint ownership annotations indicate the owner of a permission. When an endpoint e owns a permission Perm($o.x$, f), this is written as Perm[e]($o.x$, f). For example, the permission Perm[alex]($o.x$, 1) allows alex to write to field x of object o. When a user writes Perm(alex.x, 1), VeyMont infers automatically that Perm[alex](alex.x, 1) was meant. By explicitly writing Perm[bob](alex.x, 1) the user specifies that bob currently has writing access to alex.x, while alex has no access. This way, alex.x is used as shared memory. Assignments can be annotated similarly: e: $o.f$:= v denotes that endpoint e executes assignment $o.f$:= v. Again we allow shorthand notation: alex.x := 1 denotes alex: alex.x := 1. Communications are written as communicate s: v -> r: u, where endpoint s sends value v to receiver r, which stores it in u. The shorthand notation communicate alex.x -> bob.y is also supported.

Channel invariants allow access to memory to be exchanged, i.e. shared. This is done by adding a channel_invariant annotation on a communicate statement. E.g. channel_invariant Perm(alex.x, 1) gives the receiver write access to alex.x, while the sender has lost access after this communication. In other words, permissions are transferred between the sending and receiving party *if and only if* they are stated in the channel invariant.

Motivating Example. We will now further demonstrate these concepts using an example. Figure 4 shows how we annotate the program from Fig. 1b so that VeyMont can verify the program with the shared field.

Endpoints a and b are initialized at lines 2 and 3. Then, line 5 states the precondition of the run method: a has write access to a.s.x. On line 8, a increments a.s.x. This is explicitly denoted with a: at the start of the line. On lines 9 and 10, the reference to Store s is sent from a to b. In addition, the channel

```
1  choreography setter(Store s) {
2    endpoint a = Role();
3    endpoint b = Role();
4
5    requires Perm[a](s.x, 1);
6    run {
7      a: s.x := 0;
8      b: s.x := 1;
9    }
10 }
```

```
1  resource perm_x(Role e, Store s) = Perm(s.x, 1);
2
3  requires perm_x(a, s);
4  void setter_run_a(Store s, Role a, Role b) {
5    unfold perm_x(a, s);
6    s.x = 0;
7    fold perm_x(a, s);
8    unfold perm_x(b, s);
9    s.x = 1;
10   fold perm_x(b, s);   }
```

(a) An incorrect choreography   (b) Encoding of run

Fig. 5. A choreography and encoding of run using permission stratification.

invariant transfers write access for a.s.x from a to b. This is explicitly verified with the assert on line 11. On line 12, b performs an increment to a.s.x, and then proceeds with the communicate statement on line 14, to send write permission back to a. The postcondition on line 6 states these write permissions, and additionally that a.s.x is more than 2. VeyMont will verify the program, in particular that the postcondition will hold. After that, VeyMont can also be invoked to generate the corresponding concurrent program with threads for endpoints a and b.

4 Choreography Verification

VeyMont generates an encoding of a choreography such that VerCors can verify it. This encoding essentially collapses all endpoint behaviors into one implementation. To prevent permissions of different endpoints from being accidentally combined, permissions are stratified (Sect. 4.1). This also allows encoding the transfer of the message and permissions between two endpoints (Sect. 4.2).

4.1 Permission Stratification

To encode permissions labeled with an endpoint owner into PVL, we use PVL predicates to label a permission with its endpoint owner. For each permission annotated with an endpoint owner, we create a predicate wrapping that permission. To this predicate we add an argument that models the endpoint owner. In essence, this argument enforces that a predicate can only be unwrapped if the current endpoint owner is specified. We call this technique "permission stratification". For example, the permission on line 5 of Fig. 5a results in the predicate on line 1 in Fig. 5b, where [a] in the annotation causes creation of the argument e in the predicate. The argument e is only used to distinguish stratified permissions with different owners, and therefore does not occur in the predicate.

Adding an extra argument to the predicate, to encode which endpoint owns the permission, works because of the following: unfolding a predicate only succeeds if the correct arguments are used. In this case, unfolding means exchanging a predicate instance for its body, which in turn modifies the verification state. For example, on line 3 in Fig. 5b, the predicate perm_x(a, s) is required. Within the method, the permission within the predicate can only be accessed using unfold perm_x(a, s). Conversely, the statement unfold perm_x(b, s) would fail, as there is only a predicate perm_x(a, s) present. Because the arguments have to be stated explicitly to unfold the predicate, the extra argument effectively acts as a "key" to access the permission within the predicate.

VeyMont unfolds wrapper predicates automatically when the endpoint owner of a permission is known, for example, in the case of assignment. This makes the permission in the predicate available for verification. Later, VeyMont folds the predicate, possibly with a new endpoint owner. The fold and unfold steps are generated by VeyMont according to inferred or user-supplied annotations, and are checked by VerCors. For example, VeyMont generates unfold and fold annotations before and after assignment to fields. This is shown on lines 5 and 7 of Fig. 5b.

The example in Fig. 5a shows an incorrect choreography. The two endpoints share a Store s and each writes to it. The user specifies that a owns the store on line 5. This program contains a data race: a and b run concurrently and write to the same location. Therefore, verification will fail, with an error on line 8.

The example in Fig. 5b shows the encoded choreography with all permissions stratified. Line 1 defines a wrapping predicate for when the field x is owned by a given endpoint Role e. Line 4 encodes the choreography parameter Store s, and endpoints a and b. Verification with VerCors yields that on line 8 it cannot unfold predicate perm_x(b, s) because it is not present in the verification state. Indeed, after line 7, the verification state holds exactly perm_x(a, s), and not perm_x(b, s)! One way to fix this example is to send the permission Perm(s.x, 1) from a to b between the two assignment statements using a communicate statement. This will exchange perm_x(a, s) with perm_x(b, s), at the cost of synchronization at run-time (see Sect. 4.2).

By wrapping permissions in predicates, VeyMont can verify the behavior of multiple endpoints within one program. This is the key ingredient that allows verification of choreographies with shared memory.

4.2 Encoding of Choreographic Communication

Figures 6b and 6c show how VeyMont encodes the communicate statement and channel_invariant of Fig. 6a. This is an example to illustrate the encoding, it is not meaningful on its own. All line numbers in this subsection refer to Fig. 6c. Summarizing, the encoding consists of 4 steps: line 6 encodes message evaluation, line 9 encodes channel invariant checking, lines 12 and 13 encode the transfer of the channel invariant from a to b, and lines 15 and 17 encode message reception. The fold annotations are required for handling stratified permissions, following the explanation in the previous section.

```
1  choreography incr(int i) {
2    endpoint a = Role(i); endpoint b = Role(i);
3    requires Perm(a.x, 1) **
4      (c() ==> Perm(a.z, 1) ** a.z == a.x);
5    requires Perm(b.y, 1);
6    run {
7      channel_invariant
8        c() ==> Perm(a.z, 1) ** \msg == a.z;
9      communicate a.x -> b.y;
10   } }
```

(a) Input choreography

```
1  // For each field f ∈ {c, x, y, z}, define:
2  resource perm_f(Role e, Role r) = Perm(r.f, 1);
3  int get_f(Role e, Role r) =
4    (\unfolding perm_f(e, r) \in r.f)
```

(b) Background definitions for encoding

```
1   requires perm_x(a, a) **
2     (c() ==> perm_z(a, a) **
3     get_z(a, a) == get_x(a, a));
4   requires perm_y(b, b);
5   void incr_run(int i, Role a, Role b) {
6     // Evaluate message
7     int m = get_x(a, a);
8     // Assert invariant
9     assert (c() ==> perm_z(a, a) **
10      m == get_z(a, a));
11    // Transfer invariant
12    if (c()) { unfold perm_z(a, a); }
13    if (c()) { fold perm_z(b, a); }
14    // Store message at target
15    unfold perm_y(b, b);
16    b.y = m;
17    fold perm_y(b, b);
18  }
```

(c) Encoding of choreography

Fig. 6. Encoding of a choreography with a `channel_invariant` and `communicate` statement. For brevity, method definition `incr` has been omitted in Fig. 6c.

First, the message to be sent is stored in m on line 6. To read a.x, the function get_x is used. Each get_f function unfolds the wrapper predicate perm_f to read field f. On line 9, the channel invariant is checked using assert. Note that the channel invariant was transformed: m replaces \msg, and a wrapper predicate replaces Perm(a.z, 1), following the stratified permissions approach. The owner of this wrapper predicate is a, because a is the sender of the communication.

The channel invariant is transferred from a to b on lines 12 and 13 via the unfold and fold statements. The `channel_invariant` contains the condition c(), which is an abstract global condition defined for this example. Because of this condition, if statements are also necessary to conditionally unfold and fold the predicates that wrap permissions. For the boolean parts of the invariant, no annotations have to be added, as these are kept track of automatically by the symbolic execution back-end of VerCors. Finally, m is assigned to target location b.y on line 16, which models the receiving of the message by b.

5 Endpoint Projection

To generate an implementation for an endpoint of a given choreography, the endpoint projection translates each statement depending on which endpoint is currently the target. We extend the endpoint projection presented in [7] to take into account endpoint ownership annotations. This allows VeyMont to include contracts in the projection, making the generated implementation verifiable if correct annotations are provided. In addition, we show how channel invariants are included in the channel classes that implement communicate statements.

Choreography with a & b	Projection for: a	Projection for: b
a.x := 5;	→ a.x = 5;	/* skip */
communicate a.x -> b.y;	→ a_b.writeValue(a.x);	b.y = a_b.readValue();
if (a.x == 5 &&	→ if (a.x == 5 &&	if (true &&
b.y == 9) {	→ true) {	b.y == 9) {
a.foo(a.x); }	→ a.foo(a.x); }	/* skip */ }
b: a.x := 5;	→ /* skip */	a.x = 5;
communicate b: a.x -> a: b.y;	→ b.y = a_b.readValue();	a_b.writeValue(a.x);
Perm[a](x.f, 1)	→ Perm(x.f, 1)	true
(\chor v)	→ true	true
(\endpoint a; v)	→ v	true

Fig. 7. Summary of endpoint projection rules by example. Top half describes rules from [7]. Bottom half describes endpoint ownership annotations.

5.1 Statement and Expression Projection Rules

Figure 7 shows – by example – the endpoint projection rules to generate an implementation for a target endpoint. The top half of the table shows the rules identical to those in [7], the bottom half shows the new rules. Using these new rules, contracts and loop invariants can straightforwardly be transformed and preserved in the generated implementation, which was previously not possible.

We will now further discuss the rules in the bottom half of Fig. 7. If the target endpoint participates, i.e. occurs, in a statement or expression, it is transformed as follows: choreographic assignment (:=) is transformed into plain assignment, communicate statements are transformed into invocations of readValue and writeValue methods on channel objects. Perm[e](o.x, f) is included without [e] in the generated implementation, and similarly, the keyword (\endpoint e; v) causes v to be included in the generated implementation. If the target endpoint does not participate in a statement or expression, it is omitted or replaced with true. The keyword (\chor v) is handled by always discarding it. This is because \chor can freely access the memory of all endpoints, and hence cannot safely be included in the generated implementation (see Sect. 3.2).

5.2 Generating Channels

For each communicate statement (Fig. 8a) VeyMont generates a distinct channel class (Fig. 8b). An instance of this class is constructed at the start of the program, and both endpoints of the communicate statement are given a reference to it. To send and receive values, the methods writeValue and readValue can be called. The lock_invariant expresses that the channel_invariant holds at the moment of transfer, i.e. when writeValue has written the communicated value in msg and set hasMsg to true, and readValue has been called after that. Because writeValue has the channel_invariant as precondition, and readValue as postcondition, the transfer of the channel_invariant is achieved.

```
1  channel_invariant
2    Perm(\sender.z, 1) **
3    Perm(\receiver.z, 1) **
4    \sender.z == \receiver.z;
5  communicate a.x -> b.y;
```

(a) communicate with corresponding channel_invariant

```
1   lock_invariant
2     Perm(hasMsg, 1) ** Perm(msg, 1) **
3     Perm(s, 1\2) ** Perm(r, 1\2) **
4     (hasMsg ==> Perm(s.z, 1) **
5     Perm(r.z, 1) ** s.z == r.z);
6   class ChanAB {
7     boolean hasMsg; int msg;
8     Role s, r; // Sender, receiver
9
10    context Perm(s, 1\8) ** Perm(r, 1\8);
11    requires Perm(s.z, 1) ** Perm(r.z, 1) **
12      s.z == r.z;
13    void writeValue(int m);
14
15    context Perm(s, 1\8) ** Perm(r, 1\8);
16    ensures Perm(s.z, 1) ** Perm(r.z, 1) **
17      s.z == r.z;
18    int readValue(); }
```

(b) Generated channel class.

Fig. 8. Generated channel class for channel_invariant and communicate.

Since a channel invariant may refer to both \sender and \receiver, the generated class contains both endpoints as references s and r. Read permissions for these fields reside at both endpoints. This way, respective fields of \sender and \receiver, e.g. \sender.z, can be expressed as s.z, when calling writeValue or readValue. The omitted implementations of writeValue and readValue are standard, where writeValue does not block, but readValue does.

6 Case Studies

To demonstrate the VeyMont extension of this paper, we present case studies on three variants of Tic-Tac-Toe. Here TTT is the baseline case study, adapted from [7], TTT_{msg} uses ownership annotations, and TTT_{last} optimizes away a theoretically unnecessary message. We provide the full annotated programs and tool implementation in the artifact [21].

The TTT case study is a variant of the case study discussed in [7]. It is set up to simulate a game of tic-tac-toe on a 3×3 in a distributed setting. This means each endpoint has its own local copy of the board, and as the endpoints take turns they send their moves to each other so the boards stay in sync. When a winning move occurs, or the board runs out of spaces, the game ends.

While each case study has different annotations, the postcondition proven is the same: *after the game terminates, the boards of the two players are identical.* This postcondition highlights the complexity of verifying an easy to understand choreography. To prove correctness, VeyMont must prove that each move made by one player is also applied to the local board of the other player. This kind of property could also occur when e.g. executing a transaction in a distributed database. When verifying the TTT choreography and ignoring permission stratification, the property is proved automatically. However, once the endpoints are split up into threads with the endpoint projection, a problem arises: the property

```
1   choreography TTT() {
2     endpoint p1 = Player(0, true);
3     endpoint p2 = Player(1, false);
4
5     requires p1.myMark == 0 **
6       p2.myMark == 1 **
7       (\chor p1.turn != p2.turn **
8       p1.equalBoard(p2));
9     ensures (\chor p1.equalBoard(p2));
10    run {
11      loop_invariant /* omitted */ **
12        p1.equalBoard(p2);
13      while(!p1.done() && !p2.done()) {
14        if(p1.turn && !p2.turn) {
15          p1.createNewMove();
16          communicate p1.move.copy() -> p2.move;
17        } else {
18          p2.createNewMove();
19          communicate p2.move.copy() -> p1.move;
20        }
21        p1.doMove();
22        p2.doMove();
23        p1.turn := !p1.turn;
24        p2.turn := !p2.turn;
25      }
26    }
27  }
```

Fig. 9. Main choreography of the TTT case study. The loop invariant on line 11 is omitted as it is the same as the precondition of **run**.

becomes impossible to state. This is because the property requires player one to make an assertion about the state of player two, and vice versa.

Each case study solves this problem differently. The TTT case study solves the problem by using \chor. This allows violating the restriction of stratified permissions, at the cost of missing annotations in the generated implementation. Case studies TTT_{msg} and TTT_{last} use stratified permissions to pass permissions back and forth, ensuring the players can alternate reading and writing to both boards safely. Specifically, TTT_{msg} introduces an extra message at run-time, and TTT_{last} eliminates this run-time overhead by using more complicated annotations. For TTT_{msg} and TTT_{last}, the generated implementations *do* verify.

TTT. The TTT case study is similar to the case study presented in [7]. The only changes are the reduction to a 3×3 board instead of an $M \times N$ board, and minor syntactical changes. This is not a limitation of this is paper, it is merely a simplification for ease of presentation. The choreography of TTT is shown in Fig. 9. After the endpoints are initialized, the endpoints enter a loop, where they alternate taking turns. After each turn, the move is send to the other player so they can update their board. The postcondition is (\chor p1.equalBoard(p2)), meaning the board of p1 is equal to that of p2 after termination. With automatic permission generation enabled, VeyMont can verify the choreography with the initial approach presented in [7]. The projection on these (old style) choreographies yields generated implementations where the choreography properties hold [15], but verification annotations marked with \chor are not present in the generated implementations, and hence the choreography postcondition cannot be verified on it.

TTT_{msg}. We take a different approach to avoid \chor: each endpoint will only keep half permission for their own board. The other halves are pooled and used to establish and maintain board equality. After each turn, these pooled permissions are sent to the other player. Finally, when the game ends, the last player splits the pooled permissions sends half to the other player. This gives both players read permission to both boards, allowing them to state board equality.

```
1  channel_invariant
2    \msg.movePerm() **
3    ([1\2]\sender.boardPerm()) **
4    ([1\2]\receiver.boardPerm()) **
5    \sender.oneMoveAheadOf(\msg, \receiver);
```

(a) Channel invariant of the communications in while loop

```
1  if (p1.turn && !p2.turn) {
2    channel_invariant
3      [1\4]\sender.boardPerm() **
4      [1\4]\receiver.boardPerm() **
5      \receiver.equalBoard(\sender);
6    communicate p1: true -> p2;
7  }
```

(b) Communication at game end

Fig. 10. Communications in TTT_{msg} case study.

To this end, we add to both communications in the while loop the channel invariant of Fig. 10a. The sending player provides 1\2 permission for his own board, *and* the other players board, in the channel invariant (using prefix scaling notation [1\2] before the predicate on lines 3 and 4). This invariant implies that the sending player is exactly one move ahead (line 5). This makes sense as the receiving player still has to update the board with the communicated move after the communication. Each player always keeps 1\2 permission for his own board.

At each point in the game, only one of the players can read both players' boards, thus only one player is able to verify that the boards are equal. When the game ends, one of the players sends 1\4 permission for both boards to the other player. Figure 10b shows this for p1. This way, postcondition p1.equalBoard(p2) can be stated by both endpoints without \chor, and hence proven directly for the whole generated concurrent program.

TTT_{last}. We optimize away the communicate statement after the while loop, while still retaining correctness. We do this by introducing additional ghost state and reformulating the annotations to be more general. In doing so, we demonstrate a trade-off: run-time overhead can often be eliminated, at the cost of additional complexity in the contracts and ghost state.

Specifically, we use extra fields p1.lastPlayer and p2.lastPlayer. These store a reference to the same object, which stores the mark of the "last player". In Fig. 11b we see that, just before communicating a move, p1 checks if this move ended the game. If so, p1.lastPlayer is set to p2.myMark, because p2 will be the last player updating his board, before the game ends. The predicate p1.lastPlayerPerms() specifies write permission to the mark field of its lastPlayer object. If the game is not finished yet, p1 includes the full permission (1\2 + 1\2) in the channel invariant, so that p2 may (possibly) edit it. Otherwise, if the game is finished, only 1\2 permission is sent, such that both players can read their lastPlayer.mark field to see who was the last player. In Fig. 11a we show the adapted postcondition of run: the player whose mark is stored in its lastPlayer.mark field can ensure p1.equalBoard(p2). This postcondition ensures that when both endpoints terminate in the generated implementation, VeyMont will conclude that whichever endpoint is the last player, there will always be one of them that will guarantee board equality. In this way, p1.equalBoard(p2) can be proven directly for the whole generated program.

```
1  ensures (\endpoint p1;
2    ([1\2]p1.lastPlayerPerms()) **
3    p1.lastPlayer.mark == p1.myMark ==>
4      ([1\2]p1.boardPerm() **
5      ([1\2]p2.boardPerm()) **
6      p1.equalBoard(p2));
```

(a) Postcondition of **run** method.

```
1  if (p1.gameFinished()) {
2    p1.lastPlayer.mark = 1 - p1.myMark;
3  }
4  channel_invariant /* ... */
5    ([1\2]\sender.lastPlayerPerms()) **
6    (!\sender.gameFinished() ==>
7      ([1\2]\sender.lastPlayerPerms()));
8  communicate p1.move.copy() -> p2.move;
```

(b) Code for marking the last player, and the channel invariant extension.

Fig. 11. Adapted code of TTT$_{last}$ with respect to TTT$_{msg}$, stated for p1. It is symmetric for p2.

7 Related Work

Besides the works we build upon by extending VeyMont [7,15], the most similar research in the realm of VerCors is the work by Darabi et al. [2]. They introduce the **send** and **receive** statements to model loop dependencies. These statements allow sending permission to other iterations of a loop, and are similar to **communicate**. However, these statements are only supported inside loops, offer no support for sending a value, and conditional sends can only depend on variables not modified inside the loop.

Similar works in the area of choreographies are on logics to reason about the correctness of choreographies [9,10]. These works could serve as a basis for formalizing the approach outlined in this paper, but they would have to be extended with support for separation logic.

We see interesting correspondences with multiple works on session types. Generally, session types do not support implementation generation. In theory, session type results may be transferable to choreographies, but this step is non-trivial.

Hinrichsen et al. [12] introduce Actris, a Coq framework using Iris for correctness reasoning over session types. Jacobs et al. [14] introduce similar but smaller formalization of dependent session protocols, also in Iris. Both approaches are powerful, but being Coq frameworks, lack the automation we aim for in this paper. They could be good starting points for formalizing our approach.

Neykova et al. [19] present SPY, a tool that generates run-time monitors of user-defined constraints on exchanged messages and endpoint state. Our approach works without running the code, and introduces no overhead at run-time.

Bouma et al. [8] use VerCors to check conformance of Java programs to a multi-party session type (MPST). Specifically, they use permissions only at the implementation level, while we already use permissions at choreography-level.

Marques et al. present an approach to verify that C programs written using MPI [17] follow a protocol defined using a session type [16]. Their tool allows constraints to be expressed over messages sent and received, which is an extended version of session types. However, the constraints are limited to (in-)equalities of arithmetic expressions and variables, while we support general first-order logic expressions. The tool also has no support for shared memory or ghost state.

Zhou et al. [27] present Session*, a tool that extends the Scribble protocol language [26] with refinement types by compiling Session* protocols to F* [23], a functional programming language with refinement types. Because mutable memory is supported within the generated callbacks implemented in F* through an effect system, Session* supports a limited form of mutability indirectly. We support it generally, allowing sharing mutable memory across implementation callbacks and reasoning about it in contracts.

Swamy et al. [24] formalize a minimal 2-party session type framework as an example use of the SteelCore separation logic framework in F* [23]. They do not offer specialized support for correctness reasoning of session types or the transfer of resources via session types, beyond what F* offers natively. We foresee that our approach could be embedded in F* using SteelCore.

Bocchi et al. [5] present a formal framework for applying design-by-contract to session types. The "global assertions" from their work are similar to contracts in VeyMont choreographies. Besides the difference between session types and choreographies, Bocchi et al. also do not support shared memory. They do define well-assertedness of global assertions to e.g. prevent endpoints from using values they do not know about. We resolve this by using permission stratification.

Finally, Proust et al. [20] have integrated the Why3 [4] program verifier with the Bulk Synchronous Parallel (BSP) model. The version of BSP in this work shares some aspects with OpenMP, as it offers parallelized versions of common operations, such as map and fold. In addition, BSP offers choreography-like many-to-many communication. There are two differences with our work. First, code written using the BSP API can only be executed in an environment that provides such an API. VeyMont generates plain Java & PVL code that can be verified and only needs the standard library. Second, Proust et al. only consider purely functional programs, while VeyMont supports reasoning about mutable variables and shared memory.

8 Conclusion

VeyMont could already verify choreographies, auto-generate permissions, and use the endpoint projection to generate an implementation. In this work, we added endpoint ownership annotations and channel invariants to VeyMont, such that choreographies can specify concurrent programs with shared memory between threads. Additionally, we transfer verification annotations to the generated implementations, such that they can be verified directly, without the choreography. We showed the new capabilities of extended VeyMont in case studies.

For future work, we first of all aim to introduce parameterized endpoints, such that distributed systems with any n number of nodes can be formulated as choreography. Also, adding support for one-to-many or many-to-one communications would make VeyMont more expressive. While we now use verification of choreographies and the generated implementations to ensure correctness of the projection, we would also like to formalize our approach, i.e. extend [15]. Finally, by doing more case studies, we will validate our approach more extensively.

References

1. Armborst, L., et al.: The VerCors verifier: a progress report. In: Gurfinkel, A., Ganesh, V. (eds.) Computer Aided Verification - 36th International Conference, CAV 2024, Montreal, QC, Canada, July 24-27, 2024, Proceedings, Part II. Lecture Notes in Computer Science, vol. 14682, pp. 3–18. Springer (2024). https://doi.org/10.1007/978-3-031-65630-9_1
2. Blom, S., Darabi, S., Huisman, M.: Verification of loop parallelisations. In: Egyed, A., Schaefer, I. (eds.) FASE 2015. LNCS, vol. 9033, pp. 202–217. Springer, Heidelberg (2015). https://doi.org/10.1007/978-3-662-46675-9_14
3. Blom, S., Darabi, S., Huisman, M., Oortwijn, W.: The vercors tool set: Verification of parallel and concurrent software. In: Lecture Notes in Computer Science, pp. 102–110. Springer International Publishing (2017). https://doi.org/10.1007/978-3-319-66845-1_7
4. Bobot, F., Filliâtre, J.C., Marché, C., Paskevich, A.: Why3: shepherd your herd of provers. In: Boogie 2011: First International Workshop on Intermediate Verification Languages, pp. 53–64. Wrocław, Poland, August 2011
5. Bocchi, L., Honda, K., Tuosto, E., Yoshida, N.: A theory of design-by-contract for distributed multiparty interactions. In: Gastin, P., Laroussinie, F. (eds.) CONCUR 2010 - Concurrency Theory, 21th International Conference, CONCUR 2010, Paris, France, August 31-September 3, 2010. Proceedings. Lecture Notes in Computer Science, vol. 6269, pp. 162–176. Springer (2010). https://doi.org/10.1007/978-3-642-15375-4_12
6. Bornat, R., Calcagno, C., O'Hearn, P.W., Parkinson, M.J.: Permission accounting in separation logic. In: Palsberg, J., Abadi, M. (eds.) Proceedings of the 32nd ACM SIGPLAN-SIGACT Symposium on Principles of Programming Languages, POPL 2005, Long Beach, California, USA, January 12-14, 2005, pp. 259–270. ACM (2005). https://doi.org/10.1145/1040305.1040327
7. van den Bos, P., Jongmans, S.: Veymont: Parallelising verified programs instead of verifying parallel programs. In: Chechik, M., Katoen, J., Leucker, M. (eds.) Formal Methods - 25th International Symposium, FM 2023, Lübeck, Germany, March 6-10, 2023, Proceedings. Lecture Notes in Computer Science, vol. 14000, pp. 321–339. Springer (2023). https://doi.org/10.1007/978-3-031-27481-7_19
8. Bouma, J., de Gouw, S., Jongmans, S.: Multiparty session typing in java, deductively. In: Sankaranarayanan, S., Sharygina, N. (eds.) Tools and Algorithms for the Construction and Analysis of Systems - 29th International Conference, TACAS 2023, Held as Part of the European Joint Conferences on Theory and Practice of Software, ETAPS 2022, Paris, France, April 22-27, 2023, Proceedings, Part II. LNCS, vol. 13994, pp. 19–27. Springer (2023). https://doi.org/10.1007/978-3-031-30820-8_3
9. Carbone, M., Grohmann, D., Hildebrandt, T.T., López, H.A.: A logic for choreographies. In: Honda, K., Mycroft, A. (eds.) Proceedings Third Workshop on Programming Language Approaches to Concurrency and communication-cEntric Software, PLACES 2010, Paphos, Cyprus, 21st March 2010. EPTCS, vol. 69, pp. 29–43 (2010). https://doi.org/10.4204/EPTCS.69.3

10. Cruz-Filipe, L., Graversen, E., Montesi, F., Peressotti, M.: Reasoning about choreographic programs. In: Jongmans, S., Lopes, A. (eds.) Coordination Models and Languages - 25th IFIP WG 6.1 International Conference, COORDINATION 2023, Held as Part of the 18th International Federated Conference on Distributed Computing Techniques, DisCoTec 2023, Lisbon, Portugal, June 19-23, 2023, Proceedings. Lecture Notes in Computer Science, vol. 13908, pp. 144–162. Springer (2023). https://doi.org/10.1007/978-3-031-35361-1_8
11. Haack, C., Huisman, M., Hurlin, C.: Reasoning about java's reentrant locks. In: Ramalingam, G. (ed.) Programming Languages and Systems, 6th Asian Symposium, APLAS 2008, Bangalore, India, December 9-11, 2008. Proceedings. LNCS, vol. 5356, pp. 171–187. Springer (2008). https://doi.org/10.1007/978-3-540-89330-1_13
12. Hinrichsen, J.K., Bengtson, J., Krebbers, R.: Actris: session-type based reasoning in separation logic. Proc. ACM Program. Lang. **4**(POPL), 6:1–6:30 (2020). https://doi.org/10.1145/3371074
13. Honda, K., Vasconcelos, V.T., Kubo, M.: Language primitives and type discipline for structured communication-based programming. In: Hankin, C. (ed.) Programming Languages and Systems - ESOP'98, 7th European Symposium on Programming, Held as Part of the European Joint Conferences on the Theory and Practice of Software, ETAPS'98, Lisbon, Portugal, March 28 - April 4, 1998, Proceedings. Lecture Notes in Computer Science, vol. 1381, pp. 122–138. Springer (1998). https://doi.org/10.1007/BFB0053567
14. Jacobs, J., Hinrichsen, J.K., Krebbers, R.: Dependent session protocols in separation logic from first principles (functional pearl). Proc. ACM Program. Lang. **7**(ICFP), 768–795 (2023). https://doi.org/10.1145/3607856
15. Jongmans, S., van den Bos, P.: A predicate transformer for choreographies - computing preconditions in choreographic programming. In: Sergey, I. (ed.) Programming Languages and Systems - 31st European Symposium on Programming, ESOP 2022, Held as Part of the European Joint Conferences on Theory and Practice of Software, ETAPS 2022, Munich, Germany, April 2-7, 2022, Proceedings. Lecture Notes in Computer Science, vol. 13240, pp. 520–547. Springer (2022). https://doi.org/10.1007/978-3-030-99336-8_19
16. Marques, E.R.B., Martins, F., Vasconcelos, V.T., Ng, N., Martins, N.: Towards deductive verification of MPI programs against session types. In: Yoshida, N., Vanderbauwhede, W. (eds.) Proceedings 6th Workshop on Programming Language Approaches to Concurrency and Communication-cEntric Software, PLACES 2013, Rome, Italy, 23rd March 2013. EPTCS, vol. 137, pp. 103–113 (2013). https://doi.org/10.4204/EPTCS.137.9
17. Message Passing Interface Forum: MPI: A Message-Passing Interface Standard Version 4.0 June 2021. https://www.mpi-forum.org/docs/mpi-4.0/mpi40-report.pdf
18. Montesi, F.: Introduction to Choreographies. Cambridge University Press (2023). https://doi.org/10.1017/9781108981491
19. Neykova, R., Yoshida, N., Hu, R.: SPY: local verification of global protocols. In: Legay, A., Bensalem, S. (eds.) Runtime Verification - 4th International Conference, RV 2013, Rennes, France, September 24-27, 2013. Proceedings. LNCS, vol. 8174, pp. 358–363. Springer (2013). https://doi.org/10.1007/978-3-642-40787-1_25

20. Proust, O., Loulergue, F.: Verified scalable parallel computing with why3. In: Ferreira, C., Willemse, T.A.C. (eds.) Software Engineering and Formal Methods - 21st International Conference, SEFM 2023, Eindhoven, The Netherlands, November 6-10, 2023, Proceedings. Lecture Notes in Computer Science, vol. 14323, pp. 246–262. Springer (2023). https://doi.org/10.1007/978-3-031-47115-5_14
21. Rubbens, R., van den Bos, P., Huisman, M.: VeyMont permission annotations tic-tac-toe case studies and tool implementation (2024). https://doi.org/10.5281/zenodo.13348214
22. Sakar, Ö., Safari, M., Huisman, M., Wijs, A.: Alpinist: An annotation-aware GPU program optimizer. In: Fisman, D., Rosu, G. (eds.) Tools and Algorithms for the Construction and Analysis of Systems - 28th International Conference, TACAS 2022, Held as Part of the European Joint Conferences on Theory and Practice of Software, ETAPS 2022, Munich, Germany, April 2-7, 2022, Proceedings, Part II. Lecture Notes in Computer Science, vol. 13244, pp. 332–352. Springer (2022). https://doi.org/10.1007/978-3-030-99527-0_18
23. Swamy, N., Hritcu, C., Keller, C., Rastogi, A., Delignat-Lavaud, A., Forest, S., Bhargavan, K., Fournet, C., Strub, P., Kohlweiss, M., Zinzindohoue, J.K., Béguelin, S.Z.: Dependent types and multi-monadic effects in F. In: Bodík, R., Majumdar, R. (eds.) Proceedings of the 43rd Annual ACM SIGPLAN-SIGACT Symposium on Principles of Programming Languages, POPL 2016, St. Petersburg, FL, USA, January 20 - 22, 2016. pp. 256–270. ACM (2016). https://doi.org/10.1145/2837614.2837655
24. Swamy, N., Rastogi, A., Fromherz, A., Merigoux, D., Ahman, D., Martínez, G.: Steelcore: an extensible concurrent separation logic for effectful dependently typed programs. Proc. ACM Program. Lang. 4(ICFP), 121:1–121:30 (2020). https://doi.org/10.1145/3409003
25. Vercors tool homepage. https://utwente.nl/vercors. Accessed 01 Mar 2024
26. Yoshida, N., Hu, R., Neykova, R., Ng, N.: The scribble protocol language. In: Abadi, M., Lluch-Lafuente, A. (eds.) Trustworthy Global Computing - 8th International Symposium, TGC 2013, Buenos Aires, Argentina, August 30-31, 2013, Revised Selected Papers. LNCS, vol. 8358, pp. 22–41. Springer (2013). https://doi.org/10.1007/978-3-319-05119-2_3
27. Zhou, F., Ferreira, F., Hu, R., Neykova, R., Yoshida, N.: Statically verified refinements for multiparty protocols. Proc. ACM Program. Lang. 4(OOPSLA), 148:1–148:30 (2020). https://doi.org/10.1145/3428216

Correct and Complete Symbolic Execution for Free

Erik Voogd[1]([✉]), Einar Broch Johnsen[1],
Åsmund Aqissiaq Arild Kløvstad[1], Jurriaan Rot[2], and Alexandra Silva[3]

[1] University of Oslo, Oslo, Norway
erikvoogd@ifi.uio.no
[2] Radboud University, Nijmegen, The Netherlands
[3] Cornell University, Ithaca, NY, USA

Abstract. Symbolic execution is a powerful technique for program analysis. However, the formal semantics underlying symbolic execution is often developed on an ad-hoc basis and decoupled from the concrete semantics of the programming language. To overcome this issue, we introduce *symbolic SOS*: a rule format that allows us to simultaneously specify concrete *and* symbolic operational semantics. We prove that symbolic semantics, when generated from symbolic SOS, is both correct and complete with respect to the corresponding concrete semantics. The approach relies only on an algebraic signature of the source language, and is thus language-independent.

1 Introduction

Symbolic execution is an established program analysis technique with a long history [10,15,16], that is widely used for bug finding, verification and even program synthesis [1,3,11,19,21]. More recently, the systematic study of the formal foundations of symbolic execution in its own right has gained increasing interest [2,9,18,24]. In particular, De Boer and Bonsangue [8,9] introduce the notions of *correctness* and *completeness*, formalizing a correspondence between symbolic execution and concrete program execution.

Proving that a given symbolic semantics is correct and complete, however, is a tedious task that would benefit from automation. This paper provides the basis for such automation by answering the following question: *what are sufficient conditions for a language specification to define a symbolic semantics that is correct and complete by design?* We take language specifications to be defined in Structural Operational Semantics (SOS) [20,25], a standard formalism to specify programming language semantics as collections of inference rules. Our goal is to extract, for a given language with an operational semantics expressed as an SOS specification, a correct and complete symbolic semantics.

This research is partially supported by the NWO grant No. OCENW.M20.053, ERC grant Autoprobe (no. 101002697) and a Royal Society Wolfson fellowship.

© The Author(s), under exclusive license to Springer Nature Switzerland AG 2025
N. Kosmatov and L. Kovács (Eds.): IFM 2024, LNCS 15234, pp. 237–255, 2025.
https://doi.org/10.1007/978-3-031-76554-4_13

Our starting point is the *GSOS* rule format [5]. The syntactic restrictions on rules in GSOS specifications ensure that the resulting semantics is well-defined and compositional with respect to bisimilarity. The GSOS format was later generalized by Turi and Plotkin into *abstract GSOS* [25], which formalizes specifications through interaction between algebra (representing syntax) and coalgebra (representing transition systems). Goncharov et al. have recently introduced *stateful structural operational semantics* (SSOS) [13], which adapts abstract GSOS to a stateful setting.

In order to automatically obtain symbolic semantics from SOS specifications, we refine SSOS to *symbolic SOS*. A symbolic SOS specification defines both a concrete and a symbolic operational semantics, in terms of two (small-step) transition systems. Our main result is that this symbolic semantics is always correct and complete with respect to the concrete semantics. Any programming language defined in the symbolic SOS format thereby comes equipped with a corresponding correct and complete symbolic semantics. To prove this general correspondence result, we introduce the notion of *syncrete bisimulation*, which gives a sufficient condition for correctness and completeness. We then show that for every symbolic SOS specification, the induced concrete and symbolic semantics are bisimilar, and therefore the symbolic semantics is correct and complete.

Contributions. In summary, this paper introduces: (i) the *symbolic SOS* rule format (Sect. 4) from which both a concrete and a symbolic semantics can be derived; (ii) the notion of *syncrete bisimulation*, which provides a coinductive proof technique for correctness and completeness (Sect. 6); and (iii) a justification for the rule format (Theorem 1) stating that the two derived semantics from a symbolic SOS specification are always syncretely bisimilar.

2 Overview

This section summarizes the technical development and presents our key results. We also introduce our running example: the imperative toy language While. While serves as a minimal concrete example to illustrate our results, but the approach is language-independent. In Sect. 7, we consider additional common programming constructs, to showcase the power of our approach.

Example 1 (The Syntax of While). The syntax of While is given by three grammars for expressions, Boolean expressions and program statements. Let us consider the following grammar for expressions and Boolean expressions:

$$e ::= x \mid n \mid e+e \mid e-e \mid e*e \qquad b ::= \top \mid \neg b \mid b \wedge b \mid e<e \mid e=e$$

where $x \in \mathcal{X}$ ranges over program variables and $n \in \mathbb{Z}$ over integers. The syntax of the While programming language is given by the grammar

$$p ::= \text{Skip} \mid x := e \mid p \, \mathring{,}\, p \mid \text{if } b \, p \, p \mid \text{while } b \, p$$

These program statements represent inaction, assignments, sequencing, branching, and unbounded iteration.

The semantics of While can be specified using an SOS format to define a transition system that formalizes the evolution of program configurations. In particular, the SSOS format [13] considers pairs (p, s), where p is the program to be executed and s is a state. Usually, states associate values to program variables. Consider, for example, the following rules for sequencing and assignment:

$$\frac{(p, s) \downarrow_c s'}{(p \, \mathring{,}\, q, s) \longrightarrow_c (q, s')} \qquad \frac{}{(x := e, s) \downarrow_c s[x \mapsto s(e)]}$$

The transition relation $\longrightarrow_c$ denotes one step of *concrete execution*, evolving to a new program and state, and $\downarrow_c$ denotes termination. The subscript c here emphasizes that system states are *concrete*. With $[x \mapsto s(e)]$, an assignment updates the value of variable x to $s(e)$, which is the expression e evaluated in the state s according to a standard interpretation of arithmetic operations. Each rule actually represents a (potentially infinite) family of rules, one for each state. Together, these two (families of) rules describe a concrete execution model consisting of sequences of assignments to program variables.

For symbolic execution we may also define a *symbolic* semantics, again using the SSOS format. This is defined as a transition relation between states σ which are substitutions, i.e., they associate expressions to variables. The symbolic state moreover contains a set of path constraints which we add later. Symbolic rules are often identical to their concrete counterpart, up to the interpretation of states. Indeed, consider the analogous symbolic rules for sequencing and assignments:

$$\frac{(p, \sigma) \downarrow_s \sigma'}{(p \, \mathring{,}\, q, \sigma) \longrightarrow_s (q, \sigma')} \qquad \frac{}{(x := e, \sigma) \downarrow_s \sigma[x \mapsto \sigma(e)]}$$

Here, the *symbolic* transition relation $\longrightarrow_s$ denotes one step of *symbolic execution*, evolving to a new program and symbolic state, and $\downarrow_s$ denotes termination.

The rules look identical to their concrete counterparts, but the state updates differ subtly. While the concrete rule updates the state to map the variable x to a new value, namely the expression e evaluated in state s, the symbolic rule updates the state to map the variable x to a new expression: $\sigma(e)$ is the expression e with all variables substituted according to σ.

For symbolic execution to be useful, it must indeed be an abstraction of the concrete execution. That is, informally, for each concrete step there must be a symbolic step whose final state describes the state update of the concrete step. For some rules in concrete execution, however, it is unclear what the matching symbolic step should look like. Consider the concrete rules for branching:

$$\frac{s \models b}{(\texttt{if } b \, p \, q, s) \longrightarrow_c (p, s)} \qquad \frac{s \models \neg b}{(\texttt{if } b \, p \, q, s) \longrightarrow_c (q, s)}$$

These rules express that the program if $b \, p \, q$ evolves to p if s satisfies b, and to q otherwise; the state s remains unaltered in either case. These rules are deterministic: branching is resolved by checking whether or not states satisfy the Boolean expression b, guarding the control-flow of the program.

From a *symbolic* state, however, the question of whether the symbolic state satisfies b cannot be resolved. We may enable *both* transitions

$$\overline{(\text{if } b\ p\ q, \sigma) \longrightarrow_s (p, \sigma)} \qquad \overline{(\text{if } b\ p\ q, \sigma) \longrightarrow_s (q, \sigma)}$$

rendering the symbolic transition relation non-deterministic. Starting from a single state, therefore, a program generates many different sequences of transition steps, called *paths*. In contrast, concrete execution generates a *single* path. So which symbolic execution path simulates the concrete execution path?

To answer this question, states in symbolic execution are enhanced with a *path condition* and the transition relation now relates triples of programs, states, and a path condition. Path conditions aggregate the Boolean conditions that guide a program's control flow under the current substitution. In the case of conditional branching, this is realized through the following two rules:

$$\overline{(\text{if } b\ p\ q, \sigma, \varphi) \longrightarrow_s (p, \sigma, \varphi \wedge \sigma(b))} \qquad \overline{(\text{if } b\ p\ q, \sigma, \varphi) \longrightarrow_s (q, \sigma, \varphi \wedge \sigma(\neg b))}$$

Both steps augment the path condition by substituting for the variables x their associated expressions $\sigma(x)$ in the expressions b and $\neg b$.[1] The resulting system is still technically non-deterministic, but the path condition "determinizes" the symbolic execution by specifying exactly which concrete executions it simulates.

To argue that the path condition of a symbolic execution path is indeed a precondition for concrete executions, the two types of executions are connected by proving *correctness* and *completeness*. We define these notions following De Boer and Bonsangue [9]. Below, the initial configuration $(\sigma_0, \varphi_0) = (\text{id}, \top)$ consists of the identity substitution σ_0 on variables and the Boolean *truth* formula $\top$.

Correctness. Symbolic execution is *correct* with respect to concrete execution if all *symbolic* execution paths

$$(p_0, \sigma_0, \varphi_0) \longrightarrow_s (p_1, \sigma_1, \varphi_1) \longrightarrow_s \cdots \longrightarrow_s (p_k, \sigma_k, \varphi_k) \qquad (1)$$

simulate the *concrete* execution paths from (p_0, s_0) for which $s_0 \vDash \varphi_k$. Formally,

$$(p_0, s_0 \bullet \sigma_0) \longrightarrow_c (p_1, s_0 \bullet \sigma_1) \longrightarrow_c \cdots \longrightarrow_c (p_k, s_0 \bullet \sigma_k) \qquad (2)$$

is the *unique* concrete execution path starting from p_0 and $s_0 \vDash \varphi_k$. Here, $s \bullet \sigma$ denotes *evaluation of s after substitution σ*—this is made formal in Definition 5.

Completeness. Symbolic execution is *complete* with respect to concrete execution if every concrete execution path

$$(p_0, s_0) \longrightarrow_c (p_1, s_1) \longrightarrow_c \cdots \longrightarrow_c (p_k, s_k) \qquad (3)$$

---

[1] We assume that this always results in a Boolean expression; abstracting from program-level type correctness.

is simulated by a symbolic execution path as in Eq. (1), whose resulting path conditions are satisfied by s_0, i.e., $s_0 \vDash \varphi_j$ for all $j \in [0..k]$.

Correct- and completeness are properties of symbolic execution that are defined with respect to the concrete semantics: *correctness* is when every symbolic execution path corresponds to a realizable concrete computation, and *completeness* is when all concrete paths are represented by some symbolic path. In the context of program analysis, on the other hand, correctness is about *coverage* and completeness is about *precision* [2,9].

The process of defining concrete and symbolic semantics separately and then proving correctness and completeness is cumbersome. As observed, the symbolic and concrete rules are (almost) identical, leading to our key question:

Question: *Can we obtain correct and complete symbolic semantics directly from a language specification?*

We answer this question by defining a *symbolic* SOS rule format. A key insight for our work is the observation that both concrete and symbolic transition systems can arise from the same underlying specification, if this specification is sufficiently structured to obtain both semantics. In particular, the resulting state needs to be carefully constructed to ensure symbolic simulation, and care must be taken to allow building a path condition.

In symbolic SOS specifications (Sect. 4), states are meta-variables, i.e., placeholders for both concrete *and* symbolic states. In Sect. 5 we make explicit how the concrete semantics is derived from a symbolic SOS specification. Then, in Sect. 6, we derive the symbolic semantics and we define the notion of *syncrete bisimulations*. Crucially, we show that the derived semantics are related by a syncrete bisimulation relation, ensuring both correctness and completeness.

3 Preliminaries

For our programming language, we take a signature $(\Sigma, E, P, B, \sharp, \beta)$ and a fixed set of program variables $\mathcal{X}$. The signature consists of ways to generate (i) *programs* using operators in Σ; (ii) *expressions* using E-operators; (iii) *predicates* using P; and (iv) *Boolean expressions* using B. Every operator has some arity given by $\sharp \colon \Sigma + E + P + B \to \mathbb{N}$. The meaning of β is explained below.

For any set X, write $\mathcal{E}X$ for the set of terms over X using operations in E; we call these *expressions* over X. Then $\mathcal{E}\mathcal{X}$ is the set of *program* expressions, used in, e.g., assignments. With $\mathcal{V}$ a set of values (integers, rationals, lists, etc.), a family ε of maps $(\varepsilon_{\mathtt{f}} \colon \mathcal{V}^{\sharp(\mathtt{f})} \to \mathcal{V})_{\mathtt{f} \in E}$ interprets E-operators. The inductive extension $\overline{\varepsilon}$ of ε over itself, i.e., $\overline{\varepsilon} \colon \mathcal{EV} \to \mathcal{V}$ with $\overline{\varepsilon}(v) = \varepsilon(v)$, $v \in \mathcal{V}$ and $\overline{\varepsilon}(\mathtt{f}(e_1, \ldots, e_{\sharp(\mathtt{f})})) = \varepsilon_{\mathtt{f}}(\overline{\varepsilon}(e_1), \ldots, \overline{\varepsilon}(e_{\sharp(\mathtt{f})}))$ evaluates expressions over values. We will write ε for $\overline{\varepsilon}$.

States during concrete execution (or *concrete states*) are mappings $s \colon \mathcal{X} \to \mathcal{V}$ that assign values to program variables. Given $\varepsilon \colon \mathcal{EV} \to \mathcal{V}$, program expressions $e \in \mathcal{EX}$ can be evaluated in any state by inductive extension of the map $s \colon \mathcal{X} \to \mathcal{V}$ to $\overline{s} \colon \mathcal{EX} \to \mathcal{V}$ defined by $\overline{s}(x) = s(x)$ and $\overline{s}(\mathtt{f}(e_1, \ldots, e_{\sharp(\mathtt{f})})) = \varepsilon_{\mathtt{f}}(\overline{s}(e_1), \ldots, \overline{s}(e_{\sharp(\mathtt{f})}))$. Then $\overline{s} = \overline{\varepsilon} \circ \mathcal{E}s$, where $\mathcal{E}s \colon \mathcal{EX} \to \mathcal{EV}$ performs uniform substitution of variables by values in the expression according to s. Sometimes we write s for $\bar{s}$.

The set $\mathcal{P}X$ of *predicates* over X consists of expressions $\pi(e_1,\ldots,e_n)$, where $\pi \in P$ is an n-ary predicate operator, i.e., $\sharp(\pi) = n$, and each $e_i \in \mathcal{E}X$ is an expression over X. Common examples include membership, equality, and inequalities. Assume we can *interpret* predicates over values using $I: \mathcal{P}\mathcal{V} \to \{\mathsf{T},\mathsf{F}\}$. We say a concrete state $s \in \mathcal{V}^{\mathcal{X}}$ satisfies a program predicate $\pi(e_1,\ldots,e_n) \in \mathcal{P}\mathcal{X}$, written $s \vDash_{\varepsilon, I} \pi(e_1,\ldots,e_n)$ iff $I(\pi(\bar{s}(e_1),\ldots,\bar{s}(e_n))) = \mathsf{T}$. We will leave dependence on ε and I implicit by just writing $s \vDash \pi(e_1,\ldots,e_n)$.

With B as a set of logical operators such that every n-ary $\mathcal{L} \in B$ has a truth table $\{\mathsf{T},\mathsf{F}\}^n \to \{\mathsf{T},\mathsf{F}\}$, (E, P, B) is a first-order logic signature without quantification. Let $\mathcal{B}X$ be the set of *Boolean expressions* over X inductively generated by operators in B over predicates in $\mathcal{P}X$. We assume B contains binary conjunction $\wedge$ and disjunction $\vee$, and unary negation $\neg$, each with its conventional truth table. The constant $\top \in B$ (true) is satisfied by all states, and $\bot \in B$ (false) by no states. Write $s \vDash b$ if a state $s \in \mathcal{V}^{\mathcal{X}}$ satisfies $b \in \mathcal{B}\mathcal{X}$.

The set $\Sigma^*(X)$ of *programs* with free variables X is inductively generated by operators in Σ. Let $\mathcal{T} = \Sigma^*(\emptyset)$ be the set of *(closed) programs*. These are the only programs that will be equipped with a semantics. Operators in Σ may use *expressions* in $\mathcal{E}\mathcal{X}$ and *Boolean expressions* in $\mathcal{B}\mathcal{X}$. Crucial to our work, $\beta: \Sigma \to \mathcal{B}\mathcal{X}$ assigns to every operator $\mathtt{f} \in \Sigma$ an associated *guard* $\beta(\mathtt{f}) \in \mathcal{B}\mathcal{X}$ governing control flow of the semantics. For the rest of the paper, we consider the signature $(\Sigma, E, P, B, \sharp, \beta)$, the set of variables $\mathcal{X}$, and the interpretations ε and I fixed.

Example 2 (The `While` *Signature).* The signature $(\Sigma, E, P, B, \sharp, \beta)$ for the `While` language from Example 1 is as follows: Σ contains the constant `Skip` $\in \Sigma$, a binary operator for sequencing, and one constant for every pair $(x, e) \in \mathcal{X} \times \mathcal{E}\mathcal{X}$ of variable and expression representing an assignment $x\mathbin{{:}{=}}e$. Each of these operators has $\top$ as guard. Σ furthermore contains, for each Boolean expression $b \in \mathcal{B}\mathcal{X}$, a binary operator `if` $b\ \cdot\ \cdot$ for branching with guard $\beta(\mathtt{if}\ b\ \cdot\ \cdot) = b$ and a unary operator `while` $b\ \cdot$ for unbounded iteration with guard $\beta(\mathtt{while}\ b\ \cdot) = b$. The set E contains the binary operators $+$, $-$, $*$, and all integers. The set P contains binary $<$ and $=$, and B contains constant $\top$, unary $\neg$, and binary $\wedge$. We let $\mathcal{V} = \mathbb{Z}$ and ε and I are standard; e.g., $\varepsilon(6*7) = 42$ and $I(6*7 > 0 \vee \bot) = \mathsf{T}$.

4 Symbolic Rule Format

In this section, we introduce the *symbolic SOS* rule format. The format is purely syntactic, to the point that meta-variables are used as placeholders for both programs and states. This allows us to derive both concrete semantics (Sect. 5) and symbolic semantics (Sect. 6) from a single specification in the format.

Let $\mathsf{XVar} = \{\mathtt{x},\mathtt{y},\ldots\}$ and $\mathsf{SVar} = \{\mathtt{a},\mathtt{b},\ldots\}$ be sets of meta-variables that are placeholders for programs and states, respectively. An (uninterpreted) *transition* is either progressive or terminating. A *progressive* transition is an expression of the form $(x, a) \longrightarrow (y, b)$ with $x, y \in \mathsf{XVar}$ and $a, b \in \mathsf{SVar}$. Here, x is called the *source* and is said to transition to the *target* y with *input* a and *output* b. A *terminating* transition lacks a target and only produces output, written $(x, a) \downarrow b$. Terms $t \in \Sigma^*(\mathsf{XVar})$ may be used as sources and targets. Using a special termination symbol $\checkmark \in \Sigma$, we let $(x, a) \downarrow b$ be synonymous to $(x, a) \longrightarrow (\checkmark, b)$. We use ℓ to denote uninterpreted transitions, progressive or terminating. An SOS *rule* consists of a set $\{\ell_i\}_{i=1..n}$, called the *premises*, together with a *conclusion* ℓ.

Definition 1 (Symbolic SOS Rule). *A symbolic SOS rule for an operator* $f \in \Sigma$ *of arity* $n = \sharp(f)$ *is a rule* $\dfrac{\ell_1 \quad \cdots \quad \ell_n \quad \phi}{\ell}$ *where* $\phi \in \mathcal{BX}$ *is a Boolean expression called the* trigger *of the rule and*

- *the source of the conclusion ℓ is* $f(x_1, \ldots, x_n)$;
- *the source of the premise ℓ_i (each i) is x_i and its target (if progressive) is y_i;*
- *the input of each premise ℓ_i and the conclusion input is* a;
- *the output of premise ℓ_i is* b_i;
- *if ℓ is progressive, its target is in* $\Sigma^*(\{x_1, \ldots, x_n\} \cup \{y_i \mid \ell_i \text{ is progressive}\})$;
- *the conclusion output is a map* $\mathcal{X} \to \mathcal{E}(\{a, b_1, \ldots, b_n\} \times \mathcal{X}\})$.

This definition is an adaptation of the format of *stateful SOS* [13]; we have replaced states by meta-variables, added extra structure in the conclusion output, and added a Boolean trigger for control-flow. Our specification, defined just below, requires the trigger to be either the guard $\beta(f)$ of f, or its negation. The last item says that the conclusion output can store an expression over $\mathsf{SVar} \times \mathcal{X}$ for every variable, but it restricts to using meta-variables in SVar occurring in the rule. An expression in $\mathcal{E}(\mathsf{SVar} \times \mathcal{X})$ can be interpreted as a value in $\mathcal{V}$ once the meta-variables have been replaced by concrete states—this is technically outlined in Sect. 5—turning the conclusion output into a new concrete state. Replacing the meta-variables by *symbolic* states (defined later), the map $\mathcal{X} \to \mathcal{E}(\mathsf{SVar} \times \mathcal{X})$ can be interpreted as a new symbolic state, as outlined in Sect. 6.

A *symbolic SOS specification* requires each operator to have exactly *two* rules whose triggers are complementary. Letting these triggers coincide with an operator's guard and its complement, one rule has trigger $\beta(f)$, the other $\neg\beta(f)$. The behavior of a program may also depend on whether or not any of its subterms terminates (e.g. sequencing). There are therefore two rules for every operator f and every set $W \subseteq \{1, \ldots, \sharp(f)\}$ indicating which premises are progressive.

Definition 2 (Symbolic SOS Specification). *A symbolic SOS specification for a signature* $(\Sigma, E, P, B, \sharp, \beta)$ *is a set Ξ of symbolic SOS rules with the following condition: for every operator $f \in \Sigma \setminus \{\checkmark\}$ with $n = \sharp(f)$ and for every subset $W \subseteq \{1, \ldots, n\}$, there are exactly two rules $\mathcal{R}_1, \mathcal{R}_2 \in \Xi$ such that*

- *the premises $\{\ell_i\}_{i \in W}$ of both $\mathcal{R}_1$ and $\mathcal{R}_2$ are progressive, and*
- *the premises $\{\ell_i\}_{i \in [1..n] \setminus W}$ of both $\mathcal{R}_1$ and $\mathcal{R}_2$ are terminating.*

Moreover, for these rules, the triggers of $\mathcal{R}_1$ and $\mathcal{R}_2$ are $\beta(f)$ and $\neg\beta(f)$.

skip $\dfrac{}{(\texttt{Skip},\texttt{a})\downarrow\texttt{a}}$ assign $\dfrac{}{(x\mathbin{:=}e,\texttt{a})\downarrow\texttt{a}[x\mapsto\texttt{a}(e)]}$

seq-0 $\dfrac{(\texttt{x},\texttt{a})\downarrow\texttt{a}'}{(\texttt{x}\mathbin{\fatsemi}\texttt{y},\texttt{a})\longrightarrow(\texttt{y},\texttt{a}')}$ seq-n $\dfrac{(\texttt{x},\texttt{a})\longrightarrow(\texttt{x}',\texttt{a}')}{(\texttt{x}\mathbin{\fatsemi}\texttt{y},\texttt{a})\longrightarrow(\texttt{x}'\mathbin{\fatsemi}\texttt{y},\texttt{a}')}$

if-T $\dfrac{b}{(\texttt{if }b\texttt{ x y},\texttt{a})\longrightarrow(\texttt{x},\texttt{a})}$ while-T $\dfrac{b}{(\texttt{while }b\texttt{ x},\texttt{a})\longrightarrow(\texttt{x}\mathbin{\fatsemi}\texttt{while }b\texttt{ x},\texttt{a})}$

if-F $\dfrac{\neg b}{(\texttt{if }b\texttt{ x y},\texttt{a})\longrightarrow(\texttt{y},\texttt{a})}$ while-F $\dfrac{\neg b}{(\texttt{while }b\texttt{ x},\texttt{a})\downarrow\texttt{a}}$

Fig. 1. A symbolic SOS specification for the `While` language, from which both symbolic and concrete semantics can be derived.

Example 3 (Specification for `While`). A symbolic SOS specification for the language system for `While` (from Example 2) is shown in Fig. 1. We omit the trigger of a rule if it is ⊤. The rule for ¬⊤ does not matter for the semantics (see Sects. 5 and 6), because no state ever satisfies ¬⊤. The rules for branching, iteration, and sequencing are syntactic sugar for sets of rules. Rule while-F, for instance, represents two rules: one with premise $(\texttt{x},\texttt{a})\longrightarrow(\texttt{x}',\texttt{a}')$ and one with premise $(\texttt{x},\texttt{a})\downarrow\texttt{a}'$. Premise targets and outputs are not used in these instances.

When writing **a** (or **a**′) in the conclusion output of a rule, we mean the map $\mathcal{X}\to\mathcal{E}(\mathsf{SVar}\times\mathcal{X})$ that sends x to $(\texttt{a},x)$. Rule assign uses common notation for function *updates* $\texttt{a}[x\mapsto\texttt{a}(e)]$, i.e., a function that maps every y to $(\texttt{a},y)$ except x, which is mapped to $\texttt{a}(e)$. Here, $\texttt{a}(e)$ is shorthand for the expression e with every variable y substituted by $(\texttt{a},y)$.

In the following two sections, the meta-variables for states will be substituted by *concrete* states (Sect. 5) and by *symbolic* states (Sect. 6). There, the reasons for our choice of shorthand notations for **a** and $\texttt{a}(e)$ will be made clear.

5 Concrete Semantics

We now show how concrete semantics is derived from a symbolic SOS specification. We make this derivation explicit to juxtapose it with the derivation of the symbolic semantics, and to show how the meta-variables can be formally interpreted as actual states, both concrete and symbolic.

Recall that $\mathcal{T}=\Sigma^*(\varnothing)$ is the set of all programs. Usually, the meta-variables of language specification rules range over all programs. Formally, the symbolic SOS rules from the previous section are equipped with a *meta-substitution*,[2] i.e., a map $\psi_X\colon\mathsf{XVar}\to\mathcal{T}$. This mapping canonically extends to $\Sigma^*(\mathsf{XVar})\to\mathcal{T}$, performing uniform substitution on programs over meta-variables. Usually, a meta-substitution ψ_X is partially defined, namely on the sources $\{\mathrm{x}_1,\ldots,\mathrm{x}_n\}$ and the targets $\{\mathrm{y}_i \mid \ell_i$ is progressive$\}$ of a rule's premises $\ell_1,\ldots,\ell_n$. The rule format

---

[2] Not to be confused with substitutions of values or expressions.

ensures that ψ_X can also be applied to the conclusion source $f(x_1, \ldots, x_n)$ and the conclusion target t. The meta-variables in the rules are all distinct, but since meta-substitutions can be injective, programs in the rule may coincide.

The key insight here is that states, much like programs, can also be interpreted symbolically using meta-variables:

Definition 3 (Meta-Substitution of Concrete States). *A meta-substitution of concrete states is a map* $\psi_S \colon \mathsf{SVar} \to \mathcal{V}^\mathcal{X}$.

We will often combine meta-substitutions of programs $\psi_X \colon \mathsf{XVar} \to \mathcal{T}$ and of states $\psi_S \colon \mathsf{SVar} \to \mathcal{V}^\mathcal{X}$ into one meta-substitution $\psi \colon \mathsf{XVar} + \mathsf{SVar} \to \mathcal{T} + \mathcal{V}^\mathcal{X}$.

Meta-substitutions of states are usually only partially defined, namely on the input a—which is the same for all premises and for the conclusion—and on the premise outputs $\{b_1, \ldots, b_n\}$ occurring in a rule. The rule format guarantees that a meta-substitution of states ψ_S can be applied to the rule's conclusion output $u \colon \mathcal{X} \to \mathcal{E}(\mathsf{SVar} \times \mathcal{X})$, which would be of type $\psi_S(u) \colon \mathcal{X} \to \mathcal{E}(\mathcal{V}^\mathcal{X} \times \mathcal{X})$. But now that we have access to concrete states, we can use function evaluation $\mathsf{eval} \colon \mathcal{V}^\mathcal{X} \times \mathcal{X} \to \mathcal{V}, (s, x) \mapsto s(x)$, to interpret these pairs occurring in an expression as values from the concrete state. Evaluating the expression of values for each variable using $\varepsilon \colon \mathcal{EV} \to \mathcal{V}$ provides us with a new state given by $\psi_S(u) \colon \mathcal{X} \to \mathcal{E}(\mathcal{V}^\mathcal{X} \times \mathcal{X}) \xrightarrow{\mathcal{E}(\mathsf{eval})} \mathcal{E}(\mathcal{V}) \xrightarrow{\varepsilon} \mathcal{V}$ for the conclusion output.

A *concrete execution model* is a deterministic unlabeled transition system $(\mathcal{T} \times \mathcal{V}^\mathcal{X}, \longrightarrow_c)$. The concrete execution model $\longrightarrow_c$ *intended* by a symbolic SOS specification $\varXi$ for the signature $(\varSigma, E, P, B, \sharp, \beta)$ is recursively defined on the structure of programs in $\mathcal{T}$ as follows:

Definition 4 (Concrete Semantics). *Let $f \in \varSigma$ be an operator with $n = \sharp f$, let $p_1, \ldots, p_n \in \mathcal{T}$ be programs for which transitions have been defined, and let $s \in \mathcal{V}^\mathcal{X}$ be an arbitrary state. Let $W \subseteq \{1, \ldots, n\}$ indicate which transitions $(p_i, s) \longrightarrow_c (p^{(i)}, s^{(i)})$ are progressive, and let $\mathcal{R}_1, \mathcal{R}_2 \in \varXi$ be the two rules for f and W with triggers $\beta(f)$ and $\neg \beta(f)$, respectively. Then let $(f(p_1, \ldots, p_n), s) \longrightarrow_c (\psi(t), \psi(u))$ by definition, with the meta-substitution*

$$\psi \colon \mathsf{XVar} + \mathsf{SVar} \to \mathcal{T} + \mathcal{V}^\mathcal{X}, \quad x \mapsto \begin{cases} p_i & x = x_i \\ p^{(i)} & x = x'_i \end{cases} \quad b \mapsto \begin{cases} s & b = a \\ s^{(i)} & b = b_i \end{cases}$$

using conclusion target and output (t, u) of $\mathcal{R}_1$ if $s \vDash \beta(f)$ and of $\mathcal{R}_2$ otherwise.

Constants in $\varSigma$ use axioms in the specification and constitute the base cases in this recursive definition. The resulting relation is clearly deterministic: every pair (p, s) defines exactly one outgoing transition, except when $p = \checkmark$.

Example 4. Consider a program in `While` that computes absolute values:

$$p_{\mathrm{abs}} \triangleq \mathtt{if}\ (x < 0)\ \{x\mathtt{:=}0 - x\}\ \{\mathtt{Skip}\}$$

We have a specification from Example 3 which induces a concrete execution model $(\longrightarrow_c, \mathcal{T} \times \mathcal{V}^\mathcal{X})$. Let s be a concrete state that maps x to -42. Then $(p_{\mathrm{abs}}, s) \longrightarrow_c (x\mathtt{:=}0-x, s) \downarrow_c s'$, where $s' \colon x \mapsto 42$. The number 42 was obtained by evaluating the expression $0 - (\mathtt{a}, x)$ after the meta-substitution $\psi_S \colon \mathtt{a} \mapsto s$.

6 Symbolic Semantics

We develop the semantics of symbolic execution, based on the same specification as we used to derive the concrete semantics. The meta-substitution will now substitute meta-variables by *symbolic* states. After describing symbolic states and revisiting meta-substitutions, we introduce *syncrete bisimulation* to coinductively formalize correctness and completeness. Symbolic execution semantics is derived from the same specification as the concrete semantics. This semantics is both correct and complete with respect to the concrete semantics (Theorem 1).

The domain of a symbolic state $\sigma \colon \mathcal{X} \to \mathcal{E}\mathcal{X}$, like that of a concrete state, can be inductively extended from $\mathcal{X}$ to $\mathcal{E}\mathcal{X}$. This extension $\overline{\sigma} \colon \mathcal{E}\mathcal{X} \to \mathcal{E}\mathcal{X}$ is defined by $\overline{\sigma}(x) = \sigma(x)$ and $\overline{\sigma}(\mathtt{f}(e_1,\ldots,e_n)) = \mathtt{f}(\overline{\sigma}(e_1),\ldots,\overline{\sigma}(e_n))$. Now $\overline{\sigma} = \mu_{\mathcal{X}} \circ \mathcal{E}\sigma$, where $\mathcal{E}\sigma \colon \mathcal{E}\mathcal{X} \to \mathcal{E}^2(\mathcal{X})$ performs uniform substitution of variables by expressions, and $\mu_{\mathcal{X}} \colon \mathcal{E}^2(\mathcal{X}) \to \mathcal{E}\mathcal{X}$—seemingly the identity function—glues expressions together. Contrast this with the inductive extension $\overline{s}$ of a concrete state $s \colon \mathcal{X} \to \mathcal{V}$ for which $\overline{s} = \overline{\varepsilon} \circ \mathcal{E}s$: one evaluates expressions of expressions as a new expression, the other evaluates expressions of values as a value. We sometimes write σ for $\overline{\sigma}$.

Symbolic states as substitutions can be applied to predicates in $\mathcal{P}\mathcal{X}$ by letting $\sigma(\pi(e_1,\ldots,e_n)) := \pi(\sigma(e_1),\ldots,\sigma(e_n))$. Similarly, they can be applied recursively on Boolean expressions with predicates as base cases.

Definition 5 (Symbolic States as Concrete State Transformers). *Let $s \in \mathcal{V}^{\mathcal{X}}$ be a concrete state and $\sigma \in (\mathcal{E}\mathcal{X})^{\mathcal{X}}$ a symbolic state. Then s after σ is the new concrete state $s \bullet \sigma := \overline{s} \circ \sigma \colon \mathcal{X} \xrightarrow{\sigma} \mathcal{E}\mathcal{X} \xrightarrow{\mathcal{E}s} \mathcal{E}\mathcal{V} \xrightarrow{\varepsilon} \mathcal{V}$.*

The new state $s \bullet \sigma$ evaluates an expression e by inductive extension, but we can also first apply σ and then evaluate expression $\sigma(e)$ in the initial state s. These two always coincide: evaluating e in $s \bullet \sigma$ is equivalent to evaluating $\sigma(e)$ in the initial state s:

Lemma 1 (Substitution Lemma). *Let $s \in \mathcal{V}^{\mathcal{X}}$ and $\sigma \in (\mathcal{E}\mathcal{X})^{\mathcal{X}}$. Then (i) for all expressions $e \in \mathcal{E}\mathcal{X}$, $(s \bullet \sigma)(e) = s(\sigma(e))$; and (ii) for all Boolean expressions $b \in \mathcal{B}\mathcal{X}$, $s \bullet \sigma \models b$ iff $s \models \sigma(b)$.*

Example 5 (Symbolic states as concrete state transformers). Consider two variables x, y, a symbolic state $\sigma = [x \mapsto 2 * x, y \mapsto x]$ and $s_0 = [x \mapsto 21, y \mapsto 0]$ a concrete state. Then $(s_0 \bullet \sigma)(x) = \varepsilon(\mathcal{E}s(2 * x)) = \varepsilon(2 * 21) = 42$ and similarly $(s_0 \bullet \sigma)(y) = 21$. In general, for this σ, the map $s \mapsto s \bullet \sigma$ is a concrete state transformer that doubles the value of x and sets y equal to the old value of x.

Symbolic semantics is derived by interpreting meta-variables as symbolic states:

Definition 6 (Meta-Substitution of Symbolic States). *A meta-substitution of symbolic states is a map $\widehat{\psi}_S \colon \mathsf{SVar} \to (\mathcal{E}\mathcal{X})^{\mathcal{X}}$.*

The way $\widehat{\psi}_S$ acts on the conclusion output $\mathsf{u} \colon \mathcal{X} \to \mathcal{E}(\mathsf{SVar} \times \mathcal{X})$ of a symbolic SOS rule is analogous to meta-substitution of concrete states:

$$\widehat{\psi}_S(\mathsf{u}) \colon \mathcal{X} \to \mathcal{E}((\mathcal{E}\mathcal{X})^{\mathcal{X}} \times \mathcal{X}) \xrightarrow{\mathcal{E}(\mathrm{eval})} \mathcal{E}^2(\mathcal{X}) \xrightarrow{\mu_{\mathcal{X}}} \mathcal{E}\mathcal{X}$$

The meta-substitution $\widehat{\psi}_S$ is first universally applied to $\mathbf{u}$, then every pair (σ, x) is evaluated within the expressions, and finally, the resulting expression is glued.

Example 6 (Meta-substitution for assignment). Let $s_0 = [x \mapsto 21, y \mapsto 0]$ and $\sigma = [x \mapsto 2*x, y \mapsto x]$, and let $s = [x \mapsto 42, y \mapsto 21]$. In Example 5, we saw that σ transforms s_0 to s, i.e., $s_0 \bullet \sigma = s$. Suppose ψ_S and $\widehat{\psi}_S$ are concrete and symbolic meta-substitutions such that $\psi_S(\mathbf{a}) = s$ and $\widehat{\psi}_S(\mathbf{a}) = \sigma$. Consider an assignment $x := 0 - x$ as in Example 4 and its transition axiom $(x := 0 - x, \mathbf{a}) \downarrow \mathbf{u}$ in the specification from Example 3. With $\mathcal{X} = \{x, y\}$, we have $\mathbf{u} \colon \mathcal{X} \to \mathcal{E}(\{\mathbf{a}\} \times \mathcal{X})$ such that $\mathbf{u} \colon x \mapsto 0 - \mathbf{a}(x)$ and $\mathbf{u} \colon y \mapsto \mathbf{a}(y)$. Putting $s' := \psi_S(\mathbf{u})$ and $\sigma' := \widehat{\psi}_S(\mathbf{u})$, we have $s'(x) = 0 - s(x) = -42$ and $\sigma'(x) = 0 - \sigma(x) = 0 - 2*x$. For y, $s'(y) = s(y) = 21$ and $\sigma'(y) = \sigma(y) = x$. Therefore, $s_0 \bullet \sigma' = s'$.

In this example, the concrete and symbolic states are transformed concertedly by the assignment update. Specifically, $s_0 \bullet \widehat{\psi}_S(\mathbf{u}) = \psi_S(\mathbf{u})$ follows from $s_0 \bullet \widehat{\psi}_S(\mathbf{a}) = \psi_S(\mathbf{a})$ because $\mathbf{a}$ is the only meta-variable occurring in $\mathbf{u}$. Thus, the example illustrates a general inductive property of our rule format: at every step, the change in symbolic state matches the change in concrete state.

Lemma 2 (Meta-Substitution Lemma). *Let $\psi_S \colon \mathsf{SVar} \to \mathcal{V}^{\mathcal{X}}$ be a concrete and $\widehat{\psi}_S \colon \mathsf{SVar} \to (\mathcal{EX})^{\mathcal{X}}$ a symbolic meta-substitution and let $s_0 \in \mathcal{V}^{\mathcal{X}}$ be a concrete state. For all $\mathbf{u} \colon \mathcal{X} \to \mathcal{E}(\mathsf{SVar} \times \mathcal{X})$, if $s_0 \bullet \widehat{\psi}_S(\mathbf{b}) = \psi_S(\mathbf{b})$ for all $\mathbf{b} \in \mathsf{SVar}$ that occur in $\mathbf{u}$, then $s_0 \bullet \widehat{\psi}_S(\mathbf{u}) = \psi_S(\mathbf{u})$.*

A *symbolic execution model* is a nondeterministic unlabeled transition system $(\mathcal{T} \times (\mathcal{EX})^{\mathcal{X}} \times \mathcal{BX}, \longrightarrow_s)$. We now define the symbolic execution model $\longrightarrow_s$ intended by a symbolic SOS specification Ξ for the signature $(\Sigma, E, P, B, \sharp, \beta)$. For this, we let $n = \sharp(\mathbf{f})$ and, given arbitrary state σ and path condition φ, we recursively define the set of outgoing transitions for $(\mathbf{f}(p_1, \ldots, p_n), \sigma, \varphi)$, where we have already defined the sets $\mathbb{P}_i = \{(p', \sigma', \varphi') \mid (p_i, \sigma, \varphi) \longrightarrow_s (p', \sigma', \varphi')\}$ of outgoing transitions for the subterms p_i. An n-tuple $\xi \in \prod_{i \in [1..n]} \mathbb{P}_i$ contains one possible combination of targets for $p_i, \ldots, p_n$. Let $W_\xi \subseteq \{1, \ldots, n\}$ be the set of i with $p_\xi^{(i)} \neq \checkmark$, indicating progressive premises; write $\xi = (p_\xi^{(i)}, \sigma_\xi^{(i)}, \varphi_\xi^{(i)})_{i \in [1..n]}$.

Definition 7 (Symbolic Semantics). *Let $\mathbf{f} \in \Sigma$ be an operator, $\sigma \in (\mathcal{EX})^{\mathcal{X}}$ a symbolic state, $\varphi \in \mathcal{BX}$ a path condition, and $p_1, \ldots, p_n \in \mathcal{T}$ a set of programs. For $\xi \in \prod_{i \in [1..n]} \mathbb{P}_i$, let $\mathcal{R}_{\xi,1} \in \Xi$ and $\mathcal{R}_{\xi,2} \in \Xi$ be the rules for $\mathbf{f}$ and W_ξ with triggers b_f and $\neg b_f$, respectively. Let $(\mathbf{f}(p_1, \ldots, p_n), \sigma, \varphi) \longrightarrow_s (p', \sigma', \varphi')$, by definition, for all (p', σ', φ') in the set*

$$\{ (\widehat{\psi}_\xi(t_{\xi,1}), \widehat{\psi}_\xi(u_{\xi,1}), \varphi \wedge \sigma(b) \wedge \Phi_\xi), (\widehat{\psi}_\xi(t_{\xi,2}), \widehat{\psi}_\xi(u_{\xi,2}), \varphi \wedge \neg \sigma(b) \wedge \Phi_\xi) \}_{\xi \in \prod_i \mathbb{P}_i}$$

where $t_{\xi,j}, u_{\xi,j}$ ($j = 1, 2$) are the conclusion targets and outputs of $\mathcal{R}_{\xi,j}$,

$$\widehat{\psi}_\xi \colon \mathsf{XVar} + \mathsf{SVar} \to \mathcal{T} + (\mathcal{EX})^{\mathcal{X}}, \quad x \mapsto \begin{cases} p_i & \text{if } x = x_i \\ p_\xi^{(i)} & \text{if } x = x_i' \end{cases} \quad b \mapsto \begin{cases} \sigma & \text{if } b = \mathbf{a} \\ \sigma_\xi^{(i)} & \text{if } b = b_i \end{cases}$$

and $\Phi_\xi := \bigwedge_{i \in [1..n]} \varphi_\xi^{(i)}$ is the conjunction of all path conditions in the premises.

Here, Φ_ξ includes *all* premise path conditions, including conditions potentially not used in the conclusion. This condition may appear too strong for some rule instances in symbolic execution techniques. However, since $\prod_{i \in [1..n]} \mathbb{P}_i$ comprises all combinations of transitions, and since every ξ induces a step for both $\sigma(b)$ and $\neg\sigma(b)$, the resulting set of path conditions covers all of the input path condition φ. Many of the resulting steps may have coinciding continuations.

Proposition 1 (Path Condition One-Step Coverage). *Let $\longrightarrow_s$ be the intended symbolic execution system of a symbolic SOS specification, and let (p, σ, φ) be a symbolic configuration. For $A = \{\varphi' \mid (p, \sigma, \varphi) \longrightarrow_s (p', \sigma', \varphi')\}$:*

- *$\varphi_1 \wedge \varphi_2 \equiv \bot$ for all $\varphi_1, \varphi_2 \in A$ such that $\varphi_1 \neq \varphi_2$; and*
- *$\bigvee A \equiv \varphi$, where $\bigvee A$ denotes finite disjunction of all elements in A.*

Example 7. We return to program p_{abs} from Example 4 and the symbolic SOS specification from Example 3. Using the two axioms for an *if* statement, the derived symbolic execution semantics gives the two transitions $(p_{\text{abs}}, \text{id}, \top) \longrightarrow_s (x := -x, \text{id}, \top \wedge (x < 0))$ and $(p_{\text{abs}}, \text{id}, \top) \longrightarrow_s (\text{Skip}, \text{id}, \top \wedge \neg(x < 0))$. Continuing for one more step we obtain a set of four reachable configurations; the two on the left stem from $x := -x$; the other two from Skip:

$$\left\{ \begin{array}{ll} (\checkmark, x \mapsto -x, \top \wedge (x < 0) \wedge \top), & (\checkmark, \text{id}, \top \wedge \neg(x < 0) \wedge \top), \\ (\checkmark, x \mapsto -x, \top \wedge (x < 0) \wedge \neg\top), & (\checkmark, \text{id}, \top \wedge \neg(x < 0) \wedge \neg\top) \end{array} \right\}$$

The bottom configurations can be discarded: no state satisfies $\neg\top$. We further simplify path conditions by removing $\top$-conjuncts. Then $\longrightarrow_s$ reduces the *if* statement to two possible transformations: $x \mapsto -x$ if $x < 0$ and id otherwise.

Syncrete Bisimulation is a coinductive formalization of correctness and completeness for symbolic execution. We prove that our rule format induces a syncrete bisimulation relation between concrete and symbolic execution semantics, namely the identity relation: every program is syncretely bisimilar to itself.

Definition 8 (Syncrete Bisimulation). *Let $(\mathcal{T} \times \mathcal{V}^\mathcal{X}, \longrightarrow_c)$ be a concrete execution model and $(\mathcal{T} \times (\mathcal{E}\mathcal{X})^\mathcal{X} \times \mathcal{B}\mathcal{X}, \longrightarrow_s)$ a symbolic execution model. A relation $R \subseteq \mathcal{T} \times \mathcal{T}$ is a syncrete bisimulation between $\longrightarrow_c$ and $\longrightarrow_s$ if, for all $\sigma \in (\mathcal{E}\mathcal{X})^\mathcal{X}$, $\varphi \in \mathcal{B}\mathcal{X}$, and initial states $s_0 \in \mathcal{V}^\mathcal{X}$ s.t. $s_0 \vDash \varphi$, whenever pRq:*

- *if $(p, s_0 \bullet \sigma) \longrightarrow_c (p', s')$ then there is (q', σ', φ') such that (i) $(q, \sigma, \varphi) \longrightarrow_s (q', \sigma', \varphi')$ (ii) $s' = s_0 \bullet \sigma'$ (iii) $p'Rq'$ and (iv) $s_0 \vDash \varphi'$.*
- *if $(q, \sigma, \varphi) \longrightarrow_s (q', \sigma', \varphi')$ and $s_0 \vDash \varphi'$ then $(p, s_0 \bullet \sigma) \longrightarrow_c (p', s_0 \bullet \sigma')$ for some $p' \in \mathcal{T}$ such that $p'Rq'$.*

The first item makes every step in the symbolic system coinductively complete: every concrete step is matched by a symbolic step that refines the path condition in a way that the initial state s_0 remains satisfied. The second item makes every step in the symbolic system coinductively correct. Here, it may seem like any symbolic state σ can be chosen, but the updated path condition

φ' always contains the Boolean formula b that guards control-flow under substitution by σ. Hence, the condition $s_0 \vDash \varphi'$ entails $s_0 \bullet \sigma \vDash b$.

In the following results, let Ξ be a symbolic SOS specification and let $\longrightarrow_c$ be the intended concrete model and $\longrightarrow_s$ the intended symbolic model.

Theorem 1. *The identity relation on the set $\mathcal{T}$ of programs is a syncrete bisimulation between $\longrightarrow_c$ and $\longrightarrow_s$.*

By induction on the length of the transition chain, with the definitions of correctness and completeness from Sect. 2:

Corollary 1 (Correctness and Completeness). *The intended model of symbolic execution $\longrightarrow_s$ is correct and complete with respect to $\longrightarrow_c$.*

The induced small-step model provides a correct and complete core for symbolic execution. Full symbolic execution amounts to providing a search strategy for the execution tree built by $\longrightarrow_s$, and the result is guaranteed to correspond to concrete program behavior by Corollary 1.

7 Extensions

We consider two extensions to While: *arrays* (see De Boer and Bonsangue [9]) and a *probabilistic* programming constructs (see Voogd et al. [26]). We immediately obtain a concrete execution model $(\mathcal{T} \times \mathcal{V}^{\mathcal{X}}, \longrightarrow_c)$ and a symbolic execution model $\longrightarrow_s$ that is both correct and complete with respect to $\longrightarrow_c$.

Arrays. Arrays can be incorporated in While by imposing some structure on $\mathcal{X}$, E and B. Let the *variables* be a disjoint union of regular and array variables $\mathcal{X} + \mathcal{A}$ with values in $\mathbb{Z} + (\mathbb{N} \rightharpoonup \mathbb{Z})$. Regular variables $x \in \mathcal{X}$ are assigned integers and $a \in \mathcal{A}$ partial integer-valued functions with index domain $\mathbb{N}$.

Let *expressions* include $a[e]$, $a[e := e']$ and $|a|$ for $a \in \mathcal{A}$ and $e, e' \in E\mathcal{X}$. The semantics is modeled by ε; we let ε map $a[e]$ to $\varepsilon(a)(\varepsilon(e))$, and $a[e := e'](e'')$ to $\varepsilon(e')$ if $\varepsilon(e) = \varepsilon(e'')$ or $\varepsilon(a[e''])$ otherwise. We let $\varepsilon(|a|)$ be the size of the set on which $\varepsilon(a)$ is defined. Now extend Σ from Example 1 by allowing the left-hand side of an assignment to be an array expression and introduce a new constant Error to denote out-of-bounds access.

Let $\delta \in P$ be a unary predicate indicating absence of indexing errors. The semantics of the closed predicate $\delta(e)$ is inductively defined by (i) $\delta(n) := \mathsf{T}$ for all constants $n \in E$; (ii) $\delta(a[e])$ iff $(0 \leq e < |a|) \wedge \delta(e)$; (iii) $\delta(a[e := e'])$ iff $(0 \leq e < |a|) \wedge \delta(e) \wedge \delta(e')$; and (iv) $\delta(\mathtt{f}(e_1, \ldots, e_n)) \equiv \delta(e_1) \wedge \cdots \wedge \delta(e_n)$ for n-ary operation symbols $\mathtt{f} \in E$.

Now let us define a symbolic SOS specification for signature $(\Sigma, E, P, B, \sharp, \beta)$. Array assignments require a new pair of rules:

$$\frac{\delta(a[e])}{(a[e] := e', s) \downarrow s[a \mapsto a[s(e) := s(e')]]} \qquad \frac{\neg \delta(a[e])}{(a[e] := e', s) \longrightarrow (\mathtt{Error}, s)}$$

The conclusion of the left rule denotes the map $\mathcal{X} + \mathcal{A} \to \mathcal{E}(\{\mathbf{s}\} \times (\mathcal{X} + \mathcal{A}))$ that maps each variable x to $s(x)$ (including arrays) except that a is mapped to the *expression* $a[s(e) := s(e')]$ with e, e' updated to replace each variable $y \in \mathcal{X} + \mathcal{A}$ with $s(y)$. The rule on the right signals an error that may be handled by other mechanisms.

The rules in Fig. 1 with trivial triggers can be safely replaced with two rules: one with the additional trigger $\delta(e)$ for expressions in the program term and one with $\neg \delta(e)$ progressing to an error. For if- and while- rules some additional machinery is needed to maintain the requirements of Definition 2. For each Boolean expression b we introduce a new binary operator $\mathtt{sif}\ b\ \cdot\ \cdot$ (for "safe if"). We then have exactly two rules for each of $\mathtt{if}\ b$ and $\mathtt{sif}\ b$.

$$\text{if-safe}\ \frac{\delta(b)}{(\mathtt{if}\ b\ \mathtt{x}\ \mathtt{y}, a) \longrightarrow (\mathtt{sif}\ b\ \mathtt{x}\ \mathtt{y}, a)} \qquad \text{if-err}\ \frac{\neg \delta(b)}{(\mathtt{if}\ b\ \mathtt{x}\ \mathtt{y}, a) \longrightarrow (\mathrm{Error}, a)}$$

$$\text{if-T}\ \frac{b}{(\mathtt{sif}\ b\ \mathtt{x}\ \mathtt{y}, a) \longrightarrow (\mathtt{x}, a)} \qquad \text{if-F}\ \frac{\neg b}{(\mathtt{sif}\ b\ \mathtt{x}\ \mathtt{y}, a) \longrightarrow (\mathtt{y}, a)}$$

Thus an if-statement first checks if its condition contains a nil error, and only then proceeds safely to one of its branches. A "safe while" is implemented analogously by first checking its conditition, and then proceeding as before.

Randomization. For probabilistic sampling during program execution, we consider a set of logical variables $\mathcal{Y} = \{y_k\}_{k \in \mathbb{N}}$ that represent samples; states are now maps $\mathcal{X} + \mathcal{Y} \to \mathcal{V}$. We consider a signature $(\Sigma, E, P, B, \sharp, \beta)$ similar to the $\mathtt{While}$ language (see Example 2). To ensure probabilistic independence of samples, assignments $x := e$ cannot involve variables from $\mathcal{Y}$; they are still represented by a pair $(x, e) \in \mathcal{X} \times \mathcal{EX}$, but Σ is extended with a sampling statement $x \sim \mathbf{rnd}$. Consider the rule for sampling (with guard $\top$):

$$\overline{x \sim \mathbf{rnd}, a \downarrow \{x \mapsto (\mathtt{a}, y_0), y_0 \mapsto (\mathtt{a}, y_1), y_1 \mapsto (\mathtt{a}, y_2), \ldots\}}$$

which stores the first available sample y_0 in x and shifts all other samples one position. Writing (s, ρ) for the state $\mathcal{X} + \mathcal{Y} \to \mathcal{V}$, the concrete rule is

$$\overline{x \sim \mathbf{rnd}, s, \rho \downarrow (s[x \leftarrow \rho_0], \mathsf{tl}(\rho))}$$

Taking the head and tail does not work in the symbolic counterpart of this rule. A solution is to introduce a sampling index k and using the rule

$$\overline{x \sim \mathbf{rnd}, \sigma, k \downarrow \sigma[x \mapsto y_k], k+1}$$

An indexing scheme like this must be proven correct in the presence of all the rules in the programming system. The symbolic model of this language system produces symbolic states $\sigma : \mathcal{X} + \mathcal{Y} \to \mathcal{E}(\mathcal{X} + \mathcal{Y})$. Keeping k constant in other rules ensures that the part $\mathcal{Y} \to \mathcal{E}(\mathcal{X} + \mathcal{Y})$ left-shifts the stream by k, always giving a new variable in $\mathcal{Y}$.

For this to be a true randomization of programs, one assumes that the values for $\mathcal{Y}$, given by the map $\rho : \mathcal{Y} \to \mathcal{V}$, adhere to some probability law. This is a modeling issue; we argue that the symbolic system produces symbolic states that accurately represent program behavior in that they produce the same result once this initial state (randomized or not) is evaluated by the symbolic state. For a detailed account of symbolic execution of probabilistic programs, see [26].

8 Related Work

De Boer and Bonsangue formalize symbolic execution for the While language and define the notions of correctness and completeness of symbolic execution [9]. They employ a small-step transition system and inductive proofs of correctness and completeness over its transitive closure. In contrast, our work offers a coinductive alternative (allowing for non-finite computations) that captures both correctness and completeness in terms of syncrete bisimulation. We do this by quantifying over conceptual initial states s_0, and making concrete small-steps on $s_0 \bullet \sigma$ rather than big-steps on s_0 itself. A symbolic reconfiguration from σ to σ' then corresponds to a concrete reconfiguration of $s_0 \bullet \sigma$ to $s_0 \bullet \sigma'$.

Goncharov et al. developed *stateful SOS* (SSOS) for stateful programs [13], extending GSOS [5] with *state*, focusing crucially on the compositionality of the derived semantics. Via a reduction to GSOS, SSOS specifications are shown to correspond precisely to natural transformations which induce a denotational behavior that ensures compositionality in *resumption* semantics, a very fine-grained semantics in which very few programs are considered equivalent [13]. In particular, programs that induce the same state transformation—like $x:=1 \,\mathring{,}\, x:=x+1$ and $x:=1 \,\mathring{,}\, x:=x*2$—may not be equivalent under resumption semantics. Goncharov et al. consider two coarser semantics—trace and termination—which fail to be compositional in general. They therefore propose further restrictions on the SSOS format to ensure compositionality also in these settings. The unrestricted SSOS format forms the basis for symbolic SOS in our work, but we refine state transformations to ensure that they can be symbolically simulated.

The $\mathbb{K}$ framework shares our goal of defining language semantics with correct and complete analysis tools [22]. In particular, Lucanu et al. develop a language-independent coinductive description of symbolic execution [2,18], based on *Reachability Logic* [23]. They use matching logic and reachability logic to define semantics as rewrite rules, whereas we provide syntactic restrictions on the common stateful SOS format and introduce syncrete bisimulation as a useful formalization of the correspondence between symbolic and concrete (small-step) semantics. As a consequence, our proofs mostly use structural induction over programs whereas their proofs use correspondences between proof trees.

Bodin et al. propose another language-independent framework that provides analysis tools "for free" with their pretty-big-step semantics [7] and Skeletal Semantics [6]. They provide a framework of simple building blocks (bones) that assemble into programs (skeletons). Skeletons are given interpretations, and generic consistency results between interpretations are established. Finally, they define concrete and abstract interpretations and instantiate the consistency results with language-dependent lemmas. Their approach differs from ours by focusing on *structural* building blocks of semantics rather than a rule format. Additionally they focus on abstract interpretation rather than symbolic execution.

9 Discussion

We briefly consider two interesting aspects of the presented work: (1) the conditions on the rule formats to simultaneously construct concrete and symbolic semantics, and (2) extensions to more low-level state representations.

Our symbolic SOS format provides a *sufficient* condition for both concrete and symbolic semantics to be constructed simultaneously. However, identifying *necessary* conditions for rule formats that ensure correctness and completeness would be very challenging, because a lot of design choices have to be made to bridge the gap between the desired properties and the semantics specification. Our work on symbolic SOS is based on the following important design choices:

- Symbolic SOS builds on GSOS, which ensures that bisimilarity is always a congruence and that canonical operational models exist. GSOS provides a sufficient condition for this property. GSOS seems fairly close to the limits of well-behaved SOS formats. (For more liberal formats such as ntyft/ntyxt which allows both look-ahead and negative premises [14], the interpretation is more subtle [12] and it can even be difficult to decide whether a (unique) model exists [17].)
- Symbolic SOS builds on stateful SOS, which ensures that the properties above hold in a stateful setting. Symbolic SOS imposes structure such that states can be interpreted both concretely and symbolically. Lemma 2 (meta-substitution) proves that every step in one system is simulated by a step in the other. Rules in a specification must come in pairs—generalizable to complementary tuples of arbitrary size—with mutually disjoint conditions.

For our techniques to apply to a language, its operational semantics must be expressible with rules that syntactically enforce these properties: GSOS-like restrictions for compositionality and our added requirement on state structure.

The sets of variables and values, and the signatures of expressions and Boolean expressions have intentionally been kept abstract. Section 7 shows how symbolic execution correctness and completeness is maintained with additional structuring of the signatures. We believe that other extensions, e.g., for pointers or aliasing, would work similarly. Heaps could then be implemented by imposing structure on the states (both concrete and symbolic) similar to the arrays of Sect. 7. By distinguishing non-heap and heap variables and evaluating heap variables in partial maps (like the array variables), a pointer map is emulated. A predicate similar to the absence of indexing errors can be used to detect null pointer exceptions. See [9] for a discussion on aliasing. In this context, it would be interesting to further extend the path conditions with separation logic for pointers [4]. This would not affect the results presented in this paper, provided the meta-substitution lemma (Lemma 2) is maintained, ensuring that the symbolic SOS rules define matching transitions for the concrete and symbolic semantics.

10 Conclusion

We present a language-independent rule format for program semantics that induces both concrete and symbolic models. The induced models enjoy a bisimilarity relationship that ensures correctness and completeness of symbolic execution. Our approach thus allows to define operational semantics for a language and immediately obtain a symbolic execution engine that is correct by construction, providing a formal basis for analysis and verification tools.

Technically, we exploit that symbolic states represent transformations of concrete states to augment stateful SOS with a more structured notion of state, thereby obtaining *symbolic* stateful SOS. From symbolic SOS specifications, we show how to derive execution models in terms of symbolic and concrete transition systems. We formulate the novel notion of *syncrete bisimulation* and use it to prove that the derived symbolic execution model is correct and complete. The proof makes crucial use of the notion of bisimulation and a very general substitution lemma that relates symbolic states and concrete state transformations.

Our results work for concrete semantics that can be understood as *deterministic* state transformers. An interesting direction of development would be to generalize this to nondeterministic settings, such as concurrent programs. This would require a deeper investigation of the natural transformations induced by the symbolic SOS rule format and their categorical semantics. Goncharov et al. [13] also highlight this direction of research for the non-symbolic case.

Acknowledgements. The authors would like to thank the anonymous reviewers for their insightful questions and feedback.

References

1. Ahrendt, W., Beckert, B., Bubel, R., Hähnle, R., Schmitt, P.H., Ulbrich, M. (eds.): Deductive Software Verification - The KeY Book - From Theory to Practice. LNCS, vol. 10001. Springer (2016). https://doi.org/10.1007/978-3-319-49812-6
2. Arusoaie, A., Lucanu, D., Rusu, V.: A generic framework for symbolic execution. In: Erwig, M., Paige, R.F., Van Wyk, E. (eds.) SLE 2013. LNCS, vol. 8225, pp. 281–301. Springer, Cham (2013). https://doi.org/10.1007/978-3-319-02654-1_16
3. Baldoni, R., Coppa, E., D'elia, D.C., Demetrescu, C., Finocchi, I.: A survey of symbolic execution techniques. ACM Comput. Surv. (CSUR) **51**(3), 1–39 (2018)
4. Berdine, J., Calcagno, C., O'Hearn, P.W.: Symbolic execution with separation logic. In: Yi, K. (ed.) APLAS 2005. LNCS, vol. 3780, pp. 52–68. Springer, Heidelberg (2005). https://doi.org/10.1007/11575467_5
5. Bloom, B., Istrail, S., Meyer, A.R.: Bisimulation can't be traced. J. ACM **42**(1), 232–268 (1995). https://doi.org/10.1145/200836.200876

6. Bodin, M., Gardner, P., Jensen, T., Schmitt, A.: Skeletal semantics and their interpretations. Proc. ACM Program. Lang. **3**(POPL) (2019). https://doi.org/10.1145/3290357
7. Bodin, M., Jensen, T., Schmitt, A.: Certified abstract interpretation with pretty-big-step semantics. In: Proceedings of the 2015 Conference on Certified Programs and Proofs, CPP 2015, pp. 29–40. Association for Computing Machinery (2015). https://doi.org/10.1145/2676724.2693174
8. de Boer, F.S., Bonsangue, M.: On the nature of symbolic execution. In: ter Beek, M.H., McIver, A., Oliveira, J.N. (eds.) Formal Methods - The Next 30 Years, pp. 64–80. Springer, Cham (2019)
9. de Boer, F.S., Bonsangue, M.: Symbolic execution formally explained. Formal Aspects Comput.**33**(4), 617–636 (2021)
10. Boyer, R.S., Elspas, B., Levitt, K.N.: SELECT - a formal system for testing and debugging programs by symbolic execution. In: Shooman, M.L., Yeh, R.T. (eds.) Proc. International Conference on Reliable Software 1975, pp. 234–245. ACM (1975). https://doi.org/10.1145/800027.808445
11. Fragoso Santos, J., Maksimović, P., Ayoun, S.É., Gardner, P.: Gillian, part i: a multi-language platform for symbolic execution. In: Proceedings of the 41st ACM SIGPLAN Conference on Programming Language Design and Implementation, pp. 927–942 (2020)
12. van Glabbeek, R.J.: The meaning of negative premises in transition system specifications II. J. Log. Algebraic Methods Program. **60-61**, 229–258 (2004). https://doi.org/10.1016/J.JLAP.2004.03.007
13. Goncharov, S., Milius, S., Schröder, L., Tsampas, S., Urbat, H.: Stateful Structural Operational Semantics. In: Felty, A.P. (ed.) 7th International Conference on Formal Structures for Computation and Deduction (FSCD 2022). Leibniz International Proceedings in Informatics (LIPIcs), vol. 228, pp. 30:1–30:19. Schloss Dagstuhl – Leibniz-Zentrum für Informatik, Dagstuhl, Germany (2022). https://doi.org/10.4230/LIPIcs.FSCD.2022.30
14. Groote, J.F.: Transition system specifications with negative premises. Theor. Comput. Sci. **118**(2), 263–299 (1993). https://doi.org/10.1016/0304-3975(93)90111-6
15. Katz, S., Manna, Z.: Towards automatic debugging of programs. ACM SIGPLAN Notices **10**(6), 143–155 (1975)
16. King, J.C.: Symbolic execution and program testing. Commun. ACM **19**(7), 385–394 (1976)
17. Klin, B., Nachyla, B.: Some undecidable properties of SOS specifications. J. Log. Algebraic Methods Program. **87**, 94–109 (2017). https://doi.org/10.1016/J.JLAMP.2016.08.005
18. Lucanu, D., Rusu, V., Arusoaie, A.: A generic framework for symbolic execution: a coinductive approach. J. Symb. Comput. **80**, 125–163 (2017)
19. Maksimović, P., Ayoun, S.É., Santos, J.F., Gardner, P.: Gillian, Part II: real-world verification for JavaScript and C. In: Silva, A., Leino, K.R.M. (eds.) CAV 2021. LNCS, vol. 12760, pp. 827–850. Springer, Cham (2021). https://doi.org/10.1007/978-3-030-81688-9_38
20. Plotkin, G.D.: A structural approach to operational semantics. J. Log. Algebraic Methods Program. **60-61**, 17–139 (2004). originally a tech. report from Aarhus University, 1981
21. Porncharoenwase, S., Nelson, L., Wang, X., Torlak, E.: A formal foundation for symbolic evaluation with merging. Proc. ACM Program. Lang. **6**(POPL), January 2022. https://doi.org/10.1145/3498709

22. Rosu, G.: K - a semantic framework for programming languages and formal analysis tools. In: Peled, D., Pretschner, A. (eds.) Dependable Software Systems Engineering. IOS Press, NATO Science for Peace and Security (2017)
23. Ştefănescu, A., Ciobâcă, Ş, Mereuta, R., Moore, B.M., Şerbănută, T.F., Roşu, G.: All-path reachability logic. In: Dowek, G. (ed.) RTA 2014. LNCS, vol. 8560, pp. 425–440. Springer, Cham (2014). https://doi.org/10.1007/978-3-319-08918-8_29
24. Steinhöfel, D.: Abstract execution: automatically proving infinitely many programs. Ph.D. thesis, Technische Universität Darmstadt (2020)
25. Turi, D., Plotkin, G.: Towards a mathematical operational semantics. In: Proceedings of Twelfth Annual IEEE Symposium on Logic in Computer Science, pp. 280–291 (1997). https://doi.org/10.1109/LICS.1997.614955
26. Voogd, E., Johnsen, E.B., Silva, A., Susag, Z.J., Wasowski, A.: Symbolic semantics for probabilistic programs. In: Proc. 20th Intl. Conf. on Quantitative Evaluation of SysTems (QEST 2023). Lecture Notes in Computer Science, vol. 14287, pp. 329–345. Springer (2023). https://doi.org/10.1007/978-3-031-43835-6_23

Solvent: Liquidity Verification of Smart Contracts

Massimo Bartoletti[1], Angelo Ferrando[2], Enrico Lipparini[1,3](✉), and Vadim Malvone[4]

[1] Università degli Studi di Cagliari, Cagliari, Italy
enrico.lipparini@edu.unige.it
[2] Università degli Studi di Modena e Reggio Emilia, Modena, Italy
[3] Università degli Studi di Genova, Genova, Italy
[4] Télécom Paris, Palaiseau, France

Abstract. Smart contracts are an attractive target for attackers, as evidenced by a long history of security incidents. A current limitation of smart contract verification tools is that they are not really effective in expressing and verifying liquidity properties regarding the exchange of crypto-assets: for example, is it true that in every reachable state a user can fire a sequence of transactions to withdraw a given amount of crypto-assets? We propose Solvent, a tool aimed at verifying these kinds of properties, which are beyond the reach of existing verification tools for Solidity. We evaluate the effectiveness and performance of Solvent through a common benchmark of smart contracts.

1 Introduction

In recent years we have seen a steady rise of smart contracts that implement financial ecosystems on top of public blockchains, and control today more than 100 billions of dollars worth of crypto-assets [16]. The peculiarities of the setting (i.e., the absence of intermediaries, the immutability of code after deployment, the quirks in smart contract languages) make smart contracts an appealing target for attackers, as bugs might be exploited to steal crypto-assets or just cause disruption. This is witnessed by a long history of attacks, which overall caused losses exceeding 6 billions of dollars [14].

Formal methods provide an ideal defense against these attacks, since they enable the creation of tools to detect bugs in smart contracts before they are deployed. Indeed, smart contracts verification tools, often based on formal methods, have been mushrooming in the last few years: for Ethereum alone—largely the main smart contract platform—dozens of tools exist today [25]. Still, the actual effectiveness of these tools in countering real-world attacks is debatable: indeed, attacks to smart contracts have continued to proliferate, refining their strategies from exploits of known vulnerability patterns to sophisticated attacks to the contracts' business logics. As a matter of fact, the vast majority of the losses due to real-world attacks are caused by logic errors in the contract code [14], which are outside the scope of most vulnerability detection tools. In particular, several real-world attacks were based on *liquidity* weaknesses of smart contracts, which were exploited by attackers to steal or freeze crypto-assets [3]. Liquidity (also called *solvency* [24] or *enabledness* [31]) expresses the ideal behaviour of contracts in terms of the exchange of crypto-assets [13,26,36]: users want to be guaranteed that, whenever certain states are reached, they can always perform some actions that lead to a desirable assets transfer. There are two key points in this notion: the user wants to be able to constrain *who* can perform these actions, and *how many* actions are needed [31].

The current tools that support the verification of Solidity cannot verify general liquidity properties. This is due both to the design choices of Solidity, their target language, and to the complex logical structure of such properties. The difficulty of verifying Solidity is caused by several glitches of high-level abstractions over the low-level target (e.g. reentrancy [5], gas costs [19], and non-native tokens [38]). Indeed, it has been observed that existing tools already face challenges (in terms of soundness and completeness) in the verification of even simpler properties [12]. We believe that effectively verifying liquidity requires first to purify Solidity from its main semantical quirks. Once we have done this, we must deal with the peculiar logical structure of liquidity properties. Indeed, liquidity cannot be expressed in terms of safety or liveness, and bounded liveness cannot model liquidity either (see Sect. 2). To deal with liquidity, verification techniques that go beyond safety and (bounded) liveness are therefore necessary.

Contributions. We propose Solvent, a tool that verifies liquidity properties of smart contracts. Solvent takes as input a contract, written in a purified version of Solidity, and a set of user-defined liquidity properties. The tool translates them into SMT constraints [9], reducing the verification problem to an SMT-based symbolic model checking one [8]. Then, techniques such as bounded model checking and predicate abstraction are employed, relying on Z3 [15] and cvc5 [6] as back-end SMT solvers. Experiments on a benchmark of real-world smart contracts show that Solvent can efficiently verify relevant liquidity properties of their behaviour. These properties are currently out of the scope of industrial verification tools operating on the full Solidity, like e.g. SolCMC [4] and Certora [22], as well as academic tools [20,23,27,30,33,37] (we discuss such tools in [11]). Solvent provides developers with useful feedback, by detecting logical errors that would otherwise remain unnoticed. In particular, when Solvent detects a property violation, it produces a concrete execution trace that leads the contract to a state from which the desired asset exchange is unrealisable.

Summing up, the main contributions of the paper include:

- a fully automated encoding of an expressive subset of Solidity and of liquidity properties of smart contracts into SMT constraints;
- a toolchain to perform bounded model checking and predicate abstraction using Z3 and cvc5 as off-the-shelf SMT solvers, producing counterexamples (that are actually replayable in Ethereum) when the property is violated;
- a thorough evaluation of the tool effectiveness and performance on a benchmark of real-world smart contracts, which we extend with relevant liquidity properties (available on the tool github repository [10]);

- a concrete demonstration of the tool applicability, showing subtle bugs in existing smart contracts that cause crypto-assets to get frozen forever.

2 On Liquidity

In this section, we clarify our notion of liquidity, and we support our claim that it cannot be expressed in terms of safety or (bounded) liveness. Recall that safety has the form "*p always holds*", liveness has the form "*p eventually holds*", and bounded liveness "*in at most m steps p holds*". Liquidity, instead, has the form "*for certain users a, there always exists a sequence of at most m actions that a can perform to make p hold*" (where m is a parameter).

To illustrate the differences among these notions, consider a user opening a bank account. The user wants to be guaranteed that, if they deposit money in the bank, then they will always be able to withdraw their money by performing a *reasonable amount of actions*. They do not want to *always* withdraw their money (safety), or to just *eventually* withdraw their money (liveness). For example, requiring liveness but not liquidity would allow the bank to give a guarantee such as "*any client will withdraw their money after the bank has been visited overall 1 million times after the deposit*", making the liveness property "*eventually I will withdraw*" true (assuming the fairness condition that visits to the bank happen infinitely often). However, the more desirable liquidity property "*I am always able to perform at most 3 actions that make me withdraw*" would not hold. Bounded liveness would not be an appropriate requirement either. Indeed, assume that the bank guarantees that "*the user always receives their money before 3 actions have been made*". This would be undesirable, since it says that *any* sequence of 3 actions, performed by *any* user, would trigger the withdrawal.

In LTL, we have that safety properties have the form "Gp", and liveness properties have the form "GFp". Liquidity properties, however, cannot be expressed in LTL, as we need to existentially quantify over the paths ("*there exists a path where the user performs at most m actions to make p hold*"). In CTL, the closest formulation would be "$AG\ EX\ p \vee AG\ EX\ EX\ p \vee \cdots \vee AG\ (EX)^m\ p$". This, however, still does not capture the strategic aspect of liquidity, which requires that the sequence that makes p hold consists of actions made by certain users, and therefore we need to impose conditions over transition variables.

3 Verifying Liquidity Properties with Solvent

We demonstrate our tool through a simple example and provide some highlights on how it works. Solvent operates in two steps: (1) given as input a smart contract and a set of liquidity properties, it encodes the contract and the properties into constraints in the SMT-LIB standard [7]; (2) then, it issues satisfiability queries to an SMT solver to detect if the required properties are violated. If so, it produces a counterexample, in the form of a sequence of transactions leading to a state where a required property cannot be satisfied.

```
contract Crowdfund {
  int immutable end_donate;  // last block number for donations
  int immutable target;      // threshold for successful campaign
  address immutable owner;   // beneficiary of the campaign
  mapping (address => int) donors; // records users' donations
  bool target_reached;       // initialized to false

  constructor(address o, int e, int t) {
    owner = o; end_donate = e; target = t
  }
  function donate() payable {
    require (block.number<=end_donate);
    donors[msg.sender] = donors[msg.sender] + msg.value;
    if (balance>=target) { target_reached = true }
  }
  function wdOwner() {
    require (block.number>end_donate && target_reached);
    owner.trasfer(balance) // send contract balance to owner
  }
  function wdDonor() { // SUBTLE BUG HERE
    require (block.number>end_donate && balance<target);
    msg.sender.transfer(donors[msg.sender]);
    donors[msg.sender] = 0
  }
}
property donor_wd {
  Forall xa [ !target_reached && block.number>end_donate
    -> Exists tx [1,xa] // 1 = max tx length, xa = tx sender
    [ <tx>xa.balance      // balance of xa after tx is performed
      >= xa.balance + donors[xa] ] ]
}
```

Listing 1: A crowdfunding contract (with a subtle bug) and a liquidity property.

To illustrate Solvent, we consider in Listing 1 a simple crowdfunding contract. The contract is akin to a class in OO programming, with attributes that define its state and methods (triggered by blockchain transactions) that update it. The user who fires the transaction (denoted by msg.sender) can transfer some amount (msg.value) of cryptocurrency to the contract along with the call. The constructor specifies the owner of the crowdfunding campaign, the deadline for donations, and the target amount. The method donate allows anyone to donate any amount before the deadline; wdOwner allows the owner to redeem the whole contract balance if the campaign target has been reached and the deadline has expired; finally, wdDonor allows donors to withdraw their donations after the deadline, if the campaign target has not been reached.

Solvent encodes each method into an SMT constraint that, given transaction variables, ties next-state variables to current-state variables, using auxiliary variables to represent intermediate internal states. Each require is encoded as an if-then-else, where, if the condition fails, the method reverts, i.e. next-state variables coincide with current-state variables.

A crucial property of crowdfunding contracts is that donors can redeem their donations after the deadline whenever the target is not reached. We specify this property as donor_wd in Listing 1. This reads as follows: for all users xa, if the target has not been reached and the deadline has passed, then there exists a sequence tx of transactions of length 1 signed by xa such that, in the state reached after executing tx, the balance of xa is increased by st.donors[xa]. Solvent detects that this property is violated. This is correct, although surprising, because of a subtle bug in wdDonor. There, the require ensures that donors can withdraw only if the contract balance is less than the target. This would seem correct, since donate is the only method that can receive ETH (as stated by the payable tag). The quirk is that contracts can receive ETH even when there are no payable methods, through block rewards, which can send ETH to any address, or *selfdestruct*, which transfer the remaining ETH in a contract to an address at their choice [1]. Notably, an attacker could exploit a *selfdestruct* to freeze all the funds in the contract, preventing donors from withdrawing!

To translate donor_wd into an SMT constraint, Solvent considers its negation, and introduces a new existentially quantified variable for xa, and new universally quantified variables for all transaction variables in the sequence tx and for all next-state variables. Then, it reduces to checking whether there exists an xa for which, if the antecedent holds, for all transaction variables and next-state variables, either the transactions invalidly tie current and next-state, or the required consequent does not hold. If this formula is *un*satisfiable, then the property holds; otherwise, a counterexample is given. E.g., for donors_wd, the counterexample is the following sequence of transitions:

```
[1] constructor(2,0,2)   msg.sender=address(4)   msg.value=0
[2] donate()             msg.sender=address(4)   msg.value=1
[3] selfdestruct()       msg.sender=address(0)   msg.value=1
```

Here, the last transition represents a call to an adversarial contract, with a method invoking *selfdestruct* on Crowdfund.[1] This can be easily translated into a concrete Proof-of-Concept (PoC), leading the contract to a state where donors_wd cannot be satisfied.

To fix the contract, we replace the condition balance<target in wdDonor with !target_reached. With this fix, Solvent correctly detects that donor_wd holds.

Note that the fixed contract still has a liquidity vulnerability: if the target is not reached, donors can redeem their donations, but any extra funds possibly existing at contract creation, or received through block rewards or *selfdestruct* actions, will be frozen in the contract. To fix this vulnerability, we first need to quantify these extra funds: we do this by adding a variable tot_donations that we update in donate and in wdDonor, so that the extra budget is now given by balance-tot_donations. We then add a method that allows anyone to transfer any extra budget to the owner after the deadline. Solvent verifies that the revised contract still enjoys donor_wd, and transfers any extra budget to the owner, i.e.:

```
property no_frozen_funds {
  Forall xa [ balance>tot_donations && block.number>end_donate
   -> Exists tx [1, xa]
   [ (<tx>balance[owner] >= balance[owner]
                          + (balance - tot_donations)) ] ]     }
```

---

[1] Note that *selfdestruct* is still active [17].

4 Evaluation

We test our tool over a common benchmark for Solidity verification [2], which includes a representative set of real-world contracts and properties. Since this benchmark is focussed on current verification tools for Solidity, which do not deal with general liquidity properties, we extend it with relevant properties of this kind for each contract (see the github page). Overall, we end up with 107 verification tasks, which we manually check for the ground truth.

Setup. We run Solvent on each verification task on a 3GHz 64-bit Intel Xeon Gold 6136 CPU and a GNU/Linux OS (x86_64-linux) with 64 GB of RAM, with either cvc5 (v. 1.1.3-dev.152.701cd63ef) or Z3 (v. 4.13.0) as a back-end. The run-time limit for each verification task is 400s of CPU time. A subset of the results are shown in Table 1 (see github for the full results). We mark each property as: "✗(N)", if the solver finds a trace that violates the property (with N being the length of the shortest trace leading to a violation); "✓", if it proves that the property holds in all possible states; "✓(N)", if it proves that the property holds for every trace of length at most N; and "?" if it timeouts.

Results. First, we note that both solvers never return an inconsistent answer. For all non-liquid properties, except two, at least one of the solvers is able to find a counterexample. When a counterexample is found, the result is returned quite quickly, and the trace is quite short. For liquid properties, the solvers are able to prove the property only for some instances. Still, in most cases, they manage to verify the property up-to traces of significant length. Two contracts ("Payment splitter" and "Vesting wallet") are significantly tough for both solvers. This is not surprising though, as they both present non-linear behaviour, thus requiring to solve SMT formulas in the theory of Nonlinear Integer Arithmetic, which is undecidable and notoriously hard to deal with in practice for SMT solvers.[2]

Discussion. The results show that our tool is particularly good at finding counterexamples. They are witnessed by a sequence of transactions that can be replayed in the actual Ethereum, leading to a state from which the desired outcome is unreachable. On the other hand, when Solvent states that a property holds, there is no guarantee that the property is preserved "as-is". For instance, reentrancy vulnerabilities (which are abstracted away in our symbolic semantics), can falsify the property. Nonetheless, the output of Solvent guarantees that no conceptual error has been made in the business logic of the contract. Even when Solvent outputs ✓(N), the larger the N the more relevant the information given to users: indeed, empirically we observed that in the benchmark [2], property violations are already observable after short traces. Remarkably, we spot that several contracts in the benchmark [2] have liquidity vulnerabilities, i.e., crypto-assets remain frozen in the contract (in Table 1, where `no_frozen_funds` is ✗).

---
[2] Strategies to overcome the obstacles posed by NIA have been recently discussed, for the specific case of formulas coming from the verification of smart contracts, in [21].

Table 1. Solvent benchmark (subset; execution times are in seconds). For ✓(N) properties we write "—" when the prover timeouts before proving ✓(N + 1).

Contract	Property	Liquid?	cvc5 Result	cvc5 Time	Z3 Result	Z3 Time
Auction	no_frozen_funds	✗	✗(3)	1.10	✗(3)	1.15
	seller_wd	✓	✓(10)	—	✓(9)	—
	old_winner_wd	✓	✓(21)	—	✓(9)	—
Bank	deposit_not_revert	✓	✓	2.04	✓	19.79
	withdraw_not_revert	✓	✓(7)	—	✓(8)	—
Bet	any_timeout_join	✓	✓(17)	—	✓(12)	—
	oracle_win	✓	✓(14)	—	✓(7)	—
	any_timeout_win	✓	✓(39)	—	✓(9)	—
	no_frozen_funds	✗	✗(2)	0.70	✗(2)	0.74
Crowdfund (bug)	owner_wd	✓	✓	2.31	✓	26.64
	donor_wd	✗	✗(3)	1.38	✗(3)	7.78
Crowdfund (fix2)	owner_wd	✓	✓	2.34	✓	29.34
	donor_wd	✓	✓(7)	—	✓(6)	—
	no_frozen_funds	✓	✓(9)	—	✓(8)	—
Escrow	arbiter_wd_fee	✓	✓(17)	—	✓(10)	—
	buyerorseller_wd_deposit	✓	✓(16)	—	✓(41)	—
	anyone_wd	✗	✗(2)	0.70	✗(2)	0.76
	no_frozen_funds	✗	✗(3)	1.17	✗(3)	1.23
HTLC	owner_wd	✓	✓(16)	—	✓(9)	—
	verifier_wd_timeout	✓	✓(17)	—	✓(9)	—
	no_frozen_funds	✓	✓	2.37	✓	54.84
Lottery	one_player_win	✓	✓(13)	—	✓(9)	—
	p1_redeem_nojoin	✓	✓(23)	—	✓(8)	—
	p1_redeem_noreveal	✓	✓(16)	—	✓(9)	—
	p2_redeem_noreveal	✓	✓(17)	—	✓(8)	—
Payment splitter	anyone_wd_ge	✓	✓(2)	—	✓(1)	—
	anyone_wd_releasable	✓	✓(2)	—	✓(1)	—
	anyone_wd	✗	✗(1)	0.40	✗(1)	0.38
Vault	fin_owner	✓	✓(14)	—	✓(11)	—
	canc_recovery	✓	✓(20)	—	✓(10)	—
	wd_fin_owner	✗	✗(1)	0.45	✗(1)	0.44
Vesting wallet	owner_wd_expired	✓	✓	2.16	?	T/O
	owner_wd_started	✗	?	T/O	?	T/O
	owner_wd_uncond	✗	?	T/O	✗(1)	0.36
	owner_wd_beforestart	✗	?	T/O	✗(1)	0.35
	owner_wd_empty	✗	?	T/O	✗(1)	0.35
	owner_wd_released	✗	?	T/O	?	T/O

5 Related Work

The Ethereum ecosystem includes several bug detection tools that can spot *specific* forms of liquidity vulnerabilities in smart contracts. In that setting, these vulnerabilities are often referred to as "Locked Ether", which are roughly described as the absence of a mechanism to withdraw Ether from the contract. The tools capable of detecting Locked Ether bugs include Slither [18], SmartCheck [34], Maian [29], Securify2 [36], ConFuzzius [35] and sFuzz [28]. Each of these tools has its own internal encoding of the Locked Ether property, making it difficult to compare them [32]. There are two main differences between these tools and ours. First, while these tools can only spot that a predefined hard-coded Locked Ether property is violated, Solvent can verify custom liquidity properties, defined by our specification language. In particular, Solvent can verify properties that express *who* can withdraw *how much*, and under *which conditions*; not just that Ether does not get frozen in the contract. Second, bug detection tools only focus on property violations, while Solvent (a formal verification tool) is capable of verifying that a liquidity property is satisfied (always, or up to a certain bound on the number of transactions).

Other state-of-the-art formal verification tools for Solidity do not support general liquidity properties. SolCMC, the prover shipped with the Solidity compiler, as well as other verification tools such as Zeus [23], solc-verify [20], VerX [30] and SmartACE [37], only support safety properties, while other tools, such as Certora [22], VeriSolid [27], and SmartPulse [33], can also verify liveness properties. However, as discussed in Sect. 2, this is not enough for liquidity properties (see [11] for a more in-depth discussion).

6 Conclusions and Future Work

Solvent has already proven useful to spot general liquidity vulnerabilities, which are beyond the reach of current tools. Still, there is space for improvements.

First, Solvent uses off-the-shelf SMT solvers, relying on bounded model checking to find counterexamples, and on predicate abstraction to prove that the property holds. An alternative approach that we plan to investigate is to leverage advanced techniques (e.g., abstraction-refinement, k-induction, etc.) used by modern infinite-state symbolic model checkers.

Second, we plan to extend our Solidity fragment to narrow the gap with the actual Solidity (see [11] for a discussion of the main differences). In particular, we note that concretising our `transfer` into contract-to-contract calls, as in Solidity, would require to take failures and reentrancy into account. E.g., consider a contract with a method:

```
foo() { owner.transfer(1); msg.sender.transfer(1); }
```

and a property requiring that, whenever the contract balance is at least 2, any user can increase their balance by 1. In our Solidity fragment, this property is true, since both transfers will succeed under the given hypotheses. This is not the case in the concrete Solidity: e.g., `owner` could be a contract address, whose fallback method could fail under certain conditions. In this case, the second transfer in `foo` would not happen, and so the property would be violated. Since considering each transfer as potentially failing would make most contracts illiquid, a possible approach would be to allow queries to specify which transfers or addresses to be considered trusted.

Other future work include the automatic transformation of the counterexamples given by Solvent into an executable PoC (e.g., in the HardHat tool), and the formalisation of liquidity in a suitable logic.

Acknowledgments. Work partially supported by project SERICS (PE00000014) under the MUR National Recovery and Resilience Plan funded by the European Union – NextGenerationEU, and by PRIN 2022 PNRR project DeLiCE (F53D23009130001).

References

1. SMTChecker and formal verification: contract balance (2023). https://docs.soliditylang.org/en/v0.8.24/smtchecker.html#contract-balance
2. An open benchmark for evaluating smart contracts verification tools (2024). https://github.com/fsainas/contracts-verification-benchmark
3. Alois, J.: Ethereum Parity hack may impact ETH 500,000 or $146 million (2017). https://www.crowdfundinsider.com/2017/11/124200-ethereum-parity-hack-may-impact-eth-500000-146-million/. Accessed 9 Apr 2024
4. Alt, L., Blicha, M., Hyvärinen, A.E.J., Sharygina, N.: SolCMC: solidity compiler's model checker. In: Shoham, S., Vizel, Y. (eds.) CAV 2022. LNCS, vol. 13371, pp. 325–338. Springer, Cham (2022). https://doi.org/10.1007/978-3-031-13185-1_16
5. Atzei, N., Bartoletti, M., Cimoli, T.: A survey of attacks on Ethereum smart contracts (SoK). In: Maffei, M., Ryan, M. (eds.) POST 2017. LNCS, vol. 10204, pp. 164–186. Springer, Heidelberg (2017). https://doi.org/10.1007/978-3-662-54455-6_8
6. Barbosa, H., et al.: cvc5: a versatile and industrial-strength SMT solver. In: Fisman, D., Rosu, G. (eds.) TACAS 2022. LNCS, vol. 13243, pp. 415–442. Springer, Cham (2022). https://doi.org/10.1007/978-3-030-99524-9_24
7. Barrett, C., Fontaine, P., Tinelli, C.: The SMT-LIB standard: version 2.6. Technical report, Department of Computer Science, The University of Iowa (2017). https://smtlib.cs.uiowa.edu/language.shtml
8. Barrett, C., Tinelli, C.: Satisfiability modulo theories. In: Clarke, E., Henzinger, T., Veith, H., Bloem, R. (eds.) Handbook of Model Checking, pp. 305–343. Springer, Cham (2018). https://doi.org/10.1007/978-3-319-10575-8_11
9. Barrett, C.W., Sebastiani, R., Seshia, S.A., Tinelli, C.: Satisfiability modulo theories. In: Handbook of Satisfiability (2021). https://doi.org/10.3233/978-1-58603-929-5-825
10. Bartoletti, M., Ferrando, A., Lipparini, E., Malvone, V.: Solvent: liquidity verification of smart contracts. https://github.com/AngeloFerrando/Solvent
11. Bartoletti, M., Ferrando, A., Lipparini, E., Malvone, V.: Solvent: liquidity verification of smart contracts. CoRR abs/2404.17864 (2024). https://doi.org/10.48550/ARXIV.2404.17864
12. Bartoletti, M., Fioravanti, F., Matricardi, G., Pettinau, R., Sainas, F.: Towards benchmarking of solidity verification tools. In: Formal Methods in Blockchain (FMBC). OASIcs, vol. 118, pp. 6:1–6:15. Schloss Dagstuhl - Leibniz-Zentrum für Informatik (2024). https://doi.org/10.4230/OASICS.FMBC.2024.6
13. Bartoletti, M., Lande, S., Murgia, M., Zunino, R.: Verifying liquidity of recursive bitcoin contracts. Log. Methods Comput. Sci. **18**(1) (2022). https://doi.org/10.46298/LMCS-18(1:22)2022

14. Chaliasos, S., et al.: Smart contract and DeFi security: insights from tool evaluations and practitioner surveys. In: IEEE/ACM International Conference on Software Engineering (ICSE), pp. 60:1–60:13. ACM (2024). https://doi.org/10.1145/3597503.3623302
15. de Moura, L., Bjørner, N.: Z3: an efficient SMT solver. In: Ramakrishnan, C.R., Rehof, J. (eds.) TACAS 2008. LNCS, vol. 4963, pp. 337–340. Springer, Heidelberg (2008). https://doi.org/10.1007/978-3-540-78800-3_24
16. Defillama. https://defillama.com/. Accessed 9 Apr 2024
17. EIP-4758: Deactivate SELFDESTRUCT. https://eips.ethereum.org/EIPS/eip-4758. Accessed 15 June 2024
18. Feist, J., Grieco, G., Groce, A.: Slither: a static analysis framework for smart contracts. In: Workshop on Emerging Trends in Software Engineering for Blockchain (WETSEB@ICSE), pp. 8–15 (2019). https://doi.org/10.1109/WETSEB.2019.00008
19. Grech, N., Kong, M., Jurisevic, A., Brent, L., Scholz, B., Smaragdakis, Y.: MadMax: analyzing the out-of-gas world of smart contracts. Commun. ACM **63**(10), 87–95 (2020). https://doi.org/10.1145/3416262
20. Hajdu, Á., Jovanović, D.: SOLC-VERIFY: a modular verifier for solidity smart contracts. In: Chakraborty, S., Navas, J.A. (eds.) VSTTE 2019. LNCS, vol. 12031, pp. 161–179. Springer, Cham (2020). https://doi.org/10.1007/978-3-030-41600-3_11
21. Hozzová, P., Bendík, J., Nutz, A., Rodeh, Y.: Overapproximation of non-linear integer arithmetic for smart contract verification. In: International Conference on Logic for Programming, Artificial Intelligence and Reasoning. EPiC Series in Computing, vol. 94, pp. 257–269 (2023). https://doi.org/10.29007/h4p7
22. Jackson, D., Nandi, C., Sagiv, M.: Certora technology white paper (2022). https://docs.certora.com/en/latest/docs/whitepaper/index.html
23. Kalra, S., Goel, S., Dhawan, M., Sharma, S.: ZEUS: analyzing safety of smart contracts. In: Network and Distributed System Security Symposium (NDSS). The Internet Society (2018)
24. Kirstein, U.: Formal verification helps finding insolvency bugs - balancer V2 bug report. https://medium.com/certora/formal-verification-helps-finding-insolvency-bugs-balancer-v2-bug-report-1f53ee7dd4d0. Accessed 30 Aug 2024
25. Kushwaha, S.S., Joshi, S., Singh, D., Kaur, M., Lee, H.N.: Ethereum smart contract analysis tools: a systematic review. IEEE Access **10**, 57037–57062 (2022). https://doi.org/10.1109/ACCESS.2022.3169902
26. Laneve, C.: Liquidity analysis in resource-aware programming. J. Log. Algebraic Methods Program. **135**, 100889 (2023). https://doi.org/10.1016/J.JLAMP.2023.100889
27. Nelaturu, K., Mavridou, A., Stachtiari, E., Veneris, A.G., Laszka, A.: Correct-by-design interacting smart contracts and a systematic approach for verifying ERC20 and ERC721 contracts with VeriSolid. IEEE Trans. Dependable Secur. Comput. **20**(4), 3110–3127 (2023). https://doi.org/10.1109/TDSC.2022.3200840
28. Nguyen, T.D., Pham, L.H., Sun, J., Lin, Y., Minh, Q.T.: sFuzz: an efficient adaptive fuzzer for solidity smart contracts. In: International Conference on Software Engineering (ICSE), pp. 778–788. ACM (2020). https://doi.org/10.1145/3377811.3380334
29. Nikolic, I., Kolluri, A., Sergey, I., Saxena, P., Hobor, A.: Finding the greedy, prodigal, and suicidal contracts at scale. In: Annual Computer Security Applications Conference (ACSAC), pp. 653–663. ACM (2018). https://doi.org/10.1145/3274694.3274743

30. Permenev, A., Dimitrov, D.K., Tsankov, P., Drachsler-Cohen, D., Vechev, M.T.: VerX: safety verification of smart contracts. In: IEEE Symposium on Security and Privacy, pp. 1661–1677. IEEE (2020). https://doi.org/10.1109/SP40000.2020.00024
31. Schiffl, J., Beckert, B.: A practical notion of liveness in smart contract applications. In: Formal Methods in Blockchain (FMBC). OASIcs, vol. 118, pp. 8:1–8:13. Schloss Dagstuhl - Leibniz-Zentrum für Informatik (2024). https://doi.org/10.4230/OASICS.FMBC.2024.8
32. Sendner, C., Petzi, L., Stang, J., Dmitrienko, A.: Large-scale study of vulnerability scanners for Ethereum smart contracts. In: IEEE European Symposium on Security and Privacy (S&P), pp. 220–220. IEEE (2024). https://doi.org/10.1109/SP54263.2024.00230
33. Stephens, J., Ferles, K., Mariano, B., Lahiri, S.K., Dillig, I.: SmartPulse: automated checking of temporal properties in smart contracts. In: IEEE Symposium on Security and Privacy, pp. 555–571. IEEE (2021). https://doi.org/10.1109/SP40001.2021.00085
34. Tikhomirov, S., Voskresenskaya, E., Ivanitskiy, I., Takhaviev, R., Marchenko, E., Alexandrov, Y.: SmartCheck: static analysis of Ethereum smart contracts. In: Workshop on Emerging Trends in Software Engineering for Blockchain (WETSEB), pp. 9–16. ACM (2018). https://doi.org/10.1145/3194113.3194115
35. Torres, C.F., Iannillo, A.K., Gervais, A., State, R.: ConFuzzius: a data dependency-aware hybrid fuzzer for smart contracts. In: IEEE European Symposium on Security and Privacy (EuroS&P), pp. 103–119. IEEE (2021). https://doi.org/10.1109/EUROSP51992.2021.00018
36. Tsankov, P., Dan, A.M., Drachsler-Cohen, D., Gervais, A., Bünzli, F., Vechev, M.T.: Securify: practical security analysis of smart contracts. In: ACM SIGSAC Conference on Computer and Communications Security (CCS), pp. 67–82. ACM (2018). https://doi.org/10.1145/3243734.3243780
37. Wesley, S., Christakis, M., Navas, J.A., Trefler, R., Wüstholz, V., Gurfinkel, A.: Verifying SOLIDITY smart contracts via communication abstraction in SMARTACE. In: Finkbeiner, B., Wies, T. (eds.) VMCAI 2022. LNCS, vol. 13182, pp. 425–449. Springer, Cham (2022). https://doi.org/10.1007/978-3-030-94583-1_21
38. Xia, P., et al.: Trade or trick?: Detecting and characterizing scam tokens on Uniswap decentralized exchange. In: ACM SIGMETRICS/IFIP Performance, pp. 23–24. ACM (2022). https://doi.org/10.1145/3489048.3522636

StEVe: A Rational Verification Tool for Stackelberg Security Games

Surasak Phetmanee[✉], Michele Sevegnani, and Oana Andrei

School of Computing Science, University of Glasgow,
Glasgow G12 8RZ, UK
{surasak.phetmanee,michele.sevegnani,
oana.andrei}@glasgow.ac.uk

Abstract. We present StEVe, a prototype tool modelling Stackelberg Security Games (SSGs) and employing rational verification based on bespoke Stackelberg equilibrium computation. StEVe automatically extracts technical details from public vulnerability databases, transforming these into Attack Defence Trees and then into SSG models. By using the temporal logic rPATL, the tool enables the synthesis of optimal defence strategies through Stackelberg equilibrium analysis, which is implemented as a PRISM-games extension. Preliminary results demonstrate StEVe's ability to model and counteract cyber threats, reducing potential damages and financial losses.

Keywords: Rational Verification · Security Games · Temporal Logic

1 Introduction

Stackelberg Security Games (SSGs) [16,17], which utilise the concept of Stackelberg equilibrium for their solution, have proven effective for resource allocation in security contexts. In these games, the leader (typically a defender) commits to a strategy first, and the follower (the attacker) observes this strategy and responds optimally. This framework is particularly relevant in cybersecurity, where defenders must allocate finite security resources to protect multiple targets, and attackers choose targets based on the observed security measures.

To determine the optimal strategy for defenders, several factors need to be considered, including the value of the targets, the potential impact of a breach, and the evolving nature of cyber threats. One promising approach to solving this problem is Rational Verification (RV) [18], which verifies agent systems by assuming that agents act rationally to pursue their preferences. RV checks if a temporal logic formula is satisfied in some or all game equilibria, ensuring rational behaviour in the system. Recent works [1,8,11] have demonstrated the effectiveness of RV in multiple agent systems. For example, Aslanyan et al. [2] present quantitative verification methods for cybersecurity scenarios, illustrating how RV can be applied to cybersecurity. While tools like EVE [5] and PRISM-games [9] already support several types of equilibria, expanding their capabilities

© The Author(s), under exclusive license to Springer Nature Switzerland AG 2025
N. Kosmatov and L. Kovács (Eds.): IFM 2024, LNCS 15234, pp. 267–275, 2025.
https://doi.org/10.1007/978-3-031-76554-4_15

to support Stackelberg equilibria would allow their applicability to a wider set of cybersecurity scenarios, particularly those involving sequential decision making, where defenders commit to strategies in advance and attackers respond after observing these strategies.

To bridge this gap, we propose a method for computing the Stackelberg equilibrium in SSGs and introduce STEVE (**St**ackelberg Security Games and **E**quilibrium **V**erification), a tool that integrates game theory and formal verification for rationality in cybersecurity. STEVE enables defenders to compute optimal resource allocation strategies and verify rational attacker behaviour. It transforms data from public vulnerability databases (such as CVEs from NIST's National Vulnerability Database) into SSG models, automating the process of generating and verifying defensive strategies using rational verification and temporal logic. Our work also extends the PRISM-games framework to support Stackelberg equilibrium computation in cybersecurity scenarios.

2 Background

STEVE's implementation is based on the concepts introduced in this section.

Attack Defence Trees (ADTs) [6] are graphical models used to express potential security threats and their countermeasures. We restrict the ADT models to one level of child nodes and construct them solely from the perspective of a defender, which we denote as ADT(1). This is sufficient to express SSGs. The syntax of ADT(1) comprises four terms: $c^d(b', b)$; $c^d(b', f(b_1, ..., b_k))$; $c^d(f'(b'_1, ..., b'_{k'}), b)$; $c^d(f'(b'_1, ..., b'_{k'}), f(b_1, ..., b_k))$, where a represents an attacker and d is a defender, $f \in \{\vee^a, \wedge^a\}$, $f' \in \{\vee^d, \wedge^d\}$, b, $b_i \in \mathbb{B}^a$ for $1 \leq i \leq k$ and $k \geq 2$, b', $b'_j \in \mathbb{B}^d$ for $1 \leq j \leq k'$ and some $k' \geq 2$, and $\mathbb{B}^d, \mathbb{B}^a \subset A$ are disjoints sets of actions for the defender and the attacker, respectively. For example, an ADT(1) for ensuring data confidentiality against employee attacks can be represented as: c^d(firewall, $\wedge^a$(send_vurs, get_password)), where $\wedge$ represents a conjunction (both actions must occur) and $\vee$ represents a disjunction (either action can occur). The defensive action is firewall, while the attacker's actions include send_vurs and get_password. This indicates that the defender can protect the system by investing in high performance firewalls, but the system remains vulnerable to a coordinated attack involving both sending a virus and obtaining a password.

An *extensive form game* [10] $\mathcal{G}$ is a tuple $(N, A, H, Z, \chi, \pi, \gamma, u)$ where $N = \{1, ..., n\}$ is a set of players, $n \in \mathbb{N}$, $n \geq 2$, A is a finite set of actions, H is a set of non-terminal history (or choice) nodes, Z is a set of terminal history nodes disjoint from H, i.e. $H \cap Z = \varnothing$, $\chi : H \rightarrow 2^A$ maps each non-terminal history node to its possible actions, $\pi : H \rightarrow N$ is the player function, which assigns to each non-terminal history node a player $i \in N$ who chooses an action at that node, $\gamma : H \times A \rightarrow H \cup Z$ is the successor function mapping a choice node and an action to a new node, either terminal or non-terminal, and $u = (u_1, ..., u_n)$ is a profile of utility functions, where $u_i : Z \rightarrow \mathbb{R}$ is a utility function for player i that assigns a real-valued utility to each terminal node.

A *Stackelberg Security Game (SSG)* [17] is a tuple $(\mathcal{G}, AP, L)$ where $\mathcal{G}$ is a two-player (i.e., $N = \{1, 2\}$) extensive form game, AP is a set of atomic propositions, and $L : H \cup Z \to 2^{AP}$ is a labelling function. In this game, player 1 as the *defender* chooses an action and then player 2 as the *attacker* chooses an action after observing the choice of the defender. In SSGs a *strategy* is a set of actions that a player follows to make decisions in a game, based on available information and their objectives.

The logic rPATL [3], which is used within RV, is a temporal logic for expressing properties of Stochastic Multiplayer Games (SMGs), with SSGs a subclass of SMGs. This logic incorporates operators, including probabilistic (P), reward (R), next (X), bounded until ($\mathsf{U}^{\leq k}$), until (U), instantaneous reward after k steps ($\mathsf{I}^{=k}$), accumulated reward over k steps ($\mathsf{C}^{\leq k}$), and reachability reward (F). The syntax of rPATL is given by the following grammar:

$$\phi := \mathsf{true} \mid \mathsf{a} \mid \neg \phi \mid \phi \wedge \phi \mid \langle\langle C \rangle\rangle \mathsf{P}_{\sim q}[\psi] \mid \langle\langle C \rangle\rangle \mathsf{R}^r_{\sim x}[\rho] \mid \langle\langle C : C' \rangle\rangle_{max \sim x}(\theta)$$
$$\theta := \mathsf{P}[\psi] + \mathsf{P}[\psi] \mid \mathsf{R}^r[\rho] + \mathsf{R}^r[\rho] \qquad \psi := \mathsf{X}\,\phi \mid \phi\,\mathsf{U}^{\leq k}\,\phi \mid \phi\,\mathsf{U}\,\phi$$
$$\rho := \mathsf{I}^{=k} \mid \mathsf{C}^{\leq k} \mid \mathsf{F}\,\phi$$

with a an atomic proposition, $C, C' \subseteq N$ sets (or *coalitions*) of players such that $C' = N \setminus C, \sim \in \{<, \leq, \geq, >\}, q \in [0, 1], x \in \mathbb{R}, r$ a state reward structure mapping a state to a non-negative rational reward, and $k \in \mathbb{N}$. The full semantics is defined elsewhere [7].

The informal semantics for rPATL is as follows: $\langle\langle C \rangle\rangle \mathsf{P}_{\sim q}[\psi]$ indicates that coalition C has a strategy to ensure that the probability of ψ to hold meets the bound $\sim q$. $\langle\langle C \rangle\rangle \mathsf{R}^r_{\sim x}[\rho]$ means that coalition C can guarantee the expected reward r accumulated over paths satisfying ρ meets the bound $\sim x$. $\langle\langle C' \rangle\rangle_{max \sim x}(\theta)$ states that coalition C can ensure the maximum value of θ with respect to C' is within the bound $\sim x$. For the temporal operators, $\mathsf{X}\,\phi$ expresses that ϕ holds in the next state, $\phi_1\,\mathsf{U}^{\leq k}\,\phi_2$ means ϕ_1 holds until ϕ_2 holds within k steps, and $\phi_1\,\mathsf{U}\,\phi_2$ indicates ϕ_1 holds until ϕ_2 holds unbounded. $\mathsf{I}^{=k}$ represents the instantaneous reward after k steps, $\mathsf{C}^{\leq k}$ denotes the accumulated reward within k steps, and $\mathsf{F}\,\phi$ denotes the reward cumulated until eventually reaching a state where ϕ holds.

3 Rational Verification Under Stackelberg Equilibrium for Reachability Reward Properties

For an SSG $\mathcal{G}$, we extend rPATL to support rational verification under Stackelberg equilibrium for reachability reward properties in the coalition game of $\mathcal{G}$ induced by coalition $C = \{\text{defender, attacker}\}$ (denoted by $\mathcal{G}_C$), where coalition C can consist of player 1 (the defender), player 2 (the attacker), or both players 1 and 2 together. The defender selects a strategy (denoted as σ_1) that maximises their payoff, assuming that the attacker will best respond to this strategy (denoted as σ_2). On the other hand, given the defender's strategy, the attacker chooses a strategy that maximises their own payoff. In a typical SSG, the defender first selects a strategy to maximise their payoff, assuming that the attacker will respond optimally. The attacker, in response, attempts to exploit observed weaknesses. Using rPATL, we verify whether a given strategy is optimal under these conditions. We expand state formulas ϕ in the grammar by adding the syntax $\langle\langle C \rangle\rangle \mathsf{R}^r_{\mathsf{SE}=?}$ to denote the Stackelberg equilibrium (SE) and define its semantics as follows:

$$\langle\langle C \rangle\rangle \mathsf{R}^r_{\mathsf{SE}=?}[\,\mathsf{F}\phi\,] \stackrel{\text{def}}{=} \mathbb{E}^{\max,\max}_{\mathcal{G}_C,s}[\text{rew}(r,\mathsf{c},\text{Sat}(\phi))] \qquad (1)$$
$$= \sup_{\sigma_1 \in \Sigma_1} \sup_{\sigma_2 \in BR(\sigma_1)} \mathbb{E}^{\sigma_1,\sigma_2}_{\mathcal{G}_C,s}[\text{rew}(r,\mathsf{c},\text{Sat}(\phi))].$$

$\mathbb{E}^{\max,\max}_{\mathcal{G}_C,s}$ represents the expected outcome for the coalition C starting from state s, assuming that both players are acting optimally in their own interests in the game $\mathcal{G}_C$. Reward calculation is done by $\text{rew}(r,\mathsf{c},\text{Sat}(\phi))$, where r is a defined reward structure, c denotes that the reward is accumulated along the paths to the target set of states, and computes the set of states in which ϕ holds.

Σ_1 is the set of strategies for the defender, and $BR(\sigma_1)$ is the attacker's best response strategy to the defender's strategy σ_1. Given the defender's strategy σ_1, $\sup_{\sigma_1 \in \Sigma_1} \sup_{\sigma_2 \in BR(\sigma_1)}$ maximises the attacker's payoff based on this strategy, and given the attacker's strategy σ_2, it maximises the defender's payoff accordingly. For now, we only support rPATL formulas in the form $\langle\langle C \rangle\rangle \mathsf{R}^r_{\mathsf{SE}=?}[\,\mathsf{F}\,\mathsf{a}\,]$. This restriction to only reachability properties is sufficient for evaluating specific system states that are necessary for security analysis.

4 Tool Overview

STEVE is the first rational verification tool for SSGs. It can automatically extract technical exploit descriptions into ADTs, which are then transformed into SSGs for further analysis using rPATL. The overall architecture is in Fig. 1.

The tool starts analysing vulnerabilities by gathering specific CVE details and their CVSS data from public vulnerability databases in JSON format. This includes descriptions of the vulnerability, attack sequences, mitigation steps, and impact scores. Security experts can manually refine this data and consider realistic cost values before proceeding.

In creating the ADT(1), the tool extracts the mitigation steps as the defender's actions, maps attack sequences to the attacker's actions, and adds dependencies between actions using conjunctive or disjunctive operators. The obtained ADT(1) is then transformed into an SSG. Preferences are calculated using a risk estimation based on impact scores and cost, then defined at the endpoints of the game.

The tool models defensive and offensive behaviours as a PRISM-games model. A set of rPATL properties is generated to focus on security aspects such as confidentiality, integrity, or availability, based on the mitigation technique in the CVE. Security experts can specify additional security requirements as temporal formulae. The outcomes of this process include a model of the game and expressions in temporal logic.

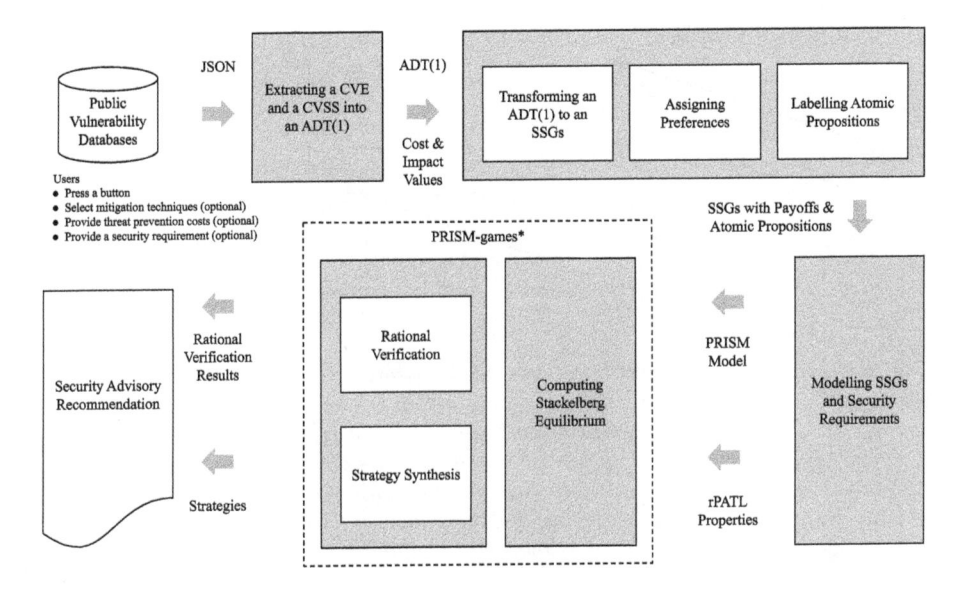

Fig. 1. Overview of STEVE's architecture and workflow. PRISM-games* is the version we patched to support Stackelberg equilibrium.

The process for computing the Stackelberg equilibrium determines the strategies for a defender and the corresponding responses from an attacker. STEVE relies on our extension of PRISM-games to support Eq. (1) for the analysis of the payoffs for both the defender and the attacker and the computation of the set of states in the equilibrium. Rational verification allows us to answer whether there is a defender strategy that comprises the equilibrium and satisfies their goals. Furthermore, we can synthesise strategies that are rational for the defender. A defender strategy that comprises the equilibrium refers to a strategy that satisfies the conditions for Stackelberg equilibrium, meaning it optimally coordinates the defender's and attacker's objectives. A rational strategy for the defender is one that minimises potential loss while considering the attacker's best response. As a final output we produce security advisory recommendations that include rational verification results and strategies.

5 Security Examples and Experiments

In this section, we present some experimental results. We select the two common vulnerabilities CVE-2017-8759 and CVE-2024-3400 due to their high severity and impact [12,13]. These have been exploited in targeted attacks, received extensive media attention, and highlight the need for robust defensive measures.

CVE-2017-8759, known as the .NET Framework remote code execution, serves as our primary example. In this CVE, the defensive solutions include the following actions: b'_1 – patch management, b'_2 – email filtering, b'_3 – backup and disaster recovery, b'_4 – application whitelisting, b'_5 – network segmentation and

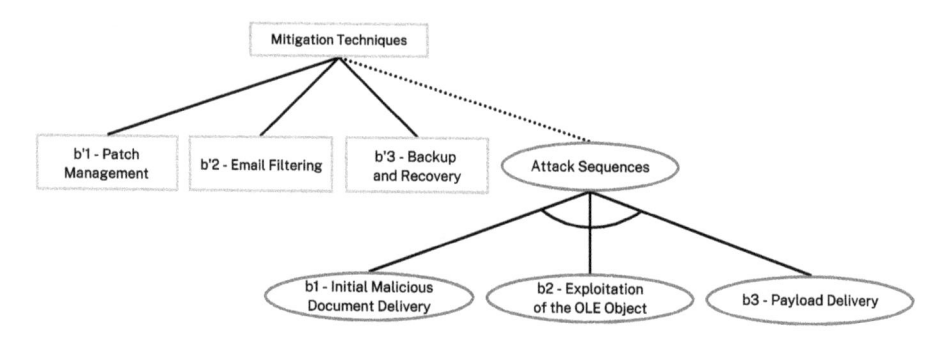

Fig. 2. Graphical representation of the ADT(1) term $c^d(\vee^d(b'_1, b'_2, b'_3), \wedge^a(b_1, b_2, b_3))$ generated from the CVE-2017-8759 example, which is then automatically transformed into an SSG. The defender (green nodes) can choose mitigation techniques for each of the following separately: b'_1 - patch management, b'_2 - email filtering, or b'_3 - backup and recovery. However, the attacker (red nodes) can initiate an attack by combining actions involving b_1 - initial malicious document delivery, b_2 - exploitation of the OLE object, and b_3 - payload delivery. (Color figure online)

monitoring, b'_6 – user training and awareness, b'_7 – multi factor authentication, b'_8 – endpoint protection, and b'_9 – regular security audits. The exploit activities involve: b_1 – malicious document delivery, b_2 – exploitation of the OLE object, b_3 – payload delivery, b_4 – execution of the HTA file, b_5 – establishment of persistence, b_6 – command and control communication, and b_7 – lateral movement and further exploitation. In this experiment, we assume that the defender takes the following disjunctive actions: b'_1, b'_2, and b'_3. The attacker uses the following conjunctive actions: b_1, b_2, and b_3. The ADT(1) term encoding this scenario is $c^d(\vee^d(b'_1, b'_2, b'_3), \wedge^a(b_1, b_2, b_3))$ and graphically represented in Fig. 2, which is then transformed into an SSG with payoffs derived from adjustment costs. Each of the defender's strategies $\sigma_1, \ldots, \sigma_8 \in 2^{\{b'_1, b'_2, b'_3\}}$ is verified against the security requirements $\rho_1 = $ F applyPatch, $\rho_2 = $ F filterEmail, and $\rho_3 = $ F backup, where applyPatch, filterEmail, and backup are user-defined atomic propositions corresponding to the actions b'_1, b'_2, b'_3 respectively. Then the tool generates the three corresponding rPATL formulae $\langle\langle C \rangle\rangle \mathsf{R}^r_{\mathsf{SE}=?}[\rho_i]$, for $i \in \{1, 2, 3\}$.

We analyse multiple defensive strategies, as shown in Table 1. The cost of each strategy is calculated from deployment and maintenance expenses, while the attacker's gain is estimated based on potential financial damages from successful exploits, including data loss and business disruption. These estimates are informed by historical data collected by the company. The strategies are evaluated based on their effectiveness in minimising the defender's loss and the attacker's gain. The Stackelberg equilibrium is highlighted in bold. Among the evaluated strategies, σ_5 (patch management) is the optimal choice as it satisfies the Stackelberg equilibrium, resulting in the least loss for the defender and a moderate gain for the attacker. Rational verification with STEVE returns "true" when a security requirement satisfies some of the rPATL formulae and the Stackelberg equilibrium, and "false" when it fails to meet these criteria or does not achieve the Stackelberg equilibrium. If the user does not provide a security requirement, STEVE will synthesise strategies that satisfy both the Stackelberg equilibrium and the applicable rPATL formulae.

Table 1. Summary of defensive & attacking strategies. Stackelberg equilibrium in bold.

Strategy	Def. Actions	Att. Actions	Def. Loss (£)	Att. Gain (£)
σ_1	$\{b'_1, b'_2, b'_3\}$	$\{b_1, b_2, b_3\}$	−85,015	1,504.5
σ_2	$\{b'_1, b'_2\}$	$\{b_1, b_2, b_3\}$	−35,900	1,770
σ_3	$\{b'_2, b'_3\}$	$\{b_1, b_2, b_3\}$	−76,018	6,018
σ_4	$\{b'_1, b'_3\}$	$\{b_1, b_2, b_3\}$	−72,537.5	3,761.25
σ_5	**$\{b'_1\}$**	**$\{b_1, b_2, b_3\}$**	**−24,750**	**4,425**
σ_6	$\{b'_2\}$	$\{b_1, b_2, b_3\}$	−43,600	7,080
σ_7	$\{b'_3\}$	$\{b_1, b_2, b_3\}$	−100,150	15,045
σ_8	∅	$\{b_1, b_2, b_3\}$	−59,000	17,700

To further validate STEVE, we conduct additional experiments on CVE-2024-3400, which affects Palo Alto Networks, potentially allowing arbitrary code execution on the firewall. Table 2 summarises the defensive strategies and their outcomes for both CVE examples. The "Securing with Stackelberg" and "Best Case" scenarios both demonstrate significantly lower defender losses and moderate attacker gains, indicating that these strategies are highly effective in mitigating damage and deterring attackers. In contrast, the "Worst Case" scenario results in the highest financial losses for defenders and the greatest gains for attackers, highlighting a critical failure in defensive measures. Additionally, strategies such as "Minimise Rewards for the Attacker" and "Exhaustive Approach" result in identical defender losses and notably low attacker gains, underscoring their effectiveness in discouraging attackers by minimising their potential rewards.

Table 2. Experimental results in various scenarios.

Scenario	CVE-2017-8759	CVE-2024-3400
Securing with Stackelberg	**−£24,750, £4,425**	**−£13,000, £3,150**
Worst Case	−£100,150, £15,045	−£60,000, £25,200
Best Case	−£24,750, £4,425	−£13,000, £3,150
Minimise for the Attacker	−£85,015, £1,504.5	−£29,000, £450
Exhaustive Approach	−£85,015, £1,504.5	−£29,000, £630
Do Nothing	−£59,000, £17,700	−£60,000, £25,200

6 Discussion and Conclusion

STEVE's capability to automatically derive ADTs from CVEs and transform them into SSG models represents a new contribution. By using the temporal logic rPATL and the extended PRISM-games framework, the tool supports the computation of Stackelberg equilibria, ensuring that the defence strategies synthesised are not only optimal but also rational given the attacker's best responses. This shows how rational verification can guide security experts in making informed decisions about the allocation of limited resources. Our experiments with two CVEs demonstrate STEVE's potential to model security scenarios and suggest optimal defensive strategies. However, further validation in practical, real world scenarios is necessary to fully assess its impact on reducing damages and financial losses. We chose PRISM-games as the backend for STEVE due to its robustness in handling game-theoretic analysis, even in non-probabilistic settings. The ability to compute Stackelberg equilibria, along with its support for rPATL, makes it the most suitable option.

There are currently some limitations to our approach. STEVE does not support social engineering attacks. Since these exploit human psychology rather than technical vulnerabilities, it is difficult to model them, within the framework of SSGs. Another limitation is that the tool cannot analyse scenarios where multiple vulnerabilities are combined by an attacker to achieve their objectives.

We plan to address these limitations in future work by extending STEVE to support a diverse range of vulnerabilities. We consider using requirements elicitation tools like FRET [4] to help users specify their logical specifications. Additionally, moving beyond single shot games to represent repeated SSGs [17] by integrating probabilistic and Bayesian games [14] will allow for better modelling of uncertainties and incomplete information prevalent in cyber-defence scenarios. We also foresee the possibility of integrating STEVE's approach into the EVE [5] framework, which would further enhance its ability to handle rational verification in cybersecurity scenarios by enabling the computation of Stackelberg equilibria. This would allow EVE to support the analysis of leader-follower interactions in security games, improving its capability to model interactions between defenders and attackers. Finally, our code and the examples presented in this paper are publicly available [15].

Acknowledgments. S.P. is supported by a Royal Thai Government Scholarship. M.S. is supported by an Amazon Research Award on Automated Reasoning.

References

1. Abate, A., et al.: Rational verification: game-theoretic verification of multi-agent systems. Appl. Intell. **51**(9), 6569–6584 (2021)
2. Aslanyan, Z., Nielson, F., Parker, D.: Quantitative verification and synthesis of attack defence scenarios. In: Proc. of CSF 2016, pp. 105–119. IEEE Computer Society (2016)

3. Chen, T., Forejt, V., Kwiatkowska, M., Parker, D., Simaitis, A.: Automatic verification of competitive stochastic systems. Formal Methods Syst. Des **43**(1), 61–92 (2013)
4. Giannakopoulou, D., Mavridou, A., Rhein, J., Pressburger, T., Schumann, J., Shi, N.: Formal requirements elicitation with FRET. In: International Working Conference on Requirements Engineering: Foundation for Software Quality (REFSQ-2020). No. ARC-E-DAA-TN77785 (2020)
5. Gutierrez, J., Najib, M., Perelli, G., Wooldridge, M.: EVE: A Tool for Temporal Equilibrium Analysis. In: Lahiri, S.K., Wang, C. (eds.) ATVA 2018. LNCS, vol. 11138, pp. 551–557. Springer, Cham (2018). https://doi.org/10.1007/978-3-030-01090-4_35
6. Kordy, B., Mauw, S., Radomirovic, S., Schweitzer, P.: Attack defence trees. J. Log. Comput. **24**(1), 55–87 (2014)
7. Kwiatkowska, M., Norman, G., Parker, D., Santos, G.: Equilibria-Based Probabilistic Model Checking for Concurrent Stochastic Games. In: ter Beek, M.H., McIver, A., Oliveira, J.N. (eds.) FM 2019. LNCS, vol. 11800, pp. 298–315. Springer, Cham (2019). https://doi.org/10.1007/978-3-030-30942-8_19
8. Kwiatkowska, M., Norman, G., Parker, D.: Probabilistic model checking and autonomy. Annu. Rev. Control. Robotics Auton. Syst. **5**, 385–410 (2022)
9. Kwiatkowska, M., Norman, G., Parker, D., Santos, G.: PRISM-games 3.0: Stochastic Game Verification with Concurrency, Equilibria and Time. In: Lahiri, S.K., Wang, C. (eds.) CAV 2020. LNCS, vol. 12225, pp. 475–487. Springer, Cham (2020). https://doi.org/10.1007/978-3-030-53291-8_25
10. Leyton-Brown, K., Shoham, Y.: Essentials of game theory: A concise multidisciplinary introduction. Morgan & Claypool Publishers, Synthesis Lectures on AI and ML (2008)
11. Najib, M.: Rational verification in multi-agent systems. Ph.D. thesis, UK (2020)
12. National Vulnerability Database (NVD): CVE-2017-8759. https://nvd.nist.gov/vuln/detail/CVE-2017-8759
13. National Vulnerability Database (NVD): CVE-2024-3400. https://nvd.nist.gov/vuln/detail/CVE-2024-3400
14. Osborne, M.J., Rubinstein, A.: A course in game theory. MIT Press (1994)
15. Phetmanee, S., Sevegnani, M., Andrei, O.: StEVe: A rational verification tool for Stackelberg security games. https://doi.org/10.5281/zenodo.11004420
16. Sinha, A., Fang, F., An, B., Kiekintveld, C., Tambe, M.: Stackelberg security games: looking beyond a decade of success. In: Proc. IJCAI18 (2018)
17. Tambe, M.: Security and game theory. Cambridge University Press (2012)
18. Wooldridge, M., Gutierrez, J., Harrenstein, P., Marchioni, E., Perelli, G., Toumi, A.: Rational verification: from model checking to equilibrium checking. In: Proc. of the AAAI Conference on Artificial Intelligence 30(1) (2016)

Learning and Reasoning

PyQBF: A Python Framework for Solving Quantified Boolean Formulas

Mark Peyrer[✉], Maximilian Heisinger,
and Martina Seidl

Johannes Kepler University Linz, Altenbergerstr. 69,
4040 Linz, Austria
{mark.peyrer,maximilian.heisinger,
martina.seidl}@jku.at

Abstract. Over the last years many solvers for quantified Boolean formulas (QBFs) have been developed. While most of these solvers support QDIMACS as a standard input format, exchanging a QBF solver within a reasoning framework is often a challenging task. Many solvers do not provide an API but they can only be used via their executable. Further, incremental solving is only supported to a limited extend.

We present PYQBF, a Python-based framework that provides a uniform programmatic interface to state-of-the-art QBF solvers. In this paper, we introduce the general architecture of PYQBF, describe the supported features and give a detailed example that illustrates how our framework can be used to implement an enumerative QBF solution counter. Our extensive experimental evaluation shows the efficiency of PYQBF. The experiments indicate that there is only little overhead compared to direct usage of the solvers.

Keywords: Quantified Boolean Formulas · Incremental Solving · Uniform API

1 Introduction

Ignatiev et al. [11] identified the low level representation of propositional logic as a limitation for wider adoption of Boolean satisfiability (SAT) solvers. To overcome this limitation, the PYSAT toolkit was presented which simplifies prototyping and working with SAT solvers. Implemented in the Python programming language, PYSAT provides a uniform interface to state-of-the-art SAT solvers allowing its users to develop SAT encodings in a user-friendly way. For SMT, PYSMT [7] offers a uniform Python interface to various SMT solvers, allowing for a straightforward combination with packages like Numpy [8] or even Machine Learning frameworks like Keras [4].

Similar or even stronger limitations concerning the usability of solvers can be observed for quantified Boolean formulas (QBF), the extension of propositional logic with existential and universal quantifiers over the Boolean variables [1].

Supported by the LIT AI Lab funded by the state of Upper Austria.

© The Author(s), under exclusive license to Springer Nature Switzerland AG 2025
N. Kosmatov and L. Kovács (Eds.): IFM 2024, LNCS 15234, pp. 279–287, 2025.
https://doi.org/10.1007/978-3-031-76554-4_16

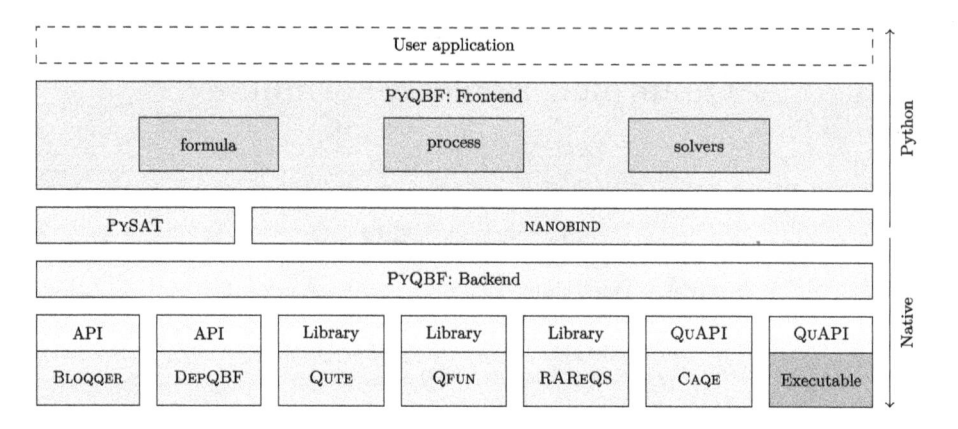

Fig. 1. Architecture of PyQBF

While there exists a growing amount of competitive QBF solvers [19] motivated by a wide range of applications [22], hardly any solver provides a programmatic interface. Only the solver DepQBF provides IPASIR-like programmatic as well as Java and Python interfaces. All the other solvers are mainly to be called via their executable. As a consequence, SMT solvers like Z3 [5] are employed for QBF solving [6]. Although they do not implement dedicated decision procedures for QBFs, they support the more general (and also harder) theory of quantified bit-vectors. Hence, those solvers tend to be less efficient for reasoning on QBF [9]. To exploit the potential of modern QBF solving technology in a user-friendly manner, we present PyQBF, a Python-based framework. It provides not only a uniform programmatic interface to recent QBF solvers, it also integrates powerful preprocessors in a seamless manner. Preprocessors rewrite QBFs in such a way that they become easier for the solvers in many cases, e.g., by eliminating certain redundancies [3]. Furthermore, PyQBF supports incremental solving, i.e., the iterative refinement of a problem by additional constraints. Our framework PyQBF is available at our GitLab instance:

https://gitlab.sai.jku.at/qbf/pyqbf

PyQBF can be installed on Linux using `pip` if `git` is available:

```
pip install --user git+https://gitlab.sai.jku.at/qbf/pyqbf.git
```

2 Architecture

In this section, we present the design and implementation of our framework PyQBF. The general architecture is shown in Fig. 1. The user application interacts with PyQBF via a Python frontend that offers three modules to access, process and solve QBFs. Between the frontend and backend we have PySAT from which we reuse some data structures and CNF processing functionality as a dependency and NANOBIND as a connection to state-of-the-art solvers. The

```
1  from pyqbf.formula import PCNF
2  from pyqbf.solvers import solve, Solver, DepQBF
3  # First approach
4  pcnf = PCNF(from_file="file.qdimacs"); print(solve(pcnf))
5  # Second approach
6  with Solver(bootstrap_with=pcnf) as s:
7          print(s.solve())
8  # Third approach
9  s = DepQBF(); print(s.solve(pcnf))
```

Fig. 2. Example usage of the solver interface

backend is written in C++ dealing with solver-specific properties and providing uniform error handling. In the following two sections, we discuss frontend and backend in detail.

2.1 Frontend of PyQBF

The frontend of PyQBF consists of three different modules, which are described in the following.

Module Formula. This module provides the functionality necessary for the manipulation of formulas in prenex conjunctive normal form (PCNF), which is the standard format supported by the majority of state-of-the-art QBF solvers. Furthermore, PyQBF reuses parts of PySAT. In particular, the class *PCNF* is directly derived from PySAT's *pysat.formula.CNF* which works only for propositional formulas. The module supports manipulation of the quantifier prefix, it provides normalization algorithms, I/O operations, and more.

Module Process. In this module, the interface to the preprocessor Bloqqer [2] is located. Most solvers strongly benefit from applying a preprocessor in their tool chain, because redundant parts in the formula are eliminated. In PyQBF, the application of a preprocessor is directly integrated and can be realized by one addition function call before a complete solver is called. In many cases, the call of a preprocessor is sufficient to solve a formula.

Module Solvers. Following a similar idea as in PySAT, PyQBF provides a uniform interface to multiple state-of-the-art QBF solvers including DepQBF (Version 6.03) [16], Qute (Version 1.1) [17], Qfun (Version 1.0) [13], Caqe (Version 4.0.1) [21] and RAReQS (Version 1.1) [14]. For each of the solver a class with the same name is provided as well as a general *Solver*-class, which can be parameterized for easier initialization. An example of how a solver is called via PyQBF is shown in Fig. 2. Here a QBF stored in a file called `file.qidmacs` is passed to the QBF solver DepQBF in three different ways.

2.2 Backend of PyQBF

We use NANOBIND [12] to connect the Python frontend with state-of-the-art QBF solvers that are mostly implemented in C/C++. The backend itself ensures that each integrated solver can be accessed in uniform manner via the frontend. Interaction with the solvers is either realized through their API (if available), by directly accessing their functions, or via QuAPI. Especially, for solvers not implemented in C/C++ (e.g., CAQE [21] which is implemented in Rust), QuAPI [10] offers a simple interface. The QuAPI framework can be seen as a wrapper for any (binary) solver executable such incremental solving under assumption becomes possible although this is not natively supported by the solver. For our case, we furthermore utilize QuAPI for the integrations of solvers, which can not be directly included in the backend. This allows the user to use additional solvers within PyQBF by simply providing a path to the solver executables.

3 Case Study

To demonstrate the usage of PyQBF, we implemented an enumerative solution counter for a given false QBF $\forall X_1 \exists Y_1 \forall Y_2 \ldots \exists Y_n.\phi$ where $X_1, Y_1, \ldots Y_n$ are disjoint sets of variables and ϕ is a propositional formula over these variables in conjunctive normal form (CNF). This counter returns the number of assignments to universal variables X_1 of the first quantifier block that falsify the QBF. The implementation follows the approach presented in [23]: A QBF solver is queried for an assignment σ of variables X_1 that falsifies the formula. This assignment is then interpreted as a conjunction of literals and added disjunctively to the formula to exclude it. The addition of such falsifying assignments is repeated until the QBF becomes true. To preserve the CNF structure, the following trick is applied. First a new variable t_1 is introduced which is defined by $t_1 \rightarrow \phi$, i.e., each clause of ϕ is extended by the literal $\neg t_1$. Now the QBF $\forall X_1 \ldots \exists Y_n \cup \{t_1\}.((t_1 \rightarrow \phi) \land t_1)$, where the last clause t_1 is only temporarily added to the formula, is solved and the falsifying assignment σ is found. Next $t_2 \rightarrow \sigma$ is added to the propositional part (where t_2 is a new variable that is included in the last existential quantifier block), clause t_1 is exchanged by clause $(t_1 \lor t_2)$ and the QBF solver is called again. The temporal addition of the clause $(t_1 \lor t_2 \lor \ldots)$ is done by the push/pop feature of DEPQBF. In this way, the power of incremental solving can be exploited and the solver does not have to restart from scratch. The implementation in PyQBF is shown in Fig. 3.

We start by loading the formula from a given file *target.qdimacs* (line 1). As previously described, we need to introduce a variable to bind the formula to (line 2) and extend each clause by its negated literal (line 5).

Next the solver has to be prepared. We use DEPQBF in incremental mode and load the formula. The current disjunction is only added temporarily. Thus a new frame is pushed before the clause is added, such that this frame can be popped and replaced at a later time (line 9). Now we have to get the result of the formula by solving it.

```
1  pcnf = PCNF(from_file="target.qdimacs") # get input formula
2  ts = pcnf.nv + 1;          # fresh variable
3  pcnf.set_quantifier(ts) # quantify variable ts
4
5  [c.append(-ts) for c in pcnf.clauses] # add -ts to all clauses
6
7  solver = DepQBF(incr=True); # init DepQBF
8  solver.load(pcnf);
9  solver.push()
10
11 root_clause = [ts];
12 solver.add(root_clause); # solve original input formula
13 result = solver.solve()
14 count = 0
15 while not result:
16     count += 1
17     a = [solver.get_assignment(abs(v)) \
18          for v in itertools.takewhile
19                (lambda x: x < 0, pcnf.prefix)]
20
21     solver.pop();
22
23     ts = pcnf.nv + 1;    # fresh variable
24     pcnf.set_quantifier(ts)
25     solver.add_var(ts);
26     root_clause.append(ts)
27
28     [solver.add([-ts, var]) for var in a]
29     solver.push();
30     solver.add(root_clause) # exclude found counter-model
31
32     result = solver.solve() # solve new formula
33 print(count)
```

Fig. 3. Counting outer-most counter-models in PyQBF.

The algorithm runs as long as the current formula is false. We compute an assignment for the outer variables in lines 17, 18 and 19, using *itertools* for a compact code. Having the assignment, we discard our temporary clause by popping the current frame. Furthermore, we encode the computed assignment as a conjunction by adding another variable to the formula as seen in line 25. This new variable will be a part of the next temporary clause, which now may be added. Thus, we push another frame and add the modified temporary clause. Finally, we solve again. This process of adding the falsifying assignment is repeated until the formula gets satisfiable.

4 Experiments

We first compare the performance of directly called solvers to the performance of solvers called via PyQBF. Secondly, we evaluate the PyQBF version of the counter-model counter presented in [23]. We use the formulas from the PCNF track of the last QBF Gallery [20]. Our experiments were run on Ubuntu 22.04 with dual-socket AMD EPYC 7313@3.7GHz CPUs and 8GB RAM per task.

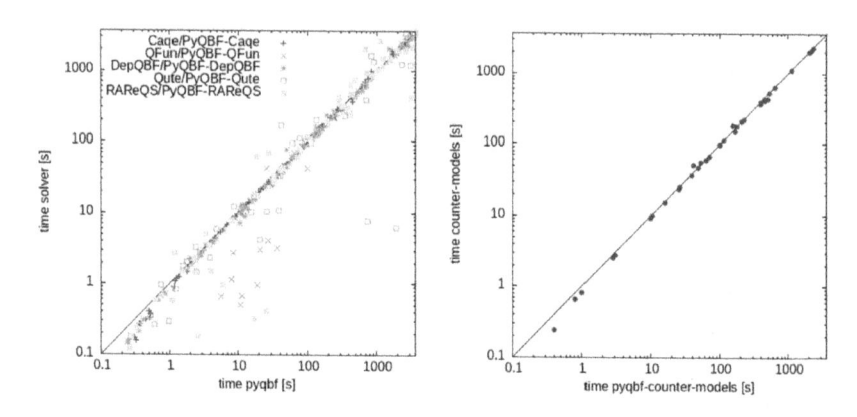

Fig. 4. Comparison between using solvers directly and through PyQBF.

QBF Solving. For these experiment, we run the five solvers currently supported by PyQBF via their PyQBF interface. We compared the resulting runtimes with the runtimes of the solvers' executables. The results are shown in Fig. 4. We observe hardly an overhead by using PyQBF, i.e., most runtime pairs are located close to the diagonal. There are a few points where mainly the executable is faster where we assume that through the different call different options are used which is beyond our control. Also almost no overhead can be observed for the preprocessor BLOQQER.

Counting Counter-Models. For the second experiment, we re-implemented the full algorithm proposed by Shukla et al. [23] in PyQBF and compared the runtime in the right part of Fig. 4. In contrast to the code presented above, the full implementation supports counting models as well as counter-models. Further, partial solutions are used for optimizing the approach. The full code is shown in the appendix. For this application, we also do not observe much overhead as indicated by the right part of Fig. 4, but the implementation of the solution counting algorithm becomes shorter. These experiments may be reproduced using our artifact [18].

5 Conclusion

In this paper, we presented PyQBF, a framework that provides uniform access to state-of-the-art QBF solvers. With PyQBF many tooling obstacles that might be an entrance barrier for application users of QBF technology are overcome. We illustrated by the implementation of a solution counter, how PyQBF is applied. Our experiments indicate that there is only neglectable overhead when calling solvers via PyQBF compared to calling them directly.

In future work, we plan to extend PyQBF to formulas that are not in prenex conjunctive normal form, but which are of arbitrary structure, i.e., which are provided in the QCIR format [15].

A PyQBF Version of Outer-Count

```
import itertools
from pyqbf.solvers import DepQBF
from pyqbf.formula import PCNF

pcnf = PCNF(from_file="unsat.qdimacs")
ts = pcnf.nv + 1; pcnf.set_quantifier(ts)
for c in pcnf.clauses:
    c.insert(0, -ts)

solver = DepQBF(incr=True); solver.load(pcnf)
solver.assume([ts])
result = solver.solve()
root_clause = [ts]

if (result and pcnf.prefix[0] < 0) or \
   (not result and pcnf.prefix[0] > 0):
    raise RuntimeError("Cannot compute (counter)models!")

relevant_prefix = list(itertools.takewhile
                (lambda x: (x > 0) == result, pcnf.prefix))

phase = result
count = 0; pushed = False
max_count = 18446744073709551615 # ULONG_MAX
while result == phase:
    a = [solver.get_assignment(abs(v)) \
            for v in relevant_prefix]
    d = 1
    dont_cares = 0
    for value in a:
        if value == 0:
            d *= 2
            dont_cares += 1
    if dont_cares >= 64:
        print("More than 2^64 models")
        exit()
    if pushed:
        solver.pop()
        pushed = False
    if count + d > max_count:
        print(f"Overflow during iterating!"\
            +" More than {count + d} models")
        exit()
    count += d
    if not phase:
        ts = pcnf.nv + 1
        pcnf.set_quantifier(ts)
        solver.add_var(ts)
        root_clause.append(ts)
        for var in a:
            if var != 0:
                solver.add([-ts, var])
        solver.push(); pushed = true
        solver.add(root_clause)
    else:
        solver.add([-x for x in a if x != 0])
        solve.assume([ts])
    result = solver.solve()
print(f"{'counter' if not phase else ''} models: {count}")
```

References

1. Beyersdorff, O., Janota, M., Lonsing, F., Seidl, M.: Quantified Boolean formulas. In: Handbook of Satisfiability, pp. 1177–1221. IOS Press (2021)
2. Biere, A., Lonsing, F., Seidl, M.: Bloqqer: blocked clause elimination for QBF (2015). https://fmv.jku.at/bloqqer/
3. Bjørner, N.S., Janota, M., Klieber, W.: On conflicts and strategies in QBF. LPAR **35**, 28–41 (2015)
4. Chollet, F., et al.: Keras. https://keras.io (2015)
5. de Moura, L., Bjørner, N.: Z3: an efficient SMT solver. In: Ramakrishnan, C.R., Rehof, J. (eds.) TACAS 2008. LNCS, vol. 4963, pp. 337–340. Springer, Heidelberg (2008). https://doi.org/10.1007/978-3-540-78800-3_24
6. Garcia-Contreras, I., Govind, V.K.H., Shoham, S., Gurfinkel, A.: Fast approximations of quantifier elimination. In: Enea, C., Lal, A. (eds.) CAV 2023, Part II, pp. 64–86. Springer, Cham (2023). https://doi.org/10.1007/978-3-031-37703-7_4
7. Gario, M., Micheli, A.: Pysmt: a solver-agnostic library for fast prototyping of SMT-based algorithms. In: SMT Workshop 2015 (2015)
8. Harris, C.R., et al.: Array programming with Numpy. Nature **585**(7825), 357–362 (2020)
9. Heisinger, M., Heisinger, S., Seidl, M.: Booleguru, the propositional polyglot (short paper). In: Benzmüller, C., Heule, M.J.H., Schmidt, R.A. (eds.) IJCAR 2024, Part I, pp. 315–324. Springer, Cham (2024). https://doi.org/10.1007/978-3-031-63498-7_19
10. Heisinger, M., Seidl, M., Biere, A.: QuAPI: adding assumptions to non-assuming sat & qbf solvers. In: PAAR@ IJCAR (2022)
11. Ignatiev, A., Morgado, A., Marques-Silva, J.: PySAT: a python toolkit for prototyping with SAT oracles. In: Beyersdorff, O., Wintersteiger, C.M. (eds.) SAT 2018. LNCS, vol. 10929, pp. 428–437. Springer, Cham (2018). https://doi.org/10.1007/978-3-319-94144-8_26
12. Jakob, W.: Nanobind: tiny and efficient C++/Python bindings (2022). https://github.com/wjakob/nanobind
13. Janota, M.: Towards generalization in qbf solving via machine learning. In: Proceedings of the AAAI Conference on Artificial Intelligence, vol. 32 (2018)
14. Janota, M., Klieber, W., Marques-Silva, J., Clarke, E.: Solving QBF with counterexample guided refinement. Artif. Intell. **234**, 1–25 (2016)
15. Jordan, C., Klieber, W., Seidl, M.: Non-CNF QBF solving with QCIR. In: Workshops at the Thirtieth AAAI Conference on Artificial Intelligence (2016)
16. Lonsing, F., Biere, A.: DEPQBF: a dependency-aware QBF solver. J. Satisfiabil. Boolean Model. Comput. **7**(2–3), 71–76 (2010)
17. Peitl, T., Slivovsky, F., Szeider, S.: Dependency learning for QBF. J. Artif. Intell. Res. **65**, 180–208 (2019). https://doi.org/10.1613/JAIR.1.11529
18. Peyrer, M., Heisinger, M., Seidl, M.: PyQBF: a python framework for solving quantified boolean formulas (2024). https://doi.org/10.5281/zenodo.13341211
19. Pulina, L., Seidl, M.: The 2016 and 2017 QBF solvers evaluations (QBFEval 2016 and QBFEval 2017). Artif. Intell. **274**, 224–248 (2019)
20. Pulina, L., Seidl, M., Heisinger, S.: QBFGallery (2023). https://qbf23.pages.sai.jku.at/gallery/
21. Rabe, M.N., Tentrup, L.: Caqe: a certifying QBF solver. In: Formal Methods in Computer-Aided Design (FMCAD), pp. 136–143. IEEE (2015)

22. Shukla, A., Biere, A., Pulina, L., Seidl, M.: A survey on applications of quantified boolean formulas. In: 31st International Conference on Tools with Artificial Intelligence (ICTAI), pp. 78–84 (2019)
23. Shukla, A., Möhle, S., Kauers, M., Seidl, M.: OuterCount: a first-level solution-counter for quantified Boolean formulas. In: Buzzard, K., Kutsia, T. (eds.) CICM 2022, pp. 272–284. Springer, Cham (2022). https://doi.org/10.1007/978-3-031-16681-5_19

Improving SAT Solver Performance Through MLP-Predicted Genetic Algorithm Parameters

Sabrine Saouli[1]($\boxtimes$), Souheib Baarir[2], and Claude Dutheillet[1]

[1] Sorbonne Université, CNRS, LIP6, 75005 Paris, France
{Sabrine.Saouli,Claude.Dutheillet}@lip6.fr
[2] Université Paris Nanterre, 92000 Nanterre, France
Souheib.Baarir@lip6.fr

Abstract. This paper improves SAT solvers by optimizing the initialization of truth values for variables in a CNF formula. It introduces a Multilayer Perceptron (MLP) model that predicts optimal Genetic Algorithm (GA) parameters based on formula characteristics. This method automates parameter tuning through machine learning, enhancing efficiency and reducing manual adjustments. Experimental results show that our MLP-guided GA approach improves SAT solver performance, indicating a promising direction for automating SAT initialization.

Keywords: Boolean satisfiability · Initialization problem · Genetic Algorithms · Machine learning · Parameters optimization

1 Introduction

Boolean satisfiability (SAT) solvers tackle combinatorial problems across diverse domains, including cryptography [15], hardware verification [8], and software analysis [6]. Given a propositional logic formula expressed in conjunctive normal form (CNF), these solvers aim at finding a model, i.e., an assignment of polarities (or truth values) to its variables that satisfies all constraints.

The choice of the initial polarities of the variables, significantly impacts the solver effectiveness. Existing approaches have explored different strategies such as Stochastic Local Search (SLS) [4] or Bayesian Moment Matching (BMM) [7].

In a recent study [16], a Genetic Algorithm (GA) for SAT Polarity Initialization (GASPI) was proposed to address the initialization problem using a GA [1]. If GASPI finds no model for the CNF formula within a predefined number of generations, it assigns the initial polarities of the variables based on the best values encountered during the GA search. Experimental results showed a superiority of GASPI compared with SLS and BMM.

Nevertheless, GASPI faces a significant challenge: the performance and efficiency of the GA heavily depend on parameter settings, which may vary across different SAT problem instances. Manual tuning of the values of these parameters is time-consuming and usually sub-optimal.

In this paper, we address this challenge with an approach that leverages machine learning techniques to automate the parameter prediction process. We design a Multilayer Perceptron (MLP) model that predicts optimal values for GASPI parameters based on the characteristics of the CNF formula. By doing so, we bridge the gap between GA-based pre-processing and effective tuning of its parameters.

The remainder of this paper is organized as follows. Section 2 provides an overview of SAT solvers and the initialization problem and reviews existing approaches tackling the initialization problem in SAT solvers. Section 3 details our proposed MLP-based parameter prediction model. Section 4 presents experimental results and performance evaluation. Finally, Sect. 5 concludes the paper and outlines future research directions.

2 Background and Related Work

2.1 Boolean Satisfiability (SAT) Solving

Boolean Satisfiability (SAT) algorithms determine the satisfiability of a propositional logic formula in Conjunctive Normal Form (CNF), which is a conjunction of clauses, each clause being a disjunction of literals. A literal is a variable or its negation. SAT solvers aim at assigning truth values to variables to satisfy all clauses. The SAT problem is NP-complete, yet practical solvers handle large, complex instances effectively.

There are two main types of SAT solvers: complete and incomplete. Complete solvers, based on the conflict-driven clause learning (CDCL) algorithm [18], guarantee a solution if one exists. Incomplete solvers, such as WalkSAT [17] and Yalsat [5], use stochastic local search (SLS) and may not find a solution.

2.2 The Initialization Problem in SAT Solving

A CDCL SAT solver starts its search on a CNF using initial truth values (polarities) assigned to variables. Selecting optimal starting polarities is crucial for solver efficiency, as it influences search space exploration. Indeed, a well-chosen initial assignment can significantly speed up the solving time.

Many state-of-the-art CDCL solvers, like Glucose [2] and MapleCOM-SPS [14], initialize all variables to false. This straightforward approach can be ineffective for certain instances, making optimal initialization a challenge.

BMM initialization [7] addresses this by using Bayesian reasoning to steer the CDCL solver towards more promising regions while SLS methods [4] iteratively adjust assignments, but risk getting stuck in local optima.

Genetic Algorithm for SAT Polarity Initialization (GASPI) evolves candidate assignments through genetic operators, aiming to satisfy all clauses. If unsuccessful, GASPI assigns polarities based on the best solution found, often outperforming BMM and SLS. However, GASPI's effectiveness is hindered by manual parameter tuning. To address this, we propose an MLP model trained on SAT problems to predict optimal GA parameters, automating the tuning process.

3 Proposed Approach

Starting from a population of potential solutions, a GA mimics natural selection. Operators like selection, crossover, and mutation generate new solutions. A fitness criterion is defined to evaluate the quality of each solution. The GA stops when a maximum number of generations is reached, an optimal solution is found, or a defined convergence level is achieved.

In GASPI, each solution is a binary vector representing a complete assignment for the CNF formula, and fitness is measured by satisfied clauses.

Configuring the population size, number of generations, crossover rate and mutation rate is crucial for the efficiency of the GA. However, finding the best parameter settings for a given problem is complex and involves extensive time and experimentation.

The following sections detail how our approach, namely GASPI-ML, tackles this issue in the context of SAT solving by using a machine learning model.

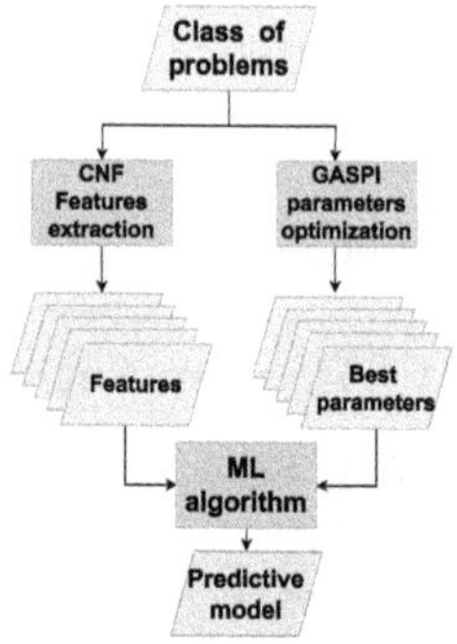

3.1 ML Training Workflow

To build a supervised learning model that predicts the best/optimal GA parameters for a given problem, a labeled dataset is needed. This dataset should contain features extracted from the problem instances and their corresponding best GA parameters. Unfortunately, such labeled data is not readily available in our context. Therefore, we developed a systematic workflow to address this gap.

Fig. 1. Tool workflow.

The first step is to collect a dataset of problem instances from a specific category of problems. Each instance represents a unique SAT problem. For each instance, we extract a set of features designed to represent the key characteristics of the underlying SAT formula. Next, we identify the best GA parameters for each problem instance through optimization techniques, establishing them as the ground truth labels for our dataset.

Using this dataset, we then train a regression model to predict the best GA parameters for new SAT instances. The model learns to map the extracted features from the SAT problems to their optimal GA parameters. The model is then used to predict the best GA parameters for unseen SAT problems (see Fig. 3).

3.2 Architecture of MLP Model

Our Approach exploits a Multi-Layer Perceptron (MLP) model. This type of artificial neural network learns to make predictions from training data. The MLP consists of an input layer, one or more hidden layers, and an output layer, with each layer containing multiple neurons connected by weighted links.

The MLP model takes various features from the SAT formula as inputs. Specifically, it utilizes 38 features which are referred to as *base features* in SATfeatPy [13]. These features are derived from the set of 48 features presented in SATzilla [19]. The selected features include key characteristics of the SAT formula, such as the number of variables, the number of clauses, the clause-to-variable ratio, and other structural properties. It then outputs four key GA parameters: *number of generations, population size, mutation rate, and crossover rate*.

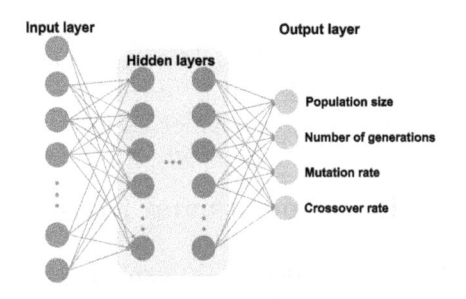

Fig. 2. MLP model.

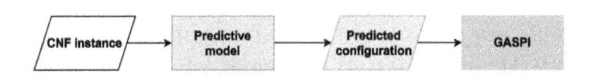

Fig. 3. Usage of the predictive model

The model consists of three hidden layers with, resp., 64, 32, and 16 neurons. The input layer receives the extracted features from the SAT problem, and the output layer provides the predicted values for the GA parameters. The hidden layers process the input features through a series of computations to predict the optimal GA parameters for a given SAT problem.

We chose this model architecture after conducting grid searches and tuning hyper-parameters to optimize performance. The training was done using the Adam optimizer [12] with an initial learning rate of 0.1, which balances convergence speed with model stability.

3.3 Tooling Support

This section outlines the tools and libraries used to implement our approach.

SMAC [10] (Sequential Model-based Algorithm Configuration) SMAC iteratively fine-tunes parameter settings based on previous evaluations, identifying optimal values to enhance the performance of GASPI on SAT instances. It handles both discrete and continuous parameters, offering flexibility in optimization.

For experiments, we run SMAC 120 times per instance, a trade-off between accurate results and excessive computation time. The optimal number of generations and population size were searched between 5 and 100, balancing convergence and memory use. The crossover and mutation rates were bounded by 0 and 1, i.e., not constrained. These ranges allowed structured fine-tuning while keeping the optimization process manageable.

SATfeatPy [13] is a library for extracting features from SAT problems in CNF format. We used features from the Satzilla paper [19] for their proven relevance in capturing SAT problem complexity. We considered two feature sets: (i) *Full Feature Set*, comprising all 38 features extracted using SATfeatPy; and (ii) *Reduced Feature Set*, derived by calculating a correlation matrix [9] and removing 13 features with a correlation coefficient ≥ 0.9, reducing redundancy.

4 Experiments and Results

This section details the experimental setup and evaluation of our approach. The evaluation includes assessing the prediction accuracy of our machine learning model and comparing its performance with state-of-the-art SAT solvers on benchmark datasets.

4.1 Experimental Setup

All our experiments are conducted on a server with an Intel(R) Xeon(R) Gold 6148 CPU @ 2.40 GHz and 1500 GB of memory. Each used solver has been run once, using the same set of benchmarks and a 7200 s timeout for each run.

Solvers: We tested our machine learning-based approach on Kissat-MAB, a SAT solver that won the 2021 SAT competition and formed the basis for subsequent winners. We replaced the SLS initialization in Kissat-MAB by GASPI-ML, keeping all other parameters default.

We trained two models: one with the full feature set and another with a subset of uncorrelated features, to examine the impact of feature selection. We also compared the predicted parameter configurations from our models with random configurations to evaluate our method's effectiveness. Hence, the analyzed solvers are: K-GASPI-ML (full feature set); K-GASPI-ML-WOC (without correlated features); K-GASPI-R (GASPI initialization with random configurations). These were compared against the baseline Kissat-MAB variants: Kissat (SLS initialization); Kissat-R (random polarities initialization). The comparison with Kissat-R aims at demonstrating that our approach offers meaningful improvements beyond random chance.

Benchmark Datasets: We collected datasets of CNF instances from the GBD benchmark library [11], including SAT problems from all SAT competitions and various other sources. We focused on problem classes from the latest SAT competition (SAT'2023) [3], selecting those with a larger number of instances in the GBD library. To ensure feasible feature extraction, we chose instances with less than 2 million clauses. We trained five models, one for each class of problems, to predict optimal GASPI parameters.

The chosen problem classes, along with their number of instances, are: Cryptography (861), Scheduling (395), Tseitin (293), Miter (331), and Argumentation (177). We used 70% of the total instances for training and 30% for testing, with features for the training instances extracted by SATfeatPy within 7200 s.

Table 1. Performance of SAT Solvers on Cryptography benchmark: Comparison of solved instances (SAT/UNSAT), PAR2 scores (hours), and preprocessing times(hours). Highlighted cells indicate best performance.

Solver	SAT	UNSAT	TOTAL(160)	PAR2	Features	GASPI
VBS	147	3	150	70.50	–	–
Kissat	133	3	136	121.26	–	–
Kissat-R	134	3	137	118.92	–	–
K-GASPI-ML	139	3	142	104.38	0.07	0.43
K-GASPI-ML-WOC	136	3	139	115.30	0.07	0.44
K-GASPI-R	128	3	131	144.54	–	0.54

Table 2. Performance of SAT Solvers on Scheduling and Tseitin benchmarks: Comparison of solved instances (SAT/UNSAT), PAR2 scores (hours), and preprocessing times (hours). Highlighted cells indicate best performance.

Class	\multicolumn{6}{c}{Scheduling (112)}	\multicolumn{6}{c}{Tseitin (88)}
Solver	SAT	UNSAT	TOTAL	PAR2	Features	GASPI	SAT	UNSAT	TOTAL	PAR2	Features	GASPI runtime
VBS	70	24	94	88.04	–	–	20	44	64	108.22	–	
Kissat	65	22	87	105.78	–	–	16	43	59	126.69	–	–
Kissat-R	67	22	89	103.41	–	–	16	43	59	125.90	–	–
K-GASPI-ML	70	24	94	101.88	4.38	2.45	18	44	62	117.99	0.013	0.0045
K-GASPI-ML-WOC	68	24	92	102.78	4.39	0.49	20	44	64	115.21	0.013	0.0005
K-GASPI-R	68	22	90	97.85	–	0.65	18	44	62	116.06	–	0.014

4.2 Experimental Results

Tables 1, 2, and 3 present the performance of the previously mentioned SAT solvers on different benchmark datasets. For each solver, we report two key metrics: The number of instances solved (SAT, UNSAT and the total number of solved instances) and the PAR2[1] score. Additionally, we provide the cumulative times for both preprocessing steps: Features extraction and GASPI initialization, reported in the "Features" and "GASPI" columns respectively. These preprocessing times are reported for both solved and timeout instances, and are included in the PAR2 calculations. All time measurements are reported in hours.

For comparison, we also include a "Virtual Best Solver" (VBS) in our results. The VBS represents a hypothetical solver that always chooses the best-performing solver for each instance. It aggregates the instances solved by at least one solver in the set, providing an upper bound on performance for reference. This presentation allows for a comprehensive comparison of solvers performance across different benchmarks, taking into account both solving capability and efficiency.

The tables show that our machine learning-based approach generally outperforms other solvers on most of the benchmark datasets. Table 1 reveals that the

---

[1] The metric used in the yearly SAT competition: the sum of runtimes for solved instances, with a penalty factor of 2 for unsolved instances. Lower PAR2 values indicate better performance.

Table 3. Performance of SAT Solvers on Miter and Argumentation benchmarks: Comparison of solved instances (SAT/UNSAT), PAR2 scores (hours), and preprocessing times (hours). Highlighted cells indicate best performance.

Class	\multicolumn{6}{c}{Miter (100)}	\multicolumn{6}{c}{Argumentation (53)}
Solver	SAT	UNSAT	TOTAL	PAR2	Features	GASPI	SAT	UNSAT	TOTAL	PAR2	Features	GASPI
VBS	10	71	81	86.74	–	–	20	13	33	86	–	–
Kissat	8	69	77	103.7	–	–	19	13	32	91.5	–	–
Kissat-R	8	69	77	103.7	–	–	19	13	32	90.88	–	–
K-GASPI-ML	8	70	78	98.84	0.35	0.36	19	13	32	91.85	0.13	0.008
K-GASPI-ML-WOC	8	71	79	96.42	0.35	0.32	20	13	33	87.31	0.13	0.012
K-GASPI-R	9	71	80	91.54	-	0.30	20	13	33	86.57	–	0.005

K-GASPI-ML solver has the highest number of instances solved. It is worth noting that, in most cases, the time spent on data preprocessing (features extraction and initialization) is relatively small compared to the overall execution time. Despite including preprocessing, both K-GASPI-ML-based approaches consistently achieves lower PAR2 values. These results demonstrate the effectiveness of our ML-based approach in predicting good Genetic Algorithm (GA) parameters.

On problem classes with less instances (e.g., "Miter" and "Argumentation"), the performance of the ML-based approach was not as good as in other benchmarks. This is likely because the ML model did not have enough data to understand the complex relationships between SAT problem features and the optimal parameters for GASPI. Despite this limitation, the solvers initialised with our approach still matched or surpassed the performance of Kissat and Kissat-R.

Additionally, we note that in all scenarios, our approach improves the VBS results. This outcome suggests the potential for developing a high-performing portfolio-based approach, combining different solvers for optimal results.

Furthermore, our solvers solved 6 instances from Cryptography, Tseitin, and Scheduling benchmarks, 5 of which were satisfiable (SAT), that were not previously solved (according to GBD). K-GASPI-ML-WOC solved 3, while K-GASPI-ML solved all 6. This outcome underscores the effectiveness of our machine learning-based approach, particularly when dealing with satisfiable instances.

5 Conclusion

This paper introduces a machine learning-based tool for automating parameter selection in Genetic Algorithms (GAs) for SAT solving. Our approach utilizes class-specific Multilayer Perceptron (MLP) models to predict optimal GA parameters based on CNF formula characteristics. Experimental results show promising outcomes, with our method outperforming other initialization techniques on most of the tested benchmarks. The class-specific nature of our models not only improves performance but also sets the stage for integration into portfolio-based SAT solving approaches. Future work will explore additional features for the MLP models, their application to other combinatorial optimization problems, aiming at developing a generalized model for optimal GA configurations across various problem classes.

References

1. Aiman, U., Asrar, N.: Genetic algorithm based solution to sat-3 problem. J. Comput. Sci. Appl. **3**(2), 33–39 (2015)
2. Audemard, G., Simon, L.: Predicting learnt clauses quality in modern sat solvers. In: Proceedings of the 21st International Joint Conference on Artificial Intelligence (IJCAI 2009), pp. 399–404 (2009)
3. Balyo, T., Heule, M., Iser, M., Järvisalo, M., Suda, M.: Proceedings of sat competition 2023: solver, benchmark and proof checker descriptions (2023)
4. Benhamou, B., Nabhani, T., Ostrowski, R., Saïdi, M.R.: Enhancing clause learning by symmetry in sat solvers. In: 2010 22nd IEEE International Conference on Tools with Artificial Intelligence, vol. 1, pp. 329–335. IEEE (2010)
5. Biere, A.: CaDiCaL, Lingeling, plingeling, treengeling, YalSAT entering the SAT competition 2017. In: Balyo, T., Heule, M., Järvisalo, M. (eds.) Proceedings of the SAT Competition 2017—Solver and Benchmark Descriptions. Department of Computer Science Series of Publications B, vol. B-2017-1, pp. 14–15. University of Helsinki (2017)
6. Clarke, E.M.: Model checking. In: Ramesh, S., Sivakumar, G. (eds.) FSTTCS 1997. LNCS, vol. 1346, pp. 54–56. Springer, Heidelberg (1997). https://doi.org/10.1007/BFb0058022
7. Duan, H., Nejati, S., Trimponias, G., Poupart, P., Ganesh, V.: Online bayesian moment matching based sat solver heuristics. In: International Conference on Machine Learning. pp. 2710–2719. PMLR (2020)
8. Gupta, A., Ganai, M.K., Wang, C.: Sat-based verification methods and applications in hardware verification. In: Bernardo, M., Cimatti, A. (eds.) Formal Methods for Hardware Verification, pp. 108–143. Springer, Heidelberg (2006). https://doi.org/10.1007/11757283_5
9. Hall, M.A.: Correlation-based feature selection for machine learning. Ph.D. thesis, The University of Waikato (1999)
10. Hutter, F., Hoos, H.H., Leyton-Brown, K.: Sequential model-based optimization for general algorithm configuration. In: Coello, C.A.C. (ed.) LION 2011. LNCS, vol. 6683, pp. 507–523. Springer, Heidelberg (2011). https://doi.org/10.1007/978-3-642-25566-3_40
11. Iser, M., Sinz, C.: A problem meta-data library for research in sat. In: Berre, D.L., Järvisalo, M. (eds.) Proceedings of Pragmatics of SAT 2015 and 2018. EPiC Series in Computing, vol. 59, pp. 144–152. EasyChair (2019). https://doi.org/10.29007/gdbb
12. Kingma, D.P., Ba, J.: Adam: a method for stochastic optimization. arXiv preprint arXiv:1412.6980 (2014)
13. Kotsiantis, S.: Feature selection for machine learning classification problems: a recent overview. Artif. Intell. Rev. **42**(1), 157–176 (2011)
14. Liang, J.H., Oh, C., Ganesh, V., Czarnecki, K., Poupart, P.: Maple-comsps, maplecomsps lrb, maplecomsps chb. In: Proceedings of SAT Competition **2016** (2016)
15. Massacci, F., Marraro, L.: Logical cryptanalysis as a sat problem. J. Autom. Reason. **24**(1), 165–203 (2000)

16. Saouli, S., Baarir, S., Dutheillet, C.: Tackling the polarity initialization problem in sat solving using a genetic algorithm. In: Benz, N., Gopinath, D., Shi, N. (eds.) NFM 2024, pp. 21–36. Springer, Cham (2024). https://doi.org/10.1007/978-3-031-60698-4_2
17. Selman, B., Kautz, H.A.: An empirical study of greedy local search for satisfiability testing. In: AAAI, vol. 93, pp. 46–51 (1993)
18. Silva, J.P.M., Sakallah, K.A.: Grasp-a new search algorithm for satisfiability. In: Proceedings of the 16th IEEE/ACM International Conference on Computer-Aided Design (ICCAD), pp. 220–227. IEEE (1997)
19. Xu, L., Hutter, F., Hoos, H.H., Leyton-Brown, K.: Satzilla: portfolio-based algorithm selection for sat. J. Artif. Intell. Res. **32**, 565–606 (2008)

Active Learning of Runtime Monitors Under Uncertainty

Sebastian Junges[1], Sanjit A. Seshia[2], and Hazem Torfah[3](✉)

[1] Radboud University, Nijmegen, Netherlands
sebastian.junges@ru.nl
[2] University of California at Berkeley, Berkeley, USA
sseshia@berkeley.edu
[3] Chalmers University of Technology and Gothenburg University, Gothenburg, Sweden
hazemto@chalmers.se

Abstract. We investigate the problem of active learning of runtime monitors for cyber-physical systems (CPS) under uncertainty. In CPS, runtime monitors need to make decisions with only partial information about the system state and cannot always rely on having a precise environment model. As a result, the learning process and resulting monitors must be able to handle this type of uncertainty. We present a framework for the active learning of monitors and discuss the challenges in implementing oracles for membership and equivalence queries. We particularly apply the framework to a setting where uncertainty models are defined by Markov decision processes. We present initial results demonstrating the efficacy of our approach in learning accurate monitors using a set of benchmarks from the domain of autonomous systems.

1 Introduction

Runtime monitors are crucial for maintaining the safety of cyber-physical systems (CPS) throughout their lifetime [3,4,14,20]. They play a vital role in detecting irregularities during runtime [12], and in evaluating the performance of the system [5,6]. Runtime monitors can also assist in maintaining situational awareness, especially in systems such as autonomous CPS [17]. Depending on the state of the system and its environment, monitors must determine if an autonomous system is within its operational design domain. If not, certain fail-safe plans need to be executed to keep the system safe. The key challenge in the construction of such monitors is to ensure that they are resilient to uncertainty in the information received about the environment. Monitors in a CPS perceive information about the environment from sensors, which are generally imperfect and may deliver data that does not accurately reflect the actual state of the environment.

In this paper, we investigate active learning of runtime monitors for CPS under uncertainty. We present a formalization of the problem and introduce a general framework for learning based on this formalization. We particularly discuss the challenges in implementing oracles for answering membership and

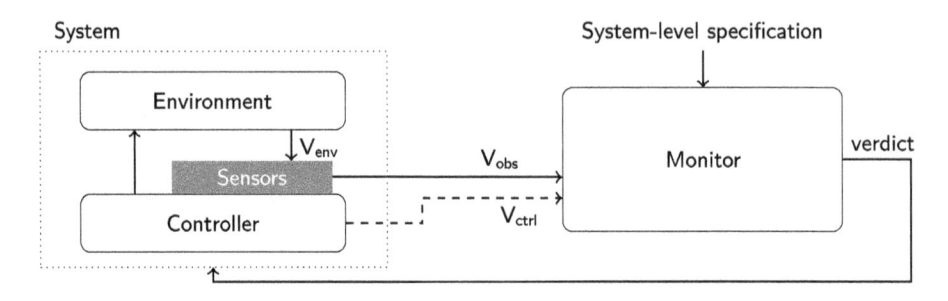

Fig. 1. A general monitoring architecture in cyber-physical systems.

equivalence queries and elaborate on the role of probabilistic and statistical verification methods in providing solutions for these problems.

Classically, runtime monitors are synthesized directly from (formal) temporal specifications [4]. The specifications are typically defined on the system level, i.e., over the joint state of system and environment. However, the monitor may only have partial observability into the current state, as shown in Fig. 1. A system-level specification is defined over the set of variables $V_{sys} = V_{env} \cup V_{ctrl}$, capturing both the state of the environment and control. A monitor, on the other hand, is defined over variables V_{obs}, capturing information about the environment as received via a set of sensors. Notice that the relation between both variables may be complex, in particular, there generally is no (deterministic) mapping between assignments to V_{sys} and V_{obs}.

Monitoring for systems with uncertainty has been studied in a variety of settings, spanning from model-based [11,15,16,18] to simulations-based approaches [7,9,19,21]. Our formalization of the monitoring problem under uncertainty generalizes over both. In our experiments, we primarily, however, work in the context of the former. The models provide a ground truth, but computing the safety can only be done via, e.g., model checking on a large model and for a single sequence of observations at a time. Given key requirements on (1) promptness, i.e., monitors must be able to issue a verdict promptly, (2) complexity, i.e., monitors themselves are safety-critical software, which means that they must be sufficiently simple, and (3) efficiency, i.e., ideally using constant memory, it is unrealistic to deploy such algorithms on a device that must be monitored.

This paper presents a work-in-progress on using supervised, active learning to extract an artifact implementing a monitor that adheres to the requirements above and that is resilient to uncertainty in the observed data. In the scope of active learning, the model-based monitor approaches yield membership oracles. We often do not have access to efficient equivalence oracles. Instead, we use statistical conformance checks. The main contribution of this paper is a statistical sound approach to do so, based on Chernoff bounds and the Bonferroni correction method. The second contribution is an empirical evaluation of this approach, using membership oracles provided by previous work on monitoring Markov decision processes (MDP) [11]. Our preliminary evaluation demonstrates the applicability of this approach.

2 Motivating Example

Consider a CPS composed of an autonomous vehicle, the *ego*, and an environment that comprises other vehicles driving on the road. At all times the ego vehicle needs to satisfy a specification φ that requires it to keep a distance larger than m meters from any other vehicle ahead of it. A monitor is integrated into the ego car, continuously checking whether this distance is maintained. The monitor has no information about the concrete positions of other cars on the road and relies in its decision making on an image-based detection module that is able to provide the monitor with information about the distances of other objects on the road. Relating this to Fig. 1, the ground truth of the positions of other vehicles on the road is part of V_{env}, and not directly observable by the monitor, whereas the distances computed by the object detection module is part of the observable feature space V_{obs}. The accuracy of a monitor for checking φ will therefore depend on the accuracy of the output of the detection module and a good monitor will have to be robust for any imperfections in the received data.

3 The Monitor Generation Problem

Before formally defining our problem, we expand on a few aspects regarding the sources of uncertainty in cyber-physical systems (CPS). Generally, systems are subject to at least two sources of uncertainty: process uncertainty that makes the evolution of states uncertain, and measurement uncertainty that yields different observations even in the same state. In this work, we consider that these types of uncertainty can be captured with a distribution. A third notion of uncertainty is that the monitor may often not have access to a precise model of the system dynamics, e.g., due to lack of data. This third notion of uncertainty is a challenge to create monitors, but not part of the monitoring problem itself. We discuss handling this type of uncertainty in our experiments.

Based on the intuition above, we can formalize the problem as follows. We use the following notation: For a countable set X, let $Distr(X) \subset (X \to [0,1])$ define the set of distributions over X. A distribution $d \in Distr(X)$ particularly satisfies, $\sum_{x \in X} d(x) = 1$. We further, define the sets Σ_{sys}^* and Σ_{obs}^* to denote the set of valuations over the variable V_{sys} and V_{obs}, respectively. We state the problem and then describe the ingredients.

Problem Statement. Given a distribution $d \in Distr(\Sigma_{sys}^*)$, a mapping $\mu: \Sigma_{sys}^* \to Distr(\Sigma_{obs}^*)$, a risk measure $r: \Sigma_{sys}^* \to \mathbb{R}$, and a constant λ, learn a monitor M such that

$$M(\sigma_{obs}) \Leftrightarrow \sum_{\sigma_{sys} \in \Sigma_{sys}^*} d(\sigma_{sys}) \cdot \mu(\sigma_{sys})(\sigma_{obs}) \cdot r(\sigma_{sys}) > \lambda$$

In our problem formulation, we assume that a system-level behavior, i.e., traces σ_{sys}, occurs according to some distribution $d \in Distr(\Sigma_{sys}^*)$. The mismatch between the system-level behavior and observations, as well as the stochastic errors in sensors is captured by the probabilistic function μ. The risk function r

defines a quantitative specification, that associates each system-level trace with a risk. Note that a qualitative specification can be represented by a measure r that returns either 0 or 1, stating whether a system-level trace satisfies (lowest risk) or violates (highest risk) the specification, respectively. A monitor then accepts an observation trace σ_{obs} if the total risk, computed as the sum of weighted risks (weighted through the probability of occurrence measured in terms d and μ) of system-level traces that may induce σ_{obs}, is larger than the threshold λ.

In our motivating example, the risk r can be described as a function that produces higher risk the closer the ego car approaches another car. The measure μ defines the error of the detection module in capturing the true distances to other cars on the road. Lastly, d is a distribution over the actions of other cars on the road. In most cases, such distribution will be unknown and will have to be approximated, for example, by performing a worst-case analysis on the non-deterministic behavior of the environment, as we show later in our experiments.

4 Active Learning Under Uncertainty

Active learning describes a process where a concept is learned by actively querying an entity about this concept. In this paper, we are interested in an active learning setting, where learning a monitor, assumes access to an entity, an *oracle*, that can answer two types of queries: *membership* and *equivalence* queries. Membership queries are used to check whether a certain observation trace is accepted by a monitor. Equivalence queries check the correctness of a learned monitor with respect to the system-level specification. If an equivalence query fails, the counterexamples computed by the oracle are used to refine the training dataset and to guide the next round of membership queries.

4.1 Membership Queries

In membership queries, the goal is to check whether a certain observation trace $\sigma_{\mathsf{obs}} \in \Sigma_{\mathsf{obs}}^*$ is an element of the language of the goal monitor. Following the problem definition above, solving a membership query for a trace σ_{obs} boils down to checking the validity of the expression

$$\sum_{\sigma_{\mathsf{sys}} \in \Sigma_{\mathsf{sys}}^*} d(\sigma_{\mathsf{sys}}) \cdot \mu(\sigma_{\mathsf{sys}})(\sigma_{\mathsf{obs}}) \cdot r(\sigma_{\mathsf{sys}}) > \lambda \qquad (1)$$

The evaluation of the above expression depends on the underlying uncertainty model, and how we can approximate the measures d and μ. In our experiments, we use an example showing how to approximate these measures for uncertainty models represented by Markov decision processes.

4.2 Equivalence Queries

Ideally, equivalence queries are solved by a model checker that checks the learned monitor against the system-level specification. This is often not feasible, as it can

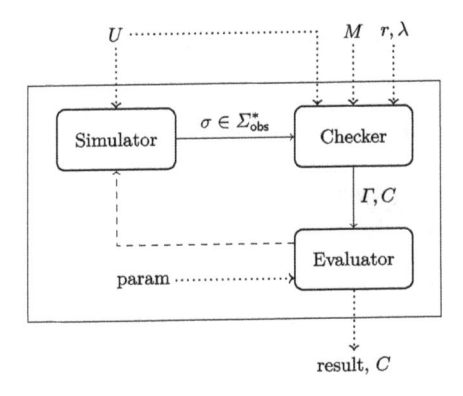

```
         U ·············   M   r, λ
         ┊              ┊   ┊   ┊
    ┌────▼──────────────▼───▼───▼────┐
    │                                │
    │  ┌───────────┐ σ ∈ Σ*_obs ┌─────────┐  │
    │  │ Simulator │───────────▶│ Checker │  │
    │  └───────────┘            └─────────┘  │
    │        ▲                      │        │
    │        ┊                    Γ, C       │
    │        ┊                      ▼        │
    │        ┊                  ┌─────────┐  │
    │    param┄┄┄┄┄┄┄┄┄┄┄┄┄┄┄┄▶│Evaluator│  │
    │                           └─────────┘  │
    └───────────────────────────────┊────────┘
                                    ▼
                               result, C
```

Fig. 2. A statistical verification approach implementing equivalence queries.

be intractable to compute or because we do not have a precise model. Instead, we will rely on conformance-based approaches that repeatedly pose membership queries and use statistical verification techniques [1] to obtain a statistical guarantee on the correctness of the monitor.

In statistical verification, we assume access to an executable system, which can be of stochastic nature, and a system-level specification. Using a (Monte Carlo) simulator, the system is executed repeatedly. Executions are checked against the specification, and a statistical result is computed aggregating the individual results.

Our statistical verification approach is depicted in Fig. 2. Given a system U (which can also be a black box), a learned monitor M, a risk function r, and a risk threshold λ, the statistical verification approach samples observation traces σ from U and checks whether the verdict of M over σ matches the result of a membership query defined in Eq. (1). After several sampling and checking rounds, the set of verdicts Γ is forwarded to an evaluator that computes a statistical verdict on the correctness of M. The evaluator can be implemented using statistical methods, such as hypothesis testing or estimation methods [1,10,13]. If M passes the statistical test, the active learning process terminates. Otherwise, a set of counterexample C is returned and used to expand the training set or guide the next learning iteration. Since monitors in each iteration are learned from a training set that includes (or is guided by) counterexamples collected in previous iterations, we lose the statistical independence and need to compensate for that by increasing the number of testing traces in each equivalence query round. A correction in the statistical parameters is therefore needed to compute a number of samples that retains statistical confidence over several learning iterations. An example of such a correction method is the Bonferroni method [8], which we will use in our experiments.

5 Preliminary Experimental Evaluation

We instantiate the active learning approach to one for learning monitors for uncertainty models given by Markov decision processes (MDPs) [11]. An MDP captures both the nondeterministic and stochastic behavior of system and environment. Particularly, the nondeterministic transitions in an MDP capture the part of the environment's behavior which is unknown (either due to the lack of data, or as a consequence of the discretization of the continuous state space). The stochastic transitions of an MDP capture any known probabilistic behavior of the environment, but foremost the stochastic error introduced by the imperfect sensors. Further, a risk function is given that associates each state in the MDP with a risk. For example, this could be the probability that our ego car in the motivating example will crash with another vehicle within a given number of steps.

In terms of our problem statement, if the nondeterminism were fixed by some policy, the MDP would become a labeled Markov chain (basically a hidden Markov model). This Markov chain can be thought of as a description of a distribution over paths $d \in \mathit{Distr}(\Sigma_{\mathsf{sys}}^*)$. In the labeled model, every state maps to a distribution over observables, which can be lifted to a mapping $\mu \colon \Sigma_{\mathsf{sys}}^* \to \mathit{Distr}(\Sigma_{\mathsf{obs}}^*)$. Finally, the risk measure $r \colon \Sigma_{\mathsf{sys}}^* \to \mathbb{R}$ is obtained by considering the last state of the sequence (the current state) and how likely it is to reach an error state from this state, i.e., by a reachability probability that can be computed for the Markov chain. The MDP with nondeterminism intuitively encodes that none of the functions are certain, but that they could be generated by any Markov chain that is induced by a policy of the MDP. The construction in [11] ensures that we overapproximate the left-hand side of Eq. (1), thereby creating a monitor that is overly cautious.

Below we explain our experimental setup, providing details on the used benchmark and the engines used to implement membership and equivalence queries.

5.1 Setup

In our experiments, we choose the class of decision trees to define the space of monitors. We use the scikit library[1] to learn decision trees with no bound on their depth. The inputs to the monitor were observation traces of a fixed length obtained from the benchmark MDPs. These ranged from traces of length 5 to 60. Our prototype was implemented in Python. All experiments where conducted on a machine with an M2 chip and with 16 GB of RAM.

Benchmarks. We applied our active learning framework on three benchmarks [11], defining MDP-based uncertainty models as described above:

- Airport: This benchmark defined a landing scenario with uncertainty about the observations of vehicles moving around the runway. The risk is defined

---
[1] https://scikit-learn.org.

by the probability of colliding with one of the on-ground vehicles. The MDP for this benchmark has 20910 states and a transition relation of size 114143.
– Evade: This benchmark defines a navigation task in a multi-agent setting in a grid. The robot moves randomly, and the risk is defined as the probability of crashing with another robot. The other robot has an internal incentive in the form of a cardinal direction, and nondeterministically decides to move or to uniformly randomly change its incentive. The MDP for this benchmark has 1001 states and a transition relation of size 5318.
– Refuel: This benchmark models a robot with a depleting battery moving on a grid with recharging stations. The world model consists of a robot moving randomly around in the grid with some dedicated charging cells The risk is to deplete the battery within a fixed horizon. The MDP for this benchmark has 45073 states and a transition relation of size 2431691.

Membership Queries. Membership queries are performed using PREMISE, a prototype tool for monitoring under uncertainty defined by Markov decision processes [11]. PREMISE computes the worst case risk over all possible policies of an MDP. It thus provides an overapproximates of the target risk in Eq. (1), as we described earlier. PREMISE comes with two algorithms for computing the risk. (1) A filtering approaches that instead of tracking the entire set of beliefs only tracks the vertices of a convex hull. (2) Another based on unrolling the MDP for the length of the observation trace and determining the risk by computing the maximal conditional reachability probability over the unrolling. In our experiments, we use the latter. Membership queries were (arbitrarily) bound to threshold equal to 0.5.

Conformance Testing. We used an estimation method based on the application of Chernoff bounds [1] and the Bonferroni correction methods. For a confidence value δ and an error margin ϵ, we can use a Chernoff bound to determine the number of samples n to obtain a monitor such that with confidence δ, the computed accuracy, $p' = \sum_{i=1}^{n} x_i/n$, where x_i represent the results of n different membership queries, does not deviate by more than ϵ from the true accuracy of the monitor. In all our experiments, we choose $\delta = 0.9$ and $\epsilon = 0.01$. The number of samples is determined by $n = \lceil ln(2\delta)/2\epsilon^2 \rceil$. We apply the Bonferonni correction by enlarging the size of the sample set in each round to $\delta' = \delta + (1-\delta)/2$, similar to [2]. We ran our experiments for at most 10 iterations. The process terminates early when a monitor with accuracy >98% is found.

5.2 Results

Initial results are presented in Fig. 3. For all three benchmarks and trace length, we were able to obtain highly accurate monitors. Accuracy was measured in terms the number of samples, chosen during conformance testing, on which both the monitor and the oracle produced matching verdicts. We also report on the rates of false positives and false negatives. The rate of false positives was computed as the ratio of 1-misclassfication, i.e., where the monitor's verdict was

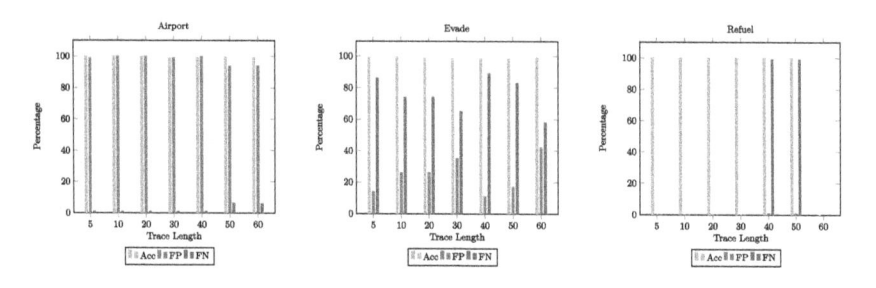

Fig. 3. Accuracy, false positives rates, and false negative rates (bars in the same order) of learned monitors for the Airport, Evade, and Refuel benchmarks. The results are presented for growing input trace lengths ranging from length 5 to 60. Statistical verification was performed using an estimation based on Chernoff bounds for values $\delta = 0.9$ and $\epsilon = 0.01$, and utilizing a Bonferroni correction. Note that the rates of false positives and negatives represent to ration with respect to the total number of misclassfications.

true and that of the oracle was false, to the total number of misclassifications. The rate of false negatives computes the complementary rate, that of the ratio of 0-misclassifications to the total number of misclassifications. Depending on the benchmark, we had variations in the false negatives and false positive rates. Note that in our current setting we are not biasing the learning towards any types of counterexamples, and thus the rates shown in our results may change if we choose to bias the training data refinement to one of the two. The number of iterations needed to learn the monitors depended on the uncertainty model. For the Evade benchmark we needed an average of 5 rounds. The average time for performing equivalence queries was about one minute testing more than 3000 samples. For larger benchmarks such as the Airport benchmark, and for traces of length 60, we required an average of 17 min to complete an equivalence query. For the Refuel benchmark, equivalence queries required less than 3min.

6 Conclusion

We investigated the problem of actively learning monitors under uncertainty. We provided a formalization for the problem and a framework for the active learning of monitors, describing challenges in implementing oracles for answering membership and equivalence queries. We further showed how the latter can be implemented for settings where uncertainty is defined by Markov decision processes, and demonstrated the potential of our methods using a prototypical implementation. With our paper, we intended to provide a foundation for defining monitor learning problems and a general framework for developing active learning approaches for different uncertainty models. In future work, we plan to investigate different instantiations of the framework and compare different statistical approaches to implementing membership and equivalence queries.

Acknowledgments. This work was partly supported by the Wallenberg AI, Autonomous Systems and Software Program (WASP) funded by the Knut and Alice Wallenberg Foundation, by DARPA contracts FA8750-18-C-0101 (AA) and FA8750-23-C-0080 (TIAMAT), and by C3DTI.

References

1. Agha, G., Palmskog, K.: A survey of statistical model checking. ACM Trans. Model. Comput. Simul. **28**(1), 1–39 (2018). https://doi.org/10.1145/3158668
2. Ashok, P., Křetínský, J., Weininger, M.: PAC statistical model checking for Markov decision processes and stochastic games. In: Dillig, I., Tasiran, S. (eds.) CAV 2019. LNCS, vol. 11561, pp. 497–519. Springer, Cham (2019). https://doi.org/10.1007/978-3-030-25540-4_29
3. Bartocci, E., et al.: Specification-based monitoring of cyber-physical systems: a survey on theory, tools and applications. In: Lectures on Runtime Verification (2018). https://api.semanticscholar.org/CorpusID:4539733
4. Bartocci, E., Falcone, Y., Francalanza, A., Reger, G.: Introduction to runtime verification. In: Bartocci, E., Falcone, Y. (eds.) Lectures on Runtime Verification - Introductory and Advanced Topics. LNCS, vol. 10457, pp. 1–33. Springer, Cham (2018). https://doi.org/10.1007/978-3-319-75632-5_1
5. Baumeister, J., Finkbeiner, B., Schirmer, S., Schwenger, M., Torens, C.: RTLola cleared for take-off: monitoring autonomous aircraft. In: Lahiri, S.K., Wang, C. (eds.) CAV 2020. LNCS, vol. 12225, pp. 28–39. Springer, Cham (2020). https://doi.org/10.1007/978-3-030-53291-8_3
6. Baumeister, J., Finkbeiner, B., Schwenger, M., Torfah, H.: FPGA stream-monitoring of real-time properties. ACM Trans. Embed. Comput. Syst. **18**(5s), 88:1–88:24 (2019).https://doi.org/10.1145/3358220
7. Cairoli, F., Bortolussi, L., Paoletti, N.: Neural predictive monitoring under partial observability. In: Feng, L., Fisman, D. (eds.) RV 2021. LNCS, vol. 12974, pp. 121–141. Springer, Cham (2021). https://doi.org/10.1007/978-3-030-88494-9_7
8. Dunn, O.J.: Confidence intervals for the means of dependent, normally distributed variables. J. Am. Statist. Assoc. **54**(287), 613–621 (1959). https://doi.org/10.1080/01621459.1959.10501524
9. Fremont, D.J., Chiu, J., Margineantu, D.D., Osipychev, D., Seshia, S.A.: Formal analysis and redesign of a neural network-based aircraft taxiing system with VerifAI. In: Lahiri, S.K., Wang, C. (eds.) CAV 2020. LNCS, vol. 12224, pp. 122–134. Springer, Cham (2020). https://doi.org/10.1007/978-3-030-53288-8_6
10. Gyori, B.M., Liu, B., Paul, S., Ramanathan, R., Thiagarajan, P.S.: Approximate probabilistic verification of hybrid systems. arXiv preprint arXiv:1412.6953 (2014)
11. Junges, S., Torfah, H., Seshia, S.A.: Runtime monitors for Markov decision processes. In: Silva, A., Leino, K.R.M. (eds.) CAV 2021. LNCS, vol. 12760, pp. 553–576. Springer, Cham (2021). https://doi.org/10.1007/978-3-030-81688-9_26
12. Pellizzoni, R., Meredith, P., Caccamo, M., Rosu, G.: Hardware runtime monitoring for dependable cots-based real-time embedded systems. In: 2008 Real-Time Systems Symposium, pp. 481–491 (2008).https://doi.org/10.1109/RTSS.2008.43
13. Sen, K., Viswanathan, M., Agha, G.: Statistical model checking of black-box probabilistic systems. In: Alur, R., Peled, D.A. (eds.) CAV 2004. LNCS, vol. 3114, pp. 202–215. Springer, Heidelberg (2004). https://doi.org/10.1007/978-3-540-27813-9_16

14. Seshia, S.A., Sadigh, D., Sastry, S.S.: Toward verified artificial intelligence. Commun. ACM **65**(7), 46–55 (2022)
15. Sistla, A.P., Srinivas, A.R.: Monitoring temporal properties of stochastic systems. In: Logozzo, F., Peled, D.A., Zuck, L.D. (eds.) VMCAI 2008. LNCS, vol. 4905, pp. 294–308. Springer, Heidelberg (2008). https://doi.org/10.1007/978-3-540-78163-9_25
16. Stoller, S.D., et al.: Runtime verification with state estimation. In: Khurshid, S., Sen, K. (eds.) RV 2011. LNCS, vol. 7186, pp. 193–207. Springer, Heidelberg (2012). https://doi.org/10.1007/978-3-642-29860-8_15
17. Torfah, H., Xie, C., Junges, S., Vazquez-Chanlatte, M., Seshia, S.A.: Learning monitorable operational design domains for assured autonomy. In: Bouajjani, A., Holík, L., Wu, Z. (eds.) ATVA 2022. LNCS, vol. 13505, pp. 3–22. Springer, Cham (2022). https://doi.org/10.1007/978-3-031-19992-9_1
18. Wilcox, C.M., Williams, B.C.: Runtime verification of stochastic, faulty systems. In: Barringer, H., et al. (eds.) RV 2010. LNCS, vol. 6418, pp. 452–459. Springer, Heidelberg (2010). https://doi.org/10.1007/978-3-642-16612-9_34
19. Yoon, H., Sankaranarayanan, S.: Predictive runtime monitoring for mobile robots using logic-based Bayesian intent inference. In: ICRA, pp. 8565–8571. IEEE (2021)
20. Zhang, P., Aurandt, A., Dureja, R., Jones, P.H., Rozier, K.Y.: Model predictive runtime verification for cyber-physical systems with real-time deadlines. In: Petrucci, L., Sproston, J. (eds.) FORMATS 2023, pp. 158–180. Springer, Cham (2023). https://doi.org/10.1007/978-3-031-42626-1_10
21. Zhao, Y., Hoxha, B., Fainekos, G., Deshmukh, J.V., Lindemann, L.: Robust conformal prediction for STL runtime verification under distribution shift. In: ICCPS 2024, pp. 169–179. IEEE (2024). https://doi.org/10.1109/ICCPS61052.2024.00022

Specify What? Enhancing Neural Specification Synthesis by Symbolic Methods

George Granberry[✉], Wolfgang Ahrendt, and Moa Johansson

Chalmers University of Technology, Gothenburg, Sweden
{georgegr,ahrendt,jomoa}@chalmers.se

Abstract. We investigate how combinations of Large Language Models (LLMs) and symbolic analyses can be used to synthesise specifications of C programs. The LLM prompts are augmented with outputs from two formal methods tools in the Frama-C ecosystem, Pathcrawler and EVA, to produce C program annotations in the specification language ACSL. We demonstrate how the addition of symbolic analysis to the workflow impacts the quality of annotations: information about input/output examples from Pathcrawler produce more context-aware annotations, while the inclusion of EVA reports yields annotations more attuned to runtime errors. In addition, we show that the method infers the programs intent, rather than its behaviour, by generating specifications for buggy programs and observing robustness of the result against bugs.

1 Introduction

The field of specification synthesis offers a possible solution to the inherent complexities involved in creating and maintaining specifications for software verification. Creating useful specifications demands a deep understanding of both the specification language and the verification process, which can often be as intricate, if not more so, than the software they aim to verify. This complexity poses a significant barrier [7,29], especially in dynamic environments where frequent updates and refactoring are the norm. Maintaining an accurate alignment between ever-evolving code and its specifications can become a cumbersome and error-prone process.

Specification synthesis potentially alleviates these concerns by automating the generation and adaptation of specifications. Instead of requiring developers to manually write detailed specifications – a task that can be both time-consuming and susceptible to human error – specification synthesis aims to infer and edit specifications directly from the codebase and associated context. The goal is to transform specifications into convenient guardrails that provide valuable insights and guidance to programmers, rather than chores performed at the end of the software pipeline.

Approaches to generating specifications typically employ a range of symbolic techniques, encompassing static as well as dynamic analyses [19]. For instance, Daikon [8], a widely recognised tool in dynamic analysis, infers properties by observing program

---

This work was supported by the Wallenberg AI, Autonomous Systems and Software Program (WASP), funded by the Knut and Alice Wallenberg Foundation.

© The Author(s), under exclusive license to Springer Nature Switzerland AG 2025
N. Kosmatov and L. Kovács (Eds.): IFM 2024, LNCS 15234, pp. 307–325, 2025.
https://doi.org/10.1007/978-3-031-76554-4_19

behaviour at runtime. On the other hand, static analysers deduce properties based on the program's structure without executing it. Despite their precision, the primary limitation of these methods is their rigidity. Symbolic techniques are constrained by a limited range of expressible properties and typically specialise in specific types of analyses which restricts their flexibility in adapting to diverse verification needs.

On the other side of specification synthesis techniques are machine-learning-based Natural Language Processing (NLP) [4] and Large Language Models (LLMs) [6]. NLP tools specialise in understanding human language, such as comments, while LLMs stand out for their flexibility and creativity in when dealing with arbitrary inputs. These models can theoretically generate any specification that can be articulated in their associated language, provided that they are appropriately trained and given the correct prompts.

However, this strength also introduces a significant challenge: the large range of potential specifications LLMs can produce often includes outputs that may not be practically useful or even plain wrong. While an LLM can generate a wide array of specifications, the lack of inherent direction means that there is no guarantee that the generated specifications will be relevant or valuable for specific verification tasks. This challenge has led users of LLM-based synthesis to rely on *prompt engineering* [33] techniques in order to increase the likelihood of the LLM to produce specifications that align with their objectives.

In this paper, we introduce a hybrid approach that combines the precision of existing symbolic tools with the flexibility and creative potential of LLMs. By integrating outputs from symbolic analysis of C programs into LLM prompts, this method aims to harness the generative capabilities of LLMs while taking into account the focus and direction of symbolic analysis. As interpreting specifications is subjective, we rely on a human-in-the-loop qualitative analysis to observe patterns in our generated specifications. From a practical sense, we cannot always expect our code to be semantically correct when generating a specification for it. Therefore, we also investigate how our proposed technique interacts with incorrect code. Ultimately, we want specification generation to contribute to the revealing of bugs in the code.

We observed that adding the output of symbolic analyses to the input of the LLM reduces the number of generated specifications. Instead, it increases the quality and the level of abstraction, such that the specification represents more intention and less low-level details. The integration acts as a directive lens, focusing the LLM on generating specifications that align with insights from symbolic analysis, thus yielding specifications that are more relevant to the user who chose said symbolic tools. Each symbolic analysis is interpreted and utilised in a unique way. In general, the analysis tools provide some extra context, and increase the likelihood that the LLM will focus on particular aspects of the behaviour.

The dominating factor for the quality of generated specifications seems to be the extent to which a program's *intent* can be identified. In the absence of a clearly inferred intent, the LLM tends to default to generating specifications based on low-level implementation details or the provided context. But whenever the LLM (partly with help of symbolic pre-analysis) successfully grasps the purpose of the program that a programmer *intended* to write, it becomes much more likely to produce specifications that align closely with that intent. This is not only true for programs which match their intent, but even for buggy programs. In our experiments, the LLM was more attentive to the intended behaviour than to the actual behaviour, as generated specifications were rather robust against bugs in the programs. This is very encouraging, and emphasizes the relevance of our approach and further work in this direction. The more we can automatically generate specifications which reflect the intended behaviour of a program, the more this can help us to reveal bugs, i.e., identify deviations from the intended behaviour.

2 Tools and Languages

Frama-C and ACSL. The Frama-C ecosystem is an open-source suite of tools designed for the analysis of the source code of software written in C [17, 18]. It integrates various static and dynamic analysis techniques to evaluate the correctness, safety, and security of C programs. It also supports the specification language ACSL [2, 25], which is used to formulate *contracts* consisting of, among others, preconditions - assumptions on the input and prestate of a function - and postconditions - requirements on the output and poststate of a function. These contracts, examples of which can be seen both in Sect. 5.2 or the appendix, provide a clear and formal framework for understanding and verifying a function's behaviour. Other ACSL annotations commonly used are *assertions* - stating a condition that needs to be true at some point in execution - and *loop invariants* which specify conditions that need to be maintained by every iteration of a loop.

Automated Testing: Pathcrawler. The PathCrawler tool is designed for the automated testing of C programs [34]. Its primary function is to generate and execute test inputs for C code, with a particular focus on achieving high code coverage. Employing a technique known as concolic testing [24]—a combination of concrete and symbolic testing—Pathcrawler efficiently explores different execution paths in the program. First it generates test inputs and then executes them, providing valuable information from the execution results across a broad spectrum of program paths. In addition, PathCrawler allows users to incorporate a test oracles, classifying the outcome of every test case of some function. However, we want to highlight that we did not make such oracle implementations available to the LLM when asking it to generate specifications. Generic oracles can be seen as executable specifications, and would have diluted the significance of our experiments. Instead, we only include input/output pairs, with the non-generic verdict.

Value Analysis: EVA. The EVA static analyzer uses abstract interpretation to approximate a set of possible values that program variables can take to avoid certain runtime errors [5]. By doing so, it can identify a range of potential issues, such as division by zero, buffer overflows, null pointer dereferences, and arithmetic overflows. EVA's analysis helps in ensuring that the code behaves correctly across all possible execution paths and input values. EVA is designed to respect, and work with, ACSL annotations when they are present.

LLM and Prompts. We have chosen to use GPT-4 (version gpt-4-0125-preview) as our LLM for generating specifications. We ran preliminary tests with Gemini as well as

GPT-3.5 but found that they returned too many syntactical and semantic errors to draw interesting conclusions from. While open source models such as Llama-3 have recently gained traction, the setup and fine tuning of such a model for our purposes remain as future work.

We prompt GPT-4 with a C program, providing instructions for how to generate ACSL annotations in a step-by-step manner. We also include a few examples of valid annotations in the prompts, leveraging a form of "few-shot learning" [6] to guide the model (see Appendix)[1]. Additionally, we employ "Chain-of-Thought" [31] reasoning, prompting the LLM to explain its thought process (seen on pages9 and 13) for generating the annotations in the same output as the actual specification. Finally, we add an "Emotional Stimulation" [20] instruction at the end of each prompt. For the core of the experiment, we augment the baseline prompt with outputs from the Pathcrawler and EVA tools to further aid the model.

3 C-Program Test Suites

For our study, we have chosen to utilise the 55 programs from the Pathcrawler test suite, which we will refer to as **pathcrawler_tests**. Note that the test suite is not available online; it was provided to us by the Pathcrawler developers. Thereby, we can assume that this test suite was not directly used in the LLM's training (although it might have seen similar ones). This suite includes a variety of program types, balancing well-known algorithms like Binary Search with more niche programs such as a Soup Heater controller. It also contains small, specially crafted programs designed to test specific capabilities of Pathcrawler, adding another layer of diversity to our tests. According to the Pathcrawler developers, the 55 programs are supposedly correct, in the sense that they are believed to correspond to their respective intention, and have no known bugs. Consequently, we examine with this suite to which extent our method produces accurate annotations for supposedly correct programs.

To also investigate to which extent our approach can help with buggy programs, we created a second suite of programs titled **mutated_set**. This comprises 8 programs from **pathcrawler_tests** but with handcrafted mutations simulating typos, designed to explore a range of programs across two key dimensions: clarity of intent and complexity. In order to study the interactions between these dimensions, this set includes various types of programs: simple programs with clear intent, complex programs with clear intent, simple programs with less clear intent, and complex programs with less clear intent.

4 Generating Annotations

For each program in our two test suites, we generate three sets of ACSL annotations:

1. **baselines_set**: Specifications generated using just the program in the prompt

---

[1] The prompts contained in the appendix of this paper have been shortened. Refer to the extended version of the paper located at https://arxiv.org/abs/2406.15540 for more detailed prompts.

2. **pathcrawler_set**: Specifications generated by including a compact representation of test-cases generated by Patchcrawler in the prompt shown in the Appendix.
3. **eva_set**: Specifications generated by running EVA on the program and including its report on potential value errors in the prompt shown in the Appendix.

The variability of LLMs like GPT-4 can be adjusted via its "temperature" setting which controls the level of determinism during generation. As we are interested in exploring what the *average* specification generated by a given prompt is, we choose to generate three distinct specifications for each program (and prompt) within our test suite, repeating the steps above with a temperature setting of 0.7. This approach allows us to both capture a spectrum of possible specifications as well as assess the consistency and variability of the model's output across multiple generations, while not being too economically costly.

Loop invariants are key for functioning specifications, and our specification generation process does indeed generate them. However, generating loop invariants is not the focus of this paper. The generation of loop invariants with LLMs calls for sophisticated prompts dedicated to this task [10, 16]. Rather, we focus on function contracts – particularly preconditions, postconditions, and assigns clauses – and our prompts are designed to generate these.

5 Evaluation

Evaluating specifications is challenging due to the absence of a definitive specification for any given program. Different users often have varying priorities and perspectives on which properties are worth verifying, making the notion of a definitive specification subjective. Similarly, a specification might be logically correct, but more or less trivial with respect to the program at hand, in which case it provides little value.

In light of these challenges, our evaluation methodology does not attempt to benchmark the generated specifications against a predefined gold standard, nor does it aim to determine the optimal approach to creating specifications. Instead, our focus is on identifying the behaviours and patterns that emerge from incorporating symbolic analysis outputs into the specification generation prompts. This approach allows to better understand the dynamics at play and what kinds of output to expect given particular prompt characteristics. In particular, we want to understand the impact of symbolic-analysis based prompt composition on the generated specifications.

We perform quantitative as well as qualitative evaluation from two different angles:

- **Types of Annotations**: First, we count the number of each type of annotation that we get for each specification set.
- **Qualitative Analysis**: Additionally we use a human-in-the-loop qualitative analysis to interpret the specification and identify trends depending on which prompt composition technique was used, to assess how the different symbolic tool outputs influence the results of the LLM. For this we use the programs in the **pathcrawler_set**.
- **Implementation vs. Intent**: Finally, we specifically examine programs in the **mutated_set** to study how errors introduced into the program affect the resultant specifications. This analysis explores how errors, symbolic analyses, intended

program functionality, and actual implementation interact in the generation of specifications.

5.1 Types of Annotations

In this section we quantify the annotations generated across all programs for our three sets: **baseline_set**, **pathcrawler_set**, and **eva_set**. While this approach does not say anything about the quality or semantics of any annotations, it does provide us with a macro-level view of which kinds of annotations are being generated and at what frequency. This systematic approach allows us to capture the influence of different symbolic contexts on the annotation generation process. It is important to note, however, that a larger number of annotations does not necessarily signify a better specification.

Figure 1 displays the number of annotations generated for each annotation type for the three prompts. For all three cases, the most common annotations are *requires* and *ensures* clauses, which are used to define pre- and post-conditions of functions, followed by *assigns* statements and *loop invariants*. More advanced ACSL annotations such as predicates or ghost-code are rarely, if ever, generated.

We observe that **eva_set** has the largest number of preconditions and postconditions, hinting that EVA reports consistently provide information that can be translated into annotations. This lines up with the contents of EVA reports as they contain both alarms that define preconditions as well as a value analysis that describes all possible output values. The report and how it is utilised will be explored further in the upcoming qualitative analysis.

We also observe that **pathcrawler_set** contains the largest number of behaviour clauses. In our experience with observing ACSL generated by GPT-4, the presence of behaviour clauses is generally an indication that the LLM has found non-trivial properties to add to its specification.

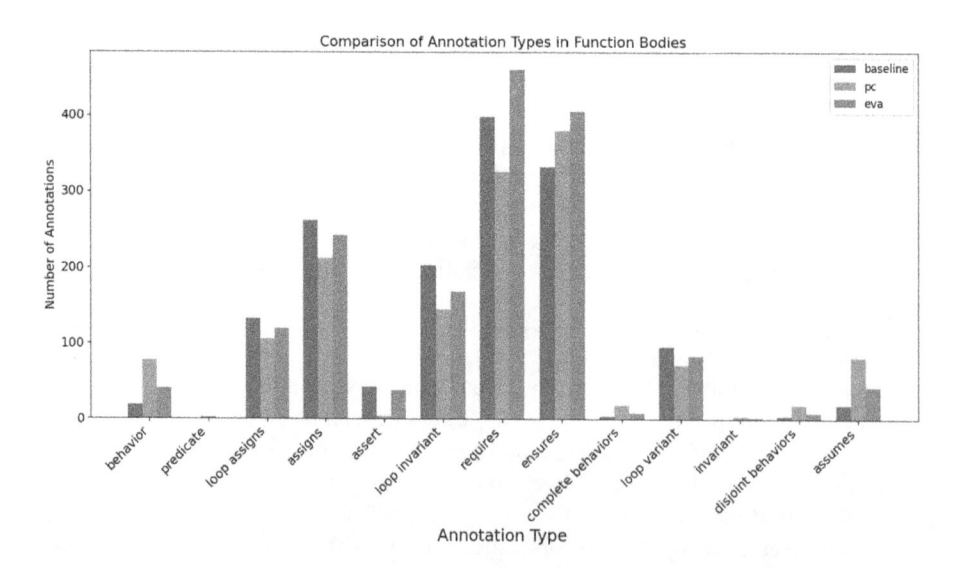

Fig. 1. Annotation-type counts for each prompt

5.2 Baseline Prompt

Many of the annotations produced with the baseline prompt, which includes no additional symbolic context, were rather simplistic. While not necessarily incorrect or completely useless, these specifications tended to focus on surface-level details of the programs, overlooking more substantive aspects. This can be seen in Fig. 2 which shows a specification generated for an implementation of binary search. The specification describes *some* properties of the program, but completely misses the semantics of a search algorithm.

```
/*@
  @ requires \valid(A + (0..9)) && \valid(&elem);
  @ ensures \result == 0 || \result == 1;
  @ assigns \nothing;
*/
int testme( int A[10], int elem) {
    ...
    /*@
      @ loop invariant high >= low;
      @ loop assigns low, high, mid, ret;
      @ loop variant high - low;
    */
    while( ( high > low ) )
    ...
}
```

Fig. 2. Specification generated for **binary search** program with the baseline prompt

CoT Inspection. Our initial intuition was that the LLM was unable to infer that the code in Fig. 2 was an implementation of binary search, however by recording the CoT process we found evidence to the contrary. For example, the following snippet that was generated along with the annotated program:

> The program seems to implement a binary search algorithm on the array A[]. It tries to find a given element elem in the array A[] and returns a boolean indicating if it was found or not.

Despite this inference made by the LLM, the specification produced did not reflect its understanding. This pattern shows up frequently where the intent is shown to be **inferred** by the LLM but not given directly to it. For example the act of naming the function *Bsearch* instead of *testme* noticeably increases the quality of the specification.

Based on the relationship between what the LLM is able to infer in the CoT and the specifications it outputs, it suggests that a weak or limited specification does not necessarily reflect the inference or logical capabilities of the LLM. Rather, it indicates that the LLM was not provided with sufficient direction or emphasis on the aspects that we were looking for.

5.3 Prompt with Pathcrawler Input/Output Pairs

In conducting a qualitative analysis on **pathcrawler_set**, we explore the efficacy of incorporating Pathcrawler input/output pairs into specification synthesis prompts. These input/output pairs are represented by a CSV string that includes the program input parameters, the output, and an optional "verdict" provided by an oracle. The rationale for this integration is grounded in the abstraction level that input/output pairs represent, which is among the most abstract representations of a program's behaviour. An example of such a CSV string can be seen in Fig. 3, which represents the inputs and outputs for an Adaptive Differential Pulse Control Modulation (ADPCM) function. Given that these pairs are utilised for synthesising programs [12], extending their use to specification synthesis is a logical progression.

```
input_n,input_valeur,input_t[0],input_t[1],output,verdict
2,0,-37,0,0,unknown
2,-91,0,62,0,unknown
2,0,0,12,1,unknown
```

Fig. 3. CSV string representing inputs and outputs generated for Adaptive Differential Pulse Control Modulation (ADPCM) by Pathcrawler

Abstract Thinking. Our observations indicate that incorporating Pathcrawler input/output pairs into the specification generation process can significantly assist LLMs in achieving specifications with more abstract properties. By "abstract properties," we mean characteristics that describe the purpose and high-level functionality of the program, rather than focusing on specific implementation details.

With the inclusion of Pathcrawler input/output pairs we observe that the LLM is able to understand the purpose of the program based on examples. Take for example the following snippet from the CoT process that we captured from the LLM during its specification generation process using Pathcrawler.

```
Next, let's analyze the PathCrawler CSV.

1. The CSV file contains test cases for 'testme'. Each
   row represents a test case, with columns representing
   the inputs 'len', 'input_buffer', and 'input_msg', and
   the output.

2. From the test cases, we can observe that if 'msg[i]'
   is '\n' and 'msg[i+1]' is '.', then 'buffer[j]' gets '
   msg[i]', 'msg[i+1]', and an extra '.'. Otherwise, '
   buffer[j]' simply gets 'msg[i]'. This behavior could
   be represented as an ACSL annotation in a
   postcondition.
```

Specifically highlighted in red, we see that the LLM noticing a pattern in the inputs and suggest a postcondition to represent it. This postcondition is then directly translated into an ACSL annotation for the specification shown in Fig. 4. This pattern is repeated throughout the comparison between **baseline_set** and **pathcrawler_set** where the test pairs will bridge some sort of logical gap that makes the LLM more likely to specify abstract properties.

```
/*@ requires \valid_range(msg, 0, len-1);
  @ requires \valid_range(buffer, 0, BUFSZ-1);
  @ requires len >= 0 && len <= BUFSZ;
  @ assigns buffer[0..BUFSZ-1];
  @ ensures \forall integer i; 0 <= i < len ==>
  @                ((msg[i] == '\n' && msg[i+1] == '.') ?
  @                  buffer[i] == msg[i] && buffer[i+1] == msg[i+1]
      && buffer[i+2] == '.' :
  @                  buffer[i] == msg[i]);
*/
void testme (char *msg, int len, char *buffer)
{...}
```

Fig. 4. BugKPath - Pathcrawler

Over-Approximation. Pathcrawler, as a structural test case generator, is designed to generate the minimal number of test cases necessary to cover all execution paths in a program. While a compact number of test cases can be considered a feature in some cases, this feature can also cause the LLM to produce over-approximated specifications. In this context, an over-approximated specification is one that makes assumptions about inputs and outputs based on a limited number of test-cases.

This behaviour can be seen in the specification generated for the program called **PointeurFonction5**, seen in Fig. 5. In this example, Pathcrawler only providing two test cases leads to a specification overly tailored to the examples.

```
...
/*@
  @ requires a >= 0 && a <= 1;
  @ requires b >= 0 && b <= 1;
  @ assigns \nothing;
  @ ensures (\result == 2 && a == 0 && b == 0) || (\result == 1
      && a == 1 && b == 0);
*/
unsigned int testme( int a, int b) {...}
```

Fig. 5. PointerFunction5 - Pathcrawler

Notice how the preconditions specified limit our inputs to $\forall a,b \in \{0,1\}$. From the implementation of the program there doesn't seem to be any specific reason why the LLM should set that precondition. However, by looking into the CoT captured during specification generation we see a clear reasoning for why the precondition was included.

1. In the functions f0, f1, and f2, I add a postcondition ('ensures') to specify the return value behavior since these functions return an integer value that is based on their input. This will allow better verification of the function behavior.
2. In the 'testme' function, I add preconditions ('requires') to limit the range of the input parameters 'a' and 'b' to prevent overflow or underflow issues. The range is derived from the PathCrawler output.
3. I add postconditions ('ensures') to specify the expected return value behavior of the 'testme' function based on the PathCrawler output.
4. I also add 'assigns' clause to the 'testme' function to specify which variables the function is allowed to modify.

The text highlighted in red clearly indicates that the preconditions were derived from the input/output pairs generated by Pathcrawler. Therefore, we should be able to look at the Pathcrawler input/output pairs to understand why the LLM came up with those preconditions. Upon examining the Pathcrawler output, we notice that there are only two test cases: one where $a = 0$ and one where $a = 1$. These inputs are not necessarily related to any of the semantics of the code, but the LLM overgeneralised based on the small number of examples.

```
input_a,input_b,output,verdict
0,0,2,unknown
1,0,1,unknown
```

State Mutation. The number of examples is not the only criterion for improved outcomes. The LLM also needs to detect recognisable patterns within these examples; without such patterns, even a large set of test cases may not lead to significant improvements in specification quality. Take for example the program titled **Apache** which edits URL strings. Based on its large number of test cases shown below, one would expect this large number of test cases to produce more useful annotations. However at a closer look, this program produces no return value and instead manipulates state.

```
input_scheme,input_uri[0],...,input_uri[14],output,verdict
1,47,47,0,0,0,0,0,0,0,0,0,0,0,0,0,,unknown
1,47,58,0,0,0,0,0,0,0,0,0,0,0,0,0,,unknown
2,108,47,47,47,0,0,0,0,0,0,0,0,0,0,0,,unknown
...
422214939,47,0,0,0,0,0,0,0,0,0,0,0,0,0,0,,unknown
5,108,100,97,112,47,47,47,63,63,63,0,0,0,0,0,,no_extra_coverage
```

Because there is no output to relate the input to, the LLM is unable to make any conclusions about the CSV file. Rather than it just not providing any benefit, we found that such additions to the prompt were actually detrimental to specification generation. This could possibly be because the CSV file takes attention away from the provided program, diverting the LLM's focus and thereby reducing the overall quality.

Are Test Cases Useful? As discussed in previous sections, adding Pathcrawler input/output pairs to prompts for specification generation is not a silver bullet that will always improve the quality of specifications. This observation raises the question: does adding input/output examples to prompts have value in general?

It is important to distinguish between the weaknesses of a specific tool and the limitations of the methodology itself. In this context, our two main weaknesses are: a small number of test cases and no representation of how state changes during test execution. These weaknesses are features of Pathcrawler (which was not designed with our use case in mind) rather than inherent flaws in the concept of using test cases for specification generation.

To address these weaknesses, we could develop a test case generator that overcomes these limitations. Such a generator would need to produce a larger quantity of test cases and include the result of state changes from before and after execution. Based on our observations, we believe that a suitable test case generator, free from these constraints, could be beneficial in increasing the quality of the generated specifications.

5.4 Prompt with EVA Annotations

EVA, a static analysis tool, specialises in conducting a comprehensive value analysis of C programs. The report that it generates includes the detailed outcomes of the value analysis but also lists alarms that signify possible runtime errors linked to these value states. Such alarms are indicators of conditions under which the program might fail or behave unexpectedly, essentially flagging areas of the code that are prone to errors due to specific input values or execution paths.

Avoiding Runtime Errors. In our analysis of the **eva_set**, a distinct characteristic emerges: the prevalence of precondition annotations that serve to help the function avoid runtime errors. These preconditions appear to be a direct result of the runtime alarms included the EVA reports. The alarms detail problematic input ranges, such as values that could cause the program to behave unpredictably or fail – common issues highlighted include index-out-of-bound errors, divide-by-zero errors, and integer overflows.

An example of these value domains can be seen in the specification generated for the program **Alias5**, seen in Fig. 6. The specification clearly aligns with the EVA report included in its synthesis prompt.

```
...
[eva:alarm] temp_files/tmphpdyn83w/eva_temp.c:8:Warning:
    signed overflow. assert -2147483648 <= x * 2;
[eva:alarm] temp_files/tmphpdyn83w/eva_temp.c:8:Warning:
    signed overflow. assert x * 2 <= 2147483647;
[eva:alarm] temp_files/tmphpdyn83w/eva_temp.c:9:Warning:
    signed overflow. assert -2147483648 <= v - y;
[eva:alarm] temp_files/tmphpdyn83w/eva_temp.c:9:Warning:
    signed overflow. assert v - y <= 2147483647;
[eva:alarm] temp_files/tmphpdyn83w/eva_temp.c:11:Warning:
    out of bounds write. assert \valid(tab + 2);
[kernel] temp_files/tmphpdyn83w/eva_temp.c:11:Warning:
    all target addresses were invalid. This path is assumed
       to be dead.
```

Notice how the alarms are utilised by the LLM in generating preconditions that ensure that the program avoids both integer overflow and index-out-of-bounds errors. These precise runtime-aware annotations are largely unique to annotations generated with EVA as the reports provide a level of direction and precision absent in the baseline prompt.

EVA Tunnel-Vision. In examining the impact of incorporating EVA reports into the specification generation process, it becomes apparent that the LLM prioritises the analysis of the EVA report over the direct reasoning about the program's implementation. This observation emerges distinctly when analysing the CoT produced by the LLM. For example, the following CoT excerpt is from the **LabelsTriTyp** program in **eva_set**

```
The provided C program is a function 'testme' that takes
   three integer inputs 'Side1', 'Side2', and 'Side3' and
      uses these inputs to calculate and return a value '
      triOut'.

From the EVA report, we can see several warnings about
   potential signed overflow in the program. This occurs
   when the sum of two sides of the triangle is close to
   the maximum value an integer can hold ('2147483647'),
   leading to a possible overfl
```

In this case we notice that while the specification in **eva_set** was able to infer that this program was a triangle classifier, its focus was clearly taken by the provided EVA report.

This observation raises concerns about the LLM's ability to balance the input from static analysis tools like EVA that provide clear direction for the LLM. While the safety and domain boundaries are well-captured, the essence of what the program is designed to do can sometimes be overshadowed by the focus on avoiding runtime errors and handling edge cases as dictated by the EVA report.

```
...
[eva:alarm] temp_files/tmphpdyn83w/eva_temp.c:8:Warning:
  signed overflow. assert -2147483648 <= x * 2;
[eva:alarm] temp_files/tmphpdyn83w/eva_temp.c:8:Warning:
  signed overflow. assert x * 2 <= 2147483647;
[eva:alarm] temp_files/tmphpdyn83w/eva_temp.c:9:Warning:
  signed overflow. assert -2147483648 <= v - y;
[eva:alarm] temp_files/tmphpdyn83w/eva_temp.c:9:Warning:
  signed overflow. assert v - y <= 2147483647;
[eva:alarm] temp_files/tmphpdyn83w/eva_temp.c:11:Warning:
  out of bounds write. assert \valid(tab + 2);
[kernel] temp_files/tmphpdyn83w/eva_temp.c:11:Warning:
  all target addresses were invalid. This path is assumed
    to be dead.
```

```
/*@ requires x >= INT_MIN/2 && x <= INT_MAX/2 && y >= INT_MIN &&
    y <= INT_MAX;
  @ requires \valid(tab + (0..2));
  @ requires y <= \length(tab) - 5;
  @ assigns tab[2], tab[y+4];
*/
int testme(int x, int y, int tab[]) {
  int v;
  int *pt;
  int **ppt;
  v = x * 2;
  v = v - y;
  pt = &tab[2];
  tab[2] = x;
  ppt = &pt;
  pt = pt + 1;
  *ppt = &tab[2];
  *(pt + v) = y;
  if (tab[y + 4] > 5)
    return 1;
  return 0;
}
```

Fig. 6. Alias5 specification generated with an EVA report as context

5.5 Implementation vs. Intent

What should a specification generation tool do if given a buggy program? Symbolic tools, such as QuickSpec [27], will simply generate some odd specification to which the buggy program adheres. The user might find this surprising, but it might not be obvious that it is due to a bug. Ideally, we would like a specification synthesis tool to generate a specification for what the program *should* do rather than blindly following what is already implemented. LLMs can sometimes help with exactly this: as illustrated in [15], GPT-4 produced the intended properties for a functional program even with a subtle bug, by inferring intent from function names rather than details of the implementation. The names provide the LLM with a high-probability cue to the program intent, allowing it to compensate for the bug, see [21] for a general discussion on this.

In the reminder of this section, we perform a small-scale experiment to investigate the question as to when GPT-4 follows the intent of the program or the implementation. We accomplish this by generating specifications from programs in **mutated_set** which contains 8 buggy programs.

Baseline Prompt - Intent Is Prioritised. While the specifications generated with the baseline prompt were in general lower quality and less likely to infer intent, we did indeed observe that **if the intent is inferred** either through a function name or from the implementation then the LLM is more likely to create a specification based on that intent even if the buggy implementation contradicts it. One clear example of this is the mutated Tritype function shown in Fig. 7. In this example, the implementation and specification are disconnected from each other as the LLM's inferred intent took priority over small yet semantically important implementation details.

```
/*@
 ...
 @ behavior not_triangle:
 @     assumes i == 0 || j == 0 || k == 0 || i+j <= k || j+k <= i
       || i+k <= j;
 @     ensures \result == 4;
 ...
*/
int tritype(int i, int j, int k){
    ...
    if ((i+j <= k) || (i+k <= i) || (i+k <= j))
        type_code = 4;
    ...
}
```

Fig. 7. Mutated Tritype where specification and implementation clearly do not agree

On the other hand, the code for calculating the Levenshtein distance shown in Fig. 8 shows us that rather than generating loop annotations from a nuanced understanding of the intent, the LLM instead only considered the implementation of nearby loop implementation.

When an obvious bug in the code is detected, the LLM responds in one of two primary ways. The more common response is that the LLM disregards the error and generates a specification using inferred intent from other language cues in the program. This lines up with observations made by Gu et al. [11] where they point out that the

```
...

int levenshtein(char *s1, char *s2) {
   /*@ loop invariant 0 <= x <= len1;
     @ loop assigns matrix[0][0 .. len1];
   */
   for (int x = 0; x <= len1; x++) matrix[0][x] = x;

   /*@ loop invariant 0 <= y <= len2;
     @ loop assigns matrix[0 .. len2][0];
   */
   for (int y = 0; y <= len2; y++) matrix[y][0] = y;
}
```

Fig. 8. Mutated Levenshtein distance with typos highlighted in red (Color figure online)

LLMs they used often had limited understandings of the semantics of the buggy program and could easily be tricked by cues such as variable or function names. On less frequent occasions the LLM might actively repair the code during the specification process, contrary to the instructions to not modify the C code. Quite likely the LLM might have seen very similar programs during training, and the corrected version is simply a more likely continuation.

Prompts with Additional Annotations. Adding information from the formal methods tools will not help much in the case of buggy programs. The inclusion of an EVA report continues to steer the LLM's towards specifications focusing on value domains, ignoring any underlying intent of the program, much like observations from bug-free scenarios. Similarly for Pathfinder, input/output pairs did not consistently aid the LLM in recognising buggy code within a program, even when an oracle was provided specifying which test cases failed. Instead, the specifications largely followed cues from names in the program, as in the baseline case.

6 Related Work

There is an ever-growing body of work exploring the opportunities of combining LLMs with various tools for formal-methods and theorem proving. In the domain of proof-assistants in particular, a few works have explored the task of synthesising properties or lemmas using neural methods [15,23,30] with varying success. More focus has been on creating models for generating proofs, with applications to most mainstream proof assistants like Isabelle/HOL, Coq and Lean [3,9,14,35]. Recent developments of proof co-pilots for Lean are ongoing, aiming to make next-tactic suggestions for the user while creating proof scripts [28,32].

For contract-based verification tools, the majority of research on annotation generation has been centred on generating loop invariants (e.g., [13,16]) needed to verify correctness of programs wrt. a *given* functional specification. Very recently (27/05/2024), there appeared work on arXiv on generating assertions by LLMs with previously encountered errors added to the input [22], to support search for correctness proofs. With the latter, we have in common that some result from symbolic analysis is used when, iteratively, prompting LLMs. However, all of these works assume a functional specification to be given. Our research, on the other hand, addresses largely the problem of *inferring* a functional specification for a program. This ability to generate specifications based on inferred intent could be particularly useful for developer productivity and user adoption. Silva et.al. [26] describe how LLMs can be leveraged to help less experienced users craft formal specifications and prove their correctness in the Dafny programming language.

7 Conclusion

In this work, we explore how two types of symbolic analyses, symbolic execution based test generation and abstract interpretation based value analysis, enhance the capability of an LLM to extract the intent of C programs and render it as ACSL specifications. The experiments show that without symbolic analysis, the LLM tends to generate lower level annotations reflecting implementation details, like assert and assigns statements. In contrast, the addition of symbolic analyses' output to LLM prompts increases the LLM's capabilities to generate specifications which capture the *intent* of the code, in particular pre- and postconditions. The experiments also show that the specification generation of high-level (intent related) properties was rather robust to bug-introducing mutations of the code. This highlights the value of the overall approach. If generated specifications of buggy code reflect the intended behaviour better than the actual behaviour, then specification generation of this kind can be of great help for revealing bugs.

We note that various limitations of the concrete tool chain we used are not inherent to the approach. For instance, for Pathcrawler sometimes outputs a very small number of input/output pairs, due to its strong focus on path coverage. In such cases, the test cases cannot contribute to more high-level specifications. Also, Pathcrawler-generated tests do not reflect pre- and post states. Both limitations can be mitigated by further development on the Pathcrawler side, or by using a different test generation facility.

Another limitation of this work is the non-determinism of the state-of-the-art LLM services like GPT-4. This makes the results of any experimentation of a tool chain involving such an LLM not fully reproducible. We share this problem with all work that uses these services in experiments. In the future, we will investigate the usage of LLM frameworks which we can deploy and control locally. Currently, these frameworks seem less competitive for our task, but that may change. Moreover, fine-tuning pre-trained models for our purpose is another direction to further investigate.

This work is aligned to the vision of trustworthy triple copiloting of implementations, tests, and specifications ('TriCo'), as co-outlined by two of the authors in [1]. However, in that vision paper, we focused on the bilateral relations of the three artefacts, whereas here, when adding the Pathcrawler output, we use implementations and tests at once when generating specifications. More generally, we see our work as a contribution to the more general aim of combining the complementary strengths of machine learning and exact analyses for effective and reliable development of trustworthy software.

A Prompts

```
You are a LLM that takes the following inputs and returns
    a C program annotated with ACSL annotations.
Inputs:
1. A C program with no ACSL annotations
GOALS:
1. Describe any abstract properties that could be
    represented as ACSL annotations
2. Generate ACSL annotations based on your analysis of
    the program
3. Returning a program with no annotation is not a valid
    solution
4. Do not edit the C code, only add annotations
5. Make sure to describe your thought process behind the
    annotations
6. Do not skip any code in the returned solution to make
    it shorter.
7. If you break any of these rules then my family will
    disown me.
...
START OF INPUT:
{program}


2. Analyze the pathcrawler CSV and describe any patterns
    that you see that could help you understand the
    behaviors of the program based on given input/output
    pairs
...
4. Generate ACSL annotations based on your analysis of
    the program and take special account of the properties
    described when analyzing the Pathcrawler CSV file
...
PathCrawler Output:
{csv}


2. Analyze the Eva report and describe how the results
    could be used in generating ACSL annotations
3. Generate ACSL annotations based on your analysis of
    the program and take special account of the properties
    described when analyzing the Eva report
...
Eva Report:
{eva}
```

References

1. Ahrendt, W., Gurov, D., Johansson, M., Rümmer, P.: TriCo—triple co-piloting of implementation, specification and tests. In: Margaria, T., Steffen, B. (eds.) ISoLA 2022, Part I, pp. 174–187. Springer, Cham (2022). https://doi.org/10.1007/978-3-031-19849-6_11
2. Baudin, P., Filliâtre, J.C., Marché, C., Monate, B., Moy, Y., Prevosto, V.: ACSL: ANSI C specification language. CEA-LIST, Saclay, France, Tech. Rep. v1 **2** (2008)
3. Blaauwbroek, L., Urban, J., Geuvers, H.: The tactician. In: Benzmüller, C., Miller, B. (eds.) CICM 2020. LNCS (LNAI), vol. 12236, pp. 271–277. Springer, Cham (2020). https://doi.org/10.1007/978-3-030-53518-6_17
4. Blasi, A., et al.: Translating code comments to procedure specifications. In: Proceedings of the 27th ACM SIGSOFT International Symposium on Software Testing and Analysis, pp. 242–253 (2018)
5. Blazy, S., Bühler, D., Yakobowski, B.: Structuring abstract interpreters through state and value abstractions. In: Bouajjani, A., Monniaux, D. (eds.) VMCAI 2017. LNCS, vol. 10145, pp. 112–130. Springer, Cham (2017). https://doi.org/10.1007/978-3-319-52234-0_7
6. Brown, T., et al.: Language models are few-shot learners. Adv. Neural. Inf. Process. Syst. **33**, 1877–1901 (2020)
7. Davis, J.A., et al.: Study on the barriers to the industrial adoption of formal methods. In: Formal Methods for Industrial Critical Systems: 18th International Workshop, FMICS 2013, Madrid, 23–24 September 2013. Proceedings 18, pp. 63–77. Springer, Heidelberg (2013)
8. Ernst, M.D., et al.: The daikon system for dynamic detection of likely invariants. Sci. Comput. Program. **69**(1–3), 35–45 (2007)
9. First, E., Rabe, M.N., Ringer, T., Brun, Y.: Baldur: whole-proof generation and repair with large language models. In: Proceedings of the 31st ACM Joint European Software Engineering Conference and Symposium on the Foundations of Software Engineering (ESEC/FSE 2023), pp. 1229–1241. Association for Computing Machinery, New York (2023). https://doi.org/10.1145/3611643.3616243
10. Flanagan, C., Joshi, R., Leino, K.R.M.: Annotation inference for modular checkers. Inf. Process. Lett. **77**(2–4), 97–108 (2001)
11. Gu, A., edt al.: The counterfeit conundrum: can code language models grasp the nuances of their incorrect generations? arXiv preprint arXiv:2402.19475 (2024)
12. Gupta, K., Christensen, P.E., Chen, X., Song, D.: Synthesize, execute and debug: learning to repair for neural program synthesis. Adv. Neural. Inf. Process. Syst. **33**, 17685–17695 (2020)
13. Janßen, C., Richter, C., Wehrheim, H.: Can ChatGPT support software verification? In: Beyer, D., Cavalcanti, A. (eds.) Fundamental Approaches to Software Engineering, pp. 266–279. Springer, Cham (2024). https://doi.org/10.1007/978-3-031-57259-3_13
14. Jiang, A.Q., : Thor: wielding hammers to integrate language models and automated theorem provers. In: Oh, A.H., Agarwal, A., Belgrave, D., Cho, K. (eds.) Advances in Neural Information Processing Systems (2022). https://openreview.net/forum?id=fUeOyt-2EOp
15. Johansson, M., Smallbone, N.: Exploring mathematical conjecturing with large language models. In: NeSy 2023, 17th International Workshop on Neural-Symbolic Learning and Reasoning (2023)
16. Kamath, A., et al.: Finding inductive loop invariants using large language models. arXiv preprint arXiv:2311.07948 (2023)
17. Kirchner, F., Kosmatov, N., Prevosto, V., Signoles, J., Yakobowski, B.: Frama-c: a software analysis perspective. Formal Aspects Comput. **27**(3), 573–609 (2015). https://doi.org/10.1007/s00165-014-0326-7
18. Kosmatov, N., Prevosto, V., Signoles, J. (eds.): Guide to Software Verification with Frama-C: Core Components, Usages, and Applications. Springer, Cham (2024)

19. Lathouwers, S., Huisman, M.: Survey of annotation generators for deductive verifiers. J. Syst. Softw. **211**, 111972 (2024)
20. Li, C., et al.: Large language models understand and can be enhanced by emotional stimuli. arXiv preprint arXiv:2307.11760 (2023)
21. McCoy, R.T., Yao, S., Friedman, D., Hardy, M., Griffiths, T.L.: Embers of autoregression: understanding large language models through the problem they are trained to solve (2023)
22. Mugnier, E., Gonzalez, E.A., Jhala, R., Polikarpova, N., Zhou, Y.: Laurel: generating Dafny assertions using large language models. arXiv preprint arXiv:2405.16792 (2024)
23. Rabe, M.N., Lee, D., Bansal, K., Szegedy, C.: Mathematical reasoning via self-supervised skip-tree training. In: Proceedings of ICLR (2021)
24. Sen, K., Marinov, D., Agha, G.: CUTE: a concolic unit testing engine for C. SIGSOFT Softw. Eng. Notes **30**(5), 263–272 (2005). https://doi.org/10.1145/1095430.1081750
25. Signoles, J.: E-ACSL: Executable ANSI/ISO C Specification Language (2011). http://frama-c.com/download/e-acsl/e-acsl.pdf
26. Silva, A.F., Mendes, A., Ferreira, J.a.F.: Leveraging large language models to boost Dafny's developers productivity. In: Proceedings of the 2024 IEEE/ACM 12th International Conference on Formal Methods in Software Engineering (FormaliSE) (FormaliSE 2024), pp. 138–142. Association for Computing Machinery, New York (2024). https://doi.org/10.1145/3644033.3644374
27. Smallbone, N., Johansson, M., Claessen, K., Algehed, M.: Quick specifications for the busy programmer. J. Funct. Program. **27**, e18 (2017). https://doi.org/10.1017/S0956796817000090
28. Song, P., Yang, K., Anandkumar, A.: Towards large language models as copilots for theorem proving in Lean. arXiv preprint arXiv:2404.12534 (2024)
29. Tyler, B.: Formal methods adoption in industry: an experience report. In: Cerone, A. (ed.) Formal Methods for an Informal World: ICTAC 2021 Summer School, Virtual Event, Astana, 1–7 September 2021, Tutorial Lectures, pp. 152–161. Springer, Cham (2023). https://doi.org/10.1007/978-3-031-43678-9_5
30. Urban, J., Jakubův, J.: First neural conjecturing datasets and experiments. In: Proceedings of CICM (2020). https://doi.org/10.1007/978-3-030-53518-6_24
31. Wang, H., Wang, R., Mi, F., Wang, Z., Xu, R., Wong, K.F.: Chain-of-thought prompting for responding to in-depth dialogue questions with LLM. arXiv preprint arXiv:2305.11792 (2023)
32. Welleck, S., Saha, R.: LLMSTEP: LLM proofstep suggestions in lean. arXiv preprint arXiv:2310.18457 (2023)
33. White, J., et al.: A prompt pattern catalog to enhance prompt engineering with ChatGPT. arXiv preprint arXiv:2302.11382 (2023)
34. Williams, N., Marre, B., Mouy, P., Roger, M.: PathCrawler: automatic generation of path tests by combining static and dynamic analysis. In: Dal Cin, M., Kaâniche, M., Pataricza, A. (eds.) EDCC 2005. LNCS, vol. 3463, pp. 281–292. Springer, Heidelberg (2005). https://doi.org/10.1007/11408901_21
35. Yang, K., et al.: LeanDojo: theorem proving with retrieval-augmented language models. In: Neural Information Processing Systems (NeurIPS) (2023)

Author Index

A
Ahrendt, Wolfgang 307
Andrei, Oana 267

B
Baarir, Souheib 288
Bartoletti, Massimo 256
Blohm, Pauline 172
Bodenmüller, Stefan 53
Bögli, Roman 24
Bos, Petra van den 217
Bucev, Mario 75

C
Chalupa, Marek 151
Chechik, Marsha 87
Ciobâcă, Ştefan 35

D
da Costa, Ana Oliveira 151
Dutheillet, Claude 288

F
Ferrando, Angelo 256
Fränzle, Martin 194
Fuhs, Carsten 75

G
Granberry, George 307
Gratie, Diana-Elena 35
Grosen, Thomas M. 194

H
Heisinger, Maximilian 279
Henzinger, Thomas A. 151
Herber, Paula 172
Huisman, Marieke 217

J
Johansson, Moa 307
Johnsen, Einar Broch 237
Junges, Sebastian 297

K
Kehrer, Timo 24
Kløvstad, Åsmund Aqissiaq Arild 237
Kunčak, Viktor 75

L
Larsen, Kim G. 194
Lerena, Leandro 24
Lipparini, Enrico 256
Loitzl, Alexander 128
Lucanu, Dorel 3

M
Malvone, Vadim 256
Milovančević, Dragana 75
Mogage, Andrei 3
Murphy, Logan 87

P
Peschanski, Frédéric 109
Peyrer, Mark 279
Phetmanee, Surasak 267

R
Reif, Wolfgang 53
Remke, Anne 172
Rot, Jurriaan 237
Rubbens, Robert 217

S
Sandro, Alessio Di 87
Saouli, Sabrine 288
Schellhorn, Gerhard 53
Seidl, Martina 279

© The Editor(s) (if applicable) and The Author(s), under exclusive license to Springer Nature Switzerland AG 2025
N. Kosmatov and L. Kovács (Eds.): IFM 2024, LNCS 15234, pp. 327–328, 2025.
https://doi.org/10.1007/978-3-031-76554-4

Seshia, Sanjit A. 297
Sevegnani, Michele 267
Silva, Alexandra 237

T
Torfah, Hazem 297
Tsigkanos, Christos 24

V
Viger, Torin 87
Voogd, Erik 237

Z
Zimmermann, Martin 194
Zuleger, Florian 128